T0214566

Lecture Notes in Computer Science   11041

Commenced Publication in 1973
Founding and Former Series Editors:
Gerhard Goos, Juris Hartmanis, and Jan van Leeuwen

More information about this series at http://www.springer.com/series/7412

Danail Stoyanov · Zeike Taylor
Duygu Sarikaya · Jonathan McLeod
Miguel Angel González Ballester
Noel C. F. Codella et al. (Eds.)

OR 2.0 Context-Aware Operating Theaters, Computer Assisted Robotic Endoscopy, Clinical Image-Based Procedures, *and* Skin Image Analysis

First International Workshop, OR 2.0 2018
5th International Workshop, CARE 2018
7th International Workshop, CLIP 2018
Third International Workshop, ISIC 2018
Held in Conjunction with MICCAI 2018
Granada, Spain, September 16 and 20, 2018
Proceedings

 Springer

Editors
Danail Stoyanov
University College London
London
UK

Zeike Taylor
University of Leeds
Leeds
UK

Duygu Sarikaya
University of Rennes
Rennes
France

Jonathan McLeod
University of Western Ontario
London, ON
Canada

Miguel Angel González Ballester
Universitat Pompeu Fabra
Barcelona
Spain

Noel C. F. Codella
IBM Research
Yorktown Heights, NY
USA

Additional Workshop Editors *see next page*

ISSN 0302-9743   ISSN 1611-3349   (electronic)
Lecture Notes in Computer Science
ISBN 978-3-030-01200-7   ISBN 978-3-030-01201-4   (eBook)
https://doi.org/10.1007/978-3-030-01201-4

Library of Congress Control Number: 2018956291

LNCS Sublibrary: SL6 – Image Processing, Computer Vision, Pattern Recognition, and Graphics

This Springer imprint is published by the registered company Springer Nature Switzerland AG
The registered company address is: Gewerbestrasse 11, 6330 Cham, Switzerland

Additional Workshop Editors

Tutorial and Educational Chair

Anne Martel
University of Toronto
Toronto, ON
Canada

Workshop and Challenge Co-chair

Lena Maier-Hein
German Cancer Research Center
Heidelberg
Germany

OR 2.0 Context-Aware Operating Theaters, OR 2.0 2018

Anand Malpani
Johns Hopkins University
Baltimore
USA

Sandrine De Ribaupierre ⓘ
University of Western Ontario
London
Canada

Marco A. Zenati ⓘ
Harvard Medical School
Boston
USA

Integrating Medical Imaging and Non-Imaging Modalities, CARE 2018

Luo Xiongbiao
Xiamen University
Xiamen
China

Tobias Reichl
KUKA Deutschland GmbH
Augsburg
Germany

Toby Collins
IRCAD
Strasbourg
France

Clinical Image-Based Procedures, CLIP 2018

Klaus Drechsler
Aachen University of Applied Sciences
Aachen
Germany

Marius Erdt
Fraunhofer IDM@NTU
Singapore

Marius George Linguraru
Sheikh Zayed Institute
for Pediatric Surgical Innovation
Washington, DC
USA

Cristina Oyarzun Laura
Fraunhofer IGD
Darmstadt
Germany

Raj Shekhar
Sheikh Zayed Institute
for Pediatric Surgical Innovation
Washington, DC
USA

Stefan Wesarg
Fraunhofer IGD
Darmstadt
Germany

Skin Image Analysis, ISIC 2018

M. Emre Celebi
University of Central Arkansas
Conway
USA

Kristin Dana
Rutgers University
Piscataway
USA

Allan Halpern
Memorial Sloan Kettering Cancer Center
New York
USA

OR 2.0 2018 Preface

Surgical robotic tools and digitally enhanced operating theaters have been giving surgeons a helping hand for years. While they provide great control, precision, and flexibility to the surgeons, they do not yet address the cognitive assistance needs in the operating theater. We are on the verge of a new wave of innovations of artificial-intelligence-powered, context-aware operating theaters. OR 2.0, Context-Aware Surgical Theaters, aimed to highlight the potential use of a broad range of topics such as machine vision and perception, robotics, surgical simulation and modeling, multi-modal data fusion and visualization, image analysis, advanced imaging, advanced display technologies, human–computer interfaces, sensors, wearable and implantable electronics and robots, visual attention models, cognitive models, decision support networks to enhance surgical procedural assistance, context-awareness, and team communication in the operating theater, human–robot collaborative systems, and surgical training and assessment in defining the technologies of the next-generation operating theaters.

OR 2.0 was held in conjunction with the Medical Image Computing and Computer Assisted Intervention (MICCAI) conference in Granada, Spain. OR 2.0 has its roots in the M2CAI workshop series that started in 2009 in London (UK) and was organized every year until 2016 in Athens; it was, however, a new movement of the domain toward multidisciplinary approaches and teamed with a focus on translation and clinical applications that define operating room technologies of the future.

The workshop featured clinicians, engineers, and industry partners. It hosted keynote speakers, oral presentations, and a poster session of accepted papers on topics such as cognitive models, process modeling, anonymization in operating theaters, smart operating rooms, surgical data science, surgical process and discrete event simulation, surgical training, perioperative process optimization, human–computer interfaces, surgical workflow analysis, surgical phase recognition, automatic length, volume estimation to aid surgical robots, motion-planning, tracking, use of RFID tags with surgical instruments, as well as technical topics such as self-supervised learning, deep learning, bidirectional rapidly exploring random trees, open research problems of nonlinear trajectories, temporal coherence, segmentation, registration. OR 2.0 also featured an open discussion forum of next-generation context-aware operating theater technologies and their clinical impact.

September 2018

Duygu Sarikaya
Anand Malpani
Marco Zenati
Sandrine de Ribaupierre

OR 2.0 2018 Organization

Organizing Board

Duygu Sarikaya	University of Rennes, France
Anand Malpani	The Johns Hopkins University, Baltimore, USA
Marco Zenati	Harvard Medical School, Boston, USA
Sandrine de Ribaupierre	University of Western Ontario, London, Canada

Advisory Board

Paolo Fiorini
Kanako Harad
Pierre Jannin
Ken Masamune
Thomas Neumuth
Nicolas Padoy
Russell H. Taylor

CARE 2018 Preface

The 5th International Workshop on Computer-Assisted and Robotic Endoscopy (CARE 2018) was held on September 16, 2018 in Granada, Spain. This half-day workshop was held in conjunction with MICCAI 2018, the 21st International Conference On Medical Image Computing and Computer-Assisted Intervention.

As in the previous four CARE workshops, our objective is to bring together researchers, clinicians, and industry to advance the field of computer-assisted and robotic endoscopy through the presentation of original research manuscripts and invited keynotes from leading experts in academia, industry, and medicine. This year we were pleased to welcome Dr. Sandrine de Ribaupierre, a distinguished pediatric neurosurgeon and professor from Western University, Canada, who gave the keynote presentation "Neuroendoscopy: What Are the Needs and Use for AR and VR?". After peer review, five papers were selected for oral presentation at CARE and the revised manuscripts are presented in these proceedings. We thank the authors for their high-quality papers and presentations at the workshop. It is their outstanding research and hard work that make this workshop a success.

We would like to express our sincere gratitude to the reviewers who contributed their time and effort in evaluating the papers. We would also like to thank KUKA Deutschland GmbH and Intuitive Surgical for their support in sponsoring the best papers and best presentation awards. Finally, we would like to thank the organizers of MICCAI for supporting and facilitating this workshop.

September 2018

Jonathan McLeod
Xiongbiao Luo
Toby Collins
Tobias Reichl

CARE 2018 Organization

Program Committee

Jonathan McLeod	Intuitive Surgical, USA
Xiongbiao Luo	Xiamen University, China
Toby Collins	IRCAD, France
Tobias Reichl	KUKA Deutschland GmbH, Germany

CLIP 2018 Preface

On September 16, 2018, the 7th International Workshop on Clinical Image-Based Procedures: From Planning to Intervention (CLIP 2018) was held in Granada, Spain in conjunction with the 21st International Conference on Medical Image Computing and Computer-Assisted Intervention (MICCAI). Following the tradition set in the past six years, this year's edition of the workshop was an exciting forum for the discussion and dissemination of clinically tested, state-of-the-art methods for image-based planning, monitoring, and evaluation of medical procedures.

Over the past few years, there has been considerable and growing interest in the development and evaluation of new translational image-based techniques in the modern hospital. For a decade or more, a proliferation of meetings dedicated to medical image computing has created a need for greater study and scrutiny of the clinical application and validation of such methods. New attention and new strategies are essential to ensure a smooth and effective translation of computational image-based techniques into the clinic. For these reasons and to complement other technology-focused MICCAI workshops on computer-assisted interventions, the major focus of CLIP 2018 continued to be on filling gaps between basic science and clinical applications.

Members of the medical imaging community were encouraged to submit work centered on specific clinical applications, including techniques and procedures based on clinical data or already in use and evaluated by clinical users. Once again, the event brought together world-class researchers and clinicians who presented ways to strengthen links between computer scientists and engineers, and surgeons, interventional radiologists, and radiation oncologists.

In response to the call for papers, 13 original manuscripts were submitted for presentation at CLIP 2018. Each of the manuscripts underwent a meticulous double-blind peer review by three members of the Program Committee, all of them prestigious experts in the field of medical image analysis and clinical translations of technology. A member of the Organizing Committee further oversaw the review of each manuscript. Eight manuscripts were accepted for oral presentation at the workshop. The accepted contributors represented a considerable diversity of countries from different continents. Judging by the contributions received, the quality of CLIP 2018 maintained the high standards of previous years.

As always, the workshop featured prominent expert keynote speakers. Vesna Prchkovska, Chief Operating Officer of the company QMENTA, provided her vision of the translation of research to industry. Dr. Elisenda Eixarch, fetal surgeon from Hospital Clínic and Hospital Sant Joan de Déu in Barcelona, presented her experience in bringing technology to real use in fetal and perinatal care.

We would like to acknowledge the invaluable contributions of our entire Program Committee, many members of whom have actively participated in the planning of the workshop over the years, and without whose assistance CLIP 2018 would not be possible. Our thanks also go to all the authors in this volume for the high quality of their work and the commitment of time and effort. Finally, we are grateful to the MICCAI organizers for supporting the organization of CLIP 2018.

September 2018

Miguel Angel González Ballester
Klaus Drechsler
Marius Erdt
Marius George Linguraru
Cristina Oyarzun Laura
Raj Shekhar
Stefan Wesarg

CLIP 2018 Organization

Organizers

Klaus Drechsler   Aachen University of Applied Sciences, Germany

Marius Erdt   Fraunhofer IDM@NTU, Singapore

Miguel González Ballester   ICREA - Universitat Pompeu Fabra, Spain

Marius George Linguraru   Children's National Healthcare System, USA

Cristina Oyarzun Laura   Fraunhofer IGD, Germany

Raj Shekhar   Children's National Healthcare System, USA

Stefan Wesarg   Fraunhofer IGD, Germany

Program Committee

Mario Ceresa   Pompeu Fabra University, Spain

Juan Cerrolaza   Children's National Medical Center, USA

Yufei Chen   Tongji University, China

Jan Egger   TU Graz, Austria

Gloria Fernández Esparrach   Hospital Clinic Barcelona, Spain

Moti Freimann   Harvard Medical School, USA

Debora Gil   Universitat Autonoma de Barcelona, Spain

Tobias Heimann   Siemens, Germany

Weimin Huang   A*STAR, Institute for Infocomm Research, Singapore

Xin Kang   Sonavex, Inc., USA

Michael Kelm   Siemens, Germany

Jianfei Liu   Duke University, USA

Diana Nabers   German Cancer Research Center, Germany

Mauricio Reyes   University of Bern, Switzerland

Akinobu Shimizu   Tokyo University of Agriculture and Technology, Japan

Awais Mansoor   Children's National Health System, USA

Xinyang Liu   Children's National Health System, USA

Sukryool (Alan) Kang   Children's National Health System, USA

Yogesh Karpate   Children's National Health System, USA

Antonio Porras   Children's National Health System, USA

Carles Sanchez Ramos   Universitat Autonoma de Barcelona, Spain

Stephan Zidowitz   Fraunhofer MEVIS, Germany

Jiayin Zhou   A*STAR, Institute for Infocomm Research, Singapore

ISIC 2018 Preface

The Third International Skin Imaging Collaboration (ISIC) Workshop and Challenge on Skin Image Analysis was held at the Granada Conference Center, Granada, Spain, on September 20, 2018, in conjunction with the 21st International Conference on Medical Image Computing and Computer-Assisted Intervention (MICCAI).

The skin is the largest organ of the human body, and is the first area of assessment performed by any clinical staff when a patient is seen, as it provides numerous insights into a patient's underlying health. For example, cardiac function, liver function, immune function, and physical injuries can be assessed by examining the skin. In addition, dermatologic complaints are also among the most prevalent in primary care. Images of the skin are the most easily captured form of medical image in health care, and the domain shares qualities with other standard computer vision datasets, serving as a natural bridge between standard computer vision tasks and medical applications.

This workshop served as a venue to facilitate advancements and knowledge dissemination in the field of skin image analysis, as well as to host a melanoma detection challenge, raising awareness and interest in these socially valuable tasks. Invited speakers included major influencers in computer vision and skin imaging, top-ranked participants of the hosted challenge, and authors of accepted manuscripts on skin image analysis.

Authors were asked to submit full-length manuscripts for double-blind peer review. A total of 28 submissions were received, and with a Program Committee composed of 31 experts in the field, reviewed by at least three reviewers. Based on the feedback and critiques, ten of the best papers (36%) were selected for oral presentation at the workshop, and included in the LNCS volume published by Springer.

For the associated challenge, participants were asked to perform three tasks on dermoscopic images: lesion segmentation, attribute detection and localization, and disease classification. Approximately 931 users registered for data download. In total, 115 submissions were made to the lesion segmentation task, 27 submissions to the lesion attribute detection task, and 159 submissions to the disease classification task, all with manuscripts supplied describing the approaches, hosted and made available on the challenge website. Six participants were selected for presentation.

We thank the authors for submitting their excellent work, our reviewers for their timely and detailed reviews, our invited speakers, challenge participants, and all our attendees. We sincerely hope that the efforts coming together to make this workshop possible will help advance the field and have a positive impact on health care around the world.

September 2018

Noel C. F. Codella
M. Emre Celebi
Kristin Dana
Allan Halpern

ISIC 2018 Organization

Steering Committee

Rogerio Feris	IBM Research, USA
Anthony Hoogs	Kitware, USA
John R. Smith	IBM Research, USA

Workshop Chairs

Noel Codella	IBM Research, USA
M. Emre Celebi	University of Central Arkansas, USA
Kristin Dana	Rutgers University, USA
Allan Halpern	Memorial Sloan Kettering Cancer Center, USA

Challenge Organizers

Harald Kittler	Medical University of Vienna, Austria
Philipp Tschandl	Medical University of Vienna, Austria
Allan Halpern	Memorial Sloan Kettering Cancer Center, USA
Brian Helba	Kitware, USA
Noel Codella	IBM Research, USA
David Gutman	Emory University, USA

Challenge Team Members

Konstantinos Liopyris	Memorial Sloan Kettering Cancer Center, USA
Michael Marchetti	Memorial Sloan Kettering Cancer Center, USA
Stephen Dusza	Memorial Sloan Kettering Cancer Center, USA
Aadi Kalloo	Memorial Sloan Kettering Cancer Center, USA

Program Committee

Anne Gattiker	IBM Research, USA
Begoña Acha	University of Seville, Spain
Bishwaranja Bhattacharjee	IBM Research, USA
Carmen Serrano	University of Seville, Spain
Catarina Barata	Instituto Superior Tecnico, Portugal
Cristina Vasconcelos	UFF, Brazil
Dwarikanath Mahapatra	IBM Research, Australia
Elena Bernardis	University of Pennsylvania, USA
Euijoon Ahn	University of Sydney, Australia

Haofu Liao	University of Rochester, USA
Harald Kittler	Medical University of Vienna, Austria
Ivan Diaz	Charles III University of Madrid, Spain
Jinman Kim	University of Sydney, Australia
Kivanc Kose	Memorial Sloan Kettering Cancer Center, USA
Lequan Yu	The Chinese University of Hong Kong, SAR China
Linlin Shen	Shenzhen University, China
Mario Guarracino	National Research Council of Italy, Italy
Olivier Gevaert	Stanford University, USA
Parneet Kaur	Rutgers University, USA
Pegah Kharazmi	University of British Columbia, Canada
Peter Soyer	University of Queensland, Australia
Philipp Tschandl	Medical University of Vienna, Austria
Reda Kasmi	University of Bejaia, Algeria
Rob Novoa	Stanford University, USA
Roberta Oliveira	University of Porto, Portugal
Sandra Avila	UNICAMP, Brazil
Suman Sedai	IBM Research, Australia
Yanhui Guo	University of Illinois at Springfield, USA
Yuexiang Li	Shenzhen University, China
Yunzhu Li	MIT, USA
Zongyuan Ge	Monash University, Australia

Contents

Proceedings of the 7th International Workshop on Clinical Image-Based Procedures: Translational Research in Medical Imaging (CLIP 2018)

Proceedings of the Third International Skin Imaging Collaboration Workshop (ISIC 2018)

Proceedings of the First International Workshop on OR 2.0 Context-Aware Operating Theaters (OR 2.0 2018)

Perioperative Workflow Simulation and Optimization in Orthopedic Surgery

Juliane Neumann[1]([⊠]) [iD], Christine Angrick[1], Daniel Rollenhagen[1], Andreas Roth[2] [iD], and Thomas Neumuth[1] [iD]

[1] Innovation Center Computer Assisted Surgery,
Leipzig University, Leipzig, Germany
`Juliane.Neumann@iccas.de`
[2] Department of Orthopaedics, Traumatology and Reconstructive Surgery,
Division of Joint Replacement and Orthopaedics,
University Hospital Leipzig, Leipzig, Germany

Abstract. Operating room management aims at the efficient coordination of surgical procedures by maximizing the number of surgical cases while minimizing the required surgery time, with the main goal of improving the patient outcome. Discrete Event Simulation can be utilized to describe, analyze and predict the impact of procedural changes in perioperative processes. The aim of this work is to provide a simulation approach for a holistic perioperative optimization. Therefore, two different process simulation techniques, namely Business Process Simulation and 3D Process Flow Simulation, were utilized. It could be shown that perioperative simulation could lead to the improvement of OR utilization, reduction of process duration and a decrease in personnel workload.

Keywords: Surgical process simulation · Discrete event simulation
Perioperative process opitimization · Operating room management

1 Motivation

The goal of the operating room (OR) management is the effective coordination and execution of surgical procedures in order to create a safe, efficient, and structured environment with the ultimate goal of optimizing the patient outcome. Due to the fact that the surgical department is the most cost-intensive department of the hospital, the OR management aims at maximizing the number of surgical cases while minimizing the required time, resources and related costs. In the last decades, numerous methods and technical approaches have been developed to improve OR scheduling and OR efficiency in order to increase capacity utilization and patient throughput, e.g. formula-based equations [1], statistical methods [2] and process- or discrete-event-simulation (DES) models. DES models aim at describing, analyzing and predicting procedural changes of dynamic systems over the time. Simulation is an essential methodology to (re-)design,

© Springer Nature Switzerland AG 2018
D. Stoyanov et al. (Eds.): OR 2.0/CARE/CLIP/ISIC 2018, LNCS 11041, pp. 3–11, 2018.
https://doi.org/10.1007/978-3-030-01201-4_1

analyze, execute and evaluate processes in respect of different perspectives, objectives, and stakeholders. DES is in the focus of widespread developments for the improvement of pre- and postoperative processes (e.g. [3,4]). However, only a few efforts have been given to the process optimization of intraoperative processes. Fernández-Gutiérrez et al. analyzed and simulated perioperative (pre-, intra- and postoperative) workflows in order to find the optimal development of new complex procedures in multimodal imaging environments [5] and for the efficient utilization of scarce medical equipment [6]. Currently, there are no simulation studies available, which focus on the streamlining of intraoperative processes and their impact on OR capacity utilization and on the execution of pre- and postoperative processes. The OR is a highly complex environment, all processes are intertwined and have a significant impact on each other. Even small delays can lead to timing problems that affect the entire surgical team and the overall OR performance. This complexity requires the analysis of processes from different perspectives. Most simulation approaches focus on temporal (process duration), behavioral (activities and interactions of personnel) and operational aspects (availability of resources, capacity of facilities) of the pre- and postoperative processes. There is no research available on how the structural perspective (environmental aspects, e.g. layout of the OR and surgical department) is influencing the perioperative processes.

The aim of this work is to provide a DES approach for a holistic perioperative process optimization with a focus on the combination of behavioral, temporal, operational and structural perspective. Two different process simulation techniques, namely Business Process Simulation (BPS) and 3D Process Flow Simulation were utilized. Process re-engineering methods based on the computer simulation are used to improve OR capacity utilization and perioperative process efficiency as well as simultaneously reduce the workload of the OR personnel by minimizing waiting times and overwork time. For this purpose, the DES models were implemented with perioperative data from Total Hip Replacement (THR) and Total Knee Replacement (TKR) surgeries. The optimization objective is to increase the number of surgeries to three cases per day by reducing the intraoperative incision-to-closure-time (ICT) through the optimization of the OR layout. Furthermore, the processes for surgery follow-up and OR preparation (closure-to-incision time (CIT)) should be streamlined in order to reduce vacancies and utilizing the available resources to capacity without overburden. To ensure a persistent high-quality patient treatment, the performance duration of perioperative activities should not be reduced.

2   Materials and Methods

2.1   Data Acquisition

THR is a orthopedic procedure in which the hip joint is replaced by a prosthetic implant to treat arthritis pain or hip fractures. During TKR the knee joint is replaced to relieve debilitating pain or osteoarthritis. For the intraoperative simulation 15 THR and 7 TKR surgeries and for pre- and postoperative simulation

30 (total or partial) knee- and hip replacement surgeries were recorded at the University Hospital Leipzig in 2016. In the pre- and postoperative environment, temporal and procedural process information for every OR staff member as well as CIT (OR turnover times) were acquired. In the intraoperative setting structural data (on-site measurement), surgical process data (surgical activities for THR and TKR), OR layout (number and the arrangement of instrument tables for left- and right side THR and TKR), instrument handover (number, duration and path of handovers between surgeon and scrub nurse), travel paths (number, duration and travel path of the circulator) as well as ICT was recorded. In addition, an ergonomic assessment was performed for every OR team member with the OWAS method (Ovako Working Posture Assessment System), which is used to evaluate the most common work postures for the back, arms, and legs.

2.2 Discrete Event Simulation

DES provides an environment for process design, analysis, re-engineering, and evaluation. It is also used to predict the impact of procedural changes over the time and to quantitatively evaluate different alternative process configurations [3]. Thereby, DES relies on the modeling of activities, which are executed by processing the transitions between a list of events. The events are usually described with instructions and a logic for executing the simulation, which enables the imitation of complex behavior. There are various DES methods and tools for different applications and objectives available. In this paper, BPS has been used for the simulation of the behavioral, temporal and operational perspective. For the assessment of structural dynamic changes and their impact on the underlying processes, 3D Process Flow Simulation has been utilized.

Business Process Simulation

For the modeling, analysis, and evaluation of complex, flexible processes, business process modeling is widely used in academic and industry. Especially, BPMN 2.0 has been proven successful in the modeling of the perioperative process environment [7]. In addition, BPMN is regarded as the most appropriate standard available for BPS. The pre- and postoperative processes in the orthopedic department were modeled with the Signavio Editor [8] in the BPMN 2.0 format. For BPS the free business process simulator BIMP [9] was used.

3D Process Flow Simulation

Following the argumentation and assessment in [5], 3D Process Flow Simulation was utilized for the intraoperative process optimization. Therefore, Delmia by Dassault Systems [10] was used, which provides a 3D Modeling environment and logical process simulation. Delmia was initially designed for manufacturing industry but has also a widespread distribution in healthcare (e.g. [4,5]).

3   Simulation Experiments

3.1   Pre- and Postoperative Simulation

Initially, the pre- and postoperative activities of all OR team members (surgeon, assistant, scrub nurse, circulator, anesthesiologist and nurse anesthetist) were modeled in BPMN format and supplemented with the recorded activity duration (mean duration and standard deviation under normal distribution). The BPMN models were simulated with BIMP in different scenarios for the whole workday with 2 or 3 surgeries. In order to analyze which and how many surgeries are feasible with the currently available OR- and personnel-capacities, different combinations of THR and TKR were simulated. According to the intraoperative data acquisition, the initial mean ICT was set to 64,24 min (std 19,74) for THR and 90,0 min (std 22,67) for TKR. The simulation scenarios were then instantiated 250 times (mean working days per year) and the minimum, average and maximum process duration (Cycle Time (CT)) for one workday were calculated via simulation. The normal working period of the OR staff is scheduled to 8 h, which has been defined as an upper boundary for the CT. In addition, waiting times in the process flow resulting from process bottlenecks or scarce resources were simulated. In order to determine the current personnel utilization, the workload of the staff was also simulated. Thereby, only the pre- and postoperative main tasks were analyzed.

In the first optimization step, the pre- and postoperative processes were streamlined with methods of Business Process Re-engineering by parallelization and summarization of activities, redistribution of responsibilities and temporal alignment of the process. After this optimization step, the BPMN models were adapted to the optimized processes and the simulation scenarios were repeated. In the second step, the intraoperative process optimization was performed. Afterwards, the simulation was repeated with improved ICTs.

3.2   Intraoperative Process Simulation

The aim of the intraoperative process optimization was to shorten the ICT by improving the OR layout, instrument table positions and setups for THR and TKR. For this purpose, the existing table setups were analyzed and simulated considering the duration, number, and paths of instrument handovers. Based on the simulation scenario, new setup suggestions are designed and compared to the initial setups. When creating the new setups, both the ergonomic aspects of the OWAS evaluation method and the average rotational movements necessary for the handovers were included. Further, a possible optimization of the circulators' travel paths was simulated together with the initial and optimized setups.

A 3D simulation environment was created with Delmia and the existing layouts and table positions were modeled and simulated based on the intraoperative recorded data (see Fig. 1). The number and the duration of handovers were included in the simulation in order to obtain the total handover time for THR and TKR. The alternative setups for the left and right side of the operated hip

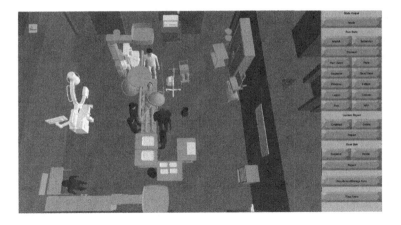

Fig. 1. 3D simluation scenario of the orthopedic OR modeled in Delmia (left TKR).

respectively the left and right side of the knee were designed, simulated, analyzed and compared with regard to the handover times and travel paths.

4 Results

4.1 Initial Situation

Conventional OR Capacity Planning
OR capacities are optimally utilized if a maximum of surgeries can be performed in the work time. Formula-based equations are the state-of-the-art (e.g. [1]) for capacity calculation and planning. These methods are used to define a baseline for the verification of the perioperative simulation:

$$Current\ Surgeries\ per\ day = \frac{Cases\ per\ year}{Working\ days\ per\ year} = \frac{581}{250} = 2,3 \quad (1)$$

Possible THR and TKR surgeries per working day (8 h-1 h for supportive tasks):

$$PossibleTHR = \frac{Work\ time - 1\,h}{meanICT(THR) + meanCIT(THR)} = \frac{420}{(64 + 60)} = 3,4 \quad (2)$$

$$PossibleTKR = \frac{Work\ time - 1\,h}{meanICT(TKR) + meanCIT(TKR)} = \frac{420}{(90 + 60)} = 2,8 \quad (3)$$

Possible surgeries per day for a combination of THR and TKR:

$$PossibleTHR/TKR = \frac{420}{(72 + 60)} = 3,2 \quad (4)$$

According to conventional planning, 3 surgeries per day should be feasible with 3THR and a combination of THR and TKR without overwork time (>8 h).

Analysis of the Initial Situation with Business Process Simulation

Firstly, the CTs of the existing situation for different THR and TKR combinations were simulated (Fig. 2 (light gray)). Two surgeries can be performed without any further process optimization with the disadvantage of an insufficient OR utilization, which results in unused resource capacities. The target of three surgeries per day could be only achieved with 3THR (avg. CT 8,2 h). All combination with one to three TKRs widely exceed the maximum CT of 8 (avg. CT: 3TKR = 9,7 h, 2TKR + 1THR = 9,2 h, 1TKR + 2THR = 8,7 h). The simulation results correspond with the calculation based on the conventional capacity planning method with minor differences for 2THR + 1TKR. In addition, the workload of the OR personnel was simulated and is presented in Fig. 3 (light gray). The upper boundary of 8 h work time per day should not be fully exploited in order to have free capacities for supportive and non-value-added tasks (e.g. supply refill, travel paths etc.). According to the recommendation of [1], the optimal workload is set to 7 h. The maximum workload is set to 4 h per day for the nurse anesthetist, who is responsible for more than one OR and acts as an anesthetist circulator. The simulation results indicate that only 3THR and the combination of 2THR + 1TKR could be performed within one work day. The optimal boundary of 7 h could not be achieved by any surgery combination without further process optimization.

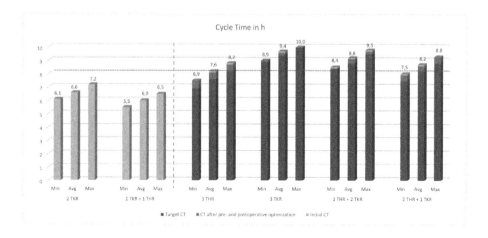

Fig. 2. CT simulation results of THR and TKR combinations: 2 surgeries (left side) and of 3 surgeries (right side). The red line marks the 8 h work time/day boundary. The results after pre-, intra- and postoperative optimization (Target CT) are numbered. (Color figure online)

4.2   Pre- and Postoperative Process Optizimation

For perioperative process optimization several process alignments, such as parallelization and summarization of activities, redistribution of responsibilities and temporal optimization of the process were proposed. Based on these optimizations a decrease of the CTs could be achieved (Fig. 2, dark gray). Still, it is not possible to perform three surgeries with at least one TKR in the time period of 8 h. In Fig. 3 (dark gray) the optimized workload is represented. Through the process optimization, a reduction and a better balancing of workload between the OR team members have been achieved. Especially, the workload of the anesthesiologist has been reduced to less than 8 h while the workload of the nurse anesthetists was slightly increased by 1 h (Fig. 3, dark blue).

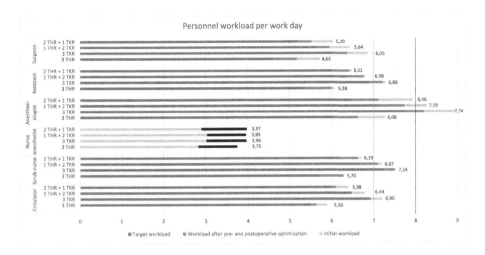

Fig. 3. Personnel workload of THR/TKR with numbered results after perioperative optimization (Target workload). Red line is the 8 h work time/day boundary and the green line is the optimal boundary. Gray: decrease and dark blue: increase of workload. (Color figure online)

4.3   Intraoperative Setup Optimization

Based on 3D Flow Simulation, optimal setups for THR and TKR were defined and evaluated in the real intraoperative OR environment. ICTs were recorded for 8 THR and TKR surgeries, which results in a decrease of 9,45 min for THR (54,75 min (std 15,04)) and 3,25 min for TKR (86,75 min (std 21,91)). The improved ICT were included in the perioperative optimization and the BPS simulation study was repeated (Fig. 2 (blue)). The results of the perioperative optimization indicate that it would be possible to perform 3THR or 2THR + 1TKR in the work time of one day (avg. CT 8,2 h). This result also corresponds with the current case mix of THR and TKR at the University Hospital, which is about 2,3:1 (409 THR, 172 TKR in 2016). Also, the workload of the OR members (Fig. 3 blue) could be decreased to the intended 7 h boundary for 3THR and 2THR + 1TKR.

5 Discussion and Conclusion

It could be shown that perioperative process optimization lead to improvement of OR utilization, reduction of CTs and a decrease in personnel workload. The simulation results of the capacity planning correspond with conventional methods. However, these metrics solely rely on parameters such as ICT and CIT and fail to asses in which way the process need to be changed for improvement. Simulation techniques enable the determination not only that perioperative processes can be improved, but also in which way processes need to be adapted and how the process efficiency is changed due to the impact of different procedural, behavioral, structural, operational or temporal parameters. In this paper different DES methods have been utilized, which were adapted to the underlying optimization problem and objective. Since 3D Flow Simulation is developed for the manufacturing industry, it is suitable for the simulation of operational and structural aspects with a high granularity. On the contrary, it lacks in the representation of complex and intertwined processes with various process actors. Thus, BPS is more suitable and flexible than other modeling methods for procedural and temporal modeling. With the proposed mixed method DES approach, aspects of both domains, could be addressed adequately. An objective time- and resource-saving assessment of different process alternatives and their impact on efficacy and potentials for perioperative process improvement could be achieved.

Acknowledgements. We would like to thank the staff of the Department of Joint Replacement for their kind support during the study. Many thanks are also owed to Fabiola Fernández-Gutiérrez for her patient assistance on Delmia.

References

1. Busse, T.: OP-Management: Grundlagen. medhochzwei Verlag (2010)
2. Dexter, F., Macario, A., Lubarsky, D.A., Burns, D.D.: Statistical method to evaluate management strategies to decrease variability in operating room utilization: application of linear statistical modeling and Monte Carlo simulation to operating room management. Anesthesiology **91**, 262–274 (1999)
3. Baumgart, A., et al.: Using computer simulation in operating room management: impacts on process engineering and performance. In: 40th HICSS, Hawaii (2007)
4. Marjamaa, A., Torkki, P.M., Hirvensalo, E.J., Kirvelä, O.A.: What is the best workflow for an operating room? A simulation study of five scenarios. Health Care Manag. Sci **12**(2), 142 (2009)
5. Fernandez-Gutierrez, F., Barnett, I., Taylor, B., Houston, G., Melzer, A.: Framework for detailed workflow analysis and modelling for simulation of multimodal image-guided interventions. JEIM **26**(1), 75–90 (2013)
6. Fernandez-Gutierrez, F., Wolska-Krawczyk, M., Buecker, A., Houston, G., Melzer, A.: Workflow optimisation for multimodal imaging procedures: a case of combined X-ray and MRI-guided TACE. Minim. Invasive Ther. Allied Technol. **26**(1), 31–38 (2016)

7. Wiemuth, M., et al.: Application fields for the new Object Management Group (OMG) standards Case Management Model and Notation (CMMN) and Decision Management Notation (DMN) in the perioperative field. Int. J. Comput. Assist. Radiol Surg. **12**(8), 1439–1449 (2017)
8. Signavio Process Editor (academic Version). https://www.signavio.com/en/bpm-academic-initiative/. Accessed 13 June 2018
9. BIMP. http://bimp.cs.ut.ee/. Accessed 13 June 2018
10. Dassault Systèmes. http://www.3ds.com/delmia/. Accessed 13 June 2018

A Method for the Context-Aware Assignment of Medical Device Functions to Input Devices in Integrated Operating Rooms

Stefan Franke[1]([✉]), Max Rockstroh[1], Martin Kasparick[2], and Thomas Neumuth[1]

[1] Innovation Center Computer Assisted Surgery, Universität Leipzig, Leipzig, Germany
stefan.franke@iccas.de
[2] Institut für Angewandte Mikroelektronik und Datentechnik, Universität Rostock, Rostock, Germany

Abstract. Operating rooms will emerge to integrated systems with a consistent, cooperative behavior. Recent developments towards context-awareness for medical devices aim to keep system's complexity manageable for the staff. In that context, we propose a modeling approach for the realization of a dynamic assignment of device functions to remote input devices. In the present experiments, we focused on the surgeon's human-machine interactions. The results of the preliminary technical validation indicate that the proposed approach has the potential to increase the surgeon's direct control with a reasonable set of already established input devices. The context-aware assignment of functions will ease the complexity where automation is not applicable due to induced risks. Thus, it contributes to the implementation of context-aware systems' behavior for a intelligent surgical working environment.

Keywords: Human-computer interfaces
Context-aware operating theatre · Intelligent operating room

1 Motivation

With the advent of medical device interoperability and of online workflow recognition, methods for configurable remote control [1,2] and context-awareness [3,4] have been discussed, and ways to automate supportive tasks and human-machine interaction [5] have been demonstrated recently. Operating rooms have begun to emerge from a set of monolithic medical devices, through an ensemble of interoperable connected devices, to a distributed system with consistent behavior. The research efforts aim to assist the surgical personnel and to keep the ever increasing complexity manageable. Instead of technology, the patient should be

© Springer Nature Switzerland AG 2018
D. Stoyanov et al. (Eds.): OR 2.0/CARE/CLIP/ISIC 2018, LNCS 11041, pp. 12–19, 2018.
https://doi.org/10.1007/978-3-030-01201-4_2

the focus. However, automation usually bears severe risks that limit the scope. Hence, we propose a method for the context-aware assignment of medical device functions to input devices in integrated operating rooms. By means of that, surgeon's direct control can be increased with a limited interaction complexity.

2 Materials and Methods

The designed approach relies on medical device interoperability and the availability of intraoperative technical context-awareness. Thus, the basic principles of both prerequisites and their existing implementations are briefly summarized.

2.1 Medical Device Interoperability and Context-Awareness

An openly integrated technical environment is an essential prerequisite for a comprehensive workflow recognition based on data from various sources as well as for the implementation of remote control. The emerging IEEE 11073 SDC standards family for medical device interoperability introduces the service-oriented architecture paradigm to operating rooms [6] and will frame the access to data and control across vendors. In this context, input devices, such as buttons and pedals [7], act as service providers analogously to medical devices offering control functionalities, such as parameter settings and operations. Following the concept discussed in [1], we developed an orchestration component that enables a dynamic configuration of remote control.

The context-aware online assignment of controls requires the intraoperative provision of information on the operational context of the medical devices. The implementation is based on an existing context-awareness pipeline that gathers data for recognition, performs a mapping to low-level tasks, processes a network of process models and additional components to provide a comprehensive situation description (*Surgical Process Context*), and shares these data via SDC network [5]. The contextual information also include predictions of upcoming work steps based on the method described in [8]. The proposed dynamic assignment is based on the situation description, especially the ongoing low-level work step and the potential upcoming tasks.

2.2 Modeling of User Interaction Needs

We propose a novel modeling approach for the realization of dynamic functionality assignment. The human-machine interaction is described as a set of interaction use cases, for instance setting the shaver's parameters and using it to remove soft tissue. The use case can be further decomposed into a set of atomic interactions, such as the step-by-step decrease or increase of the revolution limit and the continuous motor control. The interactions are described by a basic type, a target, such as the device setting, and a categorical input type to distinguish between triggers and continuous control.

The interactions are associated to the surgical workflow by mapping them to low-level tasks. To that end, the modeling approach includes pre-configuration and initiating interactions (pre-step interactions) as well as interactions during an ongoing work step (intra-step interactions). For example, the revolution limit of the shaver might be configured prior the actual work step of tissue removal. Hence, the decrease and increase interactions are required for pre-configuration. The motor control via foot pedal initiates the tissue removal work step and is thus also required prior to the work step (pre-step need). In this example, all three interactions are as well required during the actual removal work step (intra-step need).

In the formal modeling, the probability for each pre-step interaction as well as the probability of each intra-step interaction are provided. In addition, the probabilities are modeled user-dependent to represent each member of the surgical team individually. If recordings of surgeries are available, the probabilities may be determined empirically. The aspects of human-machine interaction that are essential for a dynamic assignment of controls during surgery may then be described in terms of user's interactions associated to low-level tasks. The resulting interaction use cases are user-specific and depend on the type of surgery.

2.3   Modeling of Interaction Profiles

Besides the users' needs modeled so far, a representation of available input devices, such as switches at handles or foot pedals, is necessary for a dynamic assignment. The required risk management for remote control poses considerable challenges for the modeling. For example, an input device needs to respect the risk class of the controlled medical device. Otherwise, an assignment shall be prohibited. Furthermore, the assignments should be consistent in each situation to achieve a sufficient user acceptance. For example, decreasing and increasing a device parameter should be assigned to a pair of co-located buttons.

To ensure consistent and safe configurations, a pre-definition of interaction profiles is proposed. When designing such a profile, functions are assigned to input devices allowing for a comprehensive risk management and the preservation of consistency. Whilst for each input device, the modeling complexity is reduced to the interaction assignment and an access probability for each user. By means of an access probabilities, input devices may be mainly or exclusively associated to certain users, for instance the buttons on the endoscope camera head will be used by the surgeon exclusively. The interaction profiles add another layer of specificity to the interaction use cases, as they depend on the available input devices and their accessibility by the team members.

2.4   Intraoperative Profile Selection

The dynamic assignment of functions to input devices is realized by a context-aware automated selection of the most appropriate interaction profile. The OR system performs the selection at the beginning of each low-level task. The set of interactions that the optimal profile would have to cover consists of the intra-step interactions of the actual work step and the pre-step interactions of the upcoming next task. Thus, the suitability of an interaction profile depends on the actual work step as well as on the upcoming task, which is yet not known. An online profile selection method must rely on predictions, especially a probability distribution over potentially forthcoming tasks.

We designed a score for an online assessment of the suitability of each interaction profile. The scoring uses the ongoing workflow, the prediction of forthcoming tasks, the modeled user interaction needs, and the interaction assignments of the profiles. The recently begun work step and the prediction are considered to be given as they are part of the *Surgical Process Context* [5]. For a given work step s_t and the potential upcoming tasks s_{t+1}, a score ω_u can be calculated for a profile π with pre-step interactions $\bar{i}$ and interaction during the work step i as follows for each user.

$$\omega_u(\pi) = \frac{\sum_{i \in \pi} p(i|s_t)}{\sum_i p(i|s_t)} \tag{1}$$

The required conditional probabilities $p(i|s_t)$ are given by the modeling of the user needs. Equation 1 represents the coverage of the user's current needs. By design, there should be at least one interaction profile with full coverage.

$$\bar{\omega}_u(\pi) = \sum_{s_{t+1}} \left(p(s_{t+1}|s_t) \frac{\sum_{\bar{i} \in \pi} (p_d(\bar{i}) \cdot p(\bar{i}|s_{t+1}))}{\sum_i p(i|s_{t+1})} \right) \tag{2}$$

Equation 2 represents the coverage of needs for potential upcoming tasks, which are weight by the corresponding transition probability and the accessibility of the input device $p_d(\bar{i})$ that the interaction is assigned to. The score of a profile $\omega(\pi)$ may then be calculated as a weighted sum over all user-dependent scores ω_u and $\bar{\omega}_u$ respectively. Both, ω_u and $\bar{\omega}_u$ are defined to be zero if no interaction is required for the given task. The user's priority is expressed as β_u. The parameter $\alpha \in [0; 1]$ allows to balance between the interactions needed in the ongoing work step and those required to initiate potential upcoming tasks.

$$\omega(\pi) = \sum_u \beta_u \cdot (\alpha \cdot \omega_u + (1 - \alpha)\bar{\omega}_u) \tag{3}$$

Finally, the interaction profile with the highest score is selected. To resolve inconclusive cases, an appropriate linear ordering is defined and the candidate profile with the smallest distance to the previously active profile is selected.

2.5   Technical Integration and Risk Management

The proposed scoring method needs to be integrated into the service-oriented operating room infrastructure. To that end, an orchestration component acts as a service consumer to the input devices, the medical devices, and the context provider. Based on the current interaction profile, the component must react to communicated user interactions by remote controlling the corresponding medical device. Therefore, the orchestration component becomes part of the command processing chain and must respect the risk class of the controlled device, just as the input device has to. Whenever a new low-level work step has been recognized, the most suitable interaction profile is automatically selected. However, such a dynamic changing of control assignments bears severe risks. Essentially, the user needs to be informed about the current assignment of the available input devices. This may be realized with a continuous display, as for instance proposed in [7]. To avoid an additional display, we propose a two-level risk mitigation based on a preliminary risk analysis. Whenever the interaction profile is changed, a temporary overlay is shown in the field of view of the surgeon, which displays the input device assignments. And in case of uncertainties, a static interaction can be used to show the overlay on demand. Figure 1 depicts to examples of temporary overlays provided by the orchestration component to communicate the recently changed assignments to the user.

Fig. 1. Overlays of a new interaction assignment of the spin-click wheel on the *Visus JiveX* viewer during preparation (left) and of a new assignment of the buttons at the endoscope camera head during sinus surgery (right).

Furthermore, the orchestration component needs to mitigate the risk of unintended actions due to profile changes simultaneously to user interactions. To that end, the profile is not changed while an interaction is ongoing, for instance a foot pedal is pressed down. Additionally, an input device is blocked for several seconds after its assignment has been changed automatically, and a visual feedback is given in the video overlay. The feasibility of the approach may depend on the risk management for a concrete assignment in a concrete clinical use case. For assorted functions, for instance coagulation, the blocking time might not be feasible and functions like these must be excluded from the dynamic assignment. However, we expect that a broad set of functions will be manageable.

3   Experiments

We have conducted initial experiments for the *Functional Endoscopic Sinus Surgery (FESS)* - a common surgery in ENT - in a demonstration setup. The ventilation and the drainage of the paranasal sinuses are restored under endoscopic vision with powered shavers, suction, and other instruments. Optionally, a surgical navigation system is used. The demonstration setup included all necessary devices and a viewer for medical records. For the initial technical validation presented here, recordings of twenty-four previously simulated workflows were used [5]. The workflows covered the essential surgical activities with respect to the technical limitations. The procedures consisted of thirty-five distinguishable activities including preparation tasks, tissue removal, cavity traversal, occasional endoscope cleanings, medical record access, and navigation usage.

In the present experiments, we focused on the surgeon's interactions. The technical setup included three relevant input devices: a spin-click wheel with three interactions, a foot switch with three pedals, and two buttons at the endoscope camera head. However, the spin-click wheel is not accessible to the surgeon while using the endoscope and the endoscope camera buttons are not accessible otherwise. Effectively, six input devices are available during the initial patient preparation and the final after care, and five input device are available during the endoscopic phase. The modeling of the human-machine interaction included twenty atomic interactions, among them shaver settings and motor control, displaying the navigation or the medical record viewer on the secondary display, or scrolling through documents and pages of the medical record. The useful combinations of these interactions were represented in fourteen interaction profiles. Especially the interactions for forthcoming tasks in various combinations increased the amount of required interaction profiles.

A leave-one-out cross scenario was used to evaluate the performance of the proposed scoring approach for the online selection of an appropriate interaction profile. Although the simulated workflows were based on former recordings of real interventions, the probabilities for interactions could not be determined empirically. Hence, for the technical validation we assume every interaction defined in the interaction use cases is always required, especially $p(i|s_t) \in \{0, 1\}$. Furthermore, we weighted the coverage of the current needs and the forthcoming interactions equally ($\alpha = 0.5$, see Eq. 3). We analyzed the rate of availability of the required pre-step and intra-step interactions.

4   Results

In the cross validation, 1245 work steps were analyzed, of which 1162 can include human-machine interaction, such as capture an endoscopic image for documentation purposes or configure the parameters of a medical device. Table 1 lists the availability of the interactions in the experiments with the proposed scoring approach. As already discussed, the interaction profiles are designed so that at least one profile covers all required intra-step interactions for each interaction use case. The results for intra-step interactions show that the method always selects a profile with full coverage of the intra-step needs.

Due to the limited number of available input devices (five during endoscopy, six otherwise), the method has to rely on the predictions of forthcoming steps. None of the interaction profiles is capable of providing all potentially required pre-step interactions. In 57 work steps, at least one of the required interactions

Table 1. The availability of interactions to pre-configure and initiate (pre-step) and of interactions required during the work steps (intra-step).

Interaction availability		
Interaction	Pre-step availability	Intra-step availability
Display medical record	51 of 60 (0.850)	—
Previous page in record	—	102 of 102 (1.0)
Next page in record	—	102 of 102 (1.0)
Previous document in record	—	102 of 102 (1.0)
Next document in record	—	102 of 102 (1.0)
Display navigation	38 of 59 (0.644)	—
Back in navigation wizard	—	28 of 28 (1,0)
Acquire in navigation wizard	—	28 of 28 (1.0)
Next in navigation wizard	—	28 of 28 (1.0)
Toggle reslice instrument	—	31 of 31 (1.0)
Motor control of shaver	70 of 76 (0.921)	76 of 76 (1.0)
Decrease revolution limit	70 of 76 (0.921)	76 of 76 (1.0)
Increase revolution limit	50 of 76 (0.658)	76 of 76 (1.0)
Toggle suction	158 of 159 (0.994)	235 of 235 (1.0)
Decrease suction pressure	—	159 of 159 (1.0)
Increase suction pressure	—	159 of 159 (1.0)
Toggle endoscopic light	37 of 37 (1.0)	37 of 37 (1.0)
Decrease light intensity	—	37 of 37 (1.0)
Increase light intensity	—	37 of 37 (1.0)
Capture endoscopic image	—	766 of 766 (1.0)

was not directly available for the surgeon. Overall, 2655 of the 2724 required interactions were available (97.5%). Most of the misses occurred for the increase of the shaver revolution limit during suction of nasal cavities and for the switching of the secondary screen. In the suction-related profiles, there is no input device left to also provide the revolution limit increase, which is the least critical pre-step interaction. The switching of the secondary screen is assigned to a single button in most profiles; hence, the system needs to predict whether the navigation or the medical record will be needed next, which tends to be challenging resulting in 30 misses. However, predictions significantly contribute to the availability rates by enforcing profiles with probable pre-step interactions.

5   Conclusion

The presented method for online selection of interaction profiles aims to simplify human-machine interaction in increasingly complex surgical working environments. The results of the preliminary technical validation indicate that the proposed approach has the potential to increase the surgeon's direct control while preserving operability with a reasonable amount of input devices. However, a careful design of the interaction profiles with respect to the clinical use case and the technical setting is still essential. The effectiveness of empirically determined probabilities in the model and multi-user scenarios need to be evaluated, both technically and pre-clinically on phantoms.

The integration of the method into a interoperable medical device ensemble realizes an additional aspect of context-aware assistance in the operating room. The context-aware assignment of functions to input devices will ease the complexity for the staff in cases where potential risks make automation impossible.

References

1. Kasparick, M., Schmitz, M., Golatowski, F., Timmermann, D.: Dynamic remote control through service orchestration of point-of-care and surgical devices based on IEEE 11073 SDC. In: IEEE, November 2016, pp. 121–125 (2016)
2. Vitting, A., Janß, A., Strathen, B., Strake, M., Radermacher, K.: Further development and evaluation of a universal foot switch for diverse medical disciplines within the framework of an open integration concept for the operation theatre of the future. In: Duffy, V., Lightner, N. (eds.) AHFE 2017. AISC, vol. 590, pp. 438–449. Springer, Cham (2018). https://doi.org/10.1007/978-3-319-60483-1_45
3. Feussner, H., et al.: Surgery 4.0. In: Thuemmler C., Bai C., (eds.) Health 4.0: How Virtualization and Big Data are Revolutionizing Healthcare. Springer, Cham (2017). https://doi.org/10.1007/978-3-319-47617-9_5
4. Maier-Hein, L., et al.: Surgical data science for next-generation interventions. Nat. Biomed. Eng. $1(9)$, 691–696 (2017)
5. Franke, S., Rockstroh, M., Hofer, M., Neumuth, T.: The intelligent OR: design and validation of a context-aware surgical working environment. Int. J. Comput. Assist. Radiol. Surg. (2018)
6. Kasparick, M., et al.: OR.NET: a service-oriented architecture for safe and dynamic medical device interoperability. Biomed. Eng./Biomedizinische Technik $63(1)$, p. 11 (2018)
7. Dell'Anna, J., Janß, A., Clusmann, H., Radermacher, K.: A configurable footswitch unit for the open networked neurosurgical OR - development, evaluation and future perspectives. i-com $15(3)$, 227–247 (2016)
8. Franke, S., Neumuth, T.: Adaptive surgical process models for prediction of surgical work steps from surgical low-level activities. In: 6th Workshop on Modeling and Monitoring of Computer Assisted Interventions (M2CAI) at the 18th International Conference on Medical Image Computing and Computer Assisted Interventions (MICCAI), September 2015

Interactive Training and Operation Ecosystem for Surgical Tasks in Mixed Reality

Ehsan Azimi[1]([⊠]), Camilo Molina[2], Alexander Chang[1], Judy Huang[2], Chien-Ming Huang[1], and Peter Kazanzides[1]

[1] Department of Computer Science, Johns Hopkins University,
Baltimore, MD 21218, USA
{eazimi1,pkaz}@jhu.edu
[2] Department of Neurosurgery, Johns Hopkins Hospital,
Baltimore, MD 21287, USA

Abstract. Inadequate skill in performing surgical tasks can lead to medical errors and cause avoidable injury or death to the patients. On the other hand, there are situations where a novice surgeon or resident does not have access to an expert while performing a task.

We therefore propose an interactive ecosystem for both training and practice of surgical tasks in mixed reality, which consists of authoring of the desired surgical task, immersive training and practice, assessment of the trainee, and remote coaching and analysis. This information-based ecosystem will also provide the data to train machine learning algorithms.

Our interactive ecosystem involves a head-mounted display (HMD) application that can provide feedback as well as audiovisual assistance for training and live clinical performance of the task. In addition, the remote monitoring station provides the expert with a real-time view of the scene from the user's perspective and enables guidance by providing annotation directly on the user's scene. We use bedside ventriculostomy, a neurosurgical procedure, as our illustrative use case; however the modular design of the system makes it expandable to other procedures.

Keywords: Surgical training and assessment
Medical augmented reality · Surgical simulation and modeling
Artificial intelligence

1 Introduction

The complexity of medical interventions are continuously increasing. However, due to working-hour restrictions, increasing costs, and ethical concerns regarding patient safety, clinical training opportunities are continuously decreasing [18]. Similarly, although modern tertiary care hospitals are built upon a hierarchy of novice to expert training levels, a novice resident may not always have a

© Springer Nature Switzerland AG 2018
D. Stoyanov et al. (Eds.): OR 2.0/CARE/CLIP/ISIC 2018, LNCS 11041, pp. 20–29, 2018.
https://doi.org/10.1007/978-3-030-01201-4_3

senior resident or attending immediately available for help in the setting of an emergency. This is more likely in rural areas where often there are not enough skilled surgeons to provide expert supervision or assistance.

The above factors present an opportunity to develop a practical technological solution that can support training and operation, including the ability to instantaneously connect a novice to a remote expert. Computer-based applications and augmented reality (AR) systems are increasingly popular to support the training of medical professionals, as they can result in new educational opportunities [5]. Due to recent technical advances in commercial optical see-through head-mounted display (OST-HMD) devices, there has been a considerable increase in their use for augmented reality applications and their specifications have become suitable for medical applications [12,15].

HMDs have been used in the medical domain for treatment, education, rehabilitation and surgery [6,7,9]. An early HMD research effort focused on giving the surgeon an unobstructed view of the anatomy which is rendered inside the patient's body [17]. With the advent of Google Glass around 2013, many research groups started to explore using an HMD as a replacement for traditional radiology monitors [2,19]. The use of a HMD to visualize volumetric medical data for neurosurgery planning was presented in [8]; together with a haptic device, the system allows the user to scroll through the image slices more intuitively. More recently, a generalized real-time streaming system based on OST-HMDs was proposed for image-guided surgeries, including percutaneous screw fixation of pelvic fractures [13].

Our prior work includes picture-in-picture visualization for neurosurgery navigation on a custom HMD [3,16] and the use of OST-HMDs for training two emergency medical tasks: needle chest decompression and initiating an intravenous line [4]. Our experience with the latter effort led to the conceptualization of the interactive surgical training and operation system described herein. We extend our prior approach by adding modules for content generation, remote monitoring, smart assessment, and procedure analysis. The HMD-based training application is designed to be independent of the training procedure; thus, although originally developed for emergency medical procedures, in this paper we consider ventriculostomy, which is a neurosurgical procedure that involves insertion of a drain within a cerebral ventricle for cerebrospinal fluid diversion for a variety of urgent indications. We then discuss how such technology can change the future of medical training, including by providing training data for machine learning algorithms in an artificial intelligence module.

2   System Architecture

The overall schematic of the training and practice ecosystem is shown in Fig. 1. This structure allows the expert surgeon to intuitively create a training module and the trainees to then use it for practice. It also provides real-time corrective assistance and access to the expert. We go through each element of this system and the way it operates with the other components.

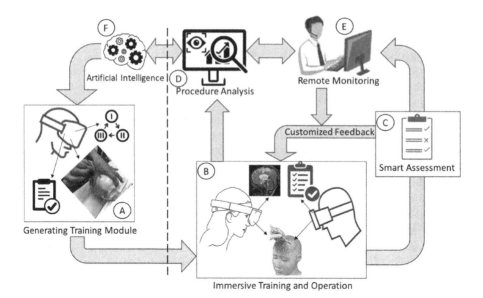

Fig. 1. Schematic overview of the interactive surgical training and operation ecosystem and its interconnections, (A) shows the application for generating tutorials, (B) is the HMD-Based immersive environment for practice and training, (C) is the automatic assessment module, (D) is the analysis of the procedure in the OR setting, (E) is the remote monitoring station for the expert, and (F) is the offline analysis (AI) based on data from multiple trainees.

2.1   Training Module Generation

As depicted in Fig. 1A, this authoring tool allows a skilled surgeon to intuitively create his/her desired training module step-by-step using voice commands, with the resulting workflow and visual elements serialized into a data asset. The dashed line in the figure separating this module from the rest of the system indicates that it does not need to be in real-time communication with its neighboring components.

2.2   HMD-Based Training and Practice

We previously developed a software framework which can provide augmented reality guidance that is agnostic to the procedure [4]. The workflow of each procedure is abstracted and represented as a sequence of steps, with associated text and visual elements. As shown in Fig. 1B, during training or actual operation of the procedure, the workflow is dynamically loaded and parsed on the OST-HMD. The trainee or practitioner can then use voice commands to go through the training steps and hide or show their desired visualizations. This mode of interaction does not involve mouse or keyboard and allows the user to focus and perform bi-manual tasks without compromising sterility. In each step, the user can see the corresponding instruction, the correct position and orientation of the tool (registered to the anatomy) if required, as well as additional information such as medical imaging (CT, MRI, etc.) if needed. The training/operation can support an individual user as well as multiple users in a collaborative setting.

2.3 Smart Assessment

The smart assessment component (Fig. 1C) uses a number of metrics to determine performance of the trainee and provide real-time feedback during the task. These metrics can include the correct positioning of an instrument or its insertion angle or even its very presence or motion pattern during a phase of the surgery. This requires software to track the motion of the instrument, which can utilize the HMD cameras, including depth camera if available, and may be facilitated by the placement of AR tags or other markers on the instrument. In some cases, it may be necessary to use an external tracking system that would then be registered to the HMD. The feedback can be turned on and off based on the skill level and/or instructor's decision in the training or evaluation phase. It is capable of both warning the user with audiovisual cues or providing guidance to the user for correction.

2.4 Procedure Analysis

There are many instances where an operation fails despite having a highly skilled surgeon and the logistics in the OR may contribute to its success. This module, which is depicted in Fig. 1D, collects data from different sources and sensors in the simulation or operative field, and provides post-training or post-surgery analysis. It differs from Smart Assessment in that it looks into the 'surgery' in the context of the OR setting rather than merely the 'surgeon' as an individual. The feedback is not provided during the task, and instead focuses on overall performance, the events in the OR, comparing to a database of similar procedures or in collaboration with others. Collected data can include eye-gaze, surgeon's location and head motion and other pertinent sensors during the surgery, in addition to the data record from the surgery. This data can also be provided to the Artificial Intelligence component (Fig. 1F) for longer-term improvements, including training of machine learning algorithms using data from multiple users. This component also processes the data provided by the expert in the remote station as well as the smart assessment for the trainee's performance.

2.5 Remote Monitoring Station

As illustrated in Fig. 1E, an expert, who is typically a skilled surgeon, monitors the trainee's actions and is able to provide real-time feedback in the form of direct annotation on the trainee's screen as well as other types of audiovisual cues. This differs from a video call because the expert has a first person view of the field, in 3D, and can provide feedback or annotation in the HMD's immersive 3D environment. Furthermore, communication is bidirectional and the trainee can also ask questions from the expert. The remote monitoring station can be advantageous in situations where additional expert assistance is critical; for example, when a particular phase of the surgery is too complex for automated assessment (e.g., via the Smart Assessment module) or when there is a scarcity of experts in a particular field, which is especially common in rural areas. The expert is able to evaluate and score the user performance for each step of the procedure. The platform subsequently saves the record and sends it to the analyzer (Sect. 2.4) and artificial intelligence (Sect. 2.6) for further processing.

2.6   Artificial Intelligence

Recorded data from multiple users is provided to the Artificial Intelligence (AI) module for the purpose of process improvement. This data can be used to further train machine learning algorithms within the Smart Assessment and Procedure Analysis modules, thereby increasing their ability to provide feedback during or immediately after the procedure. For example, the gaze tracking data can indicate where on the HMD screen and in the OR the surgeon is paying more attention; AI methods may be able to use this data to identify a novice surgeon and provide additional guidance.

3   Implementation

To verify our proposed surgical training and practice system, we selected ventriculostomy, or external ventricular drainage, which is a surgical procedure to alleviate raised intracranial pressure by inserting a tube through the skull into the ventricles to divert cerebrospinal fluid. It is done by surgically penetrating the skull, dura mater, and brain such that the ventricle of the brain is accessed. This is one of the most frequent and standardized procedures in neurosurgery. However, many first and subsequent punctures miss the target, and suboptimal placement or misplacement of the catheter is common [14]. The trajectory of the catheter must be perpendicular to the skull at the entry point. Such 3D geometrical constraints along with the described complexities make this procedure an ideal candidate for augmented reality mediated 3D visualization to enable more accurate targeting and higher success rates. Additionally, ventriculostomy, like most neurosurgical procedures, can be conceptualized and segmented into critical task components, which can be simulated independently or in conjunction with other modules to recreate the experience of a complex neurosurgical procedure [10]. Our proposed system can be used both for training on a mannequin as well as during the real operation.

3.1   System Setup

The system setup is shown in Fig. 2b, which is also a snapshot of the training environment taken from the remote station. To simulate this neurosurgical procedure, a skull model (A) was fixed by a Mayfield clamp (B). Two ARTags (C)

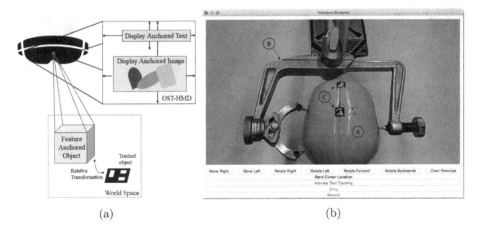

(a)   (b)

Fig. 2. (a) Representation of display anchored images and text (top), and feature anchored objects (bottom); (b) Remote monitoring station and system setup

were attached on the skull so that the camera can localize the designated landmarks. Two markers were used so that if one is occluded or out of the field of view, the camera can still see the other one.

The HMD software was developed using the cross-platform game engine Unity[1], along with C#. It was then deployed to Microsoft HoloLens[2]. The software on the remote monitoring station was developed using Python. It is cross-platform and can run on a PC, tablet, or other device.

The visual elements displayed on the HMD can be categorized based on their property (text, image, 3D object) and on their display space (display-anchored, feature-anchored), as shown in Fig. 2a. The location of a display-anchored object is defined with respect to 2D screen coordinates. For the HMD wearer, it will be fixed despite the user's head movement. In order to visualize the feature-anchored overlays in the correct pose, appropriate display calibration is performed so that the trainee can localize the designated anatomical landmark in the real world [11, 20].

3.2   Tutorial Generation

The training/operation module relies on a serialized data asset (JSON) that encodes the workflow. This module helps an expert surgeon to create this data asset. The expert wears the HMD and using voice commands starts generating the instructions step by step and adds the image (display-anchored) using the front camera of the HoloLens and uses a marker to create a landmark (feature-anchored) for the desired step, as shown in Fig. 3a.

---

[1] Unity: https://unity3d.com/.
[2] Microsoft HoloLens: https://www.microsoft.com/en-us/hololens.

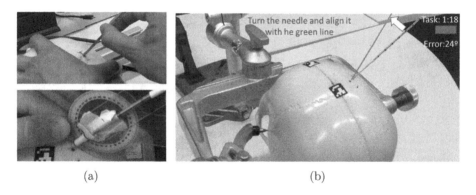

(a)   (b)

Fig. 3. Three components of the proposed ecosystem: (a) Tutorial generation by expert (top), angular calibration of needle (bottom). (b) HMD-based AR assistance for needle pose correction.

3.3   HMD-Based Training and Operation

Once the tutorial is generated, the trainee can use it as shown in Fig. 3b. Here, the HMD view of the trainee for one sample step is depicted, where the blue text is the instruction for this step, green indicates the correct orientation of the needle, and the yellow arrow guides the user toward the correct pose for the needle. The top right of the screen shows the orientation error, time on task as well as a red warning bar. Medical imaging data (CT, MRI, etc.) are also available and can be loaded by the user's voice command, eliminating the need to look at a separate monitor.

3.4   Remote Monitoring Station

A snapshot of the remote monitoring station is shown in Fig. 2b. The GUI enables the expert to stream the trainee or operator's view and send audiovisual messages to the HMD user. It communicates with the HMD wirelessly through the Internet using TCP/IP to receive HMD camera frames, and UDP to provide feedback or annotate the trainee's view on the HMD. The delay is approximately 50–100 ms (mostly for streaming images) in a local network setup, which is sufficient for this communication.

3.5   Smart Assessment

In the current implementation, Smart Assessment is integrated with the remote station and handles the tool tracking and networking. In ventriculostomy, it measures the error in the pose of the catheter at the entry point and assists the trainee to correct the pose using audiovisual cues. Tool tracking is done by computer vision and calculates the sagittal and coronal angles of the tool to determine if the needle is perpendicular to the skull. The needle is detected using a Hough line detector and segmentation in HSV color space. Measurements are calibrated using a goniometer as ground truth and interpolation (Fig. 3a).

3.6   Procedure Analysis

Eye-gaze trackers (Pupil-labs[3]) are mounted on the HMD. They depict the real-time gaze of the user to the remote station and aggregate both 2D and 3D gaze-data in the form of a heat-map and save it for analysis. Location of the operators/trainees in the OR is also tracked and saved. Other relevant data from the surgery is also fed to this module. Another method in the application logs each user's performance and its corresponding score based on the smart assessment metrics or expert feedback and saves it in a separate JSON file.

3.7   Artificial Intelligence

The Artificial Intelligence component will rely on data collected during the training/operation procedure and is an item for future work. For example, we can attempt to assess surgical skill from a heat map of the gaze-tracking data, as other studies have suggested that skill level and eye-gaze can be related [1].

4   Discussion

Modern surgical training has recognized the value of limiting weekly residency training hours. However, the limit in training hours combined with the ever increasing amount of medical knowledge an operator must master creates a significant challenge–how does one train residents to perform complex surgical procedures safely and independently if the time allotted to train residents is decreased? In order to bridge the gap of decreased clinical encounters to promote the safe delivery of care and the trainees' overall well-being, a solution that is capable of both training and supervising surgeons in training is necessary. The proposed system, presented in the context of a bedside ventriculostomy, has the potential of not only training residents how to properly execute this procedure but to also serve as a real-time platform to connect the training resident to an expert during a live clinical scenario.

   If successful, the present platform can be applied to a large variety of bedside sterile clinical procedures that residents are expected to perform independently early in their training. Examples of other applicable procedures that could be simulated for training or supervised during live clinical execution include: lumbar punctures, lumbar drains, chest tube insertion, central line insertion, intraosseous line insertion, arterial line placement, intubation, pleurocentesis, etc. All of the latter procedures, when taught conventionally, can be broken down into discrete steps that make them well suited to be adapted and presented in our training simulation platform. Similarly, all of the latter procedures can benefit from a remote clinical expert that can help a novice troubleshoot a difficult procedure by assisting with the small nuances that can only come from experience.

---

[3] Pupil-labs: https://pupil-labs.com/.

5   Conclusion

In this work, a comprehensive system for training and performing surgical tasks in mixed reality was introduced. The system includes an authoring module, training and practice setup, smart assessment, and a remote station for the expert. These have been implemented for bedside ventriculostomy and our next step is to conduct a user study with neurosurgery residents. We also plan to extend this platform for other types of procedures that can contribute to resident training and education. Moreover, the capture of data from the HMD, sensors, and remote expert further enables process improvements via data mining and training of artificial intelligence.

Acknowledgement. We thank Professor Russell Taylor for his guidance and Patrick Myers, Benjamin Pikus, Prateek Bhatnagar and Allan Wang for their assistance with the software development.

References

1. Ahmidi, N., Hager, G.D., Ishii, L., Fichtinger, G., Gallia, G.L., Ishii, M.: Surgical task and skill classification from eye tracking and tool motion in minimally invasive surgery. In: Jiang, T., Navab, N., Pluim, J.P.W., Viergever, M.A. (eds.) MICCAI 2010. LNCS, vol. 6363, pp. 295–302. Springer, Heidelberg (2010). https://doi.org/10.1007/978-3-642-15711-0_37
2. Armstrong, D.G., Rankin, T.M., Giovinco, N.A., Mills, J.L., Matsuoka, Y.: A heads-up display for diabetic limb salvage surgery: a view through the google looking glass. J. Diabetes Sci. Technol. **8**(5), 951–956 (2014)
3. Azimi, E., Doswell, J., Kazanzides, P.: Augmented reality goggles with an integrated tracking system for navigation in neurosurgery. In: Virtual Reality Short Papers and Posters (VRW), pp. 123–124. IEEE (2012)
4. Azimi, E., et al.: Can mixed-reality improve the training of medical procedures? In: IEEE Engineering in Medicine and Biology Conference (EMBC), pp. 112–116, July 2018
5. Barsom, E.Z., Graafland, M., Schijven, M.P.: Systematic review on the effectiveness of augmented reality applications in medical training. Surg. Endosc. **30**(10), 4174–4183 (2016)
6. Chen, L., Day, T., Tang, W., John, N.W.: Recent developments and future challenges in medical mixed reality. In: IEEE International Symposium on Mixed and Augmented Reality (ISMAR), pp. 123–135 (2017)
7. Cutolo, F., et al.: A new head-mounted display-based augmented reality system in neurosurgical oncology: a study on phantom. Comput. Assist. Surg. **22**(1), 39–53 (2017)
8. Eck, U., Stefan, P., Laga, H., Sandor, C., Fallavollita, P., Navab, N.: Exploring visuo-haptic augmented reality user interfaces for stereo-tactic neurosurgery planning. In: Zheng, G., Liao, H., Jannin, P., Cattin, P., Lee, S.-L. (eds.) MIAR 2016. LNCS, vol. 9805, pp. 208–220. Springer, Cham (2016). https://doi.org/10.1007/978-3-319-43775-0_19
9. Kersten-Oertel, M., Jannin, P., Collins, D.L.: DVV: a taxonomy for mixed reality visualization in image guided surgery. IEEE Trans. Vis. Comput. Graph. **18**(2), 332–352 (2012)

10. Lemole Jr., G.M., Banerjee, P.P., Luciano, C., Neckrysh, S., Charbel, F.T.: Virtual reality in neurosurgical education: part-task ventriculostomy simulation with dynamic visual and haptic feedback. Neurosurgery **61**(1), 142–149 (2007)

11. Qian, L., Azimi, E., Kazanzides, P., Navab, N.: Comprehensive tracker based display calibration for holographic optical see-through head-mounted display. arXiv preprint arXiv:1703.05834 (2017)

12. Qian, L., et al.: Comparison of optical see-through head-mounted displays for surgical interventions with object-anchored 2D-display. Int. J. Comput. Assist. Radiol. Surg. (IJCARS) **12**(6), 901–910 (2017)

13. Qian, L., et al.: Towards virtual monitors for image guided interventions-real-time streaming to optical see-through head-mounted displays. arXiv preprint arXiv:1710.00808 (2017)

14. Raabe, C., Fichtner, J., Beck, J., Gralla, J., Raabe, A.: Revisiting the rules for freehand ventriculostomy: a virtual reality analysis. J. Neurosurg. **128**(4), 1250–1257 (2018)

15. Rolland, J.P., Fuchs, H.: Optical versus video see-through head-mounted displays in medical visualization. Presence Teleoperators Virtual Environ. **9**(3), 287–309 (2000)

16. Sadda, P., Azimi, E., Jallo, G., Doswell, J., Kazanzides, P.: Surgical navigation with a head-mounted tracking system and display. Stud. Health Technol. Inform. **184**, 363–369 (2012)

17. Saucer, F., Khamene, A., Bascle, B., Rubino, G.J.: A head-mounted display system for augmented reality image guidance: towards clinical evaluation for imri-guided nuerosurgery. In: Niessen, W.J., Viergever, M.A. (eds.) MICCAI 2001. LNCS, vol. 2208, pp. 707–716. Springer, Heidelberg (2001). https://doi.org/10.1007/3-540-45468-3_85

18. Stefan, P., et al.: A mixed-reality approach to radiation-free training of C-arm based surgery. In: Descoteaux, M., Maier-Hein, L., Franz, A., Jannin, P., Collins, D.L., Duchesne, S. (eds.) MICCAI 2017. LNCS, vol. 10434, pp. 540–547. Springer, Cham (2017). https://doi.org/10.1007/978-3-319-66185-8_61

19. Yoon, J.W., Chen, R.E., Han, P.K., Si, P., Freeman, W.D., Pirris, S.M.: Technical feasibility and safety of an intraoperative head-up display device during spine instrumentation. Int. J. Med. Robot. Comp. Assisted Surg. **13**(3), 1–9 (2017)

20. Azimi, E., Qian, L., Kazanzides, P., Navab, N.:Robust optical see-through head-mounted display calibration: taking anisotropic nature of user interaction errors into account. In: IEEE Virtual Reality (VR), Los Angeles, CA, pp. 219–220 (2017)

FaceOff: Anonymizing Videos
in the Operating Rooms

Evangello Flouty[1(✉)], Odysseas Zisimopoulos[1], and Danail Stoyanov[1,2]

[1] Digital Surgery, London, UK
Evangello.Flouty@touchsurgery.com
[2] Wellcome/ESPRC Centre for Interventional and Surgical Sciences, London, UK

Abstract. Video capture in the surgical operating room (OR) is increasingly possible and has potential for use with computer assisted interventions (CAI), surgical data science and within smart OR integration. Captured video innately carries sensitive information that should not be completely visible in order to preserve the patient's and the clinical teams' identities. When surgical video streams are stored on a server, the videos must be anonymized prior to storage if taken outside of the hospital. In this article, we describe how a deep learning model, Faster R-CNN, can be used for this purpose and help to anonymize video data captured in the OR. The model detects and blurs faces in an effort to preserve anonymity. After testing an existing face detection trained model, a new dataset tailored to the surgical environment, with faces obstructed by surgical masks and caps, was collected for fine-tuning to achieve higher face-detection rates in the OR. We also propose a temporal regularisation kernel to improve recall rates. The fine-tuned model achieves a face detection recall of 88.05% and 93.45% before and after applying temporal-smoothing respectively.

Keywords: Anonymization · Face detection · Surgical data science
Smart ORs

1 Introduction

Video cameras are pervasive within the modern operating room (OR) and used extensively during surgery, for example in laparoscopic or robotic assisted surgery, but with minimal video utilization. Specifically many integrated operating rooms now incorporate surveillance cameras or documentation cameras integrated within the surgical lights or in the ceiling. The video data collected by such devices is highly sensitive because it records events during the operation and also the identities of staff and patients within the OR. Yet, the video can have multiple uses in educational material or in the analysis and automation of OR optimisation systems through surgical data science platforms [1]. To be able to use the recorded videos in the OR, video processing must take place to

D. Stoyanov et al. (Eds.): OR 2.0/CARE/CLIP/ISIC 2018, LNCS 11041, pp. 30–38, 2018.
https://doi.org/10.1007/978-3-030-01201-4_4

ensure the data is anonymized and safe to be used. It is possible to approach video anonymization through computer vision algorithms for face detection but making such systems work well in surgical environments is difficult because the OR has variable lighting conditions, multiple occlusion possibilities and also the team wears surgical drapes and masks.

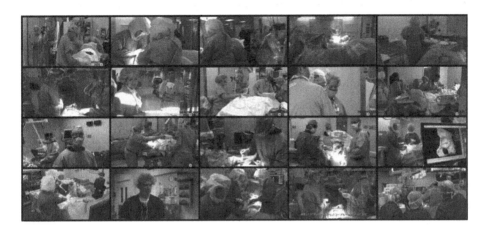

Fig. 1. FaceOff images, collected from Youtube, showing the faces in the surgical environment potentially exposing sensitive information

Real-time face detection is a mature field in computer vision [2]. As with many problems in the field, techniques using hand crafted features such as HOG [3], have recently been superseded by convolutional neural networks (CNNs) based approaches using deep learning for detection [4–6], pose estimation [7], and emotion prediction [8]. The introduction of big datasets such as FDDB [10], IJB-A [9], and WIDER [11] has empowered the use of deep learning models and enhanced robustness and efficiency, shown by the evolution of approaches from recurrent CNN (RCNN) [12], followed by Fast-RCNN [13], and finally Faster-RCNN [14]. The results for these architectures are impressive but their translation into the clinical setting faces challenges because the data needs adaptation to deal with masked faces, surgical caps and the lighting variability within the room.

In this paper, we adopt the Faster-RCNN model pre-trained on the available WIDER dataset and we adapt it for face detection in the OR. Faces in the OR are very different from the WIDER dataset due to masks, caps, and surgical magnifying glasses. Detecting such faces is difficult and requires model adaptation, which we achieve through collecting surgical data from web search engines, labelled and used to fine-tune the model. To achieve anonymization, it is important that the model catches as many faces as possible. A sliding window for temporal smoothing was implemented and then applied on the detections to have a higher chance of detecting any missed face (a false negative). Our method shows promising results on our validation dataset which will be made available to the community.

2   Methods and Data

Wider Dataset. The dataset consists of 32,203 images with 393,703 faces in 61 different environments (meetings, concerts, parades, etc.). It is also worth noting that this dataset include 166 images (in the training set) of faces in the surgical environment. This dataset is commonly used for benchmarking face detection. Faster RCNN is in the top 4 of all the submissions that used the WIDER dataset to benchmark performance [15].

FaceOff Dataset. We collected 15 videos of surgical ORs from the video search engine Youtube. All were publicly available with "Standard Youtube License" (videos can be used freely). The keywords used for searching: surgery, real-time surgery, surgery in the operating room/theatre, recorded surgery... Figure 1 shows a sample of the dataset. In total, the dataset consists of 6371 images describing 12786 faces. The images show variability in scales and occlusions of faces in the OR to achieve a good learning of the facial features in the OR.

2.1   Faster R-CNN

Faster R-CNN uses a regional proposal network (RPN) that estimates bounding boxes around regions in the input image. It is scale invariant as it proposes regions of many scales before interrogating each with one of two CNNs: ZFnet [17] and VGG-16 [16]. The convolutional layers are shared with the RPN (unlike the architecture in Fast R-CNN), making computation efficient. The CNNs evaluate regions using the intersection of union (IoU) of each anchor with the ground truth bounding boxes of the input image during training to determine if the region is used as a positive or negative sample. The RPN proposes around 21000 regions per image but after non-max filtering (NMF) around 2000 valid anchors remain and only 256 positive anchors, and 256 negative anchors are then chosen for training.

The loss function of the RPN incorporates several parts shown in the equations below:

$$\mathcal{L}(p_i, t_i) = \frac{1}{N_{cls}} \sum_i \mathcal{L}_{cls}(p_i, p_i^*) + \lambda \frac{1}{N_{reg}} \sum_i p_i^* \mathcal{L}_{reg}(t_i, t_i^*) \tag{1}$$

$$\mathcal{L}_{cls}(p_i, p_i^*) = -log(\frac{e^{f_{y_i}}}{\sum_j e^{f_j}}) \tag{2}$$

$$\mathcal{L}_{reg}(t_i, t_i^*) = smooth_{L_1}(t_i - t_i^*) = \begin{cases} 0.5 \ (t_i - t_i^*)^2, & \text{if } |t_i - t_i^*| < 1 \\ |t_i - t_i^*| - 0.5, & \text{otherwise} \end{cases} \tag{3}$$

The first part measures the error of the classifier whether the region is a class (in this case a face) or not. Where p_i is the predicted probability, p_i^* is either 0 (when the region describes the background class) or 1 (when the region describes the foreground class, in this case a face), and finally N_{cls} is the mini-batch size (in this case $2 * 256 = 512$). The classifier loss as shown in Eq. (2) is the soft-max loss of the predicted class. The second part tries to measure the error of box regressors. Where λ is a constant, p_i^* is the predicted probability (this means this part of the equation is only activated for positive anchors where $p_i^* = 1$), t_i is the predicted box, t_i^* the ground truth box, and finally N_{reg} is the total number of valid anchors (in this case around 2000). The box regressor loss is the smoothing function of the predicted box as shown in Eq. (3). It tries to minimize the difference between the predicted box and the ground truth box.

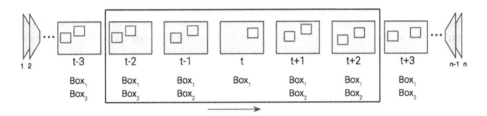

Fig. 2. The kernel size of the sliding average window is 5. The sliding average kernel estimates the missing Box_2 at frame t by averaging the corresponding detected Box_2 in the adjacent frames $\in [t - 2, t + 2]$.

2.2 Sliding Kernel Smoother

Despite the excellent performance of a per-frame face detection method, temporal discontinuities are still possible and need to be handled with a non-detection driven approach. For anonymization, having a high recall (or low false negatives) is the main target for the model to achieve. While the described Faster R-CNN captures spatial information exceptionally well it can suffer from period occlusion or failure when faces turn or enter variable illumination conditions. But since videos will be inferred using the model, valuable temporal information can potentially be lost. As illustrated in the Fig. 2 schematic, the model sometimes misses faces even though it successfully detected the same face in adjacent frames. To take advantage of that, a sliding window of kernel sizes $k = 3, 5, 7$ were applied to smooth in the detections to be able to anonymize the missed faces. Doing so will also generate more false positives as the smoothing kernel does not incorporate visual information. As described in Fig. 2, the smoothing window will apply a moving average on the centre frame t and estimates Box_2 at frame t with the aim of anonymizing a missed face.

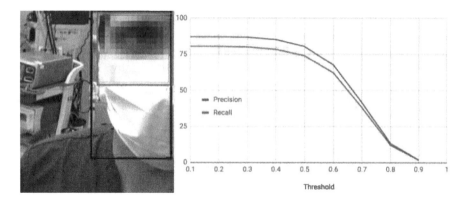

Fig. 3. Left: An example case showing the intuition of picking the right IOU threshold to calculate the metrics. The green and pink bounding boxes describes the ground truth and detected face respectively. As seen in the image, the anonymization has occurred given the area above the mask was detected. The detected region is less than half the area of the annotated face. Therefore, a threshold of $t = 0.3$ was used. **Right**: The precision and recall as a function of the value of the IOU threshold that counts a detection whether its a true positive or a false positive (Color figure online)

3   Experiments and Results

Calculating Activations: Given that the model returns a bounding box, a metric must quantify how correct is that bounding box. This section will explain how those metrics where calculated. There are 4 detection cases that occur after inferring the test set. The first case occurs when the intersection over union (IOU) between the ground truth box and the predicted box is above a certain threshold t. This detection counts as a true positive. The second case occurs when there is no detected box close to a ground truth box. This counts as a false negative. The third case happens when there is a detected box without a ground truth box around it. This case counts as a false positive. Finally in the fourth case, when the IOU of the ground truth with the detected bounding box is lower that a threshold t, it counts as a false positive and a false negative (one for missing the detection, and one for detecting something that is not a face).

To set the threshold t, the precision and recall were calculated for 9 possible values. The results can be seen in the right section of Fig. 3. Intuitively speaking, both the precision and recall will drop as the IOU threshold increase as it will be less likely for the predicted box to be more aligned with the ground truth. This graph shows that the precision and recall are stable between 0.1 and 0.3. They start slowly decreasing between $t \in [0.4, 0.5]$. A sharp drop is observed after 0.5. After evaluating the above graph, a threshold of $t = 0.3$ was chosen. 0.3 is a good value for the IOU threshold because faces are mostly covered with surgical masks. The detections sometimes only cover the eye area as shown in the left section of Fig. 3, even thought the ground truth describes the whole face including the mask. This is a good detection as it anonymizes the face and therefore it must be counted as a true positive.

WIDER Fine-Tuning Setup: For a better anonymization, detecting normal faces is also crucial in the operating room. For that, the model from [15] was used. This paper fine-tuned a VGG-16 faster r-cnn trained on Imagenet using the WIDER dataset. They used stochastic gradient descent (SGD) for 50000 iterations with base learning rate of 10^{-3} and then ran another 30000 iterations with a base learning rate of 10^{-4}.

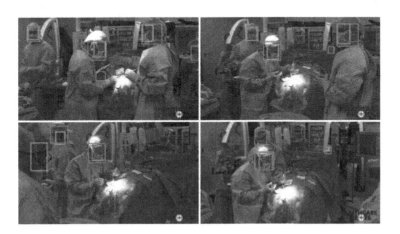

Fig. 4. Sample detections of both models. The WIDER trained model detections are shown in pink and the FaceOff fine-tuned model detections are shown in blue. (Color figure online)

FaceOff Fine-Tuning Setup: After training the model described above, we further fine-tuned the model on the newly collected dataset of faces in the OR. We trained the model on 8485 faces in the OR for 20000 iterations. The RPN generates 12000 and 2000 ROIs before and after applying NMF respectively. Model uses a mini-batch (batch of regions of ROIs) size of 64 (for normalisation), an IOU threshold of 0.7 and above to consider the ROI as an example of a face, and an IOU threshold of 0.3 and less to consider the ROI as an example of a background. The remaining ROIs (with IOU between $[0.3, 0.7]$ are discarded). Finally, a size set of 256 regions per class (256 regions for the face class, and 256 regions for the background class) is used for training.

We inferred the test set using the model trained on the WIDER dataset. The model returned a precision of 66.84%, a recall of 75.40%, and an F1 score of 70.86%. After those promising results, we fine-tuned the model using the FACE-OFF collected dataset with the setup discussed above. A precision of 82.58%, recall of 88.05%, and f1 score of 85.23% was achieved. A sample of the detections can be seen in Fig. 4.

In the surgical environment, the model must achieve a high recall since it is more important to detect a face than to falsely detect a face. In other words, the volume of false negatives should be as small as possible irrespective of the volume of false positives. To take advantage of the temporal information found in a video, the detections where smoothed around frames with no detections. Surrounding frames have very similar information with a high probability. Averaging the surrounding detections around a frame should help in detect false negatives. The disadvantage of this approach is that it is more likely to generate false positive than detecting false negatives. After getting the detections from the FaceOff fine-tuned Faster R-CNN model, a sliding window of kernel $k = 3, 5, 7$ was explored. Table 1 shows that the kernel of size 3 performed the best achieving a recall of 93.46%.

Table 1. Surgical face detection metrics of the different models tested.

Model	Precision	Recall	F1
Off-the-shelf	66.84%	75.40%	70.86%
Fine-Tuned on FaceOff	82.58%	88.05%	85.23%
Post-Smoothing k = 3	59.07%	**93.46%**	72.39%
Post-Smoothing k = 5	55.93%	93.45%	69.96%
Post-Smoothing k = 7	53.52%	93.26%	68.01%

4   Discussion and Conclusion

An increasing number of cameras are integrated in the OR (head mounted, ceiling mounted, light integrated, etc.) and anonymization of video is important in order to be able to use the recorded data for a wide range of purposes like documentation, teaching and surgical data science. In order to automatically blur faces in the recorded video, we have described a method and dataset that adapts the state-of-the-art face detection techniques. Our FaceOff method and dataset describe faces in the surgical environment and use temporal smoothing to increase the recall of detection and hence increase the effectiveness of video anonymization. We fine-tuned the Faster R-CNN pretrained on the face-detection-benchmark WIDER dataset achieving a recall of 88.05%. Taking advantage of the temporal nature of the application (anonymizing surgical video), a sliding average window was applied to the detections to smooth the missed detected faces reaching a recall of 93.46% on the collected FaceOff test-set. The work described in our study is a first step towards building the tools and capabilities needed in order to begin taking advantage of surgical data and building surgical data science pipelines.

Acknowledgements. We gratefully acknowledge the work and support received from the Innovation team at Digital Surgery.

Danail Stoyanov receives funding from the EPSRC (EP/N013220/1, EP/N022750/1, EP/N027078/1, NS/A000027/1), Wellcome/EPSRC Centre for Interventional and Surgical Sciences (WEISS) (203145Z/16/Z) and EU-Horizon2020 (H2020-ICT-2015-688592).

References

1. Maier-Hein, L., et al.: Surgical data science: enabling next-generation surgery. arXiv preprint arXiv:1701.06482 (2017)
2. Viola, P., Jones, M.J.: Robust real-time face detection. Int. J. Comput. Vis. **57**(2), 137–154 (2004)
3. Dalal, N., Triggs, B.: Histograms of oriented gradients for human detection. In: IEEE Computer Society Conference on Computer Vision and Pattern Recognition, CVPR 2005, vol. 1, pp. 886–893. IEEE, June 2005
4. Liu, Z., et al.: Deep learning face attributes in the wild. In: Proceedings of the IEEE International Conference on Computer Vision, pp. 3730–3738 (2015)
5. Parkhi, O.M., et al.: Deep face recognition. In: BMVC, vol. 1, no. 3, p. 6, September 2015
6. Farfade, S.S., et al.: Multi-view face detection using deep convolutional neural networks. In: Proceedings of the 5th ACM on International Conference on Multimedia Retrieval, pp. 643–650. ACM, June 2015
7. Ranjan, R., et al.: Hyperface: a deep multi-task learning framework for face detection, landmark localization, pose estimation, and gender recognition. IEEE Trans. Pattern Anal. Mach. Intell. (2017)
8. Kahou, S.E., Pal, C., et al.: Combining modality specific deep neural networks for emotion recognition in video. In: Proceedings of the 15th ACM on International Conference on Multimodal Interaction, pp. 543–550. ACM, December 2013
9. Klare, B.F., et al.: Pushing the frontiers of unconstrained face detection and recognition: IARPA Janus Benchmark A. In: Proceedings of the IEEE Conference on Computer Vision and Pattern Recognition, pp. 1931–1939 (2015)
10. Jain, V., Learned-Miller, E.: FDDB: a benchmark for face detection in unconstrained settings. University of Massachusetts, Amherst, Technical report UM-CS-2010-009, 2(7), p. 8 (2010)
11. Yang, S., et al.: Wider face: a face detection benchmark. In: Proceedings of the IEEE Conference on Computer Vision and Pattern Recognition, pp. 5525–5533 (2016)
12. Zhu, C., Zheng, Y., Luu, K., Savvides, M.: CMS-RCNN: contextual multi-scale region-based CNN for unconstrained face detection. In: Bhanu, B., Kumar, A. (eds.) Deep Learning for Biometrics. ACVPR, pp. 57–79. Springer, Cham (2017). https://doi.org/10.1007/978-3-319-61657-5_3
13. Girshick, R.: Fast R-CNN. In: IEEE International Conference on Computer Vision (ICCV), pp. 1440–1448. IEEE (2015)
14. Ren, S., et al.: Faster R-CNN: towards real-time object detection with region proposal networks. In: Advances in Neural Information Processing Systems, pp. 91–99 (2015)
15. Jiang, H., Learned-Miller, E.: Face detection with the faster R-CNN. In: 2017 12th IEEE International Conference on Automatic Face & Gesture Recognition (FG 2017), pp. 650–657. IEEE, May 2017

16. Long, J., et al.: Fully convolutional networks for semantic segmentation. In: Proceedings of the IEEE Conference on Computer Vision and Pattern Recognition, pp. 3431–3440 (2015)
17. Zeiler, M.D., Fergus, R.: Visualizing and understanding convolutional networks. In: Fleet, D., Pajdla, T., Schiele, B., Tuytelaars, T. (eds.) ECCV 2014. LNCS, vol. 8689, pp. 818–833. Springer, Cham (2014). https://doi.org/10.1007/978-3-319-10590-1_53

A Novel Interoperable Safety System for Improved Coordination and Communication in Cardiac Surgery

David Arney[1,2]([⊠]), Geoffrey Rance[3], Srey Rithy[3], Julian M. Goldman[1,2], and Marco A. Zenati[2]

[1] Massachusetts General Hospital, Boston, MA, USA
darney@mgh.harvard.edu
[2] Harvard Medical School, Boston, MA, USA
[3] VA Boston Healthcare System, Boston, USA

Abstract. During cardiac surgery there is an unmet need for safe transfer of responsibility for patient oxygenation back and forth from the anesthesia to the perfusion teams. Prior to cardiopulmonary bypass (CPB), lung ventilation is performed by the anesthesia machine ventilator and is the responsibility of the anesthesia team. During CPB, lung ventilation is halted and oxygenation is performed by the CPB oxygenator and perfusion team This recurrent transfer throughout the procedure introduces the rare but serious possibility of a "never event", resulting in the patient's lungs not being ventilated upon stopping the CPB and potentially leading to catastrophic hypoxemia. Monitors and alarms on the anesthesia and bypass machines would not be useful when the other device is operating so they are routinely put into a standby mode until needed. Consequently, in the event that the handoff is missed, there are no alarms to catch the situation. To solve this unmet need, we propose a novel interoperable, context-aware system capable of detecting and acting if this rare situation occurs. Our system is built on the open-source OpenICE framework, allowing it to seamlessly work with a variety of ventilator and bypass machines.

Keywords: Cardiopulmonary bypass · Never event · Interoperability Alarms · Surgical safety systems

1 Motivation

The entire cardiac surgical team (8–12 individuals) collectively takes responsibility for the patient's overall safety during cardiac surgery; it is a "team of teams", whereby four sub-teams (surgery, anesthesia, perfusion and nursing) must collaborate and coordinate their actions throughout the procedure. A mission-critical part of this responsibility is ensuring that the patient's gas exchange (oxygen and carbon dioxide) needs are met during cardiac surgery. The anesthesia team controls the function of the lung ventilator to deliver air and supplemental oxygen

D. Stoyanov et al. (Eds.): OR 2.0/CARE/CLIP/ISIC 2018, LNCS 11041, pp. 39–45, 2018.
https://doi.org/10.1007/978-3-030-01201-4_5

to the patient's lungs during inspiration and permit excretion of carbon dioxide during expiration. While the patient is being maintained on cardiopulmonary bypass (CPB), the responsibility for ensuring adequate ventilation shifts from the anesthesiologist to the perfusionist: instead of exchanging gases using the ventilator machine, the perfusionist uses the oxygenator present in-line with the CPB circuit. During the CPB "run", the ventilator machine and its monitors and alarms is turned off for the duration of the run to allow unobstructed vision of the surgical field for the surgical team. After the CPB is discontinued the responsibility of ventilation is transferred back to the anesthesia team that must restart the ventilator. These two mission-critical transitions of responsibilities back and forth from the anesthesia and perfusion team require complex human-human communication to coordinate actions involving machines that otherwise don't communicate between each other and introduce the rare but potentially lethal possibility of missing the handoff, resulting in the patient not being ventilated and suffering from anoxic brain injury (a "never event"). Communication breakdown is considered the most frequent cause of errors causing preventable adverse events in surgery. We propose an interoperable, context-aware system for cardiac surgery that specifically allows machine-machine communication and makes it hard for the surgical team to make errors and cause patient harm by detecting and alarming in case of missed handoff.

2   Methodology

In developing clinical alarms, it is important to build systems that support the existing surgical workflows and communication patterns in the care teams. In failing to do so, the new alarms are likely to cause surgical flow disruptions than of being useful. Our goal is to develop an alarm system for an extremely rare but potentially lethal situation, and therefore we need to create a system with a very low false positive rate. False positives distract the surgical team, increasing risk to the patient, and reduce confidence in the alarm system. False positives refer to situations where the alarm indicates a condition that is not actually present.

We observed and discussed the process and cardiac surgical environment with a number of subject matter experts at a cardiac surgery program of a teaching hospital of Harvard Medical School. The proposed specific alarm is most relevant to the anesthesia and perfusion teams, so we focused on interviewing domain experts of these two teams. We determined that monitoring the anesthesia machine ventilator's respiratory rate and the flow rate of the CPB machine would allow us to trigger a simple alarm for a "failure to ventilate". We read the ventilator rate and CPB pump speed and when the respiratory rate is zero and the CPB pump flow rate is also zero, we know that the patient is not being ventilated.

We prototyped this system in the Massachusetts General Hospital MD PnP lab using a combination of physical medical devices, simulated medical devices, and electronic and physical patient simulators as shown in Fig. 1. The setup includes an operating room patient monitor, an anesthesia machine, an electronic patient simulator and a physical lung simulator. The simulators allow us to see how the medical devices and our system respond to a wide variety of normal and abnormal patient conditions.

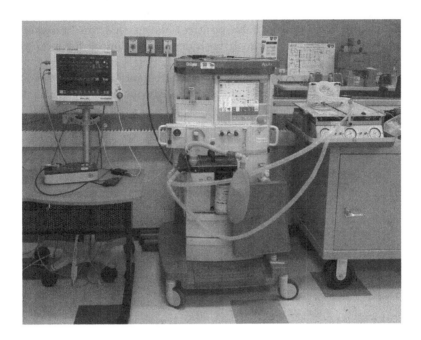

Fig. 1. Medical devices and patient simulators for algorithm development and testing

The devices were integrated using the OpenICE platform [3], which translates each device's proprietary communications protocol and data representation to a standardized format and communications middleware. This platform allows us to write applications around the device settings and vital signs of interest without having to concern ourselves with the peculiarities of specific devices. Figure 1 shows a Drager Apollo anesthesia machine, but the same respiratory rate value could be obtained from other brands and models without making any changes to the alarm application. This platform allows us to reuse device interfaces developed previously and build on safety interlock applications including PCA safety [6], x-ray and ventilator synchronization [2], [1], and detection of pulseless electrical activity. OpenICE is an implementation of the ASTM 2761-09 ICE standard [4], which includes clinical scenarios around ventilator to pump handoffs as annexes B.2.4.1 and B.2.4.2.

As an initial prototype, the purpose was to test connectivity to the required data sources and prove the feasibility of the approach. Once initial feasibility is demonstrated, we can plug in more complex algorithms to increase the specificity and sensitivity of the alarm.

We want to detect failure to ventilate with high reliability, but we only want to trigger an alarm when it is clinically relevant. Doing so perfectly would require our algorithm to know whether the clinicians already know that both the CPB machine and the ventilator are turned off. Our software can't detect what the surgical team is thinking, but we can take some steps to make the alarm more relevant and filter out real (not false positive) alarms that are irrelevant. One way to filter is to delay the alarm. If both devices remain off for more than a few seconds then there is a higher likelihood that it is not deliberate; simply delaying the alarm by a few seconds is likely to substantially reduce the number of clinically irrelevant alarms without significantly increasing the risk to the patient.

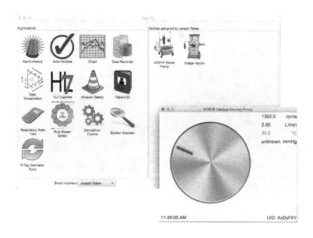

Fig. 2. The OpenICE supervisor and simulated cardiopulmonary bypass pump

We developed and tested the alarm algorithm with a mix of real and simulated medical devices. Figure 2 shows the OpenICE supervisor and the simulated cardiopulmonary bypass pump. The supervisor shows the devices that are connected (Apollo anesthesia machine and simulated pump) on the right and the available applications on the left. Our alarm application is assessed through the "Rule-Based Safety" application. The simulated bypass pump outputs pump speed in RPM, flow rate in liters/minute, blood temperature, and a pressure measurement. A full bypass machine includes several pumps and many other components. For this version of the alarm, we only use the CPB flow rate and so we have only simulated the pump.

We implemented the alarm using the OpenICE Rule-based-safety application. This allows us to write the alarm as a script that runs under OpenICE and accesses devices connected through the platform. The alarm has two states: monitoring and triggered, shown in Figs. 3 and 4.

In the monitoring mode, the alarm application shows a short description of itself, a display of the relevant device information (CPB flow rate and ventilator

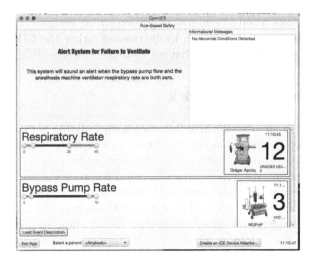

Fig. 3. The alarm system in monitoring mode

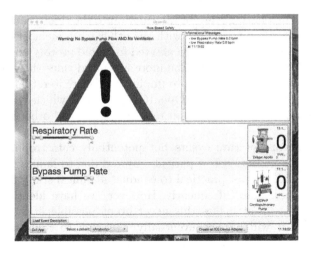

Fig. 4. The alarm system when triggered

machine respiratory rate), and a list of messages. The device information is updated as new data is available from the devices and typically refreshes in well under one second.

When the CPB machine reports a flow rate of zero and the ventilator machine reports a respiratory rate of zero simultaneously, the alarm condition is reached and the application switches to its triggered mode. In this mode, it shows an alarm symbol, changes its border to red, sounds an audible alert tone, and displays a message indicating what has happened. It also continues to show the live data from the devices and is currently configured to stop alarming without manual intervention when the alarm condition is no longer true. This allows the surgical team to stop the alarm by increasing either the CPB flow rate or ventilator respiratory rate without having to touch the OpenICE computer.

3 Results and Future Work

Having established an interoperable framework for building better alert systems for the cardiac operating room, we can build on this work by developing more advanced algorithms and by integrating the alert system with more sources of relevant information. We expect that we could improve the sensitivity of the alarm using information from hospital IT systems such as the medical records system and pharmacy systems, and that we could improve the clinical relevance using additional contextual information that would allow the algorithm to be more reactive to the unfolding situation in the operating room. Measuring and reacting to the cognitive load of the various team members would allow the alert system to be responsive without interrupting critical tasks [5]. Ideally, this system, operating through algorithms, should be viewed as an additional member of the surgical team, offering relevant information to the right people at the right time in a way that doesn't interfere with the other team members' work.

The Rule-based-safety application allowed for rapid prototyping and concept validation, but it does not support the more advanced rules that we would like to implement in the future. We plan to implement future iterations of the alarm system as full applications on the OpenICE platform, which will allow us to implement delays, thresholds based on rate of change, and other more complex rules.

Validating alarms for rare events but potentially catastrophic events is a challenge. There is no data set of patients injured due to failure to ventilate in cardiac surgery and it is not practical to conduct a clinical study to collect data on events that happen so infrequently. However, we have identified a critical system vulnerability that makes this never event possible; if making such an error is possible, it will happen eventually. We plan to continue testing our implementations using a simulation environment where we can create a wide range of clinical situations.

References

1. Arney, D., Goldman, J.M., Whitehead, S.F., Lee, I.: Synchronizing an x-ray and anesthesia machine ventilator: a medical device interoperability case study. In: BIODEVICES 2009, pp. 52–60 (2009)
2. Arney, D., Goldman, J.M., Whitehead, S.F., Lee, I.: Improving patient safety with X-ray and anesthesia machine ventilator synchronization: a medical device interoperability case study. In: Fred, A., Filipe, J., Gamboa, H. (eds.) BIOSTEC 2009. CCIS, vol. 52, pp. 96–109. Springer, Heidelberg (2010). https://doi.org/10.1007/978-3-642-11721-3_7

3. Arney, D., Plourde, J., Goldman, J.: OpenICE medical device interoperability platform overview and requirement analysis. Biomed. Eng./Biomed. Tech. **63**, 39–47 (2017)
4. ASTM F2761–09(2013): Medical Devices and Medical Systems - Essential safety requirements for equipment comprising the patient-centric integrated clinical environment (ICE) - Part 1: General requirements and conceptual model. http://www.astm.org/Standards/F2761.htm
5. Conboy, H., et al.: Cognitive support during high-consequence episodes of care in cardiovascular surgery. In: 2017 IEEE Conference on Cognitive and Computational Aspects of Situation Management, pp. 1–3, March 2017
6. Pajic, M., Mangharam, R., Sokolsky, O., Arney, D., Goldman, J.M., Lee, I.: Model-driven safety analysis of closed-loop medical systems. IEEE Trans. Ind. Inform. **10**(1), 3–16 (2014). https://doi.org/10.1109/TII.2012.2226594

Generalized Trajectory Planning
for Nonlinear Interventions

Johannes Fauser[1]([✉]), Igor Stenin[2], Julia Kristin[2], Thomas Klenzner[2],
Jörg Schipper[2], Dieter Fellner[1], and Anirban Mukhopadhyay[1]

[1] Department of Computer Science, Technische Universität Darmstadt,
Darmstadt, Germany
johannes.fauser@gris.tu-darmstadt.de
[2] Department of Oto-Rhino-Laryngology, Düsseldorf University Hospital,
Düsseldorf, Germany

Abstract. Minimally invasive procedures with flexible instruments such
as endoscopes, needles or drilling units are becoming more and more common. Their automated insertion will be standard across several applications in operation rooms of the future. In such scenarios regular re-
planning for feasible nonlinear trajectories is a mandatory step toward
automation. However, state of the art methods focus on isolated solutions only. In this paper we introduce a generalized motion planning
formulation in SE(3), regarding both position and orientation, that is
suitable for these approaches. To emphasize the generalization of this formulation we evaluate the performance of proposed Bidirectional Rapidly-
exploring Random Trees (Bi-RRT) on four different clinical applications:
Drilling in temporal bone surgery, trajectory planning for cardiopulmonary endoscopy, automatic needle insertion for spine biopsy and liver
tumor removal. Experiments show that for all four scenarios the formulation is suitable and feasible trajectories can be planned successfully.

Keywords: Motion planning · Nonlinear trajectories
Temporal bone surgery · Special Euclidean group
Bidirectional rapidly-exploring random trees

1 Motivation

Minimally-invasive procedures have been extensively studied in the last decades
and new solutions for various applications are an active research field [2]. These
include, among others, continuum robots for drilling in multi-port temporal bone
surgery [6], flexible needles for soft tissue [4] or flexible endoscopes [7] and allow
more precise interventions.

These approaches use instruments that share common constraints: they follow nonlinear curvature constrained trajectories, and rapid re-planning is necessary to ensure a continuous safe insertion. Consequently, pre- and intra-operative

D. Stoyanov et al. (Eds.): OR 2.0/CARE/CLIP/ISIC 2018, LNCS 11041, pp. 46–53, 2018.
https://doi.org/10.1007/978-3-030-01201-4_6

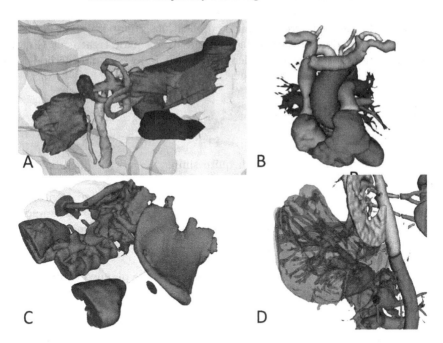

Fig. 1. Exemplary clinical applications where flexible instruments can be used: (A) temporal bone surgery for cochlear implantation (B) cardiopulmonary endoscopy, (C) spine biopsy and (D) tumor treatment in the liver.

planning in $SE(3) = \mathbb{R}^3 \times SO(3)$ is necessary to compute feasible trajectories with maximum clearance to risk structures.

Isolated solutions for the underlying motion planning problems have been proposed for many applications: computation of implant channels in intracavitary brachytherapy or trajectory planning for bevel tip needles [3], planning access paths for temporal bone surgery [5] or needle planning for liver surgery [13]. Finding feasible trajectories then requires nonholonomic motion planning where sampling based algorithms like Rapidly-exploring Random Trees (RRT) are well suited for [8]. Steering bevel-tip needles in soft tissue has been extensively studied [1] and both RRTs [9] and sequential convex optimization [10] have been shown to compute feasible trajectories. Convex Optimization has also been used to plan for automated suturing [11]. Nonlinear drilling units have been proposed to create access paths in temporal bone surgery and Bidirectional-RRT (Bi-RRT) were used to interpolate between start and goal states in $SE(3)$ [6].

However, these solution are tailored to their specific use case and do not discuss a general solution. In this paper, we propose a general motion planning formulation for nonlinear minimally-invasive interventions in OR 2.0. We extend the formulation of Bi-RRTs introduced earlier by us [6] that exploit variable curvature arcs or Bézier-splines as underlying steering functions. This extension is suitable to form a common motion planning problem for instruments that follow curvature constrained trajectories. In particular, we derive the individual specifications for four different clinical applications: temporal bone surgery, cardiopulmonary endoscopy, spine biopsy and liver tumor treatment (Fig. 1). Experiments on data sets of real patients are presented where our methods successfully plan trajectories for the respective interventions.

2   Materials and Methods

2.1   Clinical Challenges:

All mentioned interventions - though quite similar in motion planning - offer unique challenges.

Temporal Bone Surgery operates in a very small and dense environment compared to other setups. Numerous obstacles - nerves, blood vessels and the organs of the hearing and equilibrium senses - *limit* the free space and thus complicate motion planning. This raises special needs for the extension of the search tree as well as the collision detection.

In *cardiopulmonary endoscopy* trajectories have to be planned through tube-like structures. Motion planning algorithms have to find feasible paths *through* instead of around risk structures. Such narrow environments often need tailored algorithm for sufficiently fast planning [14].

Spine biopsy and *liver tumor treatment* provide environments where the spinal cord or branches of the hepatic artery and portal vein, respectively, form highly sensitive regions where precise planning is critical. In fact, Sun et al. [12] extended planning to Belief Spaces in order to limit uncertainty.

Additionally, an automatic procedure requires to continuously reevaluate the planned path. Given the latest sensory inputs, a new trajectory must be re-planned from the currently measured pose of the instrument to the target of the intervention. Depending on the success of a call to solve the motion planning problem, feedback must be given to the surgeon if the intervention can still be carried on or if it has to be canceled due to unavailability of feasible trajectories. Such feedback needs to come immediately to enforce a smooth intervention.

2.2   Problem Formulation

Planning is done in the special Euclidean group $SE(3) = \mathbb{R}^3 \times SO(3)$, to account for the instrument's position ($\mathbb{R}^3$) and its orientation ($SO(3)$), the latter represented by quaternions. The configuration space $C \subset SE(3)$ is then divided into an obstacle region $C_{Obs} \subset C$ and the free space $C_{free} = \{q \in C | q \notin C_{Obs}\}$. Valid start and goal states of trajectories are defined via subsets of C_{free}. Given, a set $M \subset C_{free}$ and the quaternion metric $\rho : SO(3) \times SO(3) \to \mathbb{R}$ (e.g. [8]),

$$\rho(h_1, h_2) = \min\{\rho_s(h_1, h_2), \rho_s(h_1, -h_2)\}$$
$$\rho_s(h_1, h_2) = \cos^{-1}(a_1 a_2 + b_1 b_2 + c_1 c_2 + d_1 d_2), \tag{1}$$

we define the approximated set $\tilde{M}(\epsilon, \phi)$ of M, $\epsilon \in \mathbb{R}^+$, $\phi \in [0, \pi]$ as,

$$\tilde{M}(\epsilon, \phi) = \{q(x, h) \in C_{free} \mid \exists\, \hat{q}(y, g) \in M : \|x - y\|_{\mathbb{R}^3} < \epsilon, \rho(h, g) < \phi\}. \tag{2}$$

Given a number of clinically ideal configurations for trajectories, such sets resemble clinically acceptable states that lie in the vicinity of the position and observe only a small perturbation in orientation. Further constraints are given by the minimum distance d_{min} to risk structures, the instrument's curvature constraint κ_{max} and the time T_{max}, in which a feedback is required. The problem formulation for an individual intervention is than expressed as:

Given,

$$M_I \subset C_{free}, \epsilon_I \in \mathbb{R}^+, \phi_I \in [0, \pi] \tag{3a}$$

$$M_G \subset C_{free}, \epsilon_G \in \mathbb{R}^+, \phi_G \in [0, \pi] \tag{3b}$$

$$d_{min} \in \mathbb{R}^+, \kappa_{max} \in \mathbb{R}^{0+}, T_{max} \in \mathbb{R}^+ \tag{3c}$$

Task: Find a path $\gamma(t) : [0, 1] \rightarrow SE(3)$ satisfying

$$\gamma(0) \in \tilde{M}_I(\epsilon_I, \phi_I) \tag{4a}$$

$$\gamma(1) \in \tilde{M}_G(\epsilon_G, \phi_G) \tag{4b}$$

$$\forall t \in (0, 1) : \|\gamma''(t)\| < \kappa_{max} \tag{4c}$$

$$\forall t \in [0, 1], o \in C_{Obs} : \|\gamma(t) - o\|_{\mathbb{R}^3} > d_{min} \tag{4d}$$

or report that no path could be found in the available time T_{max}.

Figure 2 shows examples of initial and goal regions, M_I, M_G, for a multi-port cochlear access. For preoperative planning of potential access canals, a surgeon manually defines a set of initial states at the surface of the lateral skull base (blue arrows, left image). Three goal states are defined at the round window of the cochlea as the ideal end points of the three canals for multi-port access (orange arrows, right image). Once the intervention starts, re-planning of a feasible trajectory might be necessary. Here, the current pose of the drilling unit replaces the initial region (middle image, orange arrow) and one of the three goal states is fixed as the single target state.

Fig. 2. Different initial and goal regions for cochlear implantation. *(Left)* Multiple initial states at the skull' surface (blue arrows). *(Middle)* A single initial state pointing in the robot's current direction. *(Right)* Three precise goal states for a multi-port cochlear access. (Color figure online)

Note: This definition extends our previous formulation [6] to individual approximations at both start and goal. With $\kappa_{max} = 0$ it is suitable for linear approaches. With $\phi_I = \pi$ or $\phi_G = \pi$ it falls back to more general cases where only the orientation at one end point of the trajectory is relevant.

2.3   Motion Planning

We use Bi-RRTs to solve the individual motion planning problems of the experiments (Fig. 3). Specifically, we show that two variants of Bi-RRTs - one based on circular arcs and 3D Dubins Paths, one based on Bézier-Splines [6] - are suitable for our clinical exemplary anatomies.

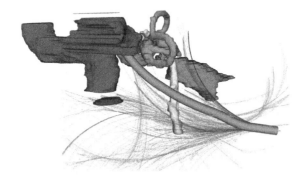

Fig. 3. Bidirectional RRTs grow two search trees - one from the initial region (blue), the other from the goal region (green) - and attempts to connect them in between. A successful connection results in a feasible nonlinear trajectory (orange). (Color figure online)

3   Experimental Results

We considered four different scenarios as shown in Fig. 1: (A) Planning of three access canals for multi-port bone surgery at the Otobasis. (B) Trajectory planning for cardiopulmonary endoscopy. (C) Flexible needle path creation for spine biopsy. (D) Access to metastases in the liver. For each scenario, expert annotations on real CT data were used to create 3D models of the individual anatomies. The obstacle regions C_{Obs} were built from the relevant risk structures of these anatomies. Adequate definitions of the general problem definition are given in Table 1. Samples of successfully planned paths in $SE(3)$ are shown as tubes in Fig. 4.

Otobasis Surgery: Our current drilling prototype has a curvature constraint of $0.05\,\mathrm{mm}^{-1}$. We considered a more flexible version to have more space for multi-port surgery. For a cochlear implant, deviations at the target should not exceed $5°$. However, as our methods allow planning with ideal orientation, we set $\epsilon = \phi = 0$ and successfully created three access canals to the cochlea with no misalignment using a bidirectional Spline-Based-RRT.

Table 1. Parameters for the different Problem Formulations.

	κ_{max} mm^{-1}	ϵ_I, ϵ_G mm	ϕ_I, ϕ_G degree	d_{min} mm	T_{max} sec
Multi-Port Bone Surgery	0.05	0.0	0.0	0.8	0.25
Cardiopulmonary endoscopy	0.1	2.0	45	3.0	3.0
Spine-biopsy	2.5	0.0	0.0	4.0	0.25
Liver tumor ablation	2.5	0.0	0.0	4.0	0.25

Cardiopulmonary Endoscopy: Trajectories were planned both with a Spline-Based-RRT and its bidirectional counterpart. We considered the use of flexible endoscopes with radius 1.0 mm. Experiments with different additional safety-distances to the vessel's inner walls showed that planning was still possible with $d_{min} = 3.0$ mm as a combined distance of radius and safety-distance. To create paths with the simpler RRT, too, we allowed a small error in target location (2.0 mm) and a quite high deviation from the supposed orientation (45°).

Spine Biopsy: Next, we planned for percutaneous needle insertion. The minimal distance to obstacles resembled a needle of radius 1.0 mm and a safety distance of 3.0 mm to keep away from vertebrae. The curvature constraint was set according

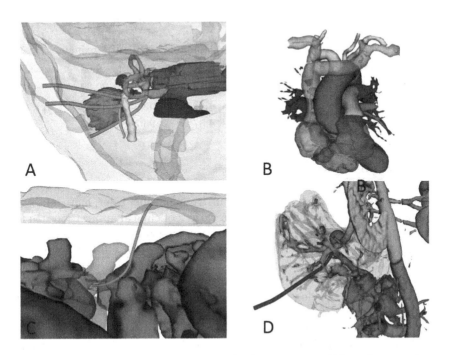

Fig. 4. Feasible paths for drilling units in Otobasis surgery (A), endoscopes in cardiopulmonary interventions (B), needles in spine biopsy and liver tumor removal (C,D).

to flexible needles currently used in research [13]. As such instruments move along circular arcs, trajectories were computed with the Bi-RRT that extends via circular arcs and attempts connection with 3D-Dubins-Paths.

Liver Tumor: Last, we planned a needle trajectory for tumor treatment in the liver. A potential tumor of spherical shape was placed within the liver (Fig. 4 **D**) and a path interpolating between a single initial state and a single goal state was computed. We again considered the use of flexible bevel-tip needles and thus chose the parameters and motion planner as in the spine biopsy experiment.

Except for the second scenario, feasible trajectories were found much quicker than the given 0.25 s. Thus, immediate feedback was possible for these scenarios. For the endoscopic access, we had to extend the given time for solving the motion planning problem. This can be explained by necessary adaptations for RRTs, when planning in narrow environments [14], a feature our planners still lack. Moreover, maximum clearance to organs in the near vicinity is often the most important clinical requirement. Thus, after successful planning, we computed distances to risk structures along the resulting paths by sampling points along the trajectories every 0.1 mm. Table 2 shows the minimum, median and maximum distances to obstacles for the four different scenarios. We observed, that the threshold d_{min} is often almost perfectly matched. This is expected, as RRTs extend their search trees randomly and no optimization is performed.

Table 2. Resulting distances to risk structures in mm.

	d_{min}	Minimum	Median	Maximum
Multi-Port Bone Surgery	0.8	0.80	3.22	9.63
Cardiopulmonary endoscopy	3.0	3.10	6.50	20.39
Spine-biopsy	4.0	4.15	6.46	30.70
Liver tumor ablation	4.0	4.37	9.92	58.78

4 Discussion and Conclusion

Minimally invasive surgeries with flexible instruments offer safer, more adaptable or completely automated procedures for a variety of clinical applications. In this paper we propose a general formulation of the necessary trajectory planning step for OR 2.0. We evaluate the theoretical definition on four clinical applications and show that the general formulation is adaptable to these scenarios. Further, we show that the proposed planning algorithms, bidirectional Rapidly-exploring Random Trees, are suitable tools to quickly compute precise nonlinear trajectories for instruments of such applications.

Currently, our planning method is purely geometric and does not consider uncertainty of any kind. In future, we want to add an optimization step to address noisy sensor measurements or dynamic constraints such as soft tissue deformation. For percutaneous needle insertion, convex optimization [10] has been shown to be an adequate technique. We expect that an adjustment of this method to interpolation in $SE(3)$ between start and goal states will further improve the proposed bidirectional approach by maximizing clearance to obstacles (Table 2). Interactive definition of the motion planning problem, subsequent trajectory planning and its visualizations shown in this paper were implemented in a custom planning tool. We also plan to publish this work as an open-source library to establish a general framework for nonlinear minimally-invasive interventions.

References

1. Alterowitz, R., Goldberg, K.: Motion Planning in Medicine: Optimization and Simulation Algorithms for Image-Guided Procedures. Springer, Heidelberg (2008). https://doi.org/10.1007/978-3-540-69259-1
2. Burgner-Kahrs, J., Rucker, D.C., Choset, H.: Continuum robots for medical applications: a survey. IEEE Trans. Robot. **31**(6), 1261–1280 (2015)
3. Duan, Y., Patil, S., Schulman, J., Goldberg, K., Abbeel, P.: Planning locally optimal, curvature-constrained trajectories in 3D using sequential convex optimization. In: 2014 IEEE International Conference on Robotics and Automation (ICRA), pp. 5889–5895, May 2014
4. Duindam, V., Alterovitz, R., Sastry, S., Goldberg, K.: Skrew-based motion planning for bevel-tip flexible needles in 3D environments with obstacles. In: IEEE International Conference on Robotics and Automation, pp. 2483–2488, May 2008
5. Fauser, J., Stenin, I., Kristin, J., Klenzner, T., Schipper, J., Sakas, G.: A software tool for planning and evaluation of non-linear trajectories for minimally invasive lateral skull base surgery. In: Tagungsb. der 15. Jahrestag. der Dtsch. Ges. f. Comput.- und Roboterass. Chirurgie e.V. (CURAC), pp. 125–126 (2016)
6. Fauser, J., Sakas, G., Mukhopadhyay, A.: Planning nonlinear access paths for temporal bone surgery. Int. J. Comput. Assist. Radiol. Surg. **13**(5), 637–646 (2018)
7. Fichera, L., et al.: Through the Eustachian tube and beyond: a new miniature robotic endoscope to see into the middle ear. IEEE Rob. Autom. Letters **2**(3), 1488–1494 (2017)
8. LaValle, S.M.: Planning Algorithms. Cambridge University Press (2006)
9. Patil, S., Burgner, J., Webster, R.J., Alterovitz, R.: Needle steering in 3-D via rapid replanning. IEEE Trans. Rob. **30**(4), 853–864 (2014)
10. Schulman, J., et al.: Motion planning with sequential convex optimization and convex collision checking. Int. J. Rob. Res. **33**(9), 1251–1270 (2014)
11. Sen, S., Garg, A., Gealy, D.V., McKinley, S., Jen, Y., Goldberg, K.: Automating multi-throw multilateral surgical suturing with a mechanical needle guide and sequential convex optimization. In: 2016 IEEE International Conference on Robotics and Automation (ICRA), pp. 4178–4185, May 2016
12. Sun, W., van den Berg, J., Alterovitz, R.: Stochastic extended lqr for optimization-based motion planning under uncertainty. IEEE Trans. Autom. Sci. Eng. **13**(2), 437–447 (2016)
13. Sun, W., Alterovitz, R.: Motion planning under uncertainty for medical needle steering using optimization in belief space. In: 2014 IEEE/RSJ International Conference on Intelligent Robots and Systems, pp. 1775–1781, September 2014
14. Yang, L., Qi, J., Jiang, Z., Song, D., Han, J., Xiao, J.: Guiding attraction based random tree path planning under uncertainty: dedicate for UAV. In: 2014 IEEE International Conference on Mechatronics and Automation, pp. 1182–1187, August 2014

Automatic Cochlear Length and Volume Size Estimation

Ibraheem Al-Dhamari[1]([✉]), Sabine Bauer[1], Dietrich Paulus[1], Rania Helal[2], Friedrich Lisseck[3], and Roland Jacob[3]

[1] Koblenz-Landau University, Koblenz, Germany
idhamari@uni-koblenz.de
[2] Ain Shams University, Cairo, Egypt
[3] Military Hospital, Koblenz, Germany

Abstract. Surgical robotics tools using real-time computer vision algorithms can detect, extract and analyze specific organs during surgery. In order to achieve successful cochlear implant surgical operation using such techniques, the exact cochlear length and size are required. We present a fast cochlear length and volume size estimation method that may be integrated in such situations. The method utilizes atlas-model-based segmentation to estimate a transformation from a model to an input volume. The result is used to transform a well-defined segmentation and a points-set of a scala tympani to the input image that segments and estimates the scala tympani length in a few seconds.

Given the lack of a publicly-available ground truth, the error is estimated using the known length of the cochlear implants. A dataset of 71 3D images of 21 patients from various age and gender groups is used. The estimated average scala tympani length is $29.54\,\mathrm{mm}$, with $0.27\,\mathrm{mm}$ standard deviation. The average scala tympani volume size is $41.56\,\mathrm{mm}^3$, with $0.19\,\mathrm{mm}^3$ standard deviation.

The method is available as an open-source 3D Slicer plug-in and the dataset is also publicly-available. Both the method and the dataset can be downloaded from a public server(https://mtixnat.uni-koblenz.de).

Keywords: Surgery robot · Cochlea · Segmentation · Registration
Length · Volume size · Automatic estimation · Fast · Surgery

1 Introduction

The cochlea is a small organ in the inner part of the ear. It has a crucial role in hearing as it filters and transfers auditory signals to the brain. Recently, Cochlear Implants (CI) have become increasingly popular as a treatment option for patients with severe to profound Sensori-Neural Hearing Loss (SNHL) [16]. These implants result in significant improvement in post-operative speech recognition. This is mostly underpinned by the adequate match between CI electrode frequency bands and their exact location inside the cochlea, as each audible

© Springer Nature Switzerland AG 2018
D. Stoyanov et al. (Eds.): OR 2.0/CARE/CLIP/ISIC 2018, LNCS 11041, pp. 54–61, 2018.
https://doi.org/10.1007/978-3-030-01201-4_7

frequency has a specific position inside the cochlea [11]. Cochlear Duct Length (CDL) can also have a significant impact on the process of pre-operative electrode selection. If the electrode has a length that is not appropriate to the cochlear length, this can result in incomplete insertion, cochlear trauma or poor cochlear coverage with poor matching between the electrodes and the cochlea [8].

Surgical robots are gaining popularity, primarily driven by improvements in nanotechnology and artificial intelligence. These robots need reliable real-time computer vision algorithms in order to detect and analyze the target organ. For instance, during a robotic cochlear surgery [17], a reliable real-time estimation of the length and size of the cochlea is needed e.g. to decide a suitable CI for a specific patient. This study proposed a fast cochlear length and volume size estimation that may benefit future surgical cochlear robots.

1.1 Related Work

By reviewing the literature, one can find major variations in the radiological human CDL measurements with regards to used methodologies. Primarily methodologies include three-dimensional (3D) processing and spiral coefficient equations, which are relatively time-consuming and require deeper radiology expertise.

Escude et al. [5] introduced an equation of spiral coefficient, which requires only one measurement. This measurement, known as the *A value*, is defined as the largest distance from the round window to the opposite cochlear lateral wall. This equation was further modified using a linear equation by Alexiades et al. [2] followed by Koch et al. [9]. Most recently, Iyaniwura et al [8], using conventional and micro-Computed Tomographic (μCT) images of cadaveric cochleaer specimens, proposed an automated method for the measure of the *A value*, with a significantly lower mean error than the manual method.

Other studies used 3D reconstructions of cross-sectional imaging such as Weurfel et al. [18], measured the cochlear length of the cone beam computed tomography of temporal bones. They measured the cochlear length with a starting point at the distal bony rim of the round window and then a 3D curve was set up from the outer edge of the bony cochlea until helicotrema [18].

This was followed by Meng et al. measuring the CDL, and the relation between the basal turn lengths and CDL using 3D multiplanar reconstructed CT images [10].

More recently, Rivas et al. [15] compared the automatic measurement of the *A value* and automatic CDL measurement by 3D reconstruction to the manually measured *A value* and CDL by two fellowship-trained neurotologists. They concluded that the automatically measured values more reproducible and less time-consuming compared to those done manually.

The 3D reconstruction is considered the most accurate method to get the CDL measurements [10]. The entirety of the complex 3D shape of the cochlea can be well evaluated and is also less liable to cutting and viewing angle errors. However, the processing time for this technique is considerably long [10].

The development of a more consistent, less time-consuming and reproducible method with no inter-observer variability, to determine CDL, is still needed.

1.2 Cochlea Segmentation

Automatic cochlear analysis requires an efficient automatic segmentation algorithm. A segmentation is the process of extracting an object from an input image. Some researchers proposed automatic cochlea segmentation methods, but they are not practical. These methods are either time consuming or they do not cover the cochlear details. Hence, they are not suitable for a surgical robot integration [6,12–14]. Atlas-based segmentation methods attempt to align an atlas to the input image. The atlas usually is a well-defined histological image or a high resolution μCT image. Model-based segmentation methods try to fit a statistical shape model to the input image [3,4]. This statistical shape model is generated using many aligned and manually segmented cochlear images.

2 Materials and Methods

The objective of this paper is to propose and to evaluate a new, relatively easy and fast methodology utilizing simple computer hardware and software to calculate the cochlear duct length and cochlear duct size. The proposal can be easily integrated into a surgical robot due to its high accuracy and fast performance. In this section, we describe briefly the dataset, the experimental design, and the proposed method.

2.1 Datasets

A part of the standard and public Human Cochlea Dataset (HCD) was used, the dataset is well described in [1]. This dataset contains Computed Tomography (CT), Magnetic Resonance (MR) and Cone Beam Computed Tomography (CBCT) modalities of patients from different age and gender groups. Each patient has 3D images of his/her cochlea before and after the cochlear implant surgery. The part used in the experiments contains 71 3D Images of 21 patients, see Fig. 2 for a sample from these images.

2.2 Atlas-Model-Based Segmentation

The proposed method combines model-based and atlas-based segmentation. A high resolution μCT image was used as a model and its manual segmentation was used as an atlas. The atlas was aligned to the input image using image registration technique. The model was obtained from public and standard μCT cochlear dataset [7].

The original μCT image was too large to process in a standard PC, hence a re-sampling procedure was necessary. The source μCT image was re-sampled from [0.008, 0.008, 0.008] mm spacing to [0.032, 0.32, 0.008] mm spacing, which reduced the image size from 13.4 GB to 806 MB. All DICOM slice files were divided into groups of 100 files, each was then loaded separately into 3D

Slicer software[1] for re-sampling. After that, all re-sampled parts were combined together to form the final re-sampled image.

Next, the image was cropped to the cochlear part only. This allows for a smaller image size of 103.2 MB with $243 \times 202 \times 1191$ voxels[2] (the original was $437 \times 412 \times 2349$ voxels). Following that, the two main cochlear scalae, i.e. scala vestibuli and scala tympani, were segmented manually, see Fig. 1. The model was the transformed manually to get a direction matrix similar to a left cochlear side. The transformed model was automatically aligned to one of the clinical CBCT images using ACIR [1]. ACIR is a registration method proposed for multi-modal cochlear images. Registration is the process of aligning two or more images. The segmentation was aligned the same way. Due to the interpolation process, a process needed by the registration procedure that find locations of pixels when images have different sizes, the segmentation needed to be corrected manually to fit the CBCT image before using it as an atlas. Following correction process, CBCT left-side cochlear atlas and its segmentation were ready to segment any CBCT left-side cochlear image automatically.

By repeating the same process above, the model and the segmentation of CT and MRI images were obtained. The right-side cochlear atlases were generated by changing the direction matrix x-direction of the previous atlases and their segmentations.

A user-friendly interface for the atlas-based segmentation method was developed as a Slicer plug-in. A summary of the segmentation process is presented in Fig. 1 left. The user inputs the cochlear image, selects any point inside the cochlea then obtains the segmentation result automatically in less than 5 s.

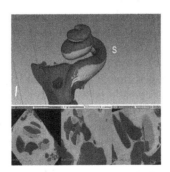

Fig. 1. Left: cochlear analysis general pipeline. Middle: Cochlea high resolution μCT model. Right: Points set model

2.3 Cochlea Points Model

Skeletonization is the process of converting an object in an image to a thinner object (skeleton) e.g. converting a rectangle to a line. It is usually used

---

[1] www.slicer.org.

[2] Voxel: volume element.

to generate curves and lines of an object in order to obtain the object related measurements e.g. the object's length.

Standard skeletonization methods did not succeed on the resulting cochlear segmentation, due to the non-regular shape of the cochlear scalae. A proposed solution was used for addressing this problem by creating a points-set model from a sorted-points set, see Fig. 1 right. This points-set model contains 55 points representing the center of the scala tympani. By applying the proposed atlas-segmentation transformation to this points-set, the length of the scala tympani can be calculated by computing the distance between each two consecutive points using the standard 3D distance equation:

$$Length = \sum_{i=1}^{n-1} \sqrt{(x_{i+1} - x_i)^2 + (y_{i+1} - y_i)^2 + (z_{i+1} - z_i)^2} \tag{1}$$

where n is the number of the points, and x, y and z, are the 3D point coordinates. Using this approach has two benefits:

A. It is faster than skeletonization as it includes only one simple matrix multiplication.
B. The points can be corrected or modified later to produce different useful measurements (e.g. measuring the inner length or the outer length of a scala).

3   Experiments and Results

A few important factors were studied in the experiments. These factors may affect the accuracy of the estimated measurements.

The only manual step in the proposed methodology is locating the cochlea in which the user provides a point inside the cochlear region (step 1 in Fig. 1 left). This point was used in the cropping phase, where the region around this point was cropped. The cropped image was used in the registration phase (step 3 Fig. 1 left). The point was considered the center of the cropping, generating a cube of 10 mm length and a 3D cropped image of about $80 \times 80 \times 80$ voxels with 0.125 mm iso spacing. These parameters were selected based on several experiments, as the cochlea was located inside this cropped size in all tested images.

The selection of this cropping point can be different from one user to another, and could be different if the same user located it multiple times. The segmentation result changes slightly if the cochlear locations point was different. For justification, the cochlear point was located 10 different times for each input image, then the average and the standard deviation of the segmentation result were recorded. In Fig. 2, and Table 1, only three cochlear location points of one patient are shown with their quantitative and visual results.

In Table 1, the points-set detection is related to the number of points that transformed to the new input image, see Sect. 2.3. Notice that the quantitative results are slightly different, while they visually look almost the same.

Table 1. Sample of Cochlear location's points and related results of patient 1

idx	Cochlea location	PointSet detection	Scala Tympani length	Scala Tympani size
a	[216 247 78]	91%	28.4032	41.1152
b	[218 250 77]	96%	29.4105	41.3886
c	[223 254 77]	98%	30.4227	41.7539

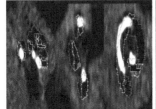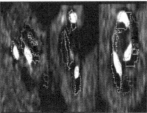

Fig. 2. Cochlear Location Change Effect, from left to right: results of point a, point b and point c. The points locations are listed in Table 1.

To find out the error resulting from the image artifact, the actual length of the CI was used as a reference point. The electrodes array was segmented out from the datasets and its length was computed. Then the estimated error is computed by comparing the computed electrodes array's length to its actual length.

Using different implants types, the estimated error average of the CI length was 0.62 mm with standard deviation of 0.27 mm. The minimum and maximum error values were 0.05 mm and 1.1 mm. It can be concluded that there will be always a small error less than 1.5 mm (0.4 was added for more justification).

Average of the estimated scala tympani length and size were computed from all the 71 volumes using the proposed methods.

The average estimated scala tympani length was 29.54 mm with a standard deviation of 0.27 mm. The minimum and maximum values were 28.39 mm and 30.71 mm. The estimated average difference error between pre-and postoperative CBCT images was 0.31 mm with a standard deviation of 0.25 mm. Similarly, the estimated average error between preoperative MRI and CBCT images was 0.30 mm with a standard deviation of 0.22 mm. The estimated average difference error between preoperative MRI and postoperative CBCT images was 0.32 mm with a standard deviation of 0.30 mm.

Average of the estimated scala tympani size was 41.56 mm^3 with a standard deviation of 0.19 mm^3. The minimum and maximum values were 40.52 mm^3 and 41.79 mm^3. The estimated average difference error between pre-and postoperative CBCT images was 0.25 mm^3 with a standard deviation of 0.27 mm^3. Similarly, the estimated average error between preoperative CBCT and MRI images was 0.16 mm^3 with a standard deviation of 0.15 mm^3. The estimated average difference error between postoperative CBCT and MRI images was 0.26 mm^3 with a standard deviation of 0.31 mm^3.

Using an ASUS ROG G751-JT notebook (Intel Core i7-4720HQ @2.6 GHz x 8, Geforce GTX970m and 32 GB Memory), the average time of computation per image, was 4.01 seconds with a standard deviation of 0.79 s. The computation time covers computing the transformation, generating the segmentation, generating the cochlear 3D model, and computing the cochlea measurements i.e. length and size.

From the results above, it seems that the CDL is long enough to accommodate a longer CI than the ones available currently. Assuming an error of 1.5 mm and a range of 28.39 mm to 30.71 mm, a suggested CI active length ranging from 26.8 mm to 29.2 mm can be used. However, to verify this suggestion, more clinical datasets from different locations are needed.

Finally, Fig. 3 shows different visual results of the segmentation and the generated 3D models from different modalities.

Fig. 3. Segmentation results and the generated 3D models. left: CBCT, middle: MR and right: CT

4   Conclusion

A real-time automatic method for cochlear images analysis is proposed. The proposed method can be integrated into a surgical cochlear robot due to high accuracy and fast performance. Due to the absence of a public ground truth, the error is estimated using the cochlear implant known length in the images.

To the best of the authors knowledge, this is the first method that uses such error estimation. The experiments showed a small length estimation error ranged from 0.15 mm to 1.1 mm. The proposed method is implanted as a public open-source plug-in for 3D Slicer software. Future works include more enhancement in terms of speed and accuracy. Using a better histological model to get a segmentation of the 3 cochlear scalae also should be considered in future research.

References

1. Al-Dhamari, I., Bauer, S., Paulus, D., Lesseck, F., Jacob, R., Gessler, A.: ACIR: automatic cochlea image registration. In: Proceedings of SPIE, Medical Imaging 2017: Image Processing, vol. 10133(10), pp. 1–5 (2017)
2. Alexiades, G., Dhanasingh, A., Jolly, C.: Method to estimate the complete and two-turn cochlear duct length. Otol. Neurotol. **36**(5), 904–907 (2015)

3. Cootes, F., Taylor, C., Cooper, D., Graham, J.: Active shape models - their training and application. Comput. Vis. Image Underst. **61**, 38–59 (1995)
4. Edwards, G.J., Taylor, C.J., Cootes, T.F.: Interpreting face images using active appearance models. In: Proceedings Third IEEE International Conference on Automatic Face and Gesture Recognition, p. 300 (1998)
5. Escude, B., James, C., Deguine, O., Cochard, N., Eter, E., Fraysse., B.: The size of the cochlea and predictions of insertion depth angles for cochlear implant electrodes. Audiol. Neurootol. **1**, 27–33 (2006)
6. Franz, D., Hofer, M., Pfeifle, M., Pirlich, M., Stamminger, M., Wittenberg, T.: Wizard-Based Segmentation for Cochlear Implant Planning. In: Deserno T., Handels H., Meinzer HP., Tolxdorff T. (eds) Bildverarbeitung für die Medizin 2014. Informatik aktuell. Springer, Heidelberg (2014). https://doi.org/10.1007/978-3-642-54111-7_49
7. Gerber, N.: A multiscale imaging and modelling dataset of the human inner ear. Sci. Data **4**, 170132 (2017)
8. Iyaniwura, J.E., Elfarnawany, M., Ladak, H.M., Agrawal, S.K.: An automated a-value measurement tool for accurate cochlear duct length estimation. J. Otolaryngol. Head Neck Surg. **47**(1), 5 (2018)
9. Koch, R.W., Elfarnawany, M., Zhu, N., Ladak, H.M., Agrawal, S.K.: Evaluation of cochlear duct length computations using synchrotron radiation phase-contrast imaging. Otol. Neurotol. **38**(6), 92–99 (2017)
10. Koch, R.W., Ladak, H.M., Elfarnawany, M., Agrawal, S.K.: Measuring cochlear duct length, a historical analysis of methods and results. Otolaryngol. Head Neck Surg. **46**(19), 1–11 (2017)
11. Mistrak, P., Jolly, C.: Optimal electrode length to match patient specific cochlear anatomy. Eur. Ann. Otorhinolaryngol. Head Neck Dis. **133**, 68–71 (2016)
12. Noble, J.H., Gifford, R.H., Labadie, R.F., Dawant, B.M.: Statistical shape model segmentation and frequency mapping of cochlear implant stimulation targets in CT. In: Ayache, N., Delingette, H., Golland, P., Mori, K. (eds.) MICCAI 2012. LNCS, vol. 7511, pp. 421–428. Springer, Heidelberg (2012). https://doi.org/10.1007/978-3-642-33418-4_52
13. Noble, J., Labadie, R., Majdani, O., Dawant, B.: Automatic segmentation of intracochlear anatomy in conventional CT. IEEE Trans. Biomed. Eng. **58**(9), 2625–2632 (2011)
14. Reda, F., Noble, J., Labadie, R., Dawanta, B.: An artifact-robust, shape library-based algorithm for automatic segmentation of inner ear anatomy in post-cochlear-implantation CT. In: SPIE 2014, Image Processing, vol. 9034(2), pp. 1–22 (2014)
15. Rivas, A., Cakir, A., Hunter, J., Labadie, R., Zuniga, M., Wanna, G., Dawant, B., Noble, J.: Automatic cochlear duct length estimation for selection of cochlear implant electrode arrays. Otol. Neurotol. **38**(3), 339–346 (2017)
16. Vaid, S., Vaid, N.: Imaging for cochlear implantation: structuring a clinically relevant report. Clin. Radiol. **69**(7), 307–322 (2014)
17. Weber, S., et al.: Instrument flight to the inner ear. Sci. Robot. **2**(4) (2017)
18. Wurfel, W., Lanfermann, H., Lenarz, T., Majdani, O.: Cochlear length determination using cone beam computed tomography in a clinical setting. Hear Res. **316**, 65–72 (2014)

Intelligent Interruption Management System to Enhance Safety and Performance in Complex Surgical and Robotic Procedures

Roger D. Dias[1,2(✉)], Heather M. Conboy[4], Jennifer M. Gabany[2,3], Lori A. Clarke[4], Leon J. Osterweil[4], David Arney[2,5], Julian M. Goldman[2,5], Giuseppe Riccardi[6], George S. Avrunin[6], Steven J. Yule[1,2,7], and Marco A. Zenati[2,3]

[1] STRATUS Center for Medical Simulation, Brigham and Women's Hospital, Boston, MA, USA
rdias@bwh.harvard.edu
[2] Harvard Medical School, Boston, MA, USA
[3] Division of Cardiac Surgery, VA Healthcare System, Boston, MA, USA
[4] University of Massachusetts, Amherst, MA, USA
[5] Massachusetts General Hospital, Boston, MA, USA
[6] Department of Information Engineering and Computer Science, University of Trento, Trento, Italy
[7] Department of Surgery, Brigham and Women's Hospital, Boston, MA, USA

Abstract. Procedural flow disruptions secondary to interruptions play a key role in error occurrence during complex medical procedures, mainly because they increase mental workload among team members, negatively impacting team performance and patient safety. Since certain types of interruptions are unavoidable, and consequently the need for multitasking is inherent to complex procedural care, this field can benefit from an intelligent system capable of identifying in which moment flow interference is appropriate without generating disruptions. In the present study we describe a novel approach for the identification of tasks imposing low cognitive load and tasks that demand high cognitive effort during real-life cardiac surgeries. We used heart rate variability analysis as an objective measure of cognitive load, capturing data in a real-time and unobtrusive manner from multiple team members (surgeon, anesthesiologist and perfusionist) simultaneously. Using audio-video recordings, behavioral coding and a hierarchical surgical process model, we integrated multiple data sources to create an interactive surgical dashboard, enabling the identification of specific steps, substeps and tasks that impose low cognitive load. An interruption management system can use these low demand situations to guide the surgical team in terms of the appropriateness of flow interruptions. The described approach also enables us to detect cognitive load fluctuations over time, under specific conditions (e.g. emergencies) or in situations that are prone to errors. An in-depth understanding of the relationship between cognitive overload states, task demands, and error occurrence will drive the development of cognitive supporting systems that recognize and mitigate errors efficiently and proactively during high complex procedures.

© Springer Nature Switzerland AG 2018
D. Stoyanov et al. (Eds.): OR 2.0/CARE/CLIP/ISIC 2018, LNCS 11041, pp. 62–68, 2018.
https://doi.org/10.1007/978-3-030-01201-4_8

Keywords: Cognitive load · Cardiac surgery · Heart rate variability
Process model

1 Introduction

Recent estimates rank medical errors leading to preventable patient harm as the third cause of death in the U.S. Fifty to 65% of complications experienced by hospitalized patients are procedural in nature and 75% of adverse events occur in the procedure/operating room [1]. Preventable errors leading to error cycles precede 80% of deaths in complex interventional care, and understanding and managing conditions leading to errors is critical to eliminate preventable patient harm [2]. The U.S. Institute of Medicine identified workflow disruptions during complex procedures as a leading contributing factor to medical errors [3]. Procedural flow disruptions secondary to interruptions have been proposed as surrogates for errors, because they increase mental workload and stress of interventional team members, negatively affect mental readiness, impair situational awareness and increase fatigue and frustration [4].

Surgical flow disruptions play a key role in preventable error generation during complex surgical procedures (e.g. robotic surgery). *Wiegmann* et al. found a linear relationship between surgical flow disruptions and errors; as the number of disruptions increased, so did the number of errors ($r = 0.47$, $p < 0.05$) [5]. A growing body of research in complex systems is aiming at manipulating the timing of information notifications in relationship to the ongoing task to minimize the preventable errors and surgical flow disruptions [6, 7]. Distractions and interruptions decrease focus and divert attention from the current task. The cost of distractions and interruptions have been widely studied in the aviation and transportation industry where it has been shown that interruption decrease performance [8, 9] and increase stress and perceived workload [10].

In a complex medical procedural environment, the smooth execution of multi-party dependencies often depends on the perfect synchronized coordination among the various members of the healthcare team, the cost of interruptions or distractions can be extremely high. Proper communication and coordination is extremely essential for the successful execution of a complex procedure. Breakdown in the communication workflow, or disruption of the smooth execution of the individual sub-steps can become critical. Therefore, there is a need to decrease peri-procedural distractions and interruptions which can increase the perceived workload among surgeons and impair team performance [11, 12].

Increase in stress levels increases the probability of making mistakes that can have potentially serious consequences to patient safety [13]. While some distractions such as noise, interruptions from communication devices and external staff may be avoidable, certain interruptions such as clinical clarifications, questions, and requests by the OR staff, may be necessary. For the essential interruptions, unless they are critical, it is important to be able to present them in between the operation steps, when the surgical workload and stress is low. From a Human Computer Interaction perspective this presents new challenges in deciding which machine generated notifications are absolutely critical, and when and how to present them without causing major disruption in the clinical workflow.

In the present study we describe a novel approach for the identification of surgical tasks imposing low vs high cognitive load during real-life cardiac surgeries. We hypothesize that timing interruptions during moments of low mental workload will be less likely to cause flow disruptions vs. interruptions during high workload moments.

2 Methods

In an initial cohort of 10 cardiac surgery cases, we have investigated the cardiac surgery team performing two different complex procedures: coronary artery bypass grafting (CABG) and aortic valve replacement (AVR). Regulatory approvals were obtained by the local Institutional Review Board (IRB), including additional protections for employees as vulnerable subjects. Both patients and staff signed an IRB approved informed consent form and separate authorization for the release of information due to audio/video recording of the procedures.

2.1 Surgical Process Modeling

A surgical team process model for two common cardiac surgery procedures (CABG and AVR) was developed by our group and described in a previous study [14]. Each procedure was segmented in 3 stages, 13–14 steps, 160–180 sub-steps, and approximately 200 tasks. The cardiac surgery process model uses a 4-level hierarchical structure involving four sub(teams): surgeon, anesthesiologist, perfusionist and nurse.

2.2 Audio and Video Recording

Two GoPro cameras (HERO4) were placed in the OR at the room corner and surgical light head, and configured to record an ultra-wide (entire team) and a narrow (surgical field) field of view at 30 frames per second and 960 pixels of video resolution. Three stereo digital voice recorders (Sony ICD-PX440) captured audio at 44.1 kHz/192 Kbps from three team members (surgeon, anesthesiologist and perfusionist) via a lapel microphone. Video and audio files were recorded in MP4 and MP3 formats respectively and synchronized during post-production.

2.3 Heart Rate Variability Analysis (HRV)

HRV is a validated measure of cognitive workload [15, 16]. A heart rate sensor (Polar H7 chest strap) was used to capture beat-to-beat (R-R) intervals from three team members (surgeon, anesthesiologist and perfusionist). We used an ultra-short-term analysis of HRV, calculating the LF/HF ratio for each 1 min epoch, as validated by previous studies [17]. We have also assessed self-reported cognitive load by applying the SURG-TLX questionnaire immediately after the procedure [18].

2.4   Dashboard for Interactive Task Analysis

A multisource database was created in Excel (format.xlsx) and connected to a data analytics software (Tableau Desktop, version 10.4), allowing us to build an interactive dashboard. Figure 1 illustrates our multimodal approach to capture, integrate, synchronize and display data for analysis.

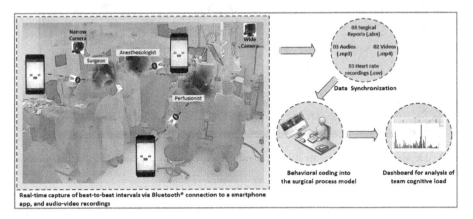

Fig. 1. Multimodal data embed into the surgical process model.

3   Results

In our initial cohort of 10 cardiac surgery procedures (8 CABG and 2 AVR), HRV parameters presenting statistically significant correlation with the SURG-TLX score were: standard deviation of normal to normal R-R intervals (SDNN) (r = −0.61, p < 0.001), HRV triangulation index (r = −0.69, p < 0.001), maximum low frequency (LF)/high frequency (HF) ratio (r = 0.55, p < 0.027), and number of episodes that LF/HF ratio was >2.0 (r = 0.80, p < 0.001).

Using HRV LF/HF ratio, we identified multiple moments of low cognitive workload throughout the recorded procedures; these moments seem to coincide with boundaries between tasks (Fig. 2). An interruption management system can time the interruptions required to exchange critical information during moments of low workload. The approach herby described also enables us to detect cognitive load fluctuations over time or in situations that are prone to errors.

4   Discussion

Complex procedural care is associated with high need for constant communication and coordination. In a recent systematic review, *Rivera-Rodriguez* and associates found that interruptions occur frequently in all healthcare settings but especially in complex procedural care and that only relatively few studies examined the cognitive implications of interruptions [19]. *Monk* et al. have proposed to manipulate the time at which

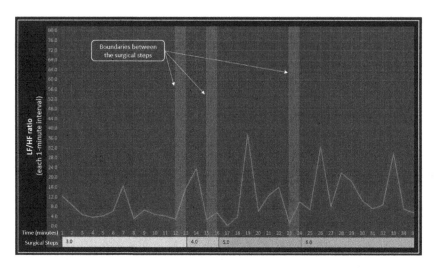

Fig. 2. Identification of moments of low cognitive workload at the boundaries between steps during cardiac surgery.

the notification of an information is delivered, relative to the execution of the ongoing task; these Authors proposed that this timing impacts on the cost of the interruption [20]. *Bailey* and associates have examined changes in mental workload during execution of interactive tasks [6]. They observed that workload exhibits transient decreases at subtask boundaries, corresponding to the completion of large chunks of the task. The majority of disrupting events in complex procedural care are related to information exchanges through communication. Since certain types of interruptions are inherent to complex procedural care, the patient safety field can benefit from an intelligent system capable of identifying in which moment workflow interference has the lowest cost.

There is lack of data describing patterns and distribution of cognitive workload among members of teams engaged in complex surgical procedural care and our ongoing research program is aimed at closing this knowledge gap and enabling new safety approaches. Procedural flow disruptions secondary to interruptions have been proposed as surrogates for errors, because they increase mental workload and stress of interventional team members, negatively affect mental readiness, impair situational awareness and increase fatigue and frustration. Awareness of the critical importance of flow interruptions on the quality of teamwork and their impact on patient outcomes has considerably increased in the last decade. Currently no interruption management system is available to the interventional team. Optimal management of flow interruptions that are required for the acquisition or notification of mission-critical information, may avoid disrupting the workflow and may lead to fewer error cycles and improved patient safety. Influential cyber-human systems research suggests that interrupting tasks during moments of lower mental workload minimizes interruption cost, as transient decrements of mental workload are present at the boundary between tasks, especially after completion of large chunks of the task. This improved understanding of variations in mental workload during complex processes offers a solution to optimally time interruptions of complex medical procedures while minimizing the cost.

Our group has demonstrated that cognitive workload during cardiac surgery procedures can be monitored in near-real time and changes throughout the procedure, alternating peaks of high workload with valleys of low workload. We have also described a context-aware cognitive interface that can predict mental workload in real-time based on physiological data. Fifty-two percent of disrupting events in complex procedural care are related to communication; [5] when individuals are disrupted by an interruption, their attention is shifted away from the primary task to the interruption task [21]. Once this shift of working memory occurs, situation awareness of the primary task begins to decay to "make room" for the process required to deal with the interrupting task; once the primary task is resumed, it is easy for the individual not to remember which part of the primary task was last completed. When attention is shifted away from the primary task, the likelihood of an error occurring upon return to the primary task is increased. Many interruptions however are required to maintain system performance and their high frequency is indicative of the high need for constant communication and coordination in healthcare.

5   Conclusions

We maintain that many medical errors are mental workload problems, that workflow disruptions are surrogates for errors, and that by timing interruptions during moments of low mental workload, the cost of the interruption (i.e. errors) can be minimized

We therefore hypothesize that a context-aware cognitive system could help manage the information flow in the procedural suite and avoid flow disruptions and error cycles leading to patient harm; such system is predicated upon monitoring changes in mental workload in real-time and delivering interruptions and notifications at the appropriate time.

Acknowledgements. The authors wish to acknowledge the contribution, dedication and commitment to excellence of the cardiac surgery team and operating room staff at the VA Boston Healthcare System. Research reported in this publication was supported by the National Heart, Lung, and Blood Institute of the National Institutes of Health under award number 1R01HL126896-01A1. The content is solely the responsibility of the authors and does not necessarily represent the official views of the National Institutes of Health.

References

1. Makary, M.A., Daniel, M.: Medical error-the third leading cause of death in the US. BMJ **353**, i2139 (2016)
2. Gawande, A.A., Zinner, M.J., Studdert, D.M., Brennan, T.A.: Analysis of errors reported by surgeons at three teaching hospitals. Surgery **133**(6), 614–621 (2003)
3. Stefl, M.E.: To err is human: building a safer health system in 1999. Front Health Serv. Manag. **18**(1), 1–2 (2001)

4. Weigl, M., et al.: Intra-operative disruptions, surgeon's mental workload, and technical performance in a full-scale simulated procedure. Surg. Endosc. **30**(2), 559–566 (2016)
5. Wiegmann, D.A., ElBardissi, A.W., Dearani, J.A., Daly, R.C., Sundt, T.M.: Disruptions in surgical flow and their relationship to surgical errors: an exploratory investigation. Surgery **142**(5), 658–665 (2007)
6. Bailey, B.P., Iqbal, S.T.: Understanding changes in mental workload during execution of goal-directed tasks and its application for interruption management. ACM Trans. Comput-Hum Interact. **14**(4), 1–28 (2008)
7. Miyata, Y., Norman, D.A.: Psychological issues in support of multiple activities. In: Norman, D.A., Draper, S.W. (eds.) User centered System Design, pp. 265–284. Lawrence Erlbaum Associates, Inc., Hillsdale (1986)
8. Latorella, K.A.: Effects of modality on interrupted flight deck performance: implications for data link. Proc. Hum. Factors Ergon. Soc. Annu. Meet. **42**(1), 87–91 (1998)
9. Oulasvirta, A., Saariluoma, P.: Surviving task interruptions: Investigating the implications of long-term working memory theory. Int. J. Hum. Comput. Stud. **64**(10), 941–961 (2006)
10. Chen, Y.: Stress state of driver: mobile phone use while driving. Procedia Soc. Behav. Sci. **96**, 12–16 (2013)
11. Wheelock, A., et al.: The impact of operating room distractions on stress, workload, and teamwork. Ann. Surg. **261**(6), 1079–1084 (2015)
12. Arora, S., et al.: Factors compromising safety in surgery: stressful events in the operating room. Am. J. Surg. **199**(1), 60–65 (2010)
13. Arora, S., Sevdalis, N., Nestel, D., Woloshynowych, M., Darzi, A., Kneebone, R.: The impact of stress on surgical performance: a systematic review of the literature. Surgery **147**(3):318–330, 330.e311–330.e316 (2010)
14. Dias, R., et al.: Embedding real-time measure of surgeons' cognitive load into cardiac surgery process modeling. In: Academic Surgical Congress: 2018, Jacksonville, FL, USA (2018)
15. Dias, R.D., Ngo-Howard, M.C., Boskovski, M.T., Zenati, M.A., Yule, S.J.: Systematic review of measurement tools to assess surgeons' intraoperative cognitive workload. Br. J. Surg. **105**, 491–501 (2018)
16. Thayer, J.F., Hansen, A.L., Saus-Rose, E., Johnsen, B.H.: Heart rate variability, prefrontal neural function, and cognitive performance: the neurovisceral integration perspective on self-regulation, adaptation, and health. Ann. Behav. Med. **37**(2), 141–153 (2009)
17. Baek, H.J., Cho, C.H., Cho, J., Woo, J.M.: Reliability of ultra-short-term analysis as a surrogate of standard 5-min analysis of heart rate variability. Telemed. J. E Health **21**(5), 404–414 (2015)
18. Wilson, M.R., Poolton, J.M., Malhotra, N., Ngo, K., Bright, E., Masters, R.S.: Development and validation of a surgical workload measure: the surgery task load index (SURG-TLX). World J. Surg. **35**(9), 1961–1969 (2011)
19. Rivera-Rodriguez, A.J., Karsh, B.T.: Interruptions and distractions in healthcare: review and reappraisal. Qual. Saf. Health Care **19**(4), 304–312 (2010)
20. Monk, C.A., Boehm-Davis, D.A., Trafton, J.G.: The attentional costs of interrupting task performance at various stages. Proc. Human Factors Ergon. Soc. Annu. Meet. **46**(22), 1824–1828 (2002)
21. Flin, R., Youngson, G., Yule, S.: Enhancing Surgical Performance. CRC Press, Boca Raton, FL, US (2016)

Performance Evaluation to Improve Training in Forceps-Assisted Delivery

Mónica García-Sevilla[1,2(✉)], Juan De León-Luis[3,4], Rafael Moreta-Martínez[1,2], David García-Mato[1,2], Rubén Pérez-Mañanes[2,5], José Calvo-Haro[2,5], and Javier Pascau[1,2]

[1] Department of Bioengineering and Aerospace Engineering, Universidad Carlos III de Madrid, Madrid, Spain
{mongarci,rmoreta}@pa.uc3m.es, {dgmato,jpascau}@ing.uc3m.es
[2] Instituto de Investigación Sanitaria Gregorio Marañón, Madrid, Spain
[3] Department of Obstetrics and Gynecology, Hospital General Universitario Gregorio Marañón, Madrid, Spain
[4] Departamento de Salud Publica y Materno Infantil, Facultad de Medicina, Universidad Complutense de Madrid, Madrid, Spain
jaleon@ucm.es
[5] Department of Traumatology and Orthopaedic Surgery, Hospital General Universitario Gregorio Marañón, Madrid, Spain

Abstract. The World Health Organization recommends a rate of cesareans inferior than 15%. However, the actual rates in the US double this value, while the use of obstetrical instruments, a recommended alternative to cesareans but which requires high skill and experience, has significantly decreased in the latest years. In this context there is a clear demand for simulators, with special interest in learning the correct use of Kielland's forceps. In this work we present a virtual instrumented simulator to improve training in the correct use of forceps proposing a three-step protocol which guides users along the process while evaluating their performance. We validate this protocol, following principles based on previously published guidelines, on two types of manikins. Our results show that the proposed solution successfully detects the incorrect positioning of the forceps in most steps, guiding the user during the training process and providing feedback on wrong maneuvers.

Keywords: Training · Forceps delivery · Tracking system
Performance evaluation · Assessment

1 Motivation

According to the World Health Organization (WHO), the number of cesareans performed in deliveries should be inferior to 15% due to their associated intraoperative complications and morbidity [4]. Fifty years ago, this rate in the US was 4.5%. However, in 2009 it ascended to 32.9% and by 2015 the registered rate

© Springer Nature Switzerland AG 2018
D. Stoyanov et al. (Eds.): OR 2.0/CARE/CLIP/ISIC 2018, LNCS 11041, pp. 69–77, 2018.
https://doi.org/10.1007/978-3-030-01201-4_9

was 32.0% [7]. These fluctuations and the significant increment recorded over the last decades seem to be a consequence of the practice style.

The correct use of obstetrical instruments during the second stage of labor is a good alternative to cesarean, as it has demonstrated to reduce morbidity without increasing complications in the fetus. This reduction is especially significant when deliveries are forceps-assisted. However, the rates of operative vaginal delivery (OVD) have suffered an important reduction over the last decades, decreasing in the US from 9.01% in 1990 to 3.14% in 2015 [7]. The use of these tools for assistance requires high clinical experience and training, as poor performance can cause damage to both mother and fetus (skull or scalp trauma, facial nerve palsy or ocular trauma among others). Nowadays, health care providers seem to have a lack of experience when confronting real clinical cases which require the use of obstetrical instruments and, consequently, they may end up performing cesareans instead. A survey conducted among resident physicians upon completion of their residency showed that 55% of them did not feel competent to perform forceps and vacuum deliveries [9]. These results could explain the cesareans rate increment and the decrease of OVD.

A cross sectional study conducted in 2017 in the UK reported that more than two-thirds of specialist trainees in obstetrics and gynecology think simulators could improve training significantly in this area, showing special interest in the safe use of Kielland's forceps [12]. In our hospital, the number of cesareans in complicated cases has been reduced in recent years while the use of forceps (specially Kielland's) has increased considerably. This seems to be a consequence of the special attention given to train residents in the correct use of obstetrical instruments through manikins, actors and simulators.

Several simulators of childbirth have been developed over the years to complete novice obstetricians' formation. These simulators can be realistic and focus on different roles of childbirth. According to their components or features they can be classified as: anatomical or virtual and instrumented or non-instrumented. Anatomical simulators are useful for demonstration of obstetrical maneuvers and for learning how to handle specific scenarios. Instrumented anatomical simulators are more realistic, incorporating some interesting functionalities like the ability to replicate vaginal delivery by an ejection system [5]. On the other hand, virtual non-instrumented simulators include three-dimensional visualization, useful to illustrate the fetus descent, but are more theoretical than practical. Lastly, the virtual instrumented simulators are the most complex ones, including interaction between simulator and student by visual and/or haptic feedback.

Many virtual-instrumented simulators have focused on measuring shoulder extraction forces [8] while others simulate delivery with visual and haptic feedback [1]. Among these, some include a navigation component where the position of obstetrical instrumentation can be displayed in real time with respect to the manikins by means of a tracking system. The first to implement this functionality were Lapeer et al. in 2005 [6], developing an augmented reality interface where the forceps placement in the fetus manikin head could be visualized in a virtual scene using an optical tracking system. The purpose of their work was to evaluate skull deformations. In 2009 a new simulator called BirthSIM was presented including also instrumented forceps, tracked by means of an electromagnetic tracking system. Up to date, this seems to be the best augmented reality simulator for delivery training. However, their use of the tracked forceps has been limited to assess the improvements of junior obstetricians [2].

In this work we present a virtual instrumented simulator to improve training in the correct use of forceps. We propose a protocol composed of three steps which guide the users along the process while evaluating their performance. The evaluation principles applied are based on guidelines found in the literature as well as experts indications. The software has been developed in 3DSlicer [3] (a free and open-source platform for medical image analysis and visualization) for use in combination with delivery manikins. Forceps, fetus and mother are navigated through an electromagnetic tracker, while displaying their relative position in real time on a 3D virtual scene. To evaluate the protocol, two experiments were performed: one using a fixed manikin of a fetus head; the second, in a real scenario with delivery manikins and performed by an expert.

2 Materials and Methods

The 3D Guidance electromagnetic tracking system (EMTS) from NDI (Northern Digital Inc.) was used to track the position of the baby, mother and forceps blades in real time. We chose this type of positioning device instead of an optical tracking system as the former does not require direct view of the markers. As the baby is initially inside the mother and covered by the belly, the use of the EMTS was considered a better approach. However, the forceps are made of stainless steel, which alters the field generated by the EMTS due to its ferromagnetic properties. To overcome this issue, we 3D printed a replica of the forceps in Alumide, a non-ferromagnetic material commonly used in 3D printing composed of nylon filled with aluminum dust. Its model, extracted from a CT, was then modified to include in the handle endings a special case for the sensors. Also, four holes were added to the design of each blade for an accurate registration between sensor and model.

The PROMPT Flex - Advanced mother and fetus manikins (Limbs and Things) employed in our hospital for training workshops were used for experiments and for generation of the 3D models (from CT scan) visualized in the virtual scene. Also, a stand with the baby's head in occiput anterior (OA) position was 3D printed in polylactic acid (PLA) to carry out the initial experiment.

The software was implemented as an extension inside the open-source platform 3DSlicer. The extension is composed of different modules, each with a specific task: a registration module for setup, used to register each model with their corresponding sensor in a fast and semi-automatic way; a learning module to visualize the correct movement for each step; a training module to perform the process step by step while checking if the placements are correct; an evaluation module to record the whole process and analyze it afterwards.

In the following section, the steps taken during the process of forceps application will be explained, together with the description of how the verification has been implemented. By convention, the blade with the lock is referred to as left blade and the other as right. Figure 1 represents the reference system for each model present in the virtual scene.

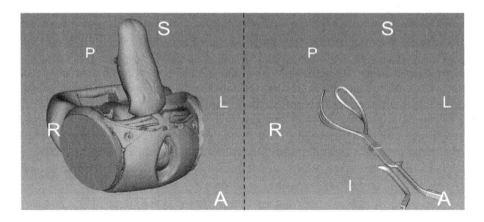

Fig. 1. Coordinate systems for mother and baby (left) and for forceps (right)

2.1   Protocol for Forceps Placement

Assembly and Presentation: Before the application, forceps are held outside the pelvis correctly assembled and presented in the position they will have once applied to the fetal head. For a correct assembly, the right shank must be above the left one and below the lock. The forceps should be placed symmetrically, being the handles at the same level. In the validation of this step, the relative position of the shanks is compared, taking the left forceps as reference frame. If the distances in horizontal or forwards are higher than 0.5 cm, the assembly is considered incorrect.

For a correct presentation, if the baby is placed in OA, the forceps should be parallel to the floor and the lock should be looking towards the fetal occiput (upwards). If the baby is in left OA or right OA position, the blades should form an angle of 45° with the floor. We defined a reference ideal position of the forceps with this criterium, and then calculated the registration between its actual position and this reference, extracting the rotational component of the resulting transform. For the presentation to be correct, the AP angle (measured in the reference frame of the baby) from the rotation matrix should be close to 0. As 45° would represent another position for the fetus, a margin of 22.5° (45/2) was established.

Forceps Application: The application of the forceps can be divided in three stages: initial placement, insertion and final placement. This is done firstly with the left branch and then with the right one in order to avoid them crossing once inserted, which can cause damage to the mother.

In the initial placement, the left blade is placed vertically and in contact with the fetus head. For detecting this contact, the distance between the tip of the forceps and the baby's head was computed and a maximum distance of 1 cm was defined as correct. The correct angle of the forceps was defined by an expert and settled to be 10° from the vertical (SI axis of the baby) with a 10° margin. For evaluation, the angle of a vector defined in the direction of the shank is compared with the ideal one.

Then, the insertion is performed. When completed, the blades should lie over the cheeks of the fetus covering the area between eyes and ears [10]. A study performed on 50 full term neonates showed that a margin of at least 3 cm should be kept between the tip of the blade and both the eye and facial nerve [2]. To verify a correct application, the distances from the tip to the outside eye corner and to the facial nerve (area behind the ear) are computed. Also, the distance from the tip to the cheeks is obtained, where values greater than 1 cm are considered incorrect.

Traction: Finally, after application both blades should be easily locked. Although the blades do not necessarily lock perfectly, the gap between the handles must be always below 1 cm [11]. Before performing the traction, the final position of the blades must be checked and the following conditions must be satisfied [10]: the midline of the forceps must coincide with the sagittal suture; the posterior fontanelle must be one finger breadth (2 cm) above the plane of the shanks; the space between the heel and the baby's head should admit no more than a fingertip (1 cm); the distance to eyes and facial nerve must be greater than 2.9 cm.

For validating that the forceps lie evenly against both sides of the baby's head and that the gap between them is 1 cm or less, the distance of each shank to the AP axis from the baby's reference frame is measured. The value should be between 0 and 0.5 cm for the left blade and between −0.5 and 0 for the right one. For measuring the distance to the posterior fontanelle, a plane is created in the shank, whose normal is defined by the vertical axis of the forceps coordinates system (SI). The distance between the fontanelle and the plane must be of at least 2 cm. The last two conditions enumerated are checked as explained in Step 2.

3   Experiments

For the protocol validation, an initial experiment was carried out by one of the members of the developers team using the printed forceps and the 3D printed head. Maneuvers for assembly, presentation and initial placement were repeated a total of 8 times, from which 4 were correctly placed while the other 4 were deliberately placed incorrectly. For final placement and traction, 4 correct placements were recorded.

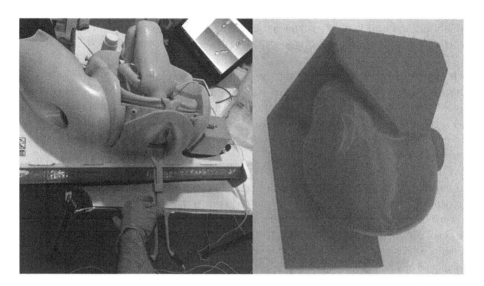

Fig. 2. Experiments with commercial manikins (left) and 3D printed head (right).

A second experiment was implemented in a real scenario, where maneuvers were performed by an expert (clinician with more than 14 years of experience in the field of obstetrics and gynecology) using the 3D printed forceps and the commercial manikins (Fig. 2). The number of recorded repetitions was the same as in the first experiment. For the deliberate incorrect placements and assemblies, the expert focused on common mistakes novices do when training. These examples were only for the first steps (before insertion) as common errors are easier to identify in these stages.

The precision and recall for each experiment were computed. In this application, precision is considered more relevant than recall as it is better for the training to inform the novice that the placement is incorrect when it is not than the opposite. For that reason, an $F_{0.5}$ score was evaluated defined as:

$$F_\beta = (1 + \beta^2)\frac{Precision \cdot Recall}{\beta^2 Precision + Recall} \tag{1}$$

4   Results

Tables 1 and 2 show for each experiment the placements detected correctly (true positives and true negatives) and incorrectly (false positives and false negatives). These values are obtained for each phase of the procedure: assembly, presentation, initial and final placement (for left and right blades) and traction placement. Table 3 shows the resulting $F_{0.5}$ scores.

Table 1. Rates of success from experiment 1

	Step 1		Step 2				Step 3	Total
	Assembly	Presentation	Init L	Final L	Init R	Final R	Traction	
TP	2	4	4	2	4	1	3	**20**
TN	4	4	4	2	4	2	0	**20**
FP	0	0	0	0	0	0	0	**0**
FN	2	0	0	0	0	1	1	**4**

TP: true positive, TN: true negative, FP: false positive, FN: false negative
Init L(R): initial placement for left(right) branch
Final L(R): final placement for left(right) branch

Table 2. Rates of success from experiment 2 (expert)

	Step 1		Step 2				Step 3	Total
	Assembly	Presentation	Init L	Final L	Init R	Final R	Traction	
TP	3	4	4	1	3	0	0	**15**
TN	4	4	4	0	4	0	0	**16**
FP	0	0	0	0	0	0	0	**0**
FN	1	0	0	3	1	4	4	**13**

TP: true positive, TN: true negative, FP: false positive, FN: false negative
Init L(R): initial placement for left(right) branch
Final L(R): final placement for left(right) branch

Table 3. $F_{0.5}$ scores

	Precision	Recall	$F_{0.5}$
Experiment 1	1	0.83	**0.96**
Experiment 2	1	0.54	**0.85**

5   Conclusions

A new protocol for training in the correct application of forceps is presented. The implemented software goes through every step of the process and relies in the conditions presented in the literature and defined by experts to characterize the correctness of each step. An electromagnetic tracking system is used to track the position in real-time of forceps and manikins.

An initial evaluation of the software has been performed, firstly with a fixed manikin of a baby head in OA position and later in a real scenario with an expert using delivery commercial manikins. The results obtained from these experiments demonstrate high performance, especially for the initial steps. Yet, some limitations were found in the real scenario regarding the final placements. Once inserted, the forceps are slightly deformed, which implies an incorrect representation of the blades position in the virtual scene and therefore a wrong computation of the distances. This would explain the increase in the false negative rate for the final placement in step 2 and for step 3 during the second experiment, since the real manikin deformed the forceps during these phases.

In the lights of these promising results, a further study will be performed to assess the advantages in learning of forceps placement using this protocol. Also, an alternative more rigid material for the forceps will be tested to avoid deformation once inserted.

Acknowledgments. Supported by projects PI15/02121 (Ministerio de Economía y Competitividad, Instituto de Salud Carlos III and ERD Funds), TOPUS-CM S2013/MIT-3024 (Comunidad de Madrid) and GEER.

References

1. Abate, A.F., Acampora, G., Loia, V., Ricciardi, S., Vasilakos, A.V.: A pervasive visualhaptic framework for virtual delivery training. IEEE Trans. Inf. Technol. Biomed. **14**(2), 326–334 (2010). https://doi.org/10.1109/TITB.2010.2043678
2. Dupuis, O., et al.: Does forceps training on a birth simulator allow obstetricians to improve forceps blade placement? Eur. J. Obstet. Gynecol. Reprod. Biol. **159**(2), 305–309 (2011). https://doi.org/10.1016/j.ejogrb.2011.09.002
3. Fedorov, A., et al.: 3D Slicer as an image computing platform for the Quantitative Imaging Network. Magn. Reson. Imaging **30**(9), 1323–1341 (2012). https://doi.org/10.1016/j.mri.2012.05.001
4. Gibbons, L., Belizán, J.M., Lauer, J.A., Betrán, A.P., Merialdi, M., Althabe, F.: The Global Numbers and Costs of Additionally Needed and Unnecessary Caesarean Sections Performed per Year: Overuse as a Barrier to Universal Coverage. World Health Report. Background Papers, pp. 1–31 (2010). https://doi.org/10.1017/CBO9781107415324.004
5. Knapp, C.F., Eades, G.S.: Dynamic childbirth simulator for teaching maternity patient care (1974). http://www.freepatentsonline.com/3826019.html
6. Lapeer, R., Chen, M.S., Villagrana, J.: An augmented reality based simulation of obstetric forceps delivery. In: ISMAR 2004: Proceedings of the Third IEEE and ACM International Symposium on Mixed and Augmented Reality (ISMAR), pp. 274–275 (2004). https://doi.org/10.1109/ISMAR.2004.13
7. Martin, J.A., Hamilton, B.E., Osterman, M.J., Driscoll, A.K., Mathews, T.J.: Births: final data for 2015. Natl. Vital Stat. Rep. **66**(1), 1 (2017). https://www.ncbi.nlm.nih.gov/pubmed/28135188
8. Moreau, R., Pham, M.T., Redarce, T., Dupuis, O.: Simulation of forceps extraction on a childbirth simulator. In: Proceedings of IEEE International Conference on Robotics and Automation, pp. 1100–1105 (2008). https://doi.org/10.1109/ROBOT.2008.4543351
9. Powell, J., Gilo, N., Foote, M., Gil, K., Lavin, J.P.: Vacuum and forceps training in residency: experience and self-reported competency. J. Perinatol. Off. J. Calif. Perinat. Assoc. **27**(6), 343–346 (2007). https://doi.org/10.1038/sj.jp.7211734
10. Rather, H., Muglu, J., Veluthar, L., Sivanesan, K.: The art of performing a safe forceps delivery: a skill to revitalise. Eur. J. Obstet. Gynecol. Reprod. Biol. **199**, 49–54 (2016). https://doi.org/10.1016/j.ejogrb.2016.01.045

11. Simpson, A.N., et al.: Learning from experience: development of a cognitive task list to perform a safe and successful non-rotational forceps delivery. J. Obstet. Gynaecol. Can. **37**(7), 589–597 (2015). https://doi.org/10.1016/S1701-2163(15)30196-1
12. Wattar, B.H.A., Mahmud, A., Janjua, A., Parry-Smith, W., Ismail, K.M.: Training on Kielland's forceps: a survey of trainees' opinions. J. Obstet. Gynaecol. **37**(3), 280–283 (2017). https://doi.org/10.1080/01443615.2016.1196476

Clinical Trial of Information Acquisition System for Surgical Instruments in Digital Operation Room

Kaori Kusuda[1(✉)], Kazuhiko Yamashita[2], Yoshitomo Ito[3],
Kiyohito Tanaka[4], Ken Masamune[1], and Yoshihiro Muragaki[1]

[1] Tokyo Women's Medical University, Tokyo, Japan
kusuda.kaori@twmu.ac.jp
[2] Graduate School of Medicine, Osaka University, Osaka, Japan
[3] Saiseikai Kurihashi Hospital, Saitama, Japan
[4] Kyoto Second Red Cross Hospital, Kyoto, Japan

Abstract. To prevent incidents in which surgical items are retained in a patient's body, a unique device system (UDS) of surgical instruments in the operation room is required. In our previous study, we developed surgical instruments with radio-frequency identification (RFID) tags and a UDS antenna to assign unique identification to each instrument in operation room. The purposes of the present study were to evaluate the recognition accuracy of the antenna system during surgery and determine the usage rate of preoperatively prepared surgical instruments. The experiments were conducted in four inguinal hernia surgeries. The recognition accuracy of data acquisition was 97.7%. The one cause that decreased this rate by 2.3% was occasional placement of the RFID tags outside the radio communication range of the antenna. However, when the surgical instruments were moved by a nurse and returned to the antenna, the system could detect all instruments. The system could detect RFID tags during surgery, and the accuracy was maintained when the scrub nurses placed the instruments on the antenna unconsciously. The total usage rate of the preoperatively prepared surgical instruments was 50.0%. Thus, half of the surgical instruments were not used during surgery and underwent a repeated sterilization and washing process. These instruments are exposed to high pressure and temperature, increasing the risk of instrument defects. The system described herein can clarify these rates and help to optimize the number of surgical instruments that are prepared before surgery.

Keywords: RFID tags · Surgical instrument · Antenna

1 Background

Surgical items are retained in a patient's body once in every 10,000 operations, and 30% of the items are surgical instruments [1, 2]. This problem is caused by complex counts and defects of surgical instruments. First, a nurse conducts a surgical count, and the medical staff repeatedly counts all sponges and instruments in the perioperative period. The scrub nurse who passes the instruments to the surgeons must also

© Springer Nature Switzerland AG 2018
D. Stoyanov et al. (Eds.): OR 2.0/CARE/CLIP/ISIC 2018, LNCS 11041, pp. 78–84, 2018.
https://doi.org/10.1007/978-3-030-01201-4_10

simultaneously conduct surgical counts and provide support during the surgery. The surgical count depends heavily on a manual count method, which has a risk of miscounting. The World Health Organization reported that manual counting is not foolproof [1] and that support by a counting system is required. Second, because the surgical instruments are not managed individually, the causes of surgical instrument defects are not always clear. To prevent these issues, a unique device system (UDS) that can recognize each instrument individually in the operation room (OR) is required.

In a general hospital, a surgical instrument set is assembled before surgery to streamline preparation of the OR. A set consists of multiple types and numbers of instruments, and the total number of instruments is 10 to 200. The lists of instruments are fixed for each surgical type in each hospital. However, the list of surgical instruments that are prepared before surgery is not optimized; instead, the instruments are compiled at the surgeon's discretion. Un-optimized sets lead to an overloaded washing and sterilization process for surgical instruments. Too many instruments in the set will lead to a complicated surgical count for medical staff in OR and potentially impact risks of miscounts.

In our previous study, we developed surgical instruments with radio-frequency identification (RFID) tags (Fig. 1) and software to recognize each instrument in the OR [3]. Each RFID tag has a unique ID (UID) for easy identification, and each instrument can be recognized automatically. The tag is covered by ceramic and can tolerate the processes of washing and sterilization in the hospital. An antenna system was also developed in that study. The system detects the RFID tag and obtains a UID when nurses place the surgical instruments on the antenna plate. The system allows for recording of the number of uses and defect history of each instrument. The frequently used data of instruments being transferred from one set to another are recorded. The results of that study suggest that this system can trace each instrument [4].

The purposes of the present study were to evaluate the recognition accuracy of the antenna system during surgery and determine the usage rate of surgical instruments that were prepared before surgery. Finally, we discuss the possibility of applying our system to a workflow model and digital OR.

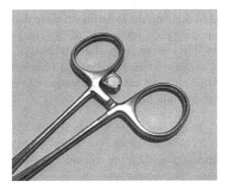

Fig. 1. Surgical instrument with RFID tag [3]

2 Methods

Our system was placed on a Mayo table, which is an instrument table positioned over the patient, and the table was then covered by a sterilized surgical drape. As the RFID surgical instruments are placed on the table (Fig. 2), the system can automatically detect these tags and obtain a UID. To obtain the correct number of instruments in the present study, the instruments were visually counted using a video camera at the same time as control data. The accuracy of the system was calculated by the following formula (1):

$$Accuracy\,of\,system\,[\%] \;=\; Sn/Vn \times 100 \tag{1}$$

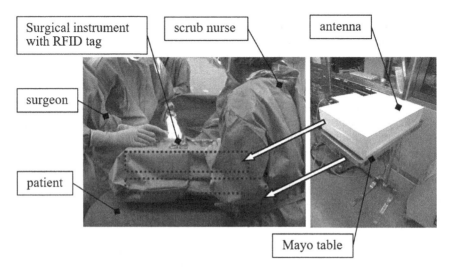

Fig. 2. Antenna system on Mayo table, covered with a sterilized surgical drape

Vn: total number of instruments counted using video camera
Sn: total number of instruments counted using system
To obtain a gold standard number, the experiments were conducted in four inguinal hernia surgeries. Sixty-one surgical instruments of 20 types with RFID tags were prepared for hernia surgery. Fifty-seven surgical instruments of 18 types were used for calculation of the accuracy because 3 towel forceps and 1 knife holder were not used on the instrument table in these surgical cases. The usage rate of the instruments was calculated by the following formula (2):

$$Usage\,rate\,[\%] \;=\; Un/In \times 100 \tag{2}$$

Un: number of instruments placed on the antenna
In: number of instruments in a hernia set

3   Results

Figure 3 shows the number of surgical instruments that were placed on the Mayo table during surgery. The number of instruments placed on the antenna plate at the same time ranged from 1 to 10 in this case. The data of the four hernia surgeries are shown in Table 1; the total average accuracy of data acquisition was 97.7%. Because the RFID tags were sometimes placed outside the radio communication range on the antenna, they could not always be detected. However, when the surgical instruments were moved by a nurse and returned to the Mayo table, the system could detect all instruments.

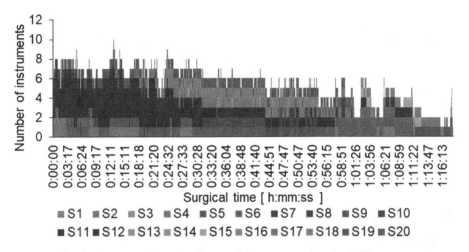

Fig. 3. Count number of each type of instrument using the RFID system

Table 1. Results of clinical trial of the system

#	Surgical time [minutes]	System accuracy [%]	Usage rate of instruments [%]
1	79	96.8	50.9
2	60	99.4	43.9
3	67	97.1	49.1
4	78	97.7	56.1

The total usage rate of the surgical instruments in the surgical sets was 50.0%. Nevertheless, the sets contained 57 surgical instruments including 18 types. 10 Halsted mosquito forceps were included in the set; however, the usage rate was around 22%. Additionally, some instrument types were not used during surgery.

4 Discussion

4.1 Recognition Accuracy of Surgical Instruments Using the UDS

Several previous studies have been performed in an attempt to detect surgical instruments separately by image processing or barcodes [5, 6]. However, these methods fail to detect some instruments because of overlap and the presence of blood. To recognize barcodes, nurses must scan it one by one and wipe blood from the surface of the instrument. This operation leads to human error and is not adequate for use in OR. In the present study, the RFID tags communicated by radio-frequency, and the system could detect instruments that overlapped and contained blood.

As an RFID mechanism, tags can send and receive information when the tags and antenna are set in parallel. Scrub nurses place instruments on the table unconsciously, and RFID tags become perpendicular to the plane of the instrument table. Therefore, the magnetic flux from the system cannot pass the tag. This technical issue should be resolved to acquire data of surgical instruments in the OR.

In general, the antenna structure is a single-loop antenna, and the magnetic flux is uneven on the antenna plate. Therfore, a reader can detect the UID of instruments when the RFID and antenna are only in parallel. The system that was developed in our previous study used multiple antennas, resulting in multi-magnetic flux. In the present antenna, the magnetic flux becomes smooth (Fig. 4) [7]. The system maintains an adequate communication distance and detects RFID tags during surgery, and the accuracy remains high when the scrub nurses set the instruments down unconsciously.

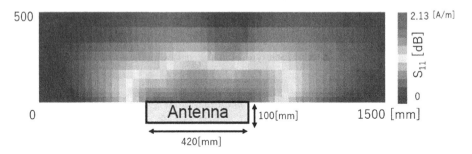

Fig. 4. Magnetic flux using antenna of UDS [7]

4.2 Usage Ratio of Surgical Instruments in a Set

In each hospital, surgical sets of sterilized instruments are prepared preoperatively for specific types of procedures. There is no established list of instruments to include, and medical staff make independent judgments about decreasing or increasing the number of instruments. In fact, most surgical sets contain more than the required number of instruments. However, defects of instruments have been reported despite the fact that the instruments were not used during surgery. The inclusion of the extra instruments in the surgical set is associated with defect formation.

In this study, the rate of surgical instrument use in each set was 50%. Most of the surgical instruments in the sets were not used during surgery, and the washing and sterilizing processes were repeated. To prevent defects of instrument, the number of surgical instruments must be minimized. However, because each set includes extra instruments for emergency situations, unused instruments cannot simply be removed from the set. Continuing clinical trials will clarify the optimal number of instruments.

The period and frequency of instrument breakdowns can be approximated by a bathtub curve. Medical equipment (e.g., syringe pumps, electric knives) are maintained routinely and managed individually. The period and frequency of breakdowns cannot be estimated for surgical instruments because these instruments are not individually managed [8]. Therefore, instrument defects unexpectedly occur during surgery. Our UDS provides new insight into the defect rate of surgical instruments as determined by the management method.

4.3 Digitalization of Workflow and Medical Device Data

Several previous studies involved digitalization of the surgical scenario to develop a scrub nurse robot and optimize workflow. Motion of medical staff was detected automatically during laparoscopic surgery, and the workflow was analyzed [9]. Image processing and an RFID system were used, and the system detected phases automatically [10].

In this study, each surgical instrument was detected automatically, and the UID of instruments and date of detection were obtained. Additionally, we are developing a Smart Cyber Operating Theater (SCOT) as part of our project. This system connects medical devices that are made by various companies using OPeLiNK [11]. Connecting our system with OPeLiNK will allow for detection of surgical instruments and digitalization of surgical items.

4.4 Limitation of This Study

A limitation of this study is that some surgical instrument skipped Mayo table could not detect. Usually, two surgical tables are used in a surgery. Often used instruments are placed on Mayo table, and unused instruments at the surgical phase are placed on another instruments table. For example, a knife holder was usually skipped Mayo table to prevent cutting unconsciously, so it omitted from the calculations in this study. Our study is developing new antenna for surgical table. The system will be developed, and surgical instruments can be counted automatically.

Additionally, the described system cannot be used to attach an RFID tag to certain instruments, such as the small clips used for brain surgery or a strip retractor that bends at the point of RFID tag attachment. These instruments still need to be counted manually. Miniaturization of RFID tags or coexistence of the tags with another detection system may help to realize total management of instruments.

5 Conclusion

Incidents in which surgical instruments are retained in a patient's body occur even today, and the causes are miscounting and defective surgical instruments. The final goal of this study was to establish a surgical instrument management protocol for use in the OR. Such an individual management system was developed in this study, and a clinical trial was conducted to evaluate the accuracy of recognition of RFID tags and determine the usage rate of surgical instruments. The total accuracy of data acquisition was 97.7%, and the total usage rate of the instruments in surgical sets was around 50.0%. Our system can automatically detect these tags and obtain information during surgery; these data can then be utilized when devising instrument sets.

References

1. World Health Organization.: WHO Guidelines for Safe Surgery 2009 (2009)
2. Gawande, A., Studdert, D., Orav, E., Brennan, T., Zinner, M.: Risk factors for retained instruments and sponges after surgery. N. Engl. J. Med. **348**(3), 229–235 (2003)
3. Yamashita, K., et al.: Identification of information surgical instrument by ceramic RFID tag. In: World Automation Congress Proceedings of a Meeting 28 September–2 October, pp. 1–6 (2008)
4. Kusuda, K., et al.: Management of surgical instruments with radio frequency identification tags: A 27-month in hospital trial. Int. J. Health Care Qual. Assur. **29**(2), 236–247 (2016)
5. Lincourt, A.E., Harrell, A., Cristiano, J., Sechrist, C., Kercher, K., Heniford, B.T.: Retained foreign bodies after surgery. J. Surg. Res. **138**(2), 170–174 (2007)
6. Williams, H., Harris, R., Turner-Stokes, L.: Work sampling: a quantitative analysis of nursing activity in a neurorehabilitation setting. J. Adv. Nurs. **65**(10), 2097–2107 (2009)
7. Kusuda, K., et al.: Measurement of magnetic field from radio-frequency identification antenna for use in operation room. In: 2017 IEEE Conference on Antenna Measurements & Applications (CAMA), pp. 414–415 (2017)
8. Yasuhara, H., Fukatsu, K., Komatsu, T., Obayashi, T., Saito, Y., Uetera, Y.: Prevention of medical accidents caused by defective surgical instruments. Surgery **151**(2), 153–161 (2012)
9. Miyawaki, F., Masamune, K., Suzuki, S., Yoshimitsu, K., Vain, J.: Scrub nurse robot system—intraoperative motion analysis of a scrub nurse and timed-automata-based model for surgery. IEEE Trans. Industr. Electron. **52**(5), 1227–1235 (2005)
10. Neumuth, T., Meißner, C.: Online recognition of surgical instruments by information fusion. Int. J. CARS **7**, 297–304 (2012)
11. Okamoto, J., Masamune, K., Iseki, H., Muragaki, Y.: Development concepts of a Smart Cyber Operating Theater (SCOT) using ORiN technology. Biomed. Tech. **63**(1), 31–37 (2018)

Temporal Coherence-based Self-supervised Learning for Laparoscopic Workflow Analysis

Isabel Funke[1(✉)], Alexander Jenke[1], Sören Torge Mees[2], Jürgen Weitz[2], Stefanie Speidel[1], and Sebastian Bodenstedt[1]

[1] Department for Translational Surgical Oncology, National Center for Tumor Diseases (NCT), Partner Site Dresden, Dresden, Germany
{Isabel.Funke,Alexander.Jenke,Stefanie.Speidel, Sebastian.Bodenstedt}@nct-dresden.de
[2] Department of Visceral, Thoracic and Vascular Surgery, Faculty of Medicine, University Hospital Carl Gustav Carus, TU Dresden, Dresden, Germany

Abstract. In order to provide the right type of assistance at the right time, computer-assisted surgery systems need context awareness. To achieve this, methods for surgical workflow analysis are crucial. Currently, convolutional neural networks provide the best performance for video-based workflow analysis tasks. For training such networks, large amounts of annotated data are necessary. However, collecting a sufficient amount of data is often costly, time-consuming, and not always feasible. In this paper, we address this problem by presenting and comparing different approaches for self-supervised pretraining of neural networks on unlabeled laparoscopic videos using temporal coherence. We evaluate our pretrained networks on Cholec80, a publicly available dataset for surgical phase segmentation, on which a maximum F_1 score of 84.6 was reached. Furthermore, we were able to achieve an increase of the F_1 score of up to 10 points when compared to a non-pretrained neural network.

Keywords: Self-supervised learning · Temporal coherence
Surgical workflow analysis · Surgical phase recognition · Pretraining
CNN-LSTM

1 Introduction

The aim of a computer-assisted surgery (CAS) system is to provide the surgeon with the right type of assistance at the right time. To achieve this, context awareness is crucial. This means that the system must be able to understand the processes currently taking place in the operating room (OR) and adapt its behavior accordingly. *Surgical workflow analysis* covers the challenging topic of perceiving, understanding, and describing surgical processes [11].

I. Funke and S. Bodenstedt—Both authors contributed equally to this work.

© Springer Nature Switzerland AG 2018
D. Stoyanov et al. (Eds.): OR 2.0/CARE/CLIP/ISIC 2018, LNCS 11041, pp. 85–93, 2018.
https://doi.org/10.1007/978-3-030-01201-4_11

A common approach is to analyze surgical processes by interpreting a time series of signals that are recorded by sensors – in some cases also by humans – in the OR. As laparoscopic surgeries are performed via camera, methods that require only video as input sensor data are of special interest, since the video can be collected effortlessly during surgery.

State-of-the-art video-based approaches for workflow analysis rely on deep neural networks [1,2,9,15,18]. However, deep learning-based methods require large amounts of labeled data for training. Especially in surgery, obtaining a sufficient amount of annotated video data is difficult and costly.

To alleviate the problem of limited training data, it is common to *pretrain* neural networks and fine-tune them afterwards. Often, networks are pretrained using labeled data coming from another domain, such as ImageNet [4]. Another way is to use unlabeled data from the same domain and train on a proxy task using labels inherent in the data, which is called *self-supervised* learning.

For self-supervised learning from video, a number of ideas have been proposed [5,8,12,13,16]. Most exploit the *temporal coherence* of video, which implies that (i) consecutive frames are in temporal order, (ii) frames change slowly over time, and (iii) frames change steadily, i.e., abrupt motions are unlikely.

The studies [12,13] propose proxy tasks based on the temporal order between frames. In line with this, [2] use the task to order pairs of laparoscopic images for pretraining a network for surgical phase segmentation. *Surgical phase segmentation* [14] is the problem of recognizing the surgical phase being performed by the surgeon at each point during surgery. Another proxy task for this problem is to predict the progress and remaining duration of a surgery [18].

Intuitively, these tasks encourage the network to learn discriminative features that are useful to infer the absolute or relative temporal position of a video frame. In contrast, [5,8,16] aim at learning features that are *invariant* to typical alterations occurring between adjacent frames, such as slight rotations or deformations. To this end, they aim to ensure that temporally close frames, which most likely depict the same semantic scene, are mapped to similar representations in feature space. This idea goes back to *Slow Feature Analysis (SFA)* [17].

In this paper, we describe and compare different approaches to exploit temporal coherence while pretraining a convolutional neural network (CNN) for surgical phase segmentation. We assume the pretraining encourages the CNN to learn features that are invariant to irrelevant changes between adjacent frames, such as slight movements of instruments or of the endoscope, while being discriminative enough to distinguish between semantically different frames.

To promote reproducibility and to fuel future research, we made our code available at https://gitlab.com/nct_tso_public/pretrain_tc.

Experiments using the Cholec80 dataset [15] demonstrate that a CNN pretrained to exploit the temporal coherence of unlabeled laparoscopic video outperforms a non-pretrained CNN after being fine-tuned for surgical phase segmentation. When only 20 labeled videos are available, the proposed pretraining achieves an increase from 67.8 to 78.6 as measured by F_1 score.

2   Methods

The core of our neural network architecture for surgical phase segmentation is a ResNet-50 CNN [6]. We initialize it with ImageNet [4] pretrained weights and further train it on unlabeled videos of laparoscopic surgeries, using an SFA-based approach for self-supervised learning. This encourages the CNN to map temporally close video frames to similar representations in feature space.

More formally, the CNN learns an embedding $f : \mathbb{R}^{3 \times h \times w} \rightarrow \mathbb{R}^d$, where $\mathbb{R}^d$ is the d-dimensional feature space and $\mathbb{R}^{3 \times h \times w}$ is the space of laparoscopic video frames with height h, width w, and three color channels (RGB). Let $I_t \in \mathbb{R}^{3 \times h \times w}$ denote the frame at time step t. To suffice temporal coherence, we require that $f(I_t) \approx f(I_{t+\Delta})$ for a small Δ with $|\Delta| < \delta$. To learn an embedding that is discriminative and to avoid trivial solutions such as $f(I_t) := 0$, we require that $f(I_t)$ and $f(I_{t+\Gamma})$ lie further apart in feature space when Γ is large, i.e., $|\Gamma| > \gamma$ (see Subsect. 2.1 for details). δ and γ are non-negative real-valued parameters.

To evaluate the efficacy of the proposed self-supervised pretraining approach, we extend the CNN into a recurrent neural network (RNN) and fine-tune the CNN-RNN for surgical phase segmentation using annotated laparoscopic videos (see Subsect. 2.2). We can then compare the performance of the pretrained CNN-RNN to the performance of a CNN-RNN that has been trained solely for the surgical phase segmentation task (see Sect. 3).

2.1   Self-supervised Pretraining

For self-supervised pretraining, the output layer of the ResNet-50 CNN is replaced with a fully connected layer with $d = 4096$ output neurons (*FeatureNet*). As the CNN has been pretrained on ImageNet, we only adjust the weights of the *conv5_x* layers and of the newly added fully connected layer during training.

Given a frame I_t, we calculate the embedding $F_t := f(I_t)$ by forwarding the frame through *FeatureNet* and taking the output $(o_1, o_2, ..., o_d)^T \in \mathbb{R}^d$ at the last layer. We train *FeatureNet* to learn a temporally coherent video frame embedding using one of the following methods. Throughout this section, D denotes a distance function, in our case the L2 norm.

(a) Training with **contrastive** loss
   Given a video with T frames, we create a tuple $(I_t, I_{t+\Delta}, I_{t+\Gamma})$ by sampling t from $[0, T-1]$, Δ from $[-\delta, \delta]$, and Γ from $[-(T-1), -\gamma] \cup [\gamma, T-1]$ uniformly at random. Regarding *FeatureNet* as a Siamese network [3], we propagate the temporally close pair $(I_t, I_{t+\Delta})$ through the CNN and calculate $D(F_t, F_{t+\Delta})$. Likewise, we propagate the temporally distant pair $(I_t, I_{t+\Gamma})$ and calculate $D(F_t, F_{t+\Gamma})$. Finally, we calculate the contrastive loss [5]

$$L_c(F_t, F_{t+\Delta}, F_{t+\Gamma}) = D(F_t, F_{t+\Delta}) + \texttt{max}\{0, m_c - D(F_t, F_{t+\Gamma})\}.$$

This loss function encourages F_t to be close to $F_{t+\Delta}$, while F_t and $F_{t+\Gamma}$ are enforced to be separated by margin m_c.

(b) Training with **ranking** loss

A training tuple $(I_t, I_{t+\Delta}, I_{t+\Gamma})$ is created the same way as in method (a). Regarding *FeatureNet* as a Triplet Siamese Network, we propagate the triplet $(I_t, I_{t+\Delta}, I_{t+\Gamma})$ through the CNN and calculate the ranking loss [16]

$$L_r(F_t, F_{t+\Delta}, F_{t+\Gamma}) = \max\{0, D(F_t, F_{t+\Delta}) - D(F_t, F_{t+\Gamma}) + m_r\}.$$

This loss function considers the distance between F_t and $F_{t+\Delta}$ relative to the distance between F_t and $F_{t+\Gamma}$ and encourages F_t and $F_{t+\Delta}$ to be closer together than F_t and $F_{t+\Gamma}$ by a margin of m_r.

(c) Training with **1st & 2nd order contrastive** loss

While (first order) temporal coherence requires the first order temporal derivatives in the learned feature space to be small, i.e., $F_t \approx F_{t+\Delta}$, *second order temporal coherence* [8] requires the second order temporal derivatives to be small, i.e., $F_t - F_{t+\Delta} \approx F_{t+\Delta} - F_{t+2\Delta}$ for a small value of Δ. Intuitively, first order temporal coherence ensures that embeddings do not change quickly over time, while second order temporal coherence ensures that the changes are consistent, or steady, across neighboring frames. Applying the contrastive loss function to second order temporal coherence yields

$$L_{c_2}(F_t, F_{t+\Delta}, F_{t+2\Delta}, F_{t+\Gamma}) = L_c(F_t - F_{t+\Delta}, F_{t+\Delta} - F_{t+2\Delta}, F_{t+\Delta} - F_{t+\Gamma})$$

In practice, we create a training tuple $(I_t, I_{t+\Delta}, I_{t+2\Delta}, I_{t+\Gamma})$ by sampling t, Δ, and Γ as described in method (a). Regarding *FeatureNet* as a Triplet Siamese Network, we propagate the triplets $(I_t, I_{t+\Delta}, I_{t+2\Delta})$ and $(I_t, I_{t+\Delta}, I_{t+\Gamma})$ through the network and calculate L_{c_2}. We then combine it with the first order contrastive loss L_c into an overall loss $L_{c+c_2} = L_c + \omega L_{c_2}$, where $\omega = 0.5$ is a non-negative real-valued weight parameter.

2.2 Supervised Fine-Tuning for Surgical Phase Segmentation

Once pretrained, we modify the CNN for surgical phase segmentation by extending it into an RNN using a long short-term memory unit (LSTM) [7] with 512 neurons. The LSTM is followed by a fully connected layer, which has one output neuron per surgical phase. We refer to this CNN-LSTM as *PhaseNet*. During fine-tuning, the weights of the CNN and the LSTM are jointly optimized. However, the weights of the ResNet-50 layers below *conv5_x* stay frozen.

3 Evaluation

For evaluation, we used the publicly available Cholec80 dataset [15]. It consists of 80 videos from laparoscopic cholecystectomies, annotated with surgical phase labels. We divided the dataset into four sets A, B, C, and D of equal size and similar average procedure length. A, B, and C were used for training, while D was withheld for testing. For pretraining, we extracted video frames at 5 Hz.

Training and testing for phase segmentation was performed at 1 Hz. Each frame was downsized to 384×216 px.

We trained three different versions of *FeatureNet*, one with each of the pre-training variants described in Sect. 2.1. The union of sets A, B, and C (i.e., 60 videos in total) was used as training data, ignoring the labels. Each CNN was trained for 25 epochs. Per epoch, we randomly sampled 250 tuples per video, which were processed in batches of size 64. δ was set to 30 s (15 s for variant (c)), γ to 120 s and $m_c = m_r = 2$. We used the Adam optimizer [10] with a learning rate of 10^{-4}. All newly added layers were initialized with random values from the range $(\frac{-1}{\sqrt{n}}, \frac{1}{\sqrt{n}})$, with n being the number of neurons in the layer.

To evaluate the suitability of the proposed pretraining approach for surgical phase segmentation, each of the pretrained CNNs (**contrastive, ranking**, and **1st & 2nd order contrastive**) was extended into a *PhaseNet* and fine-tuned using the labeled videos from either set A (#OPs = **20**), sets A and B (#OPs = **40**), or sets A, B, and C (#OPs = **60**). As baseline, a *PhaseNet* without self-supervised pretraining (**no pretraining**) was fine-tuned in the same manner. Note that the underlying ResNet-50 CNN had still been pretrained on ImageNet.

For fine-tuning the networks, we used the Adam optimizer [10] with a learning rate of 10^{-4} and a batch size of 128. After every batch, the content of the LSTM's hidden state was saved and restored for the next batch. Due to hardware restraints, gradients were only accumulated for three batches before applying the optimizer. Training was stopped once the accuracy on the training set climbed above 99.9%. All newly added layers were initialized as described above.

The results of evaluating each *PhaseNet* on test set D can be found in Table 1. We calculated the metrics *accuracy*, *recall*, and *precision* as defined in [14]. The F_1 score is the harmonic mean of precision and recall. The metrics were

Table 1. Performance of the baseline (first row) and the pretrained models on the surgical phase segmentation task. *#OPs* denotes how many labeled OPs were used.

	#OPs	Accuracy	Recall	Precision	F_1 score
No pretraining	20	78.8 ± 12.5	72.3 ± 11.4	73.4 ± 12.9	67.8 ± 14.1
	40	88.8 ± 7.7	83.2 ± 8.4	83.8 ± 9.2	80.4 ± 10.3
	60	89.7 ± 6.6	82.8 ± 9.4	85.8 ± 7.6	80.8 ± 10.3
Contrastive	20	84.4 ± 10.6	77.2 ± 8.4	78.8 ± 5.3	73.9 ± 8.9
	40	91.7 ± 5.5	85.4 ± 6.1	88.2 ± 5.6	83.8 ± 7.1
	60	92.0 ± 4.5	86.2 ± 4.2	85.5 ± 4.8	83.6 ± 4.9
Ranking	20	86.1 ± 7.2	79.4 ± 6.5	82.9 ± 5.9	77.2 ± 7.4
	40	90.2 ± 6.4	85.6 ± 6.2	85.2 ± 5.9	82.5 ± 7.3
	60	90.3 ± 5.4	85.2 ± 6.2	86.1 ± 5.2	82.9 ± 6.9
1st & 2nd order contrastive	20	88.1 ± 5.8	80.7 ± 5.7	83.8 ± 5.6	78.6 ± 6.1
	40	90.7 ± 10.4	86.3 ± 7.5	86.9 ± 6.1	83.4 ± 10.1
	60	92.7 ± 4.3	87.0 ± 4.0	87.6 ± 5.3	84.6 ± 5.4

averaged over all operations in the test set. Table 2 presents the phase-wise results of the best performing pretrained *PhaseNet* (**1ˢᵗ & 2ⁿᵈ order contrastive**) compared to the *PhaseNet* that did not undergo self-supervised pretraining.

Table 2. Comparison of the baseline and the best performing pretrained model. We report the average F_1 scores calculated for each of the phases P1 to P7.

	#OPs	P1	P2	P3	P4	P5	P6	P7
No pre-training	20	64.5± 35.7	83.4± 15.9	59.0± 33.4	80.8± 14.2	62.0± 24.0	62.8± 20.2	62.4± 18.3
	40	88.7± 21.6	92.3± 10.8	75.3± 29.4	90.3± 14.3	74.0± 17.6	71.7± 19.4	71.0± 14.3
	60	82.4± 25.3	94.9± 5.7	81.1± 18.5	92.0± 10.9	76.1± 15.3	73.7± 17.9	65.4± 24.6
1ˢᵗ & 2ⁿᵈ order	20	79.3± 25.7	92.2± 7.6	81.9± 14.4	91.3± 8.0	72.4± 17.5	72.8± 17.5	60.0± 24.4
contrastive	40	87.6± 15.3	95.7± 7.1	86.3± 13.3	91.4± 18.1	78.5± 18.4	73.2± 21.7	71.6± 18.1
	60	90.2± 14.7	97.6± 2.7	89.3± 9.9	95.9± 3.7	75.4± 19.3	76.9± 18.2	67.8± 16.6

4 Discussion

Table 1 clearly shows that all three pretrained models outperform the baseline when being fine-tuned on the same set of labeled training data. The performance boost is especially apparent when only 20 labeled videos are available. Here, in terms of F_1 score, pretraining achieves an increase from 67.8 to up to 78.6 while halving the standard deviation. Pretraining still improves performance when more labeled videos are available. Notably, the pretrained models fine-tuned on only 40 labeled videos outperform the baseline trained on 60 videos. We conclude that the proposed SFA-based pretraining enables a CNN to learn feature representations that are beneficial to the task of surgical phase segmentation.

Comparing the three pretraining variants, we do not find big differences. All in all, using a combination of first and second order temporal coherence for pretraining seems to offer the largest boost to performance, especially when only few (20) labeled videos are used.

Looking at the results with respect to each surgical phase (Table 2), we see that most phases benefit greatly from pretraining (variant **1ˢᵗ & 2ⁿᵈ order contrastive**) when only 20 labeled videos are available. The effect of pretraining diminishes when the number of labeled videos is increased, but is still noticeable in the majority of phases. Only the benefit to phase P7 seems negligible.

P7 contains visual similarities with P5 and P6, which makes them difficult to distinguish. Since the phase is short (about 1 to 3 min), frames that we label as close during pretraining may belong to previous phases. Likewise, frames that belong to previous phases but are temporally close are not selected as distant pair. Hence, the network learns features that are rather invariant than discriminative with regard to phase P7 and P6 or P5.

To shed some light on the features learned during pretraining, we investigated which images the network considers similar. We selected query frames $\{I^q\}$ from a video used during pretraining. Then, for each frame I^q and each video v in the test set, we identified the frame $I^{q,v}$ in v that is most similar to I^q, i.e., closest to I^q in feature space. More formally, $I^{q,v} = \text{argmin}_{I_t \in v} D(f(I^q), f(I_t))$, where D was chosen to be the L2 norm. To calculate the embedding f, we used the **1st & 2nd order contrastive** pretrained *FeatureNet* (before fine-tuning).

Figure 1 presents four selected queries. Generally, it can be seen that images that are close in feature space show similar scenes with regard to anatomical structures and/or tool presence. The first and second query frames depict scenes that only differ in the amount of blood visible, a trait also observed in the retrieved frames. Likewise, the third and fourth query frames show similar scenes. However, the third query frame is unusual as the specimen bag is closed. Observing that the retrieved images are semantically not closely related to the query frame, we assume that its embedding does not reflect the presence of the specimen bag. For the fourth query frame, which is visually similar but more representative, semantically similar frames are retrieved.

We refrain from comparing temporal coherence-based learning to other pretraining methods for surgical phase segmentation [2,18] since these studies were conducted using other datasets, namely EndoVis2015 (7 cholecystectomies) in [2] and 120 cholecystectomies in [18].

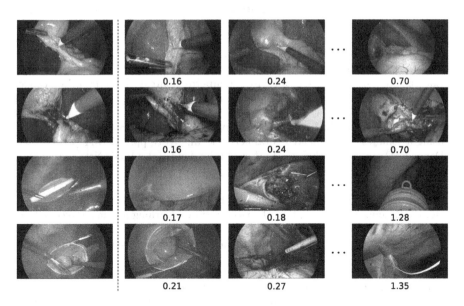

Fig. 1. Image retrieval task. Each row represents one query. Left-most: Query frame. Right: The frames closest in feature space, one per test video. Numbers denote distance to query frame. The depicted frames are sorted with regard to this distance.

5 Summary

In this paper, we show that the temporal coherence of unlabeled laparoscopic video can be exploited for self-supervised pretraining by training a CNN to map temporally close video frames onto embeddings that are close in feature space. When extended into a CNN-LSTM architecture for surgical phase segmentation, all pretrained models outperform the non-pretrained baseline when being fine-tuned on the same labeled dataset. Using a combination of first and second order temporal coherence, the pretrained models even perform similarly or better than the baseline when less labeled data is used. Combining our approach with temporal order-based concepts into a more holistic temporal coherence-based pretraining method could possibly enhance the discriminative properties of the learned embedding and improve performance even further.

Future work will address the question whether the learned embeddings can be used for unsupervised detection of more fine-grained video segments, such as surgical activities or steps. Furthermore, we will investigate whether the notion of slow and steady features is beneficial for regularization during supervised training compared to using the concept during a separate pretraining phase.

References

1. Aksamentov, I., Twinanda, A.P., Mutter, D., Marescaux, J., Padoy, N.: Deep neural networks predict remaining surgery duration from cholecystectomy videos. In: Descoteaux, M., Maier-Hein, L., Franz, A., Jannin, P., Collins, D.L., Duchesne, S. (eds.) MICCAI 2017. LNCS, vol. 10434, pp. 586–593. Springer, Cham (2017). https://doi.org/10.1007/978-3-319-66185-8_66
2. Bodenstedt, S., et al.: Unsupervised temporal context learning using convolutional neural networks for laparoscopic workflow analysis. arXiv preprint arXiv:1702.03684 (2017)
3. Bromley, J., Guyon, I., LeCun, Y., Säckinger, E., Shah, R.: Signature verification using a "siamese" time delay neural network. In: NIPS, pp. 737–744 (1994)
4. Deng, J., Dong, W., Socher, R., Li, L.J., Li, K., Fei-Fei, L.: ImageNet: a large-scale hierarchical image database. In: CVPR, pp. 248–255 (2009)
5. Goroshin, R., Bruna, J., Tompson, J., Eigen, D., LeCun, Y.: Unsupervised learning of spatiotemporally coherent metrics. In: ICCV, pp. 4086–4093 (2015)
6. He, K., Zhang, X., Ren, S., Sun, J.: Deep residual learning for image recognition. In: CVPR, pp. 770–778 (2016)
7. Hochreiter, S., Schmidhuber, J.: Long short-term memory. Neural Comput. **9**(8), 1735–1780 (1997)
8. Jayaraman, D., Grauman, K.: Slow and steady feature analysis: higher order temporal coherence in video. In: CVPR, pp. 3852–3861 (2016)
9. Jin, Y., et al.: SV-RCNet: workflow recognition from surgical videos using recurrent convolutional network. IEEE Trans. Med. Imaging **37**(5), 1114–1126 (2018)
10. Kingma, D., Ba, J.: Adam: a method for stochastic optimization. In: ICLR (2015)
11. Lalys, F., Jannin, P.: Surgical process modelling: a review. Int. J. Comput. Assist. Radiol. Surg. **9**(3), 495–511 (2014)
12. Lee, H.Y., Huang, J.B., Singh, M., Yang, M.H.: Unsupervised representation learning by sorting sequences. In: ICCV, pp. 667–676 (2017)
13. Misra, I., Zitnick, C.L., Hebert, M.: Shuffle and learn: unsupervised learning using temporal order verification. In: Leibe, B., Matas, J., Sebe, N., Welling, M. (eds.) ECCV 2016. LNCS, vol. 9905, pp. 527–544. Springer, Cham (2016). https://doi.org/10.1007/978-3-319-46448-0_32

14. Padoy, N., Blum, T., Ahmadi, S.A., Feussner, H., Berger, M.O., Navab, N.: Statistical modeling and recognition of surgical workflow. Med. Image Anal. **16**(3), 632–641 (2012)
15. Twinanda, A.P., Shehata, S., Mutter, D., Marescaux, J., de Mathelin, M., Padoy, N.: EndoNet: a deep architecture for recognition tasks on laparoscopic videos. IEEE Trans. Med. Imaging **36**(1), 86–97 (2017)
16. Wang, X., Gupta, A.: Unsupervised learning of visual representations using videos. In: ICCV, pp. 2794–2802 (2015)
17. Wiskott, L., Sejnowski, T.J.: Slow feature analysis: unsupervised learning of invariances. Neural Comput. **14**(4), 715–770 (2002)
18. Yengera, G., Mutter, D., Marescaux, J., Padoy, N.: Less is more: surgical phase recognition with less annotations through self-supervised pre-training of CNN-LSTM networks. arXiv preprint arXiv:1805.08569 (2018)

Proceedings of the 5th International Workshop on Computer Assisted Robotic Endoscopy (CARE 2018)

Endo3D: Online Workflow Analysis for Endoscopic Surgeries Based on 3D CNN and LSTM

Weixiang Chen[1,2,3], Jianjiang Feng[1,2,3(✉)], Jiwen Lu[1,2,3], and Jie Zhou[1,2,3]

[1] Department of Automation, Tsinghua University, Beijing, China
jfeng@tsinghua.edu.cn
[2] State Key Lab of Intelligent Technologies and Systems,
Tsinghua University, Beijing, China
[3] Beijing National Research Center for Information
Science and Technology, Beijing, China

Abstract. Surgical workflow analysis is an important topic of computer-assisted intervention and phase recognition is one of its important tasks. Features extracted from video frames by 2D convolutional networks were proved feasible for online phase analysis in former publications. In this paper, we propose to extract fine-level temporal features from video clips using 3D convolutional networks (CNN) and use Long Short-Term Memory (LSTM) networks to capture coarse-level information. By combining fine-level and coarse-level information, our proposed method outperforms state-of-the-art online methods without using specific knowledge of surgeries and almost reaches the state-of-the-art offline performance.

1 Introduction

Computer-assisted surgery system (CAS) is an important topic of computer-assisted intervention, which assists surgeons by giving some advice or guidances in surgeries. To achieve this aim, Surgeries Workflow Analysis (SWA) is an important task. Endoscopic surgery workflow analysis progresses rapidly these years because this kind of surgeries are all performed under an endoscopic cameras so that the videos are always available. In addition, endoscopic surgeries need CAS more than other surgeries because of the limited field of view in endoscopic camera. With such limited field of view, it is very difficult for surgeons to recognize the detailed positions of the camera, the targets, and some special vessels or nerves.

Existing publications on SWA have described various types of features which can be roughly divided into image-based features and signal-based features. Signal-based features are extracted from signals like tool usage [14], some manually defined surgical activities [11], and kinematic data [13]. Although signal-based features yield good performance, it requires some additional devices (e.g. RFID tags for tool signals and daVinci system for kinematic data), which is inconvenient for many online situations. Since surgery videos are always available,

D. Stoyanov et al. (Eds.): OR 2.0/CARE/CLIP/ISIC 2018, LNCS 11041, pp. 97–107, 2018.
https://doi.org/10.1007/978-3-030-01201-4_12

image-based features can be more universal. At first, image-based features were mainly extracted by manually designed rules. [2] used pixels value and its gradients; [4] designed descriptors combining color, shape and texture information. However, manually selected image features are suboptimal.

A better solution to this problem is selecting features by convolutional neural networks (CNN) instead of manually. With appropriate setup, CNN can learn highly distinctive features from training data. EndoNet [15] used AlexNet to extract features and fed them to hybrid Hidden Markov Models (HMM) for phase recognition. On the dataset of the EndoVis 2015 Workflow Challenge, EndoNet performed the best. A recent method SV-RCNet [9], which combines ResNet [7] and Long Short-Term Memory (LSTM) [6], is now the state-of-the-art on Cholec80 dataset[1] [15].

EndoNet used AlexNet as the basic network and extracted features from a single frame. This limited the expressiveness of features because they contain no temporal information. SV-RCNet used LSTM to mix shot features into clip features, but since all convolutions were still in single shot, it ignores edges in time domain. EndoNet used HMM for global optimization which performs well in its offline version. However, online analysis is important in many applications, such as giving doctors some advice during surgery or in emergency situations. SV-RCNet's LSTM method can work online, but clips of 2s are too short to cover coarse-level temporal features. Without prior knowledge inference (PKI) which is specific to certain surgeries [9], its accuracy is 85.3%, only slightly higher than EndoNet's.

We proposes an online SWA method Endo3D which is based on C3D networks [8] and LSTM. It extracted 3-D CNN features from a clip of video rather than a single frame, which encodes fine-level temporal information. Besides, we proposed a three-layer LSTM with sequences long enough to encodes coarse-level temporal information into our prediction. Our proposed method outperforms SV-RCNet (whose accuracy without PKI is 85.3%) in online recognition with 91.2% online accuracy on Cholec80. In addition, it can also predict tool usage with 86% Mean Average Precision (mAP). The main contributions of our method are:

1. Extract spatial-temporal features from surgery videos with an extended C3D network.
2. Extract coarse-level information by LSTM which plays important role in phase recognition.
3. Combine fine-level and coarse-level temporal information in an online mode.
4. Achieve state-of-the-art online phase recognition accuracy without using specific knowledge.
5. Achieve high accuracy in tool presence detection.

2   Methodology

2.1   Endo3D Network Architecture

Our model is trained in two steps (as Fig. 1 shows). The first step is fine tuning process on a network derived from C3D. We use the fine tuned network to extract

---

[1] http://camma.u-strasbg.fr/datasets.

features and predict tool presences. In the second step, the features are arranged into sequence which is then be fed to 3-layer LSTM to predict workflow phases. For every time step in sequence, our model gives a prediction for phases. The two parts of Endo3D separately introduce fine-level (for about 4.6 s) and coarse-level (for all the past frames) temporal information into recognition, together with spatial information.

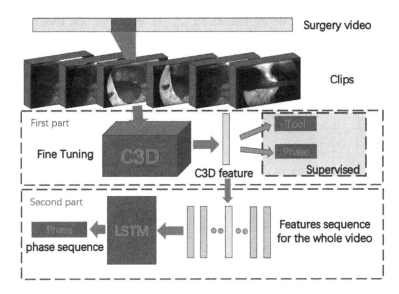

Fig. 1. Diagram of the proposed Endo3D method.

2.2   First Part: Video Feature Extraction

The first part of our model is shown in Fig. 2. The C3D's fc7 layer is supposed to compute tool presence. There is a concatenation layer fc8 after fc7 which concatenates tool layer and fc7 for phase prediction. After training, the phase and tool layer are left away and we use fc8 as a $l_v = 4103$ dimensional feature. In other words, phase layers are only used as supervisions in training. The input of our network are $16 \times 112 \times 112 \times 3$ RGB video clips and the output feature vectors is denoted as V_f. We downsample videos from 25 fps to 2.5 fps, and arrange contiguous 16 frames as a clip in length of 4.6 s and with a sampling interval of 1 s. As a result, fine-level temporal texture is introduced when doing three-dimensional convolution in this step.

This part is trained using Adam [12]. Our tool layer's output is activated by sigmoid function, because tool presence detection is a multi-labeled task. We write it as V_t whose length is the number of tools denoted as n_t. V_p denotes the phase layer's output which is activated by softmax function. For a batch of size N, loss function can be defined as:

$$L = c_1 \times L_t + c_2 \times L_p + c_3 \times L_{regu} + c_4 \times L_w \tag{1}$$

$$L_t = -\frac{1}{N} \sum_{i=1}^{N} \sum_{t=1}^{n_t} [T_t^{(i)} \log(V_t^{(i)}) + (1 - T_t^{(i)}) \log(1 - V_t^{(i)})] \tag{2}$$

$$L_p = -\frac{1}{N} \sum_{i=1}^{N} \sum_{p=1}^{n_p} T_p^{(i)} \log(V_p^{(i)}) \tag{3}$$

where T_p and T_t is groundtruth of phase and tool respectively; c_is are weighting coefficients; L_w is weight decay loss and L_{regu} is regularization loss, which are set to prevent overfitting; (i) means the i-th sample in the batch.

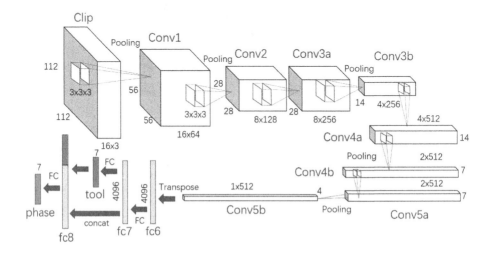

Fig. 2. The first part: C3D network of the proposed method.

2.3   Second Part: Coarse-Level Temporal Information

Since C3D captures only fine-level temporal information we introduce LSTM to deal with long term temporal information, which is shown in Fig. 3. fc8 vectors are arranged into sequences and fed to LSTM. For every time step in the sequence, the output will only be influenced by all the past inputs, so our method is online. $V_{f,t} \in \mathbb{R}^{l_v \times 1}$ denotes the value of fc8 layer of t-th timestep (the outputs of former networks are strided with 1 s, so the timestep of LSTM is 1 s). The sequence is denoted as $S^{(T)} = [V_{f,1}, V_{f,2}, ..., V_{f,T}]$, where T denotes the sequence at T-th second. Because LSTM networks care nothing about the length of sequences, we use feature sequence of all past clips as input and get output of the same number of clips. Only the output of last timestep is used as the newest coming prediction in testing procedure.

In order to simplify training, we expand all sequences to the same length of n_s with 0 and set their labels with background class which is different from

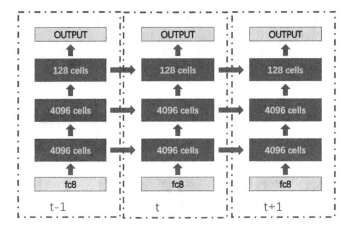

Fig. 3. The second part: LSTM network of the proposed method

real phases. We also introduce a mask to mark background frames. Expanded sequence is denoted as $\widehat{S^{(T)}} = [S^{(T)}, O_{l_v, n_s - T}]$ and all the sequences are now in the same shape of $l_v \times n_s$. Output sequences are $n_p \times n_s$ dimensional binary vectors, which is denoted as $P_{t,p}$ corresponding to phase p and timestep t. Mask is also a vector denoted as M_t. $M_t = 0$ if timestep t is background, otherwise $M_t = 1$.

The sequence learning loss can be denoted as:

$$
L_s = -\frac{1}{N} \sum_{i=1}^{N} \frac{\sum_{t=1}^{n_s} \sum_{p=1}^{n_p} M_t^{(i)} T_{t,p}^{(i)} \log(P_{t,p}^{(i)})}{\sum_{t=1}^{n_s} M_t^{(i)}}. \tag{4}
$$

It is a cross-entropy loss with mask to filter out background. When computing accuracy, background results are not taken into account. Output of LSTM can be directly used after softmax function as the confidence value without other classifiers.

We trained the whole network from scratch. We choose 3-layer LSTM because the number of its parameters is suitable for the difficulty of the problem and the size of training set. If new SWA tasks are defined, the complexity of this part can be changed.

3 Experiment

3.1 Dataset

Experiments are done on Cholec80 dataset [15], which contains 80 videos of cholecystectomy surgeries performed by 13 surgeons. All the videos are captured at 25 fps and are sampled to 2.5 fps. The whole set is labeled with tool presences and phases. Video frames are annotated with 7 phases (see Fig. 4) in 2.5 fps. Phases are notated as P0 to P6 following the order above. For most videos, transformations between phases follow some disciplines. Unlike Jin *et al.* [9], we do not use this prior knowledges. Tools are annotated in 1 fps which also have 7 kinds[2].

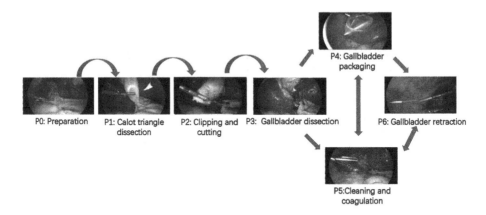

Fig. 4. Surgery workflow of cholecystectomy for dataset Cholec80.

For the first part, we use first 40 videos to train Endo3D feature extraction network and the other 40 videos for validation and test. For the second part, 40 validation videos are divided to do 4-fold cross-validation, which is the same as the division of EndoNet. In training set, there are over 200K frames with their annotations. We arrange them into 16 frames length clips with 1 s stride and finally get about 86K clips. The labels of clips are defined by label of the last frame in the clip, because we want to use only past frames to extract features. In the second step, videos are transformed into feature sequences and fit into n_s, the length of the longest one in our dataset. Only complete sequences are used in training.

3.2   Training Parameters

Our C3D network is pretrained on sport1M dataset [10]. The fc7 and fc8 layers are trained at the learning rate of 10^{-3} and initialized randomly. The layers defined in original C3D networks are initialized using pretrained parameters and trained at 10^{-4}. Training for this part is setup on 2 NVIDIA GeForce 1080Ti cards. The batch size is 24 per card. Our process is carried out using Tensorflow [1] and training process takes 16 h for all 10K iterations. Feature extraction takes approximately 156 ms per clip on one card.

For the last 40 videos of Cholec80 dataset, $n_s = 5983$. The output of LSTM network is 8D feature vector, because $n_p = 7$ for Cholec80. We trained our

---

[2] Seven tools: Bipolar, Clipper, Grasper, Hook, Irrigator, Scissors, Specimen bag.

model for 80 epochs with batch size 2 and initial learning rate 0.01. LSTM process is carried out on Keras [3] and executed on a 1080Ti card. Training process takes approximately 90 s for an epoch and it takes about 2 s to predict a sequence, which is related to n_p. Because Keras implementation can not predict dynamically with timesteps, for every new coming timestep, it computes from the first timestep to the last one and only updates the new coming timestep's prediction. Changing some Keras' backend code or implementing the method with C language can accelerate this process.

3.3   Results

Phase Recognition. Phase recognition is measured by precision, recall, and accuracy which are defined in [13]. The results are shown in Tables 1 and 2. Results of EndoNet and SC-RCNet are cited from the reference paper [9,15]. Notations of all baselines are defined as follow:

- **EndoNet SVM**: EndoNet [15] without its HMM, which are the recognition results feeding fc8 of EndoNet into SVM.
- **EndoNet ON**: the online phase recognition results of EndoNet [15]
- **EndoNet OFF**: the offline phase recognition results of EndoNet [15].
- **SV-RCNet+PKI**: the phase recognition result of SV-RCNet with prior knowledge inference process [9].
- **SV-RCNet**: the phase recognition result of SV-RCNet without prior knowledge inference process [9].
- **C3D**: the results of our phase layer's output fine-tuned with only phase supervision.
- **Endo3D**: results of our phase layer's output fine-tuned with proposed tool and phase supervisions.
- **Endo3D SVM**: results of our fc8 after a SVM classifier.
- **Endo3D LSTM**: results of our proposed Endo3D process.

Table 1. Phase recognition results (%).

Method	Precision	Recall	Acc.
EndoNet no-HMM	70.1	66.7	75.3
EndoNet ON	75.1	80.0	81.9
EndoNet OFF	85.7	89.1	92.2
SV-RCNet+PKI	90.6	86.2	92.4
SV-RCNet	80.7	83.5	85.3
C3D	63.5	59.9	69.9
Endo3D	66.4	67.0	74.7
Endo3D SVM	72.8	68.4	78.7
Endo3D LSTM	81.3	87.7	91.2

Table 2. Compare for every phase on precision and recalls (%).

Phase	Method (Precision/Recall)	
ID	EndoNet ON	Endo3D LSTM
P0	**90.0**/85.5	82.8/**99.8**
P1	96.4/81.1	**96.9/97.8**
P2	**69.8/71.2**	69.5/71.0
P3	82.8/86.5	**97.3/88.8**
P4	55.5/75.57	**92.3/91.7**
P5	**63.9**/68.7	58.2/**81.6**
P6	57.5/**88.9**	**72.1**/82.5

Endo3D with LSTM outperforms other online methods and is almost comparable to offline version of EndoNet. Only for some short phases like P0, P2 and P6, the proposed method does not perform as well as EndoNet. The result without LSTM is comparable to EndoNet no-HMM method (which uses SVM), and our Endo3D SVM method outperformed it. SV-RCNet without prior knowledge is not as good as our method and our method can almost reach its result with prior knowledge. C3D features perform a little worse than the proposed method, which proves that using tool information as supervision in training and as features in predicting phases has positive influences.

LSTM in our method and HMM in EndoNet can both improve results a lot. According to our result, the contribution of LSTM is greater than HMM. Theoretically, HMMs are based on transition matrix, emission matrix, whose representation ability may be lower than LSTM. LSTM use forget gates to manage memories from far before, which improves performances in long sequences learning. Besides, LSTM can be easily extended to multi-layers.

Prior Knowledge Inference (PKI) helps SV-RCNet a lot in accuracy, but we suppose that such knowledge should be better learnt by network from videos. As an automatic method, prior knowledge for specific dataset might not always be available. Data-driven methods can be extended to new surgery datasets without manually defined knowledge, which we suppose is a desirable property.

Figures 5 and 6 show the confusion matrix of 7 phases and the background for C3D features without and with LSTM, respectively. Predictions spread on less phases after LSTM, which shows LSTM does help filter out impossible transformations. P5 is the only phase getting worse after LSTM and it is predicted as P3 for many cases. As Fig. 4 shows, P5 is next to P3, P4 or P6 which is the most complex phase from the perspective of coarse-level phase transformations. Irrigators are mainly used in P5 which is detected with high accuracy, so from the perspective of tool evidences, P5 is not that difficult and our prediction before LSTM is a little higher.

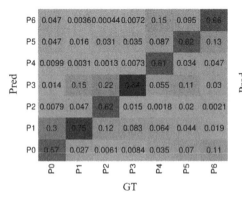

Fig. 5. Confusion matrix before LSTM.

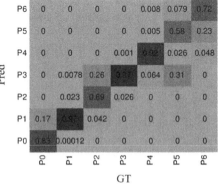

Fig. 6. Confusion matrix after LSTM.

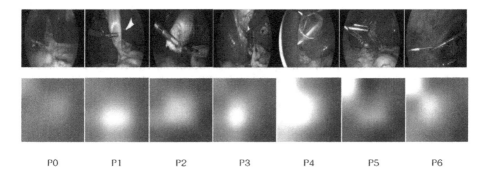

PO   P1   P2   P3   P4   P5   P6

Fig. 7. Average feature maps from Conv5b layer.

Figure 7 shows average feature maps extracted by the proposed C3D networks. The maps come from the last pooling layer of network and are average between channels. We arrange feature maps according to their groundtruth phases as Fig. 7 shows. Eventhough it is hard to describe the detailed meanings of deep features, we can find out that feature maps have different reaction regions for different phases.

Table 3. Tool presence detection result (%).

Tool	DPM	EndoNet	Endo3D
Bipolar	60.6	**86.9**	69.72
Clipper	68.4	80.1	**95.12**
Grasper	82.3	**84.8**	71.32
Hook	93.4	**95.6**	87.81
Irrigator	40.5	74.4	**96.43**
Scissors	23.4	58.6	**87.33**
Specimen bag	40.0	86.8	**94.97**
MEAN	58.4	81.0	**86.1**

Tool Presence Detection. The tool presence performance is measured by mAP. Results about EndoNet are reported in [15]. Deformable Part Model (DPM) [5], one of the most popular object detection method, is used as a baseline for tool presence detection.

The results are shown in Table 3. The mAP for Bipolar, Grasper and Hook of proposed method is lower than EndoNet, but for the other 4 tools its mAP is higher. For Irrigator, Scissors and Clipper, the mAPs are higher for more than 15% points. As a result, average mAP for all tools of our proposed method is about 5 points higher than EndoNet. In fact, Grasper and Hook might occur in almost all phases, because surgeons need them to move or grasp tissues. So these two tools are less important as phase features. The proposed method is more sensitive to tools like scissors and irrigator, whose occurrences are key information for phase, because we train tool detection together with phase recognition.

4   Conclusions

In this paper, we focus on online phase recognition of endoscopic surgery videos and propose a method to learn 3-D CNN features from video clips called Endo3D. With the help of C3D and LSTM network, we combine fine-level and coarse-level temporal texture together and use temporal-spatial information to recognize phases. In addition, Endo3D uses tool and phase groundtruth to do multi-target training. The proposed method outperformed the previous state-of-the-art on public domain dataset without using specific knowledge.

Reducing the time consumption is the first thing to do in the future. As an online method, the current processing time limits the output rate. Keras consumes most of time because this implementation doesn't support dynamical input and output of LSTM nodes. Engineering improvements like a C version test script will help a lot because average time to compute per node of LSTM is less than 40 ms.

Acknowledgement. This work is supported by the National Natural Science Foundation of China under Grant 61622207.

References

1. Abadi, M., Agarwal, A., Barham, P., Brevdo, E., et al.: TensorFlow: large-scale machine learning on heterogeneous systems (2015). Software available from http://tensorflow.org/
2. Blum, T., Feußner, H., Navab, N.: Modeling and segmentation of surgical workflow from laparoscopic video. In: Jiang, T., Navab, N., Pluim, J.P.W., Viergever, M.A. (eds.) MICCAI 2010. LNCS, vol. 6363, pp. 400–407. Springer, Heidelberg (2010). https://doi.org/10.1007/978-3-642-15711-0_50
3. Chollet, F., et al.: Keras (2015). https://github.com/keras-team/keras
4. Dergachyova, O., Bouget, D., Huaulmé, A., Morandi, X., Jannin, P.: Automatic data-driven real-time segmentation and recognition of surgical workflow. IJCARS **11**(6), 1–9 (2016)
5. Felzenszwalb, P.F., Girshick, R.B., Mcallester, D., Ramanan, D.: Object detection with discriminatively trained part-based models. IEEE T-PAMI **32**(9), 1627 (2010)
6. Graves, A.: Long short-term memory. Neural Comput. **9**(8), 1735–1780 (1997)
7. He, K., Zhang, X., Ren, S., Sun, J.: Deep residual learning for image recognition. In: CVPR, pp. 770–778 (2016)
8. Ji, S., Yang, M., Yu, K.: 3D convolutional neural networks for human action recognition. IEEE T-PAMI **35**(1), 221–231 (2012)
9. Jin, Y., et al.: SV-RCNet: workflow recognition from surgical videos using recurrent convolutional network. IEEE T-MI **37**(5), 1114–1126 (2018)

10. Karpathy, A., Toderici, G., Shetty, S., Leung, T., Sukthankar, R., Li, F.F.: Large-scale video classification with convolutional neural networks. In: CVPR, pp. 1725–1732 (2014)
11. Katić, D., et al.: Knowledge-driven formalization of laparoscopic surgeries for rule-based intraoperative context-aware assistance. In: Stoyanov, D., Collins, D.L., Sakuma, I., Abolmaesumi, P., Jannin, P. (eds.) IPCAI 2014. LNCS, vol. 8498, pp. 158–167. Springer, Cham (2014). https://doi.org/10.1007/978-3-319-07521-1_17
12. Kingma, D., Ba, J.: Adam: a method for stochastic optimization. Comput. Sci. (2014)
13. Padoy, N., Blum, T., Ahmadi, S.A., Feussner, H., Berger, M.O., Navab, N.: Statistical modeling and recognition of surgical workflow. Med. Image Anal. $16(3)$, 632–641 (2012)
14. Stauder, R., et al.: Random forests for phase detection in surgical workflow analysis. In: Stoyanov, D., Collins, D.L., Sakuma, I., Abolmaesumi, P., Jannin, P. (eds.) IPCAI 2014. LNCS, vol. 8498, pp. 148–157. Springer, Cham (2014). https://doi.org/10.1007/978-3-319-07521-1_16
15. Twinanda, A.P., Shehata, S., Mutter, D., Marescaux, J., Mathelin, M.D., Padoy, N.: EndoNet: a deep architecture for recognition tasks on laparoscopic videos. IEEE T-MI $36(1)$, 86–97 (2016)

Unsupervised Learning of Endoscopy Video Frames' Correspondences from Global and Local Transformation

Mohammad Ali Armin[1,2(✉)], Nick Barnes[1,4], Salman Khan[1],
Miaomiao Liu[1], Florian Grimpen[3], and Olivier Salvado[2]

[1] CSIRO (Data61), Canberra, Australia
m.a.armin@gmail.com
[2] Biomedical Informatics Group, Brisbane, Australia
Olivier.Salvado@csiro.au
[3] Department of Gastroenterology and Hepatology,
Royal Brisbane and Women's Hospital, Brisbane, Australia
[4] College of Engineering and Computer Science (ANU), Canberra, Australia

Abstract. Inferring the correspondences between consecutive video frames with high accuracy is essential for many medical image processing and computer vision tasks (e.g. image mosaicking, 3D scene reconstruction). Image correspondences can be computed by feature extraction and matching algorithms, which are computationally expensive and are challenged by low texture frames. Convolutional neural networks (CNN) can estimate dense image correspondences with high accuracy, but lack of labeled data especially in medical imaging does not allow end-to-end supervised training. In this paper, we present an unsupervised learning method to estimate dense image correspondences (DIC) between endoscopy frames by developing a new CNN model, called the EndoRegNet. Our proposed network has three distinguishing aspects: a local DIC estimator, a polynomial image transformer which regularizes local correspondences and a visibility mask which refines image correspondences. The EndoRegNet was trained on a mix of simulated and real endoscopy video frames, while its performance was evaluated on real endoscopy frames. We compared the results of EndoRegNet with traditional feature-based image registration. Our results show that EndoRegNet can provide faster and more accurate image correspondences estimation. It can also effectively deal with deformations and occlusions which are common in endoscopy video frames without requiring any labeled data.

Keywords: Convolutional neural network · Unsupervised learning
Image correspondences · Registration

1 Introduction

Estimating image correspondences is the base of many medical image processing and computer vision algorithms. Traditional methods such as SIFT [1] or KLT [2] have shown remarkable results in estimating image correspondences and registering

© Springer Nature Switzerland AG 2018
D. Stoyanov et al. (Eds.): OR 2.0/CARE/CLIP/ISIC 2018, LNCS 11041, pp. 108–117, 2018.
https://doi.org/10.1007/978-3-030-01201-4_13

endoscopy frames [3, 4], yet they are computational expensive, may fail for frames with sparse textures, and become unreliable when objects deform (one example of correspondences estimation by SIFT feature tracking [5], SIFT flow [1] and our method (EndoRegNet) is shown if Fig. 1).

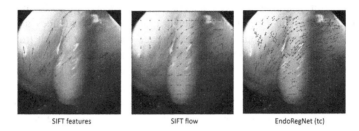

SIFT features   SIFT flow   EndoRegNet (tc)

Fig. 1. Example of correspondences estimation by the SIFT feature tracker, SIFT flow, and our proposed method (EndoRegNet) from consecutive colonoscopy frames, frames are overlaid, SIFT flow and EndoRegNet are shown sparsely for better visualization of the motion.

In recent years, methods based on deep Convolutional Neural Networks (CNN) have been shown to be accurate in image correspondence estimation. Ji et al. [6] developed a deep view morphing network that can predict the middle view and image correspondences between two frames. Fischer et al. proposed FlowNet [7] which can predict dense motion flow between two frames. However, these methods need a large amount of labeled data for training and testing, which hamper performance when not available because it is very difficult to generate a ground-truth for correspondences of endoscopy images (even when using a simulator). The lack of ground-truth to allow end-to-end network training, especially in medical imaging, has increased the popularity of unsupervised or semi-supervised CNNs. For instance, Zhou et al. [8] and Garg et al. [9] have estimated depth, and Yin and Shi [10] estimated depth, camera pose and optical flow from images without using labeled data. Meister el al. [11] and Wang et al. [12] however, focused mainly on unsupervised flow estimation by estimating back and forth motion using FlowNet architecture and introducing an loss function to deal with occlusion. Although, they have shown remarkable results in comparison to supervised methods (e.g. FlowNet), for a more challenging dataset such as Sintel [13] which include deformation and occlusion, their method cannot outperform supervised methods, and needs improvements. Besides, using FlowNetS as the base of their network structure means a requirement of a huge dataset for training. In our method, we tackled deformation by learning parameters of a global polynomial transformation between consecutive frames, and inspired by deep view morphing [6] we developed a CNN that can be trained with smaller dataset. In medical imaging, De vos et al. [14] registered cardiac MRI images through implementing a cubic B-spline transformer and spatial transformer network [15]. Although their method can deal with deformable MRI images, it cannot handle occlusion, which is common in colonoscopy images.

In this paper, we propose a novel CNN architecture to predict correspondences of deformable, sparse texture endoscopy images through image registration while being robust to occluded areas. Our method does not require labeled data. We achieved this by developing a network comprising three components: (i) a Dense Image Correspondences (DIC) sub-network that predicts pixel displacement between two frames as (dx, dy) and allows local deformation; (ii) a Polynomial Transformer Parameters (PTP) sub-network, which estimates polynomial parameters between two frames and can produce a global motion flow which is used to regularize the output of the DIC network; (iii) and a Visibility Mask (VM) sub-network, which predicts occluded areas in the second frame. The output of the dense image correspondences and the polynomial subnetwork are the input to a bilinear image transformer which transforms the second image to the first one. The loss function is computed as absolute difference between first image I_1 and a transformation of second image I_2 to I_1 based on both motion and polynomial transformation estimated by the DIC and PTP networks, along with absolute difference between correspondences obtained by the PTP and DIC network. Since our model performs image registration for endoscopy, we call our network EndoRegNet. The EndoRegNet is unsupervised and there is no need for any labeled data for training. We train the network with both simulated and real colonoscopy video frames. Our results show excellent performance in image registration of colonoscopy frames that are non-rigid and have sparse texture. Further, EndoRegNet can be used to register any endoscopy video frames, or indeed other non-rigid scenes. We test EndoRegNet on vivo datasets [16, 17]. The key contributions of the EndoRegNet can be summarized as (i) using a polynomial transformation to regularize local pixel displacement (a polynomial transformation unlike affine transformation can model deformation between two frames, which is a main difference between our method and other unsupervised method such as [11]); (ii) dealing with deformation by using absolute pixel-by-pixel transformations regularized by a polynomial transformation; (iii) refining image correspondences for occluded areas by calculating a visibility mask. We could obtain good results by training our network even on a small medical image dataset. The overview of our method is shown in Fig. 2.

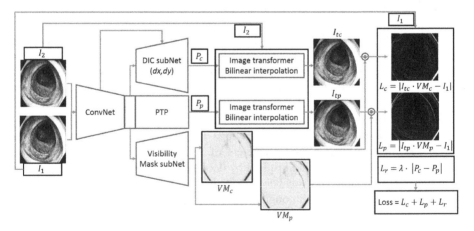

Fig. 2. The endoscopy image registration network (EndoRegNet). DIC and PTP are dense image correspondences and polynomial transformer parameters sub-network, $P_c(x_{c2}, y_{c2})$ and $P_p(x_{p2}, y_{p2})$ are image correspondences estimated by DIC and PTP.

2 Method

Our goal is to register colonoscopy frames and estimate dense image correspondences between consecutive frames through image registration. This can be performed by estimating pixel displacement between two frames, however a network that only estimates pixel displacement can result in outliers and consequently a poor image registration. Here we introduce a new approach to address this through regularizing local pixel displacement by estimating a global transformation. In this paper, we introduce a polynomial function of second order (as it can deal with deformations) to determine the global transformation between two frames. Colonoscopy frames include haustral folds which lead to occlusions, so a visibility mask similar to [6] is also included in the model to improve registration performance by omitting occluded areas. The EndoRegNet is introduced in the following.

2.1 Dense Image Correspondence (DIC) Sub-network

Image correspondences or the dense flow field between two consecutive frames (I_1, I_2) can be estimated as a relative offset of (dx, dy) for each point pair. Each pair of points from I_1 as target image $P(x_1, y_1)$ can be mapped to source image point $P_c(x_{c2}, y_{c2})$ through:

$$x_{c2} = x_1 + dx, y_{c2} = y_1 + dy \tag{1}$$

Our DIC sub-network accepts two consecutive images as input, and estimates pixel displacement (dx, dy) for each pixel. By finding the mapping relation between I_1 and I_2 from Eq. (1), bilinear sampling which is explained in [15] can be used to generate a transformed image I_{tc} which is a transformation of I_2 onto I_1. The DIC sub-network minimizes the L_1 norm; the absolute difference between I_{tc} and I_1, known as photometric loss, which has been used in unsupervised view synthesis algorithms (e.g. [18]): $L_c = |I_{tc} - I_1|$.

2.2 Polynomial Transformation Parameters (PTP)

Similarly to the view synthesis approach, if we only use DIC, we will be highly subject to outliers where individual point pairs have better matches on photometric loss but that are not consistent with their local regions. Here, we introduce a polynomial transformation to regularize the motion of images points between I_1 and I_2. We map a set of grid points $P(x_1, y_1)$ which indicate pixel position in a target image I_1 to a source image I_2 points $P_p(x_{p2}, y_{p2})$ by finding second degree polynomial transformation coefficients (θ_{ij}) between them as $P_p = \theta_{ij} \cdot P$ and can be extended as follows:

$$\begin{bmatrix} x_{p2} \\ y_{p2} \end{bmatrix} = \begin{bmatrix} \theta_{11} & \theta_{12} & \theta_{13} & \theta_{14} & \theta_{15} & \theta_{16} \\ \theta_{21} & \theta_{22} & \theta_{23} & \theta_{24} & \theta_{25} & \theta_{26} \end{bmatrix} \cdot \begin{bmatrix} x_1 & y_1 & x_1 y_1 & x_1^2 & y_1^2 & 1 \end{bmatrix}^t \tag{2}$$

Here, P_p determines where to sample pixels from I_2 to obtain transformed image I_{tp} which is a transformation of I_2 onto I_1. The PTP sub-network estimates polynomial coefficients θ_{ij} by minimizing a photometric loss similar to DIC sub-network: $L_p = |I_{tp} - I_1|$. Again we incorporate bilinear sampling [15] in a similar manner to DIC to infer I_{tp}.

2.3   Visibility Mask (VM) Sub-network

Colonoscopy frames include haustral folds which cause occlusions. This occlusion prevents a full view of next frame and therefore increases the number of outliers between two consecutive frames. The effect of occlusion has been reduced by determining the visible area between two frames through a visibility mask (VM) [6, 19]. The last layer of VM sub-network has a sigmoid function that assigns one for existing correspondences and zero when correspondences are not found by the DIC sub-network or PTP. We modify the L_c and L_p to learn VM_c and VM_p which are the visibility masks for the DIC and PTP respectively:

$$L_c = |I_{tc} \cdot VM_c - I_1|, \quad L_p = |I_{tp} \cdot VM_p - I_1| \tag{3}$$

2.4   Regularized DIC and Final Objective Function

To regularize local pixel displacement estimated by the DIC, we reduce the absolute difference between global positions estimated by the PTP sub-network P_p and local position estimated by the DIC sub-network P_c as $L_r = \lambda \cdot |P_c - P_p|$. Here λ is a weight, and empirically $\lambda = 0.9$ shows good results.

In general, the objective function for whole network can be calculated as sum of L_c and L_p which are estimated from Eq. 3 and L_r as a regularization term:

$$Loss = L_c + L_p + L_r \tag{4}$$

2.5   Architecture and Training Details

The first part of EndoRegNet consists of 6 convolutional layers which are shared among other sub-networks. EndoRegNet takes two consecutive RGB frames as input of size 224×224 pixels. PTP consists of three convolution layers followed by a fully connected layer to estimate θ_{ij}. The DIC sub-network is formed by three convolutional layers, and five de-convolutional layers. The VM sub-network has six de-convolutional layers and its last layer is a convolutional layer with a sigmoid activation function. The EndoRegNet architecture is shown in Fig. 3.

The whole network was implemented and trained using the GPU version of Tensorflow [20]. We used ADAM solver [21] with the initial learning rate of 0.0001, β_1 and β_2 were 0.9 and 0.999 respectively. We used multi-GPU (Nvidia). Our network began to converge after 150,000 iterations.

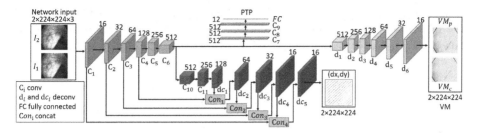

Fig. 3. The EndoRegNet architecture

3 Dataset

Simulated and Real Colonoscopy Frames. Our dataset includes 29,000 pairs of frames which were extracted from simulated and real colonoscopy videos. The simulated frames were generated by a simulator described in [22]. The simulations were of ten different colons, and formed 72% of the data. The real frames extracted from six colonoscopy videos (six different patients). A 190HD Olympus endoscope was used to perform real colonoscopy procedures, which could capture 50 frame/sec (frame size was 1352 × 1080 pixels). We only used the informative frames for training and validation and removed uninformative frames (e.g. out of focus frames or blurry or those close to the colon wall) [23] from our computation.

Real Colonoscopy Frames. We used a colonoscopy dataset from Hamlyn Center Laparoscopic (HCL) [24] to validate the generalization performance of our trained network. The video frames were captured either by Olympus NBI endoscope, or a Pentax i-scan endoscope [17]. From HCL colonoscopy videos, the video number 10 (vn10) has been chosen for our test as it contained 1250 pairs of consecutive frames. 25% of these frames were uninformative and ignored in our experiments.

Laparoscopy Video Frames. In addition to the above, we trained the EndoRegNet with 80% of two set of laparoscopic in vivo video frames [16]. The first set contained 1220 pairs of stereo video frame, and the second set contained 5626 consecutive frames with deformation due to tools interaction.

4 Experiments and Results

EndoRegNet was trained with 80% of our colonoscopy data, which was a mix of real and simulated colonoscopy frames (46476 frames). The trained EndoRegNet was then validated on real colonoscopy test data by computing mean absolute difference (MAD) and structural similarity index map (SSIM) (please see [25]) between I_1 and resgitered image. Note that we used default parameters for SSIM as stated in original paper [25]. Examples of SSIMs are presented in Fig. 4(a) and results as the mean of SSIM and MAD are reported in Fig. 6. We evaluated the performance of our trained network on real colonoscopy video frames vn10 which were obtained from [24] (b.1, b.2) in Fig. 4. The results are presented in Fig. 6.

We trained each set of laparoscopy video frames with the pre-trained EndoRegNet. 80% of data was used for training. Examples of stereo pairs and tool interaction are shown in Figs. 4(c, d) and 5.

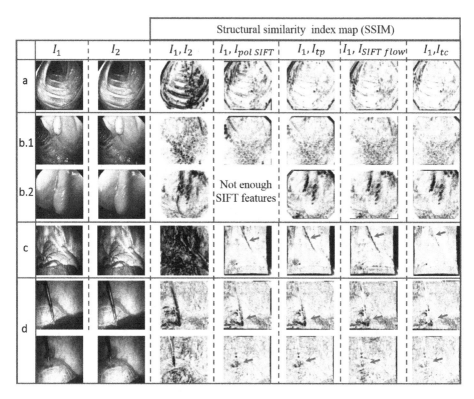

Fig. 4. Examples of images and SSIM between I_1, I_2 and I_1 and registered images by traditional feature-based method polynomial (I_{pol}) transformation when SIFT is used as feature detector, EndoRegNet PTP (I_{tp}), SIFT flow ($I_{SIFTflow}$), and DIC (I_{tc}). Real colonoscopy from our dataset (a), colonoscopy frames from Hamlyn (vn10) [17] (b.1, b.2), laparoscopy frame [16] (c), laparoscopy frame when tool interacts with organs and results in deformations (d). The red arrows show areas with deformation. Note that higher similarity leads to brighter area. (Color figure online)

In addition, we compared the results of our network with traditional image registration using polynomial transformation and SIFT flow. The correspondences were estimated by using SIFT features explained in [5]. Results are reported in Fig. 6. Note that the test set has not been used in training phase and for the sake of comparison we did not apply visibility masks on registered images obtained by EndoRegNet.

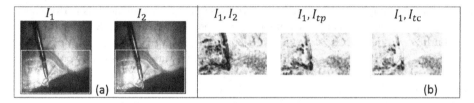

Fig. 5. Sample of deformed endoscopy sequences, two consecutive frames when a tool interacts with organ (deformed region is cropped for better perception, yellow rectangle) (a), SSIM between I_1, I_2 and I_1 and registered image with EndoRegNet (b). (Color figure online)

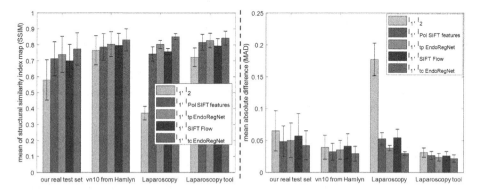

Fig. 6. The mean of SSIM and MAD error of different image registration method including polynomial (I_{pol}) transforms when SIFT is used as feature detector, EndoRegNet PTP (I_{tp}), SIFT flow, and DIC (I_{tc}) over endoscopy frames. Our real colonoscopy test set, vn10 from Hamlyn [17], laparoscopy test set [16], and deformed laparoscopy test set. Higher the SSIM and lower the MAD is better.

5   Discussion and Conclusion

In this paper, we present an unsupervised method to register deformable endoscopy video frames and estimate their correspondences. This is achieved by introducing a novel CNN model, called EndoRegNet, which has three main parts; (i) a dense image correspondences (DIC) sub-network, which estimates local displacement of pixels; (ii) polynomial transformation parameters (PTP) estimator, which is used to regularizes correspondences estimated by DIC, it can also deal with global deformations; (iii) and a visibility mask VM sub-network, which can refine correspondences in case of an occlusion (this is very common in colonoscopy video frames).

We trained all parts of EndoRegNet at the same time. At the test time, only DIC and VM could be used to predict correspondences between two consecutive frames and refine them. The results of EndoRegNet were compared with feature-based image registration for different set of endoscopy video frames. Our results presented in Fig. 6. show high performance of EndoRegNet and its ability to generalize to new datasets.

Note that we trained EndoRegNet on a training set and then evaluated its performance on data that has not been observed in the training phase by computing SSIM and MAD.

Further, EndoRegNet showed excellent performance in registering deformed sequences (e.g. Fig. 5). As shown in Fig. 5(b) warping functions such as polynomial are inadequate to deal with the deformed images. We used a combination of local pixel displacement DIC and a second degree polynomial transformation PTP to deal with deformation. Particularly in Fig. (4)(b, d) it can be seen that some local strong deformation artefacts are better handled by the combination.

Other unsupervised flow estimation methods introduced by Meister el al. [11] and Wang et al. [12] are using FlowNet architecture but they have over 150 million parameters and thus require a huge training dataset. This is not feasible for our application. Instead, our proposed method provides excellent performance without requiring a large training data. We plan to improve our deformation model by using different objective function and convolution layers to better model long displacement and deformation.

Acknowledgement. We gratefully acknowledge the support of NVIDIA Corporation with the donation of the Titan X Pascal GPU used for this research.

References

1. Liu, C., Yuen, J., Torralba, A., Sivic, J., Freeman, W.T.: SIFT flow: dense correspondence across different scenes. In: Forsyth, D., Torr, P., Zisserman, A. (eds.) ECCV 2008. LNCS, vol. 5304, pp. 28–42. Springer, Heidelberg (2008). https://doi.org/10.1007/978-3-540-88690-7_3
2. Shi, J., Carlo, T.: Good features to track. In: Presented at the Computer Vision and Patern Recognition, Seattle, WA (1994)
3. Armin, M.A., Chetty, G., De Visser, H., Dumas, C., Grimpen, F., Salvado, O.: Automated visibility map of the internal colon surface from colonoscopy video. Int. J. Comput. Assist. Radiol. Surg. **11**, 1599–1610 (2016)
4. Bell, C.S., Puerto, G.A., Mariottini, G.-L., Valdastri, P.: Six DOF motion estimation for teleoperated flexible endoscopes using optical flow: a comparative study. Presented at the May (2014)
5. Puerto-Souza, G.A., Mariottini, G.L.: Hierarchical Multi-Affine (HMA) algorithm for fast and accurate feature matching in minimally-invasive surgical images. Presented at the October (2012)
6. Ji, D., Kwon, J., McFarland, M., Savarese, S.: Deep view morphing. In: CVPR 2017 (2017)
7. Dosovitskiy, A., et al.: FlowNet: learning optical flow with convolutional networks. In: 2015 IEEE International Conference on Computer Vision (ICCV), pp. 2758–2766. IEEE (2015)
8. Zhou, T., Brown, M., Snavely, N., Lowe, D.G.: Unsupervised learning of depth and ego-motion from video. Presented at the July (2017)
9. Garg, R., Vijay Kumar, B.G., Carneiro, G., Reid, I.: Unsupervised CNN for single view depth estimation: geometry to the rescue. In: Leibe, B., Matas, J., Sebe, N., Welling, M. (eds.) ECCV 2016. LNCS, vol. 9912, pp. 740–756. Springer, Cham (2016). https://doi.org/10.1007/978-3-319-46484-8_45
10. Yin, Z., Shi, J.: GeoNet: unsupervised learning of dense depth, optical flow and camera pose. In: CVPR (2018)

11. Meister, S., Hur, J., Roth, S.: UnFlow: unsupervised learning of optical flow with a bidirectional census loss. In: AAAI (2018)
12. Wang, Y., Yang, Y., Yang, Z., Zhao, L., Xu, W.: Occlusion aware unsupervised learning of optical flow. In: CVPR (2018)
13. Butler, D.J., Wulff, J., Stanley, G.B., Black, M.J.: A naturalistic open source movie for optical flow evaluation. In: Fitzgibbon, A., Lazebnik, S., Perona, P., Sato, Y., Schmid, C. (eds.) ECCV 2012. LNCS, vol. 7577, pp. 611–625. Springer, Heidelberg (2012). https://doi.org/10.1007/978-3-642-33783-3_44
14. de Vos Bob, D., Berendsen, F.F., Viergever, M.A., Staring, M., Išgum, I.: End-to-end unsupervised deformable image registration with a convolutional neural network. In: Cardoso, M.J., et al. (eds.) DLMIA/ML-CDS -2017. LNCS, vol. 10553, pp. 204–212. Springer, Cham (2017). https://doi.org/10.1007/978-3-319-67558-9_24
15. Jaderberg, M., Simonyan, K., Zisserman, A., Kavukcuoglu, K.: Spatial transformer networks. In: Cortes, C., Lawrence, N.D., Lee, D.D., Sugiyama, M., Garnett, R. (eds.) Advances in Neural Information Processing Systems, vol. 28, pp. 2017–2025. Curran Associates Inc, Red Hook (2015)
16. Mountney, P., Stoyanov, D., Yang, G.-Z.: Three-dimensional tissue deformation recovery and tracking. IEEE Signal Process. Mag. **27**, 14–24 (2010)
17. Ye, M., Giannarou, S., Meining, A., Yang, G.-Z.: Online tracking and retargeting with applications to optical biopsy in gastrointestinal endoscopic examinations. Med. Image Anal. **30**, 144–157 (2016)
18. Zhou, T., Tulsiani, S., Sun, W., Malik, J., Efros, A.A.: View synthesis by appearance flow. In: Leibe, B., Matas, J., Sebe, N., Welling, M. (eds.) ECCV 2016. LNCS, vol. 9908, pp. 286–301. Springer, Cham (2016). https://doi.org/10.1007/978-3-319-46493-0_18
19. Zhou, T., Krahenbuhl, P., Aubry, M., Huang, Q., Efros, A.A.: Learning dense correspondence via 3D-guided cycle consistency. In: Proceedings of the IEEE Conference on Computer Vision and Pattern Recognition, pp. 117–126 (2016)
20. Abadi, M., et al.: TensorFlow: large-scale machine learning on heterogeneous distributed systems. ArXiv:160304467 Cs. (2016)
21. Kingma, D.P., Ba, J.: Adam: a method for stochastic optimization. ArXiv:14126980 Cs. (2014)
22. De Visser, H., et al.: Developing a next generation colonoscopy simulator. Int. J. Image Graph. **10**, 203–217 (2010)
23. Armin, M.A., et al.: Uninformative frame detection in colonoscopy through motion, edge and color features. In: Luo, X., Reichl, T., Reiter, A., Mariottini, G.-L. (eds.) CARE 2015. LNCS, vol. 9515, pp. 153–162. Springer, Cham (2016). https://doi.org/10.1007/978-3-319-29965-5_15
24. Hamlyn Centre Laparoscopic/Endoscopic Video Datasets. http://hamlyn.doc.ic.ac.uk/vision/
25. Wang, Z., Bovik, A.C., Sheikh, H.R., Simoncelli, E.P.: Image quality assessment: from error visibility to structural similarity. IEEE Trans. Image Process. **13**, 600–612 (2004)

Learning to See Forces: Surgical Force Prediction with RGB-Point Cloud Temporal Convolutional Networks

Cong Gao$^{(\boxtimes)}$, Xingtong Liu, Michael Peven, Mathias Unberath, and Austin Reiter

The Johns Hopkins University, Baltimore, MD 21218, USA
cgao11@jhu.edu

Abstract. Robotic surgery has been proven to offer clear advantages during surgical procedures, however, one of the major limitations is obtaining haptic feedback. Since it is often challenging to devise a hardware solution with accurate force feedback, we propose the use of "visual cues" to infer forces from tissue deformation. Endoscopic video is a passive sensor that is freely available, in the sense that any minimally-invasive procedure already utilizes it. To this end, we employ deep learning to infer forces from video as an attractive low-cost and accurate alternative to typically complex and expensive hardware solutions. First, we demonstrate our approach in a phantom setting using the da Vinci Surgical System affixed with an OptoForce sensor. Second, we then validate our method on an *ex vivo* liver organ. Our method results in a mean absolute error of 0.814 N in the *ex vivo* study, suggesting that it may be a promising alternative to hardware based surgical force feedback in endoscopic procedures.

1 Introduction

Robot-assisted clinical systems have been increasingly adopted due to their advantages during surgical procedures. However, obtaining haptic feedback of a teleoperated surgical system still constitutes a hard problem due to practical challenges such as control loop stability. In the current version of the da Vinci Surgical System [1] (Intuitive Surgical, Inc., Sunnyvale, CA, USA), there is no haptic technology and no feedback on the grip forces. Surgeons depend on visual cues to infer the forces to avoid damage to tools and anatomy since excessive mechanical force can lead to the breakage of an end-effector string, serious artery or nerve injury, and even post-operation trauma [2]. As a result, there is a critical need to design force sensing systems in the field of surgical robotics.

Recently, many researchers have focused their efforts on solutions to this problem. For instance, numerous tactile sensing devices have been developed to estimate tactile information during static (point based) measurements, including indentation-based contact devices, aspiration devices, optical fiber devices, and

© Springer Nature Switzerland AG 2018
D. Stoyanov et al. (Eds.): OR 2.0/CARE/CLIP/ISIC 2018, LNCS 11041, pp. 118–127, 2018.
https://doi.org/10.1007/978-3-030-01201-4_14

non-contact devices [3]. Such devices are capable of providing accurate tactile information during static measurements of a single point, but they cannot scan soft tissue in a dynamic way, which is not a real-time solution [4]. Another area of investigation is directed towards using a torque sensor to model and compensate for grip force. This may provide a consistent internal force compensation based on the quantitative model, but it largely relies on the surgeon's skills and experience [2]. In addition, most of these hardware-based solutions have delicate and expensive components, which often cannot withstand sterilization.

Vision based approaches are one way to overcome above limitations of hardware solutions. Starting from [5], computer vision has been used to measure the deformed object and recover the applied force from linear elasticity equations. Recent advances in deep learning bring opportunities to such vision based force prediction in real surgical scenarios [6–9]. For example, researchers in [6] extract the 3D deformable structure of the heart and use a neural network with the architecture of LSTM-RNN to predict the applied force.

In this paper, we propose a vision-based surgical force prediction model called RGB-Point Cloud Temporal Convolutional Network (RPC-TCN). The model is based on a spatial block that encodes information at individual time-steps from a video and a temporal block to reason over sequences of observations. The spatial block combines 2D features (e.g., from an RGB image) and 3D features (e.g., from a 3D point cloud) for a given time, while the temporal block makes use of multiple static features via the Temporal Convolutional Network [10] (TCN) to model force change over time. To better abstract the core feature, we apply a pre-trained VGG16 image model [11] along with a pre-trained 3D point cloud-based architecture called PointNet [12] to extract features from raw visual data and then concatenate these two features to train a TCN time-series model. We evaluate our approach on internally-collected da Vinci surgical video, and show that our model produces highly accurate results. Figure 1 shows representative test result on an *ex vivo* liver.

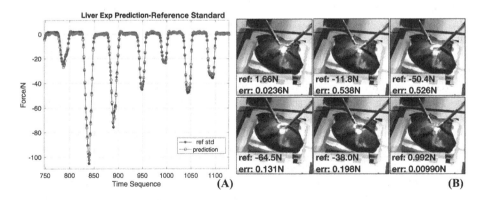

Fig. 1. Results of the *ex vivo* liver study: (A) Test result w.r.t time sequence. The blue line represents the reference standard force and the red curve are the model predictions. (B) A set of screenshots of the RGB image and their reference standard force and error. (Color figure online)

Related Work. Much work has focused on modeling tissue deformation during force prediction, since for reasonably soft material the applied force is positively correlated to the deformation of the tissue surface [6, 8, 13]. Therefore, accurately measuring surface deformation in 3D is vitally important for vision-based force estimation. Furthermore, depth data can then be converted to 3D point cloud. The recently proposed PointNet [12] directly works on 3D unordered point cloud data, which essentially breaks the pixel order limit of the 2D depth image. The unordered point cloud is robust to camera view points and invariant to transformations, which brings the potential ability to generalize to different objects.

In prior work, Temporal Convolutional Networks (TCN) have been proposed to improve video-based analysis models [10]. The input feature vector is the latent encoding of a spatial CNN which corresponds to each frame of the video sequence. Here, we define an observation window which has n frames backward and forward, centered at the current time-step t. The label for each window is the force at time t, which corresponds to the middle vector in this window. The intuition behind utilizing a time-series model lies with the observation that anatomical surfaces are often deforming continuously. It is then reasonable to introduce time-varying features to determine these forces.

In this paper, our RPC-TCN coalesces the above mentioned features to fully grasp the vision-based properties and then make the force prediction.

2   Methodology

2.1   Dataset Collection

Since there is no open source dataset for this task, we conduct experiments both in a phantom study and *ex vivo* study to generate our internal dataset. Figure 2 presents the setup details.

To collect force data, we fix the OptoForce 3D Force Sensor underneath the phantom object to record force data. The sensor measures the force a robotic tool applies to the phantom rather than the force at the tool tip itself. The force sensor is accurate up to 12.5×10^{-3} N and collects 3D force observations (including x, y, and z in the force sensor coordinate). We only use the z-component, which is perpendicular to the planar surface the specimen is placed upon. It will automatically re-bias each time we place an object.

RGB images and depth images are collected using a Kinect2 RGB+D camera. This setup is convenient to demonstrate feasibility of the proposed fusion of RGB images and point clouds for force prediction. In a clinical scenario, a dedicated depth camera is not yet available. However, previous research has validated a learning-based method to estimate dense depth images and surface normal maps from endoscopic surgical video, which results in high-resolution spatial 3D reconstructions to an average error of 0.53 mm to 1.12 mm [14]. Based on this result, obtaining 3D point cloud and depth information from endoscopic video is realistically achievable.

The object is fixed in the working area of a standard dual arm da Vinci system [1]. As the image stream flows at 30 fps, the RGB data, depth data, and

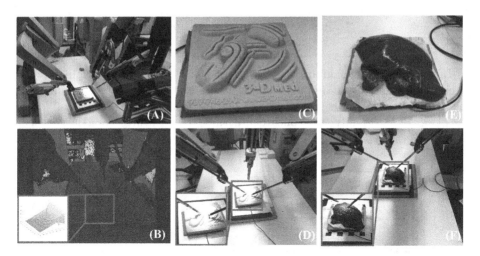

Fig. 2. (A) The experimental environment. (B) The depth image from the Kinect2 camera. (C) The phantom used in the experiment. The force sensor is placed under the phantom. (D) RGB image of the phantom. (E) A fresh piece of pig liver. (F) RGB image of the liver.

force data are synchronized to be within 10 ms. The Kinect2 RGB+D camera is placed at four different positions to collect multiple points of view to test against model overfitting.

2.2 RPC-TCN

Spatial Block. Figure 3 shows the overall structure of our RPC-TCN. We use $X_{RGB} \in \mathbb{R}^{224 \times 224}$ and $X_D \in \mathbb{R}^{151 \times 151}$ to denote RGB image and depth image. The pre-trained VGG16 network has shown good performance at localization and classification tasks [11]. In our task, we assume that the movement of the da Vinci tool and the feature change of the phantom is relevant for the force prediction. Thus, we choose to fine tune the pre-trained VGG Network from the ImageNet dataset for later regression. The output feature comes from the 2nd classifier layer, which contains more representative variants than the last layer, such that $X_{VGG} \in \mathbb{R}^{4096}$. Depth image X_D is converted to point cloud data in the depth camera's coordinate system.

Depth Image to Point Cloud. In the following formula, x_D and y_D refer to the coordinate pixel index in the depth image, and z_D is its depth value. $\bar{x}_D$, $\bar{y}_D$, and $\bar{z}_D$ refer to the mean values. c_x, c_y and f_x, f_y are the intrinsic parameters of principal point and focal length of the depth camera. We use the maximum length in depth image to normalize the point cloud into a unit sphere. The normalized coordinates are

$$x_{pc} = (x_D - c_x)\frac{z_D}{f_x} - \bar{x}_D, \tag{1}$$

$$y_{pc} = (y_D - c_y)\frac{z_D}{f_y} - \bar{y}_D, and \qquad (2)$$

$$z_{pc} = z_D - \bar{z}_D. \qquad (3)$$

In order to fit the input vector size of the PointNet, the original point cloud is uniformly downsampled from 22801 to 2048 points. Next, we fine tune the pre-trained PointNet to select the feature from the second-to-last layer, $X_{ptnet} \in \mathbb{R}^{512}$. Finally, we concatenate these two features to a larger one, $X_{cat} = [X_{VGG}, X_{ptnet}] \in \mathbb{R}^{4608}$.

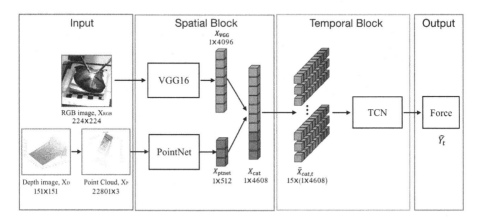

Fig. 3. The basic architecture of RPC-TCN. The spatial block extracts features from the pre-trained VGG net and PointNet and concatenates two features. The temporal block expands this feature to be 15 frames in a window and predict the force corresponding to the middle frame.

Temporal Block. Figure 4 presents the hierarchical structure of the temporal block. Here, we denote the concatenated feature X_{cat} with respect to time as $X_{cat,t}$, then $\bar{X}_{cat,t} = [X_{cat,t-n}, \ldots, X_{cat,t-1}, X_{cat,t}, X_{cat,t+1}, \ldots, X_{cat,t+n}]$. We define the collection of filters in each convolutional layer as $W = \{W^{(i)}\}_{i=1}^{F_l}$ for $W^{(i)} \in \mathbb{R}^{d \times F_{l-1}}$ with a corresponding bias vector $b \in \mathbb{R}^{F_l}$, where $l \in \{1, \ldots, L\}$ is the layer index. Given the signal from the previous layer, $E^{(l-1)}$, we compute activations $E^{(l)}$ with

$$E_{(0)} = f(W * \bar{X}_{cat,t} + b), \qquad (4)$$

$$E_{(l)} = f(W * \bar{E}_{(l-1)} + b), \qquad (5)$$

where $f(\cdot)$ is a non-linear activation function and $*$ is the convolution operator. We also perform batch normalization after each convolutional layer. We compare different activation functions and find that the Rectified Linear Units (ReLU) perform best in our experiments. Finally, we use a linear regression at the last fully-connected layer to predict the force, $\hat{Y}_t \in \mathbb{R}$. We define U as the filter for the last linear layer L and c as the bias. The process is

$$\hat{Y}_t = Linear(UE^{(L)} + c). \qquad (6)$$

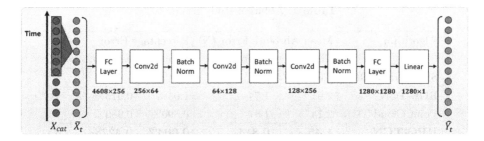

Fig. 4. Hierarchical structure of the temporal block.

3   Experiment and Result

3.1   Experimental Setting and Dataset

In total, we obtain 61,473 samples in our phantom study and 44,413 samples in our *ex vivo* liver study. The training data is randomly split to 80% of the full dataset and 5% for validation, 15% for test in both experiments (e.g., the phantom and *ex vivo* were trained and tested separately). The loss function is Mean Squared Error (MSE) and the learning rate is initialized to be 1×10^{-5} and multiplied by 0.1 every 1000 epochs.

To test the power of the proposed algorithm, we compare to multiple algorithms in both the phantom and *ex vivo* study. We first conduct experiments on traditional single-frame based methods on the RGB images, called Single-frame RGB. In this setup, we use the same VGG16 network to abstract the feature and then construct a convolutional neural network to perform regression. Then we compare the temporal methods, RGB-TCN and Point Cloud-TCN. In these experiments, the features from the spatial block are the same as discussed before, but we test the performance by separately passing them to the same TCN structure. We finally test on the RPC-TCN.

3.2   Results and Analysis

Table 1 displays the prediction accuracy of various algorithms as a comparison on the same dataset. The percentage error is based on the maximum force magnitude in the dataset, which is -239 N for the phantom study and -190 N for the *ex vivo* liver study. The single-frame RGB is worse than the TCN type methods, which supports the hypothesis that the time-scaled feature is critical to force prediction. Compared to the other two TCN methods, our RPC-TCN presents the best mean absolute error result with 1.45 N, corresponding to 0.604% for the phantom study and 0.814 N, corresponding to 0.427% for the *ex vivo* liver study.

Figure 5(A) and (B) displays a correlation plot of our RPC-TCN result. The correlation coefficient is 0.995 and 0.996 for our predictions on the phantom and liver data, respectively, implying a strong relationship between the prediction and the reference standard data. From the test error trend in Fig. 5(C) and (D),

Table 1. Ablation study results.

Algorithm	Mean Absolute Error (N)		Percentage Error	
	Phantom	*Ex vivo* Liver	Phantom	*Ex vivo* Liver
Single-frame RGB	7.06	10.4	3.01%	5.45%
RGB-TCN	2.51	1.74	1.05%	0.913%
Point Cloud-TCN	2.14	1.87	0.896%	0.983%
RPC-TCN	**1.45**	**0.814**	**0.604%**	**0.427%**

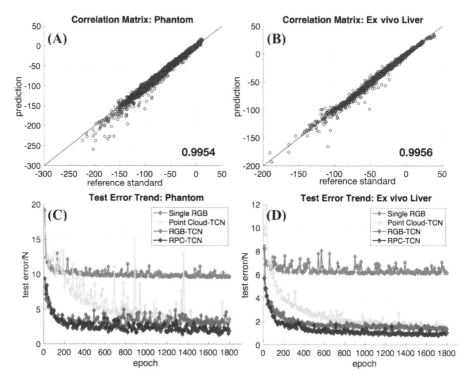

Fig. 5. (A), (B) Illustration of the correlation matrix between reference standard force and the prediction force. (C), (D) Test Error trend with training epochs. The error is calculated as mean absolute error of all test data.

we find that the single RGB image method presents much higher error, which indicates overfitting. All three TCN based methods can converge to a relatively low test error, while the PC-TCN and the RGB-TCN perform similarly well, but are outperformed by the proposed RPC-TCN suggesting that the use of information from multiple sources is indeed beneficial for vision-based force prediction.

To better understand the error distribution, we divide the force magnitude into 7 bins, each of which spans a 20 N force interval. Figure 6(A) and (B) show the phantom study result. We calculate the mean absolute error and the standard deviation error in each bin and plot them as comparison. Compared to the Point Cloud-TCN and the RPC-TCN, RGB-TCN shows smaller error in lower force, but it has large error and variation when the force becomes large. This comparison indicates that the RGB-TCN is good at predicting small forces, but it does not perform well for large force prediction.

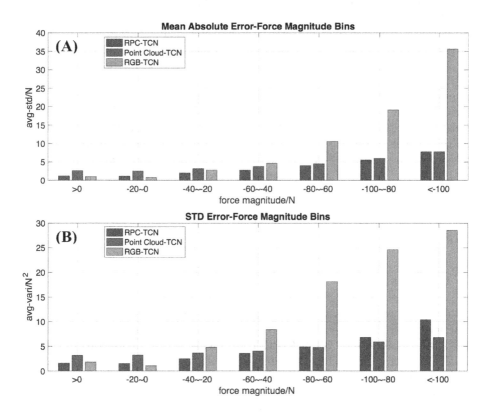

Fig. 6. (A) Illustration of mean absolute error distribution w.r.t 7 bins. (B) Illustration of standard deviation error distribution w.r.t 7 bins.

One of the reasons to this phenomenon is that the training data is biased in force distribution. There are more training samples for smaller forces. A more uniformly-distributed dataset will improve large force prediction. The Point Cloud-TCN shows higher error in low forces, but its prediction error is more uniformly distributed. The reason that Point Cloud-TCN is more steady than RGB-TCN is that features of 3D point cloud are more directly related to deformation than 2D features. This Point Cloud-TCN experiment also shows that only with 3D data, our model achieves good performance, validating the power of depth data. Our proposed RPC-TCN takes advantage of these two information and presents a more consistent error distribution trend regardless of absolute scale.

The *ex vivo* liver study is much closer to a human-organ application compared to the phantom study. Our model still reaches a low error when training and testing in this real organ scenario. We intentionally test large force magnitudes that could cause damage to tissues to be able to predict the onset of excessively large force and, thus, warn clinicians. Training and testing images include specularities, which improves the generalization ability to different surgical scenarios.

Our current model does not evaluate the transferability to different organs. Current results are reached by training and testing on one single phantom and *ex vivo* liver. We assume the liver properties are similar across different sources, but it still indicates a degree of overfitting to such object. Future study will include testing on multiple organs and considering tissue biomechanical properties. The Kinect camera and OptoForce are convenient tools to demonstrate feasibility of vision-based force estimation. The objects in our experiments are overall flat and thin, which enable the underneath force sensor to measure the applied force change, but the soft tissues are still absorbing part of the touch force. Going forward, however, we will consider setups that are more realistic regarding clinical practice. This includes monocular depth estimation from RGB endoscopic video as in [14] and slave-side force sensors to accurately measure tool tip contact force. These must be carefully designed as obtaining ground truth forces *in vivo* is non-trivial.

4   Conclusion

In this paper, we discuss a proof-of-principle system to infer forces during surgical activity from RGB+D video. We propose a convolutional neural network called RGB-Point Cloud TCN (RPC-TCN). This network combines the information from traditional RGB+D images obtained from dense depth imagery, and time series analysis for surgical force prediction in a robotic surgical system. Phantom and *ex vivo* liver experiments yield a mean prediction error to 0.814 N. Our results on this proof-of-principle prototype are promising and encourage further research on 3D sensing in endoscopy to realize the proposed force sensing approach in clinical practice.

Acknowledgement. This work was funded by an Intuitive Surgical Sponsored Research Agreement.

References

1. DiMaio, S., Hanuschik, M., Kreaden, U.: The da Vinci surgical system. In: Rosen, J., Hannaford, R. (eds.) Surgical Robotics, pp. 199–217. Springer, Boston (2011). https://doi.org/10.1007/978-1-4419-1126-1_9
2. Lee, C., et al.: A grip force model for the da Vinci end-effector to predict a compensation force. Med. Biol. Eng. Comput. **53**(3), 253–261 (2015)

3. Konstantinova, J., Jiang, A., Althoefer, K., Dasgupta, P., Nanayakkara, T.: Implementation of tactile sensing for palpation in robot-assisted minimally invasive surgery: a review. IEEE Sens. J. **14**(8), 2490–2501 (2014)

4. McKinley, S., et al.: A single-use haptic palpation probe for locating subcutaneous blood vessels in robot-assisted minimally invasive surgery. In: 2015 IEEE International Conference on Automation Science and Engineering (CASE), pp. 1151–1158. IEEE (2015)

5. Greminger, M.A., Nelson, B.J.: Vision-based force measurement. IEEE Trans. Pattern Anal. Mach. Intell. **26**(3), 290–298 (2004)

6. Aviles, A.I., Alsaleh, S.M., Hahn, J.K., Casals, A.: Towards retrieving force feedback in robotic-assisted surgery: a supervised neuro-recurrent-vision approach. IEEE Trans. Haptics **10**(3), 431–443 (2017)

7. Karimirad, F., Chauhan, S., Shirinzadeh, B.: Vision-based force measurement using neural networks for biological cell microinjection. J. Biomech. **47**(5), 1157–1163 (2014)

8. Aviles, A.I., Alsaleh, S.M., Sobrevilla, P., Casals, A.: Force-feedback sensory substitution using supervised recurrent learning for robotic-assisted surgery. In: 2015 37th Annual International Conference of the IEEE Engineering in Medicine and Biology Society (EMBC), pp. 1–4. IEEE (2015)

9. Gessert, N., Beringhoff, J., Otte, C., Schlaefer, A.: Force estimation from OCT volumes using 3D CNNs. Int. J. Comput. Assist. Radiol. Surg., 1–10 (2018)

10. Lea, C., Vidal, R., Reiter, A., Hager, G.D.: Temporal convolutional networks: a unified approach to action segmentation. In: Hua, G., Jégou, H. (eds.) ECCV 2016. LNCS, vol. 9915, pp. 47–54. Springer, Cham (2016). https://doi.org/10.1007/978-3-319-49409-8_7

11. Simonyan, K., Zisserman, A.: Very deep convolutional networks for large-scale image recognition. arXiv preprint arXiv:1409.1556 (2014)

12. Qi, C.R., Su, H., Mo, K., Guibas, L.J.: Pointnet: Deep learning on point sets for 3d classification and segmentation. In: Proceedings of Computer Vision and Pattern Recognition (CVPR), vol. 1(2), p. 4. IEEE (2017)

13. Aviles, A.I., Alsaleh, S.M., Casals, A.: Sight to touch: 3D diffeomorphic deformation recovery with mixture components for perceiving forces in robotic-assisted surgery. In: 2017 IEEE/RSJ International Conference on Intelligent Robots and Systems (IROS), pp. 160–165. IEEE (2017)

14. Reiter, A., Léonard, S., Sinha, A., Ishii, M., Taylor, R.H., Hager, G.D.: Endoscopic-CT: learning-based photometric reconstruction for endoscopic sinus surgery. In: Medical Imaging 2016: Image Processing. vol. 9784, p. 978418. International Society for Optics and Photonics (2016)

Self-supervised Learning for Dense Depth Estimation in Monocular Endoscopy

Xingtong Liu[1]([✉]), Ayushi Sinha[1], Mathias Unberath[1], Masaru Ishii[2],
Gregory D. Hager[1], Russell H. Taylor[1], and Austin Reiter[1]

[1] The Johns Hopkins University, Baltimore, USA
xliu89@jh.edu
[2] Johns Hopkins Medical Institutions, Baltimore, USA

Abstract. We present a self-supervised approach to training convolutional neural networks for dense depth estimation from monocular endoscopy data without *a priori* modeling of anatomy or shading. Our method only requires sequential data from monocular endoscopic videos and a multi-view stereo reconstruction method, e.g. structure from motion, that supervises learning in a sparse but accurate manner. Consequently, our method requires neither manual interaction, such as scaling or labeling, nor patient CT in the training and application phases. We demonstrate the performance of our method on sinus endoscopy data from two patients and validate depth prediction quantitatively using corresponding patient CT scans where we found submillimeter residual errors. (Link to the supplementary video: https://camp.lcsr.jhu.edu/miccai-2018-demonstration-videos/)

1 Introduction

Minimally invasive procedures, such as functional endoscopic sinus surgery, typically employ surgical navigation systems to visualize critical structures that must not be disturbed during surgery. Computer vision-based navigation systems that rely on endoscopic video and do not introduce additional hardware are both easy to integrate into clinical workflow and cost effective. Such systems generally rely on the registration of preoperative data, such as CT scans, to intraoperative endoscopic video data [1]. This registration must be highly accurate in order to guarantee reliable performance of the navigation system. Since the accuracy of feature-based video-CT registration methods is dependent on the quality of reconstructions obtained from endoscopic video, it is critical for these reconstructions to be accurate. Further, in order to solve for the additional degrees of freedom required by deformable registration methods [2], these reconstructions must also be dense. Our method satisfies both of these requirements (Fig. 1).

Russell H. Taylor is a paid consultant to and owns equity in Galen Robotics, Inc. These arrangements have been reviewed and approved by JHU in accordance with its conflict of interest policy.

© Springer Nature Switzerland AG 2018
D. Stoyanov et al. (Eds.): OR 2.0/CARE/CLIP/ISIC 2018, LNCS 11041, pp. 128–138, 2018.
https://doi.org/10.1007/978-3-030-01201-4_15

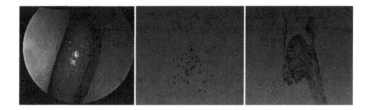

Fig. 1. Visual comparison of reconstructions: the green dots in the endoscopic image (left) are 2D projections of the sparse reconstruction (middle) from a recent SfM-based method [1]. In this example, SfM only yields 67 3D points. Our method (right) produces a dense reconstruction with 125369 3D points, shown here from approximately the same viewpoint as the SfM reconstruction. The higher the resolution of the input image, the greater the number of points our method is able to reconstruct. (Color figure online)

Several reconstruction methods have been explored in the past. Multi-view stereo methods, such as Structure from Motion (SfM) [1] and Simultaneous Localization and Mapping (SLAM) [3], are able to simultaneously reconstruct 3D structure and estimate camera poses in feature-rich scenes. However, the paucity of features in endoscopic images of anatomy can cause these methods to produce sparse reconstructions, which can lead to inaccurate registrations.

Mahmoud et al. [4] propose a quasi-dense SLAM method for minimally invasive surgery that is able to produce dense reconstructions. However, it requires careful manual parameter tuning. Further, the accuracy of the reconstruction is lower than that required for sinus surgery, where low prediction errors are critical due to the proximity of critical structures such as the brain, eyes, carotid arteries, and optic nerves. Shape from Shading (SfS) based methods explicitly [5,6] or implicitly [7] model the relationship between appearance and depth. These methods generally require *a priori* modeling of the lighting conditions and surface reflectance properties. Since the true lighting and reflectance conditions are hard to model, SfS-based methods rely on simplified models that can result in noisy and inaccurate reconstructions, e.g., in the presence of specular reflections.

Convolutional neural networks (CNNs) have shown promising results in high-complexity problems including general scene depth estimation [8] which benefits from local and global context information and multi-level representations. However, using CNNs directly in endoscopic videos poses several challenges. First, dense ground truth depth maps are hard to obtain inhibiting the use of fully supervised methods. Hardware solutions, such as depth or stereo cameras, often fail to acquire dense and accurate depth maps from endoscopic scenes because of the non-Lambertian reflectance properties of tissues and paucity of features. Software solutions, such as those discussed above, do not produce reconstructions with the density or accuracy required for our application. More recent CNN-based methods [9] use untextured endoscopy video simulations from CT to train a fully supervised depth estimation network and rely on another trained transcoder network to convert RGB video frames to texture independent frames required for depth prediction. This procedure requires per endoscope photometric calibration and complex registration which may only work well in narrow tube-like structures. It is unclear whether this method will work on in-vivo images since it is only validated on two lung nodule phantoms. Second, endoscopic images do not provide the photo-constancy that is required by unsupervised methods for depth estimation of general scenes [10]. This is because the camera and light source move jointly and, therefore, the appearance of the same anatomy can vary substantially with different camera poses. In addition, texture-scarce regions make it hard to provide valuable information to guide the unsupervised network training even if the appearance was preserved across camera poses.

In this work, we present a self-supervised approach to training deep learning models for dense depth map estimation from monocular endoscopic video data. Our method is designed to leverage improvements in SfM- or SLAM-based methods since our network training exploits reconstructions produced by these methods for self-supervision. Our method also uses the estimated relative camera poses to ensure depth map consistency in the training phase. While this approach requires the intrinsic parameters of the corresponding endoscope, it does not require any manual annotation, scaling, registration, or corresponding CT data.

2 Methods

We introduce a method for dense depth estimation in unlabeled data by leveraging established multi-view stereo reconstruction methods. Although SfM-based methods are only able to produce sparse reconstructions from endoscopic video data, these reconstructions and relative camera poses have been shown to be reliable [1]. Therefore, we use these reconstructions and camera poses to supervise the training of our network using novel loss functions. Doing so enables us to produce reliable dense depth maps from single endoscopic video frames.

2.1 Training Data

Our training data consists of pairs of RGB endoscopic images, 3D reconstructions and coordinate transformations between the image pairs from SfM, and the rectified intrinsic parameters of the endoscope. The training data generation is completely autonomous given the endoscopic and calibration videos and could, in principle, be computed on-the-fly with SLAM-based methods.

For each frame, we compute a sparse depth map to store the 3D reconstructions. By applying perspective geometry, 3D points can be projected onto image planes. Since SfM- or SLAM-based methods do not consider all frames when triangulating one particular 3D point, we only project the 3D points onto associated image planes. $b_{i,j} = 1$ indicates frame j is used to triangulate the 3D point i and $b_{i,j} = 0$ indicates otherwise. $\left(u_i^j, v_i^j\right)$ are projected 2D coordinates of the 3D point i in frame j. The sparse depth map Y_j^* of frame j is

$$Y_j^* \left[\left[v_i^j \right], \left[u_i^j \right] \right] = \begin{cases} z_i^j & \text{if } b_{i,j} = 1 \\ 0 & \text{if } b_{i,j} = 0 \end{cases}, \quad \text{where} \tag{1}$$

z_i^j is the depth of 3D point i in frame j. Since the reconstruction is sparse, large regions in Y_j^* will not have valid depth values.

We also compute sparse soft masks to ensure that our network can be trained with these sparse depth maps and mitigate the effect of outliers in the 3D reconstructions. This is achieved by assigning confidence values to valid regions in the image while masking out invalid regions. Valid regions are 2D locations on image planes where 3D points project onto, while the remaining image comprises invalid regions. The sparse soft mask, W_j, of frame j is defined as

$$W_j \left[\left[v_i^j \right], \left[u_i^j \right] \right] = \begin{cases} c_i & \text{if } b_{i,j} = 1 \\ 0 & \text{if } b_{i,j} = 0 \end{cases}, \quad \text{where} \tag{2}$$

c_i is a weight related to the number of frames used to reconstruct 3D point i and the accumulated parallax of the projected 2D locations of this point in these frames. Intuitively, c_i is proportional to the number of frames used for triangulation and the accumulated parallax. Greater magnitudes of c_i reflect greater confidence.

2.2   Network Architecture

Our overall network architecture (Fig. 2) is a two-branch Siamese network [11] with high modularity. For instance, our single-frame depth estimation architecture can be substituted with any architecture that produces a dense depth map. We introduce two custom layers in this network architecture.

The *Depth Map Scaling Layer* scales the predicted dense depth map from the single-frame depth estimation architecture to remain consistent with the scale of the coordinate transformation. It uses the corresponding sparse depth map as the anchor point for scale computation.

The *Depth Map Warping Layer* warps a scaled dense depth map to the coordinate frame of the other input to the Siamese network using the relative camera pose between the two frames. We implement this layer in a differentiable manner so that the training loss can be backpropagated. These two layers work together to generate data that is used to enforce depth consistency, described in the following section.

2.3   Loss Functions

In the training phase, we use two loss functions that leverage the sparse depth annotations and relative camera poses between frames produced by SfM.

The first loss function, *Scale-invariant Weighted Loss*, allows the network to train with sparse depth annotations because it uses sparse soft masks as weights to ignore regions in the training data where no depth values are available. Given a

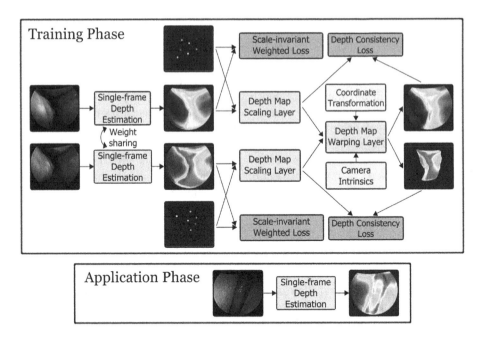

Fig. 2. Network architecture: our training network (top) is a self-supervised two-branch Siamese network that uses sparse 3D points and relative camera poses from SfM to estimate dense depth maps from pairs of images and enforce depth consistency, respectively. The soft sparse mask and sparse depth map are represented as a single blue square with dots. During the application phase (bottom), we use the trained weights of the single-frame depth estimation architecture (Fig. 3) to predict a dense depth map that is accurate up to a global scale. (Color figure online)

sparse depth map, Y^*, a predicted dense depth map, Y, and a sparse soft mask, W, the Scale-invariant Weighted Loss is defined as

$$L_{sparse}\left(Y, Y^*, W\right) = \frac{1}{\sum_i w_i} \sum_i w_i d_i^2 - \frac{1}{\left(\sum_i w_i\right)^2} \left(\sum_i w_i d_i\right)^2, \quad \text{where} \quad (3)$$

w_i is the value of the sparse soft mask at pixel location i and $d_i = \log y_i - \log y_i^*$ is the difference between the predicted and ground truth depth at location i [12]. The scale-invariance of this loss function is advantageous given the inherent scale ambiguity of single-frame depth estimation. It makes the network potentially generalizable to different patients, endoscopes, and anatomy because the network simply needs to estimate correct depth ratios without having to estimate the correct global scale. The global scale can vary considerably across different scenarios and is almost impossible for the network to estimate solely from endoscopic frames with no additional *a priori* information as input. Finally, it makes the automatic training data generation in our method feasible. If the depth estimation network is set up to predict global scale, the results from

SfM- or SLAM-based methods must resolve scale ambiguity first. This requires additional steps, e.g. registration to preoperative CT data, to recover the correct global scale. However, registration usually requires manual initialization and, therefore, user interaction. Alternatively, external tracking devices can record data that reflects global scale information but are often not accurate and can change the clinical workflow. With the Scale-invariant Weighted Loss, the automatically generated 3D reconstructions and camera poses are directly usable for network training. This allows our method to use all existing endoscopic videos as training data in a fully automatic manner as long as the intrinsic parameters of the corresponding endoscopes are known.

The second loss function, *Depth Consistency Loss*, adds spatial constraints among frames in the training phase. By using the Scale-invariant Weighted Loss only, the network does not gain any information from regions where no sparse depth annotations are available and the training is prone to overfitting to the measurement noise or outliers from SfM- or SLAM-based methods. The Depth Consistency Loss helps gain more information and mitigate the overfitting issues. It requires inputs from the Depth Map Scaling Layer and the Depth Map Warping Layer. We denote the predicted depth map of frame k as Z_k and the warped depth map, warped from its original coordinate frame j to the coordinate frame k, as $\check{Z}_{k,j}$. Pixels in $\check{Z}_{k,j}$ and Z_k at location i are denoted $\check{z}_i^{k,j}$ and z_i^k, respectively. The Depth Consistency Loss of frame j w. r. t. k is defined as

$$L_{consist}(j,k) = \frac{1}{N}\sum_{i=1}^{N}|\check{z}_i^{k,j} - z_i^k|, \quad \text{where} \tag{4}$$

N is the number of pixels in the region where both maps have valid depths.

The network overall loss is a weighted combination of the two loss functions defined above. Given the predicted dense depth map, Y, and sparse depth map, Y^*, the overall loss for network training with a single pair of training data from frame j and k is defined as

$$L(j,k) = L_{sparse}\left(Y_j, Y_j^*, W_j\right) + L_{sparse}\left(Y_k, Y_k^*, W_k\right)$$
$$+ \omega\left(L_{consist}(j,k) + L_{consist}(k,j)\right), \quad \text{where} \tag{5}$$

ω is used to control how much weight each type of loss function is assigned.

3   Experimental Setup

Our network is trained using an NVIDIA TITAN X GPU with 12 GB memory. We use two sinus endoscopy videos acquired using the same endoscope. Videos were collected from anonymized and consenting patients under an IRB approved protocol. The training data consist of 22 short video subsequences from Patient 1. We use the methods explained above to generate a total of 5040 original image pairs. The image resolution is 464×512, and we add random Gaussian noise to image data as an augmentation method. We use 95% of these data for training

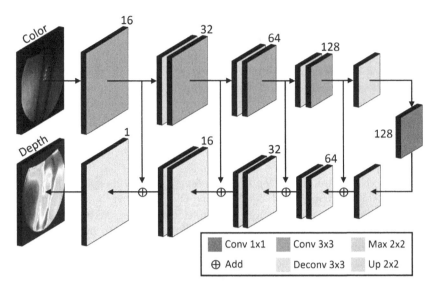

Fig. 3. Single-frame depth estimation architecture: with the encoder-decoder architecture and symmetric connection skipping mechanism, the network is able to extract global information while preserving details.

and 5% for validation. The learning rate and the weight, ω, of the loss function are empirically set to $1.0e^{-4}$ and $2.0e^{-4}$, respectively. For evaluation, we use 6 different scenes from Patient 1 and 3 scenes from Patient 2, each containing 10 test images as input to the network in the application phase. These depth maps are converted to point clouds that were registered [13] to surface models generated from corresponding patient CTs [14]. We use the residual error produced by the registration as our evaluation metric for the dense reconstructions. The single-frame depth estimation architecture we use is an encoder-decoder architecture with symmetric connection skipping (Fig. 3) [15].

4   Results and Discussion

The mean residual error produced by registrations over all reconstructions from Patient 1 is $0.84\,(\pm 0.10)$ mm and over all reconstructions from Patient 2 is $0.63\,(\pm 0.19)$ mm. The mean residual error for Patient 1 is larger than that for Patient 2 due to the larger anatomical complexity in the testing scenes of Patient 1. The residual errors for all 9 testing scenes are shown in Fig. 4. Since our method relies on results from SfM or other multi-view stereo reconstruction methods, improvements in these methods will be reflected immediately in our dense reconstructions. However, if these methods are not able to reconstruct any points from training videos or if the reconstructed points and estimated camera poses have large systematic errors, our method will also fail.

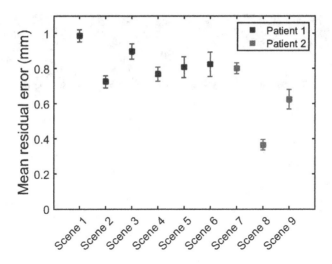

Fig. 4. Mean residual errors for all testing scenes from Patients 1 and 2.

We are able to detect and ignore frames where no reconstructions are estimated as well as individual outliers in reconstructions when the number of outliers is small relative to the number of inliers. However, there are cases where all reconstructed points and estimated camera poses are incorrect because of the extreme paucity of features in certain regions of the nasal cavity and sinuses. Currently, we rely on manual checking to ensure that 2D projections of SfM reconstructions are locked onto visual features in order to ignore erroneous reconstructions. However, in the future, we hope to develop an automatic method to detect these failures. Further, with training data from a single patient and evaluation on only two patients, it is unclear whether our method is able to generalize or is overfitting to this particular endoscope. Our current results also do not allow us to know whether or not fine-tuning the network in a patient-specific manner will improve the accuracy of reconstructions for that particular patient. In the future, we hope to acquire a larger dataset in order to investigate this further.

Samples from our current dense reconstruction results are shown in Fig. 5 for qualitative evaluation. There are several challenges in these examples where the traditional SfS methods are likely to fail. For example, shadows appear in the lower middle region of the second sample and the upper right region of the fourth sample. There are also specular reflections from mucus in the first, third and fourth samples. With the capability of extracting local and global context information, our network recognizes these patterns and produces accurate predictions despite their presence. Figure 1 also shows a comparison between a sparse reconstruction obtained using SfM and a dense reconstruction obtained using our method.

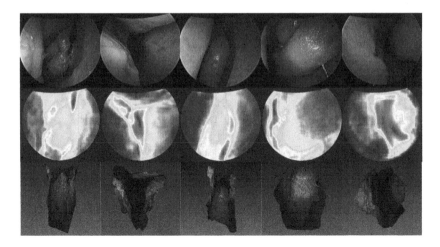

Fig. 5. Examples of dense photometric reconstructions from Patients 1 and 2: each column captures a different region in the nasal cavity and sinuses. The top row shows the color endoscopic images, the middle row shows the corresponding depth images where red maps to high values and blue to low values, and the bottom row shows the photo-realistic 3D reconstructions produced by our method. (Color figure online)

5   Conclusion

In this work, we present an approach for dense depth estimation in monocular endoscopy data that does not require manual annotations for training. Instead, we self-supervise training by computing sparse annotations and enforcing depth prediction consistency across multiple views using relative camera poses from multi-view stereo reconstruction methods like SfM or SLAM. Consequently, our method enables training of depth estimation networks using only endoscopic video, without the need for CT data, manual scaling, or labeling. We show that this approach can achieve submillimeter residual errors on sinus endoscopy data. Since our method can generate training data automatically and directly maps original endoscopic frames to dense depth maps with no *a priori* modeling of anatomy or shading, more unlabeled data and improvements in SfM- or SLAM-based methods will directly benefit our approach and enable translation to different endoscopes, patients, and anatomy. This makes our method a critical intermediate step towards accurate endoscopic surgical navigation. In the future, we hope to evaluate our method on different endoscopes, patients, and anatomy and compare with other methods. Substituting the single-frame depth estimation architecture with a multi-frame architecture is also a potential future direction to explore.

Acknowledgement. The work reported in this paper was funded in part by NIH R01-EB015530, in part by a research contract from Galen Robotics, and in part by Johns Hopkins University internal funds.

References

1. Leonard, S., et al.: Evaluation and stability analysis of video-based navigation system for functional endoscopic sinus surgery on in-vivo clinical data. IEEE Trans. Med. Imaging **62**(c), 1–10 (2018). https://doi.org/10.1109/TMI.2018.2833868

2. Sinha, A., Liu, X., Reiter, A., Ishii, M., Hager, G.D, Taylor, R.H.: Endoscopic navigation in the absence of CT imaging. Med. Image Comput. Comput. Assist. Interv. (2018, in press). https://arxiv.org/abs/1806.03997

3. Grasa, O.G., Bernal, E., Casado, S., Gil, I., Montiel, J.M.M.: Visual SLAM for handheld monocular endoscope. IEEE Trans. Med. Imaging **33**(1), 135–146 (2014). https://doi.org/10.1109/TMI.2013.2282997

4. Mahmoud, N., Hostettler, A., Collins, T., Soler, L., Doignon, C., Montiel, J.M.M.: SLAM based quasi dense reconstruction for minimally invasive surgery scenes. arXiv:1705.09107 (2017)

5. Tatematsu, K., Iwahori, Y., Nakamura, T., Fukui, S., Woodham, R.J., Kasugai, K.: Shape from endoscope image based on photometric and geometric constraints. Procedia Comput. Sci. **22**, 1285–1293 (2013). https://doi.org/10.1016/j.procs.2013.09.216

6. Ciuti, G., Visentini-Scarzanella, M., Dore, A., Menciassi, A., Dario, P., Yang, G.Z.: Intra-operative monocular 3D reconstruction for image-guided navigation in active locomotion capsule endoscopy. In: 4th IEEE RAS & EMBS International Conference on Biomedical Robotics and Biomechatronics (BioRob), pp. 768–774 (2012). https://doi.org/10.1109/BioRob.2012.6290771

7. Reiter, A., Leonard, S., Sinha, A., Ishii, M., Taylor, R.H., Hager, G.D.: Endoscopic-CT: learning-based photometric reconstruction for endoscopic sinus surgery. In: Proceedings of SPIE Medical Imaging 2016: Image Processing, vol. 9784, p. 978418–6 (2016). https://doi.org/10.1117/12.2216296

8. Laina, I., Rupprecht, C., Belagiannis, V., Tombari, F., Navab, N.: Deeper depth prediction with fully convolutional residual networks. In: Fourth International Conference on 3D Vision (3DV), pp. 239–248 (2016). https://doi.org/10.1109/3DV.2016.32

9. Visentini-Scarzanella, M., Sugiura, T., Kaneko, T., Koto, S.: Deep monocular 3D reconstruction for assisted navigation in bronchoscopy. Int. J. Comput. Assist. Radiol. Surg. **12**(7), 1089–1099 (2017). https://doi.org/10.1007/s11548-017-1609-2

10. Zhou, T., Brown, M., Snavely, N., Lowe, D.G.: Unsupervised learning of depth and ego-motion from video. In: IEEE Conference on Computer Vision and Pattern Recognition (CVPR), vol. 2, no. 6, pp. 6612–6619 (2017). https://doi.org/10.1109/CVPR.2017.700

11. Chopra, S., Hadsell, R., LeCun, Y.: Learning a similarity metric discriminatively, with application to face verification. In: IEEE Conference on Computer Vision and Pattern Recognition (CVPR), vol. 1, pp. 539–546 (2005). https://doi.org/10.1109/CVPR.2005.202

12. Eigen, D., Puhrsch, C., Fergus, R.: Depth map prediction from a single image using a multi-scale deep network. In: Proceedings of International Conference on Neural Information Processing Systems, vol. 2, pp. 2366–2374 (2014). http://dl.acm.org/citation.cfm?id=2969033.2969091

13. Billings, S., Taylor, R.: Generalized iterative most likely oriented-point (G-IMLOP) registration. Int. J. Comput. Assist. Radiol. Surg. **10**(8), 1213–1226 (2015). https://doi.org/10.1007/s11548-015-1221-2

14. Sinha, A., Reiter, A., Leonard, S., Ishii, M., Hager, G.D., Taylor, R.H.: Simultaneous segmentation and correspondence improvement using statistical modes. In: Proceedings of SPIE Medical Imaging 2017: Image Processing, vol. 10133, p. 101331B–8 (2017). https://doi.org/10.1117/12.2253533
15. Mao, X., Shen, C., Yang, Y.B.: Image restoration using very deep convolutional encoder-decoder networks with symmetric skip connections. In: Proceedings of International Conference on Neural Information Processing Systems, pp. 2802–2810 (2016). https://dl.acm.org/citation.cfm?id=3157412

Wide-Area Shape Reconstruction by 3D Endoscopic System Based on CNN Decoding, Shape Registration and Fusion

Ryo Furukawa[1]([envelope]), Masaki Mizomori[1], Shinsaku Hiura[1], Shiro Oka[2], Shinji Tanaka[2], and Hiroshi Kawasaki[3]

[1] Hiroshima City University, Hiroshima, Japan
{ryo-f,hiura}@hiroshima-cu.ac.jp, mizomori@ime.hiroshima-cu.ac.jp
[2] Hiroshima University Hospital, Hiroshima, Japan
{oka4683,colon}@hiroshima-u.ac.jp
[3] Kyushu University, Fukuoka, Japan
kawasaki@ait.kyushu-u.ac.jp

Abstract. For effective *in situ* endoscopic diagnosis and treatment, dense and large areal shape reconstruction is important. For this purpose, we develop 3D endoscopic systems based on active stereo, which projects a grid pattern where grid points are coded by line gaps. One problem of the previous works was that success or failure of 3D reconstruction depends on the stability of feature extraction from the images captured by the endoscope camera. Subsurface scattering or specularities on bio-tissues make this problem difficult. Another problem was that shape reconstruction area was relatively small because of limited field of view of the pattern projector compared to that of the camera. In this paper, to solve the first problem, learning-based approach, *i.e.*, U-Nets, for efficient detection of grid lines and codes at the detected grid points under severe conditions, is proposed. To solve the second problem, an online shape-registration and merging algorithm for sequential frames is proposed. In the experiments, we have shown that we can train U-Nets to extract those features effectively for three specimens of cancers, and also conducted 3D scanning of shapes of a stomach phantom model and a surface inside a human mouth, in which wide-area surfaces are successfully recovered by shape registration and merging.

1 Introduction

Endoscopic diagnosis and treatment on digestive tracts have become popular and widespread because of effectiveness on finding tumors in early-stage or little suffering on surgery. For this reason, an easy to deploy, accurate tumor size estimation technique is required for endoscopic systems and has been intensively researched. On our continuous works on the development of a 3D endoscope system to automatically measure the shape and size of living tissue based on active stereo, we made non-contact measurement systems by making ultra-small projectors which are possible to be inserted through the instrument channel of

© Springer Nature Switzerland AG 2018
D. Stoyanov et al. (Eds.): OR 2.0/CARE/CLIP/ISIC 2018, LNCS 11041, pp. 139–150, 2018.
https://doi.org/10.1007/978-3-030-01201-4_16

ordinary endoscopes [1–5]. Using those devices, we have successfully measured several *ex vivo* human tumor samples. One significant limitation of the current systems is that it easily fails to recover shapes because of strong subsurface scattering and specular effects which is common in internal tissue. Another issue is that shape reconstruction area was relatively small because of limited field of view of pattern projector compared to that of the camera of the endoscope.

In this paper, to solve the pattern detection problems caused by complicated surface reluctances, such as sub-surface scattering and specularities, we propose a learning-based approach, which is based on CNNs (convolutional neural networks). To apply CNN to oneshot scan, we used two types of U-Nets for line detections (horizontal and vertical) and code detection, since each of the tasks is simplified and easy to learn. Then, at a decoding phase, two outputs of the U-Nets from the single captured image are integrated to make the final output, *i.e.*, detected lines with ID. Using the final output, 3D shapes are reconstructed by light sectioning method using decoded IDs.

Since each region of reconstruction is small, online shape-registration and merging algorithm for sequential frames is required to recover the wide structures of the entire shape. For the purpose, we propose a shape registration and merging algorithm in the paper. In the method, we introduce RBF-based shape densifing algorithm to fill holes between grid lines. Then, ICP based registration is applied followed by incremental fusion of the shape of each frame to the global space, *i.e.*, TSDF in our technique. Final shapes are reconstructed by marching cubes algorithm.

In the experiments, a learning-based technique is evaluated by comparing several real tissues with previous techniques [5], proving the effectiveness of our method. Then, our online shape-registration and merging algorithm is applied to a shape model, *i.e.*, phantom model, of a stomach and a part of a real human body, *i.e.*, inside mouth, to show the successful results of the technique.

2   Related Work

For 3D reconstruction method using endoscopes, techniques using shape from shading (SFS) [6] or binocular stereo [7] have been proposed. However, these techniques often have stringent assumptions on the images that can be processed, or, in the case of binocular stereo, require specialized endoscopes. As an example of active stereo applications in endoscopy, in [8] a single-line laser scanner attached to the head of the scope was used to measure tissue shapes, however, the scope head needed to be directed in parallel to the target, which limited the practical applicability of the technique. Lin *et al.* proposed 3D endoscope system using colored, middle-sized circle dots [9]. Compared to their work, our system uses structured light composed of sharp lines, which can be used for accurate 3D reconstruction using light sectioning triangulation. This is important for obtaining small shape details of the target. Recently, Furukawa *et al.* extended their grid pattern based active stereo system by using DOE (diffractive optical element) with "gap coding" technique solving typical issues for endoscopic

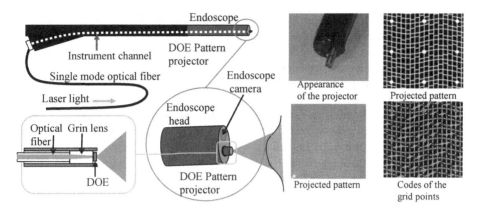

Fig. 1. The system configuration (the left image), the DOE pattern projector (the middle column), and the projected pattern (the right column). The images of the middle column are the appearance of the projector (inserted through the instrument channel) and the pattern illumination projected on a white wall. The images of the right column are the projected pattern and the codewords embedded into the pattern, where S colored in red, L in blue, and R in green. S means edges of the left and the right sides have the same height, L means the left side is higher, and R means the right is higher. (Color figure online)

systems [4,5]. This paper solves practical issues for applying the technique to real bio tissues.

For integrating multiple shapes, registering multiple shapes by ICP algorithm [10] has been a widely-used solution. Similarly, signed distance field (SDF) representation has been widely used for fusing multiple shapes [11]. Recently, Kinect-Fusion [12] integrates those methods so that online shape reconstruction can be realized, where sequentially-captured 3D shapes are incrementally registered and fused into a single model.

3   Overview

3.1   System Configuration

A projector-camera system is constructed by inserting a fiber-shaped, micro pattern projector into the instrument channel of a standard endoscope as shown in Fig. 1. For our system, we used a FujiFilm VP-4450HD system coupled with a EG-590WR scope. The DOE-based pattern projector is inserted through the instrument channel of the endoscope the projector slightly protrudes from the endoscope head as shown in Fig. 1 and emits the structured light.

The light source of the projector is a green laser module with a wavelength of 517 nm. The laser light is transmitted through a single-mode optical fiber to the head of the DOE projector. In the head, the light is collimated by grin lens, and go through the DOE. The DOE can project a fine, complex pattern at a greater depth range.

In terms of pattern design, we use a grid pattern with gapped lines, whose features are reported to be robust to blurring [4]. The pattern is shown in Fig. 1. The vertical lines of the pattern are all connected and straight, whereas the horizontal line segments are designed so that adjacent line segments have variable vertical gaps at the grid points. With this configuration, a higher-level ternary code emerges from the design with the following three codewords: S (the endpoints of both sides have the same height), L (the end-point of the left side is higher), and R (the end-point of the left side is higher). The codes of the pattern of Fig. 1 (right column, top) are shown by color in Fig. 1 (right column, bottom).

Since the vertical lines of the pattern are straight lines, we can apply light sectioning method for 3D triangulation using these lines. By using light sectioning method, we can get accurate 3D points on these lines, which is important for capturing small details of the target surface.

3.2   Algorithm Overview

We record sequence of images captured by the endoscope camera, while projecting the structured light shown in Fig. 1. Then, every image the captured sequence is analyzed to obtain shape information of the frame. The reconstructed shapes are 3D curves corresponding to the vertical lines of the grid pattern. Since the 3D curves are sparse, we convert the shape information to frame-wise depth images, then, process the depth images with the KinectFusion algorithm.

The 3D reconstruction of each frame consists of two stages, such as pattern decoding stage and 3D reconstruction stage as shown in Fig. 2. The pattern decoding stage is processed by CNNs, which are trained to extract grid-like structures, and the gap codes in the captured images. In the 3D reconstruction stage, the extracted grid structures and code information are analyzed, and the IDs of all the detected vertical lines are decided, and 3D curves are reconstructed by light-sectioning method.

For training CNNs (learning phase in Fig. 2), actual patterns are projected onto the strong subsurface scattering objects and captured by a camera. Then, correct lines and code IDs are manually given as the ground truth. It is a tough task even for humans, thus, learning data augmentations such as image translations or rotations are used to decrease the burden. Then, parameters and kernels of U-Net [13] are estimated for lines and IDs independently using deep learning framework so that cost functions are minimized. The cost function is basically a difference between an output of U-Net and the ground truth.

In the decoding phase, the captured image is first applied to CNNs for vertical and horizontal line detections. At the same time, the image is also applied to CNN for region-wise classification of local feature codes embedded into the pattern. Then, both results are combined to produce final output, *i.e.*, detected lines with estimated local codes in the pattern. By using the image with detected lines with pattern ID as the input, 3D shapes are recovered in the 3D reconstruction stage. Since a single local code is not sufficient for unique decision of correspondences, information of connectivity and the epipolar constraints are used with a voting scheme to increase robustness, similarly as [14]. Once correspondences of

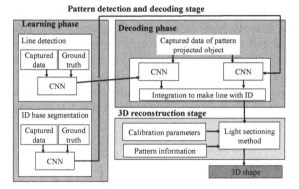

Fig. 2. Overview of CNN-based decoding and 3D reconstruction for oneshot scan. Note that we have two CNNs for vertical and horizontal line detections, and another CNN for decoding IDs of grid points.

the detected curves are retrieved, 3D shapes are reconstructed by light sectioning method.

Since many of the KinectFusion implementations require depth images, we generate depth images from the sparse 3D curves. Then, the depth images are processed by KinectFusion algorithm. Within the module, the depth images are fused to a volume, where shapes are represented as TSDF (truncated signed distance field). Once all the frames are fused into one volume, the module outputs the fused surface.

4   CNN-based Feature Detection and Decoding for Active Stereo

A major feature of the projected pattern is a grid-like structure and discrete codes given to each grid point. The grid-like structure is composed of vertical and horizontal line segments. In the pattern, a discrete feature (gap code) is attached to each of the grid point represented by the level gap between the left and right edges of the grid point. The classes of the code are either of S/L/R as shown in Fig. 1 (right column, bottom).

We extract grid-structure and gap-code information using U-Nets [13]. We use U-Nets because this network structure can use global image structures to detect local image features. Because the projected pattern has global structure of grid, we can expect U-Nets use this structure information for detecting local line features to improve performance.

4.1   Detection of Grid Structures

The training process of a U-Net for detecting vertical lines is as follows. First, image samples of the pattern-illuminated scene is collected. Then, the vertical line locations for the image samples are designated manually as curves of 1-dot widths. The 1-dot width curves such as shown in Fig. 3(b) and (d) are too sparse and narrow to be directly used as regions of training data. Thus, regions with 5-dot width of left and right side of the thin curves are extracted, and labeled as 1 and 2, respectively, as shown in Fig. 3(c) and (e). The rest of the pixels are labeled as 0. These 3 labeled images are used as training data. Then, a U-Net is trained to produce such labeled regions using the loss function of the softmax entropy between the 3-labeled training data and the 3-D feature map produced by the trained U-Net.

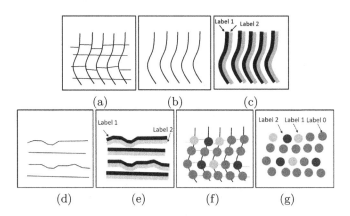

Fig. 3. Training data for U-Nets: (a) An example of captured pattern. (b) Manually annotated vertical line. (c) Manually annotated horizontal line. (d) Training labels for horizontal-line detection. (f) Manually annotated gap codes. (g) Training labels for code detection. In the training data for horizontal-line detection, the discontinuity at the grid points are intentionally connected in the training data. In the training data for code detection, background pixels are treated as "don't care" data for the loss function.

By applying the trained U-Net to the image, we can get the 3-labeled image, where left and right side of the vertical curves are labeled as 1 and 2, respectively. Thus, by extracting the 2 horizontally-adjacent pixels where the left is 1 and the right is 2, and connecting those pixels vertically, vertical curve detection is achieved.

The horizontal curve detection is achieved similarly. However, the horizontal edges may be disconnected due to the gaps at the grid points. Even in those cases, training data is provided as continuous curves that go through the center point of the gaps as shown in Fig. 3(e). By optimizing a U-Net using such training data, we can expect results where horizontal curves are detected as continuous at grid points, even if they are actually disconnected by gap codes.

An advantage of using U-Net for line detection of the grid structure is that the U-Net can be implicitly trained to use not only local intensity variation, but also more global information such as repetitive information of grid-like structures. A supporting evidence, that we have experienced is that, if we process an image sample that is scaled so that the training image set does not include the similarly-scaled images, the line-detection performance noticeably worsens.

4.2 Detection of Pattern Codes

In the proposed method, identification of gap codes is processed by directly applying U-Net to the image signal, not from the line detection results. Thus, the gap code estimation does not depend on line segment detection, which is advantageous for stable detection of gap codes. Note that such a direct method is not easy to implement by conventional image processing.

The training data generation is shown in Fig. 3 (bottom row). In the training process, the white background pixels of Fig. 3 (bottom row, right column) are treated as "don't care" regions.

The advantage of directly detecting the pattern code is that the stability of the code detection. Since, in the previous work [14], identification of gap codes have been achieved by using results of line detection, failure of line detection or failure of grid-structure analysis consequently leads to code-detection failures. The proposed method is free from such problems of sequential processing.

5 Registration and Fusing Multiple Captured Frames

For the KinectFusion implementation, we use Kinfu module of point cloud library [16]. Since this module requires depth images for inputs, we generate depth images from the sparse 3D curves.

To convert the sparse 3D curves into a dense depth image, we use Radial basis function for interpolation of the 3D curves. Radial basis function (RBF) has been a common tool for 3D shape interpolation from point sets [15]. In the case of the proposed system, we only require 2D depth map for the camera viewpoint of the frame, not a general 3D shape; thus, the problem becomes much simpler.

First, the reconstructed 3D curves are stored in 2D maps in camera view. Then, for each 3D point on the curves, a tangent plane is estimated by fitting the neighbor point set (neighbor points are defined by 2D distances on the 2D view) to a 2D plane by 2D linear regression.

Then, the tangent planes of all the curve points are fused using the weights of the radial basis function. In the proposed system we use 2D Gaussian kernel for the RBF. The resulting height function $h(x, y)$ is

$$h(x,y) = \frac{\sum_i k(x - x_i, y - y_i)\{a_i(x - x_i) + b_i(y - y_i) + z_i\}}{\sum_i k(x - x_i, y - y_i)}, \tag{1}$$

where $k(x, y)$ is an RBF kernel defined by $k(x, y) = \exp(-\frac{x^2 + y^2}{2\sigma^2})$, (x_i, y_i) is the 2D position of the i-th point in the camera view, z_i is the depth of the i-th point from the camera view, a_i and b_i are the coefficients of the tangent plane fit by the linear regression, σ is a scale parameter of RBF. In our case, we set this value to about average apparent size of the grid in captured images. We calculate the value of (1) for each pixel of the depth image.

Then, the depth images are processed by KinectFusion algorithm. We used Kinfu module of PCL (point cloud library) [16]. The view pose of the depth image is registered with the volume 3D shape represented as TSDF by ICP algorithm using depth error and normal error criterion. Then the depth data is fused into the TSDF. The fused points are extracted after all the frames are processed.

6   Experiment

6.1   Evaluation of CNN Based Line Detection

To show effectiveness of the proposed pattern-feature extraction for endoscope images, we measured specimens of cancers that are resected from patients. The appearance, captured image by the 3D endoscope, outputs of the U-Nets for line detection and code labels are shown in Fig. 4(a)–(d) respectively. The grid structures and codes that are extracted from the U-Net results are shown in Fig. 4(e). For comparison, grid-structures and codes detected by a previous method [4] are shown in Fig. 4(f). The 3D reconstruction results of this sample are shown in Fig. 4(g). Although the captured image (Fig. 4(b)) is low-resolution and includes significant noises, the extracted grid structure (Fig. 4(e)) is stable. By comparing Fig. 4(e) with Fig. 1(right column, bottom), we can confirm that the gap codes extracted by the U-Net is reasonably accurate. The manually counted code-detection error rate of Fig. 4(e) was 4.5%, whereas that of the result of baseline method [4] (Fig. 4(e)) was 18.6%. Using the decoded pattern, the 3D shape of the pattern-projected regions are mostly reconstructed as shown in Fig. 4(f).

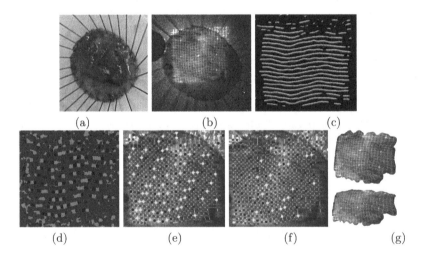

(a)   (b)   (c)

(d)   (e)   (f)   (g)

Fig. 4. Grid and code detection results for a specimen of a cancer: (a): The appearance of the sample. (b) The captured image. (c) U-Net output for horizontal-line detection. (d) U-Net output of code detection. (e) Extracted grid-structures and codes. Compare (e) with pattern codes shown in Fig. 1. The counted error rate of (e) was 4.5%. (f) Grid-structures and codes extracted by a previous method [4]. Compare (f) with Fig. 1. The counted error rate of (f) was 18.6%. (g) The reconstructed 3D shape.

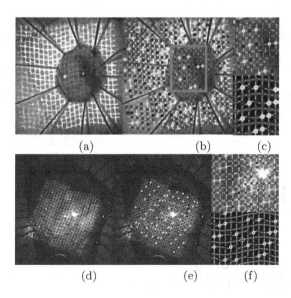

(a)   (b)   (c)

(d)   (e)   (f)

Fig. 5. Grid and code detection results for two specimens of cancers: (a, d) Captured images. (b, e) Extracted grid-structures and codes. (e, f) Magnified regions of (b) and (e), and the corresponding pattern regions.

Grid and code extraction results for other two specimens are shown in Fig. 5, where (a) and (d) are the captured images, (b) and (e) are the extracted grid and code structures, and (c) and (f) are the magnified code structures and the corresponding pattern regions. The regions of (c) and (f) are shown as cyan rectangles of in (b) and (e). The specimen of (a–c) was affected by strong subsurface scattering, however, the extracted codes were reasonably accurate. The image (d) has highly affected by highlights, and the grid structure was missing at the saturated area itself. However, the grids and codes around the saturated area became accurate enough so that the 3D shape can be successfully reconstructed. Those results confirm the stability of our feature-extraction method even if the data condition is low.

6.2   Simultaneous Localization and 3D Mapping

Then, we apply our online shape registration and merging algorithm to both a phantom model of a stomach and a part of a real human body, *i.e.*, inside a mouth. About calibration, we pre-calibrated the projector-camera system using sphere-based calibration [2].

We first captured shapes of the stomach model for evaluation purpose. Results are shown in Fig. 6. In Fig. 6(a), the area of the recovered shape from a frame of the captured sequence is shown by the red rectangle. Figure 6(b) is the captured image of the red rectangle where the grid pattern is projected to the surface. In the image, we can observe that grid lines are disconnected by the complicated shape of the surface of the model, however, curves and IDs detected

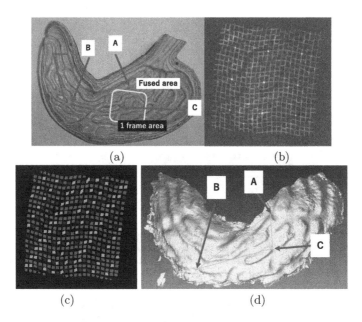

(a)   (b)

(c)   (d)

Fig. 6. An example of capturing a phantom model of a stomach: (a) The appearance of the phantom model. (b) A captured image of red rectangle in (a). (c) The CNN result of grid and code detection of (b). Compare (c) with Fig. 1. (d) Fused shape (the region of blue polygon in (a)). (Color figure online)

by our method resulting in grids and codes shown in Fig. 6(c). The integrated shape generated by the online registration and merging algorithm is shown in Fig. 6(d). We can confirm that a large area is successfully recovered as well as keeping high-frequency shape details. For quantitative evaluation, we selected three points that can be identified from shape features on the merged surface (A, B, and C in Fig. 6(d)), and compared lengths of them with the ground truth values measured from the real model (A, B and C in Fig. 6(a)). The results shown in Table 1 confirm that the scale of the shape is correct.

Table 1. Estimated and true lengths of line segments shown in Fig. 6.

Line segments in Fig. 6	Real distance	Estimated distance
$\overline{AB}$	67 mm	63 mm
$\overline{AC}$	25 mm	25 mm
$\overline{BC}$	55 mm	56 mm

Finally, we captured shapes inside a mouth of a human. A captured image, the pattern detection result, the single-frame shape from the shown image, and the final integrated shape are shown in Fig. 7. With this experiments, we can confirm that the grid-structure and codes are robustly detected even with live tissues captured by an ordinary endoscopic system. In addition, a large area is successfully recovered without losing high-frequency shape details, which are clearly observed in Fig. 7(h) where small shape details in the top (a subimage of (a)) is also shown in the right 3D CG shading results (a subimage of (d)).

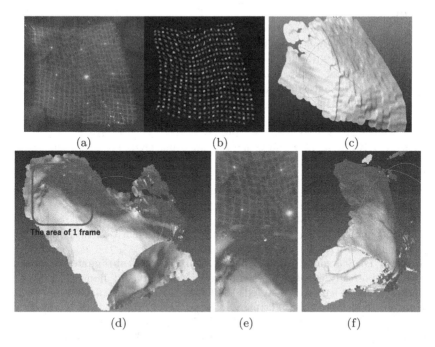

(a)   (b)   (c)

(d)   (e)   (f)

Fig. 7. An example of capturing surfaces inside a mouth: (a) A captured image. (b) The extracted grid-structures and codes of (a). Compare (b) with Fig. 1. (c) The reconstructed shape from (a). (d) The merged shape. (e) Small shape details restored by shape fusion (top: subimage of(a), bottom: subimage of (d)). (f) The merged shape from another viewpoint.

7   Conclusion

This paper proposed a CNN-based grid pattern detection algorithm for active stereo to solve pattern degradation problem caused by subsurface scattering and specularities. Two independent networks, $i.e.$ U-Nets, are constructed and trained for both line detection and code based segmentation purposes, respectively. They are integrated to retrieve robust and accurate line detection results with pattern IDs. With our experiments using several target objects with strong subsurface scattering and specular effects, the proposed method shows stable detection of the grid structure and codes that are embedded into the grid points. In addition, 3D shapes of strong subsurface scattering objects are successfully reconstructed, which is only scarcely reconstructed even with the previous technique which is designed to robust to blurring effects. In the future, $in\text{-}vivo$ experiments for test and real diagnosis purposes are important for real system.

Acknowledgment. This work was supported by JSPS/KAKENHI 16H02849, 16KK0151, 18H04119, 18K19824, and MSRA CORE14.

References

1. Aoki, H., et al.: Proposal on 3D endoscope by using grid-based active stereo. In: The 35th EMBC (2013)
2. Furukawa, R., et al.: Calibration of a 3D endoscopic system based on active stereo method for shape measurement of biological tissues and specimen. In: The 36th EMBC, pp. 4991–4994 (2014)
3. Furukawa, R., et al.: 2-DOF auto-calibration for a 3D endoscope system based on active stereo. In: The 37th EMBC, pp. 7937–7941, August 2015
4. Furukawa, R., et al.: 3D endoscope system using DOE projector. In: The 38th EMBC, pp. 2091–2094 (2016)
5. Furukawa, R., Naito, M., Miyazaki, D., Baba, M., Hiura, S., Kawasaki, H.: HDR image synthesis technique for active stereo 3D endoscope system. In: The 39th EMBC, pp. 1–4 (2017)
6. Visentini-Scarzanella, M., Stoyanov, D., Yang, G.: Metric depth recovery from monocular images using shape-from-shading and specularities. In: ICIP, Orlando, USA, pp. 25–28 (2012)
7. Stoyanov, D., Scarzanella, M.V., Pratt, P., Yang, G.-Z.: Real-time stereo reconstruction in robotically assisted minimally invasive surgery. In: Jiang, T., Navab, N., Pluim, J.P.W., Viergever, M.A. (eds.) MICCAI 2010. LNCS, vol. 6361, pp. 275–282. Springer, Heidelberg (2010). https://doi.org/10.1007/978-3-642-15705-9_34
8. Grasa, O., Bernal, E., Casado, S., Gil, I., Montiel, J.: Visual slam for handheld monocular endoscope. IEEE Trans. Medical Imaging **33**(1), 135–146 (2014)
9. Lin, J., Clancy, N.T., Stoyanov, D., Elson, D.S.: Tissue surface reconstruction aided by local normal information using a self-calibrated endoscopic structured light system. In: Navab, N., Hornegger, J., Wells, W.M., Frangi, A.F. (eds.) MICCAI 2015. LNCS, vol. 9349, pp. 405–412. Springer, Cham (2015). https://doi.org/10.1007/978-3-319-24553-9_50
10. Besl, P.J., McKay, N.D.: Method for registration of 3-d shapes. In: Robotics-DL tentative, International Society for Optics and Photonics, pp. 586–606 (1992)
11. Curless, B., Levoy, M.: A volumetric method for building complex models from range images. In: Proceedings of the 23rd Annual Conference on Computer Graphics and Interactive Techniques, pp. 303–312. ACM (1996)
12. Newcombe, R.A., et al.: KinectFusion: real-time dense surface mapping and tracking. In: 2011 10th IEEE International Symposium on Mixed and Augmented Reality (ISMAR), pp. 127–136. IEEE (2011)
13. Ronneberger, O., Fischer, P., Brox, T.: U-net: Convolutional networks for biomedical image segmentation. In: MICCAI, Springer (2015) 234–241
14. Furukawa, R., Morinaga, H., Sanomura, Y., Tanaka, S., Yoshida, S., Kawasaki, H.: Shape acquisition and registration for 3D endoscope based on grid pattern projection. In: The 14th ECCV. Volume Part VI. (2016) 399–415
15. Carr, J.C., Fright, W.R., Beatson, R.K.: Surface interpolation with radial basis functions for medical imaging. IEEE transactions on medical imaging **16**(1), 96–107 (1997)
16. Rusu, R.B., Cousins, S.: 3d is here: Point cloud library (pcl). In: Robotics and automation (ICRA), 2011 IEEE International Conference on, IEEE (2011) 1–4

Proceedings of the 7th International Workshop on Clinical Image-Based Procedures: Translational Research in Medical Imaging (CLIP 2018)

Patch-Based Image Similarity for Intraoperative 2D/3D Pelvis Registration During Periacetabular Osteotomy

Robert B. Grupp[1](✉), Mehran Armand[2,3], and Russell H. Taylor[1]

[1] Department of Computer Science, Johns Hopkins University, Baltimore, MD, USA
grupp@jhu.edu
[2] Department of Mechanical Engineering, Johns Hopkins University,
Baltimore, MD, USA
[3] Johns Hopkins Applied Physics Laboratory, Laurel, MD, USA

Abstract. Periacetabular osteotomy is a challenging surgical procedure for treating developmental hip dysplasia, providing greater coverage of the femoral head via relocation of a patient's acetabulum. Since fluoroscopic imaging is frequently used in the surgical workflow, computer-assisted X-Ray navigation of osteotomes and the relocated acetabular fragment should be feasible. We use intensity-based 2D/3D registration to estimate the pelvis pose with respect to fluoroscopic images, recover relative poses of multiple views, and triangulate landmarks which may be used for navigation. Existing similarity metrics are unable to consistently account for the inherent mismatch between the preoperative intact pelvis, and the intraoperative reality of a fractured pelvis. To mitigate the effect of this mismatch, we continuously estimate the relevance of each pixel to solving the registration and use these values as weightings in a patch-based similarity metric. Limiting computation to randomly selected subsets of patches results in faster runtimes than existing patch-based methods. A simulation study was conducted with random fragment shapes, relocations, and fluoroscopic views, and the proposed method achieved a 1.7 mm mean triangulation error over all landmarks, compared to mean errors of 3 mm and 2.8 mm for the non-patched and image-intensity-variance-weighted patch similarity metrics, respectively.

Keywords: X-ray navigation · 2D/3D registration
Periacetabular osteotomy

1 Introduction

Developmental dysplasia of the hip (DDH) is a condition with lower than normal coverage of the femoral head. Patients with DDH frequently exhibit significant discomfort and are consequently less mobile. Severe arthritis is a common

D. Stoyanov et al. (Eds.): OR 2.0/CARE/CLIP/ISIC 2018, LNCS 11041, pp. 153–163, 2018.
https://doi.org/10.1007/978-3-030-01201-4_17

long-term consequence of untreated DDH, therefore surgical treatment is expected during the lifetime of a patient [1]. The periacetabular osteotomy (PAO) is a surgical procedure designed to preserve the natural joint of young patients with DDH [2]. In order to relocate the joint and increase femoral head coverage, the acetabulum must be freed from the remainder of the pelvis by performing osteotomies along the ilium, ischium, posterior column, and pubis. Many clinicians use intraoperative fluoroscopy to manually navigate osteotomes while performing the cuts. Even with fluoroscopic guidance, the ischial and posterior osteotomies introduce the risk of joint breakage due to their closeness to the acetabulum. Furthermore, the fluoroscopic views are difficult to mentally interpret and accurate determination of femoral head coverage remains a challenge after its relocation [3]. A simulated set of PAO osteotomies with fragment movement, along with corresponding simulated fluoroscopic images, are shown in Fig. 1.

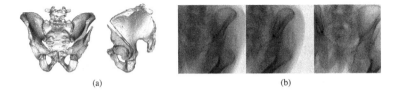

(a)   (b)

Fig. 1. A simulated example of periacetabular osteotomies and a fragment reposition is shown in (a). The corresponding simulated fluoroscopic images are shown in (b).

Leveraging optical tracker navigation systems, several computer-assisted PAO approaches have been proposed to either track the osteotomes or estimate the pose of the acetabular fragment [4–6]. These systems require the attachment of at least one rigid body fiducial to a patient's bone and, in order to perform an accurate registration of the pelvis, require a tracked pointer tool to be swept across the surface of the relevant bone structures. This requires a larger incision than typically used for PAO and eliminates the use of more modern, minimally invasive, approaches [7]. Taking into account these limitations and the prevalence of fluoroscopy use in PAO, we believe X-Ray navigation is a more prudent approach for computer-assisted navigation of osteotomes and bone fragment pose.

The pose of a patient's anatomy with respect to the fluoroscopy coordinate frame may be estimated using intensity-based 2D/3D, X-Ray/CT, registration [8]. Using multiple views, 3D points with respect to the pelvis coordinate frame may be triangulated. The motion of the fragment may be captured and reported by measuring the positions of landmarks prior to fragment relocation and afterwards. Navigation of the osteotome with respect to the pelvis is feasible by estimating the locations of an osteotome's landmarks. Most C-Arm models do not report the relative pose information of each view, therefore a fiducial object is typically used to establish a common coordinate frame and recover the multi-view geometry. By using the pelvis as a fiducial, we avoid the introduction of new objects into the surgical workflow and fluoroscopic field of view.

Many methods exist to accurately register an intact pelvis with a single X-Ray view [8], however PAO requires registration of the fractured pelvis with a relocated acetabulum. Poor triangulation performance may result from irregular mis-registrations across views, since a fractured pelvis for PAO yields an intraoperative reality that is inconsistent with the preoperative model. For example, registration of a particular view may be drawn to the pelvis fragment with iliac crest, while registration of another view may be drawn to the acetabulum. In [9,10], 2D/3D registration of fractured bone fragments was proposed, both requiring preoperative CT of the bone fragments. However, for PAO the fracture is created intraoperatively when 3D imaging is generally not available. Manual masking of the model discrepencies in 2D is time consuming and will delay the surgical workflow. By dividing the similarity computation across patches, and weighting each patch proportionally to the variance of image intensities, [11] demonstrated registrations robust to the presence of metallic objects. Since intensities corresponding to the relocated acetabular region have significant variance, this weighting is not effective for PAO pelvis registration.

In this paper, we use a preoperative weighting of 3D anatomical regions representing each region's expected contribution to an accurate registration of the fractured pelvis. Using the current estimate of the pelvis pose, this weighting is projected into 2D at each optimization iteration and, after some additional processing, applied as weights for a patched similarity metric. To the best of our knowledge, iterative adjustment of patch weightings has not been done in this way for 2D/3D registration. By treating the patch weightings as a distribution over the most useful pixels during registration, computation in early optimization iterations may be restricted to small random subsets of patches, resulting in reduced runtimes. These methods were evaluated with a simulation study accounting for various fragment shapes and movements. With respect to rotation and translation registration errors and landmark triangulation error, the methods using iteratively adjusted weights outperformed existing similarity metrics.

2 Methods

2.1 2D/3D Registration Overview

The primary objective of X-Ray/CT, single-view, single-object, rigid registration is to compute the rigid transformation between the coordinate frame of a preoperative model and the coordinate frame of the X-Ray imager. In this paper, we use an intensity-based registration approach, formulated as the optimization problem in (1). $\mathcal{S}$ represents a similarity metric between 2D images: the intraoperative fluoroscopic image, I_X, and a digitally reconstructed radiograph (DRR). DRRs are created via the projection operator, $\mathcal{P}$, which uses a 3D volume of attenuations, I_{CT}, and the volume's pose with respect to the imaging coordinate frame, θ. $\mathcal{R}$ applies a regularization in order to penalize less plausible poses.

$$\underset{\theta \in SE(3)}{\arg \min} \mathcal{S}\left(I_X, \mathcal{P}\left(I_{CT}; \theta\right)\right) + \mathcal{R}\left(\theta\right) \tag{1}$$

In this paper, we follow a multi-resolution approach, solving (1) at a low 2D resolution and using that solution as the initialization for (1) at a higher resolution. The initialization to the low resolution level is determined by a 2D/3D paired-landmark registration. We follow the approach of [12] and use the CMA-ES optimizer at the lower resolution. At the second resolution, the BOBYQA optimization algorithm is used and regularization is replaced with box constraints. The object pose is parameterized by the $\mathfrak{se}(3)$ Lie algebra with $SE(3)$ reference point at the previous estimate of the object's pose with respect to the perspective · projection coordinate frame and a center of rotation about the volume center.

In this work we only consider square shaped patches, defined by the center row, c_r, center column, c_c, and radius, r. A computation over an entire image is equivalent to computation on a single image patch with size equal to the entire image extent. The Normalized cross-correlation (NCC) similarity metric over a patch is defined in (2).

$$\mathcal{S}_{NCC}\left(I_1, I_2; c_r, c_c, r\right) = \sum_{i=c_r-r}^{c_r+r} \sum_{j=c_c-r}^{c_c+r} \frac{\left(I_1\left(i, j\right) - \mu_{I_1}\right)\left(I_2\left(i, j\right) - \mu_{I_2}\right)}{\sigma_{I_1} \sigma_{I_2} \left(2r + 1\right)^2} \tag{2}$$

Within the patch, the means of image intensities are denoted by μ_{I_1} and μ_{I_2}; σ_{I_1} and σ_{I_2} denote the corresponding within patch standard deviations. NCC assumes a linear relationship between the intensity values of each image, which is not satisfied by paired intraoperative fluoroscopy and DRRs derived from a CT with a single effective energy. Computing NCC on the Sobel X and Y derivatives of the 2D images attempts to overcome this limitation and is defined in (3).

$$\begin{aligned} \mathcal{S}_{GNCC}\left(I_1, I_2; c_r, c_c, r\right) = \; & \mathcal{S}_{NCC}\left(\nabla_X I_1, \nabla_X I_2; c_r, c_c, r\right) \\ & + \mathcal{S}_{NCC}\left(\nabla_Y I_1, \nabla_Y I_2; c_r, c_c, r\right) \end{aligned} \tag{3}$$

Computing (3) with a single patch, of size equal to the 2D image extent, shall be referred to as Grad-NCC. Calculating (3) over a set of patches distributed over the image, and combining the values in a weighted sum is shown in (4).

$$\mathcal{S}_{PGNCC}\left(I_1, I_2; P\left(r\right), w\right) = \sum_{(k,l) \in P(r)} w\left(k, l\right) \mathcal{S}_{GNCC}\left(I_1, I_2; k, l, r\right) \tag{4}$$

The set of all patch centers available within an image with patch radius, r, is defined as $P_{\text{complete}}(r)$. The similarity metric using $P_{\text{complete}}(r)$ with a constant weighting shall be referred to as P-Grad-NCC. Non-uniform patch weightings are used to emphasize that specific pixels should have more influence over the registration process. As in [11], the variances of image intensities within patches may be used as a weighting; this method will be referred to as P-Grad-NCC-Var.

2.2   Iterative Calculation of Patch Weights

An ideal weighting will have largest values at 2D locations that are both feature-rich and consistent with the preoperative model. Weights at locations expected to confound the registration will be assigned lower values. To help achieve this, we rely on a preoperative 3D labeling which divides the pelvis into regions that are expected to produce useful and model-consistent features when forward projected. A 3D weight image is computed using a manually specified lookup table defined over 3D labels. Regions about the iliac crest, pubis ramus, sacrum-ilium junction, and vertebrae are assigned large weights, while areas corresponding to the ilium wing and soft-tissue are given smaller weights. Very low weights are assigned to regions which are expected to change intraoperatively, such as the femur or any potential location on the acetabular fragment.

Several projection operations are performed using the current estimate of the pelvis pose. A mask, M, of 2D pixel locations where it is likely for a mismatch with our preoperative model to occur, is computed by casting rays and checking for collision with possible fragment or femur regions in the preoperative plan. A 2D boundary edge map of the pelvis is derived by checking for rays which intersect the intact pelvis' surface, and also have an adjacent ray not intersecting the surface. Edges overlapping with expected mismatch locations in M are pruned. Next, the edge map is dilated and pruned once more. An initial 2D weighting is produced through a maximum intensity projection of the 3D weight image. Every 2D weight value corresponding to an edge pixel is scaled by 10. This allows edge features consistent with the model to dominate the registration. Weight values at locations overlapping in M are scaled by 0.1. This effectively serves as

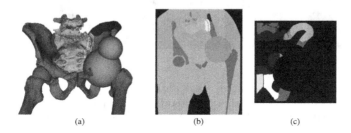

(a)   (b)   (c)

Fig. 2. The surface rendering of a preoperative set of 3D labels used for iterative weight computation is shown in (a); (b) depicts a corresponding coronal slice. The light green spheres encompass possible acetabular fragment and femoral head relocations, and are most likely to project to 2D pixels inconsistent with the preoperative model. The iliac crest, left and right pubis rami, vertebrae, ilium wing, soft-tissue, etc. are all assigned different labels, allowing for a diverse assignment of 3D weightings. An example of the 2D weights is shown in (c). In areas expected to represent a relocated acetabular fragment, the femur, soft-tissue, or air, the weightings are very low. Areas expected to contain the pubis ramus and iliac crest are weighted the largest, since we believe those features will be most helpful. Other areas, such as vertebrae are given moderate weights, since they are expected to help with registration, but not be as helpful as the iliac and pubis regions. (Color figure online)

an automatic masking of regions which are believed to be inconsistent with our preoperative pelvis model. The set of 2D weights is normalized to sum to 1.

The method employing this strategy is referred to as P-Grad-NCC-Pr. The 3D preoperative labels used throughout this paper, along with a corresponding 2D weighting, is shown in Fig. 2.

2.3   Randomly Selecting a Subset of Patches

We may treat the complete set of weightings as a categorical distribution over the available patches in an image. A subset of patches, $P'(r) \subseteq P_{complete}(r)$ may be sampled using this distribution. An updated weighting is obtained by re-normalizing the subset of original weights corresponding to the patches in $P'(r)$. Computation is restricted to patches that are perceived to contain the most useful information for registration, by iteratively calculating weightings and then sampling random patches. In order to achieve convergence, after each optimization iteration the number of patches is grown by a factor equal to the golden ratio: $(1 + \sqrt{5})/2$. Once the number of random patches exceeds the maximum number of patches in the image, the metric reverts to using all patches. Random patch sampling is only incorporated at the lower resolution level; the full set of patches is used at the second resolution level. This method using randomly selected patches is referred to as P-Grad-NCC-Pr-R. An example of randomly selected patches during a registration is shown in Fig. 3.

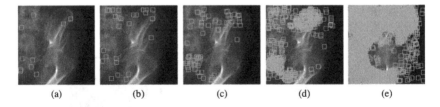

| (a) | (b) | (c) | (d) | (e) |

Fig. 3. Randomly sampled patches used during a registration. (a) iteration 1; 10 patches. (b) iteration 3; 26 patches. (c) iteration 5; 68 patches. (d) iteration 9; 466 patches. (e) iteration 17; 21,892 patches. All patches were used after iteration 17. In (a)–(d), the patches are concentrated in areas consistent with the preoperative model, and which also have strong edge features and high contrast.

2.4   Simulated Data

Simulated data is derived from pre and postoperative CT scans of a cadaveric specimen (male, 88 years), for which a PAO was performed by an experienced clinician. Initial segmentations of the preoperative pelvis and femurs were obtained through an automated method [13], and refined manually. A rigid registration was performed to map the postoperative CT to the preoperative CT. Points along each of the osteotomies in the postoperative CT were manually digitized and transformed into the preoperative coordinate frame. Planes were fit to the transformed osteotomy points to obtain a baseline set of osteotomies. The segmentation of the acetabular fragment is determined by the set of pelvis labels contained within the convex hull defined by the cutting planes. Various fragment shapes were created by randomly rotating each cutting plane normal and translating by a random amount in the updated normal direction. Collision detection against other bones was conducted to ensure randomly sampled movements of the fragment and femur were valid. Soft-tissue is incorporated into the fluoroscopic image simulation by warping fragment and femur voxels within the volume and overwriting any overlapping soft-tissue voxels. Random intensities in the HU range of muscle are used to fill any "holes" left by relocating the acetabulum and femur. Fluoroscopic images were simulated similar to the procedure described in [14]. Figure 1 shows a relocated simulated fragment, and the corresponding set of 2D fluoroscopic images.

2.5 Evaluation Metrics

Registration rotation and translation errors are reported in the perspective projection coordinate frame with center of rotation located at the true location of the volume centroid. The anatomical landmarks used for triangulation evaluation were the relocated femoral head (FH), the anterior superior iliac spine (ASIS), anterior inferior iliac spine (AIIS), greater sciatic notch (GSN), inferior obturator foramen (IOF), and the superior pubis symphysis (SPS). These landmarks are useful as they correspond to the relocated fragment and measurement of possible BB locations, or are in close proximity to possible osteotomies and the measurement of osteotome positions. For each fragment movement, the relative poses of three fluoroscopic views were estimated using pelvis registration transformations. The previous imaging world frame was replaced with the pelvis frame and each landmark position was triangulated.

3 Experiments and Results

3.1 Simulation Study Parameters

CT scans were acquired using a Toshiba Aquilion One with both 0.5 mm slice spacing and thickness, and resampled to 1 mm isotropic spacings. Using the left side of the specimen, 15 random fragments were sampled, and 20 random movements were sampled for each fragment. Three fluoroscopy images were simulated from soft-tissue volumes created for each fragment movement. The first view was initialized as an anterior-posterior view, followed by a random perturbation of the pelvis pose. To obtain the second and third views, random orbital rotations in opposite directions were applied to the first view, followed by a small rigid perturbation. This resulted in a total of 900 simulated fluoroscopy images.

Five random registration initializations were created for each fluoroscopic image by simulating a point picking process, followed by a landmark-based registration. Human error was simulated by adding random noise to each 3D landmark and to each landmark visible in the 2D image. Each initialization was used to run a registration for the following similarity metrics: Grad-NCC, P-Grad-NCC, P-Grad-NCC-Var, P-Grad-NCC-Pr, P-Grad-NCC-Pr-R. A total of 4500 total registrations per similarity metric were completed.

Simulated fluoroscopic images were 1536×1536 pixels, with $0.194 \, mm/pixel$ isotropic spacing. A source to detector distance of $1020 \, mm$ and principal point at the center of the detector were used.

For CMA-ES, a population size of 100 was used for all registrations, across all similarity metrics. Downsampling of $8\times$ was done in each 2D dimension for the CMA-ES stage and $4\times$ for the BOBYQA stage. Patches of size 11×11 pixels were used at the lower resolution level, and patches of 19×19 pixels were used at the higher resolution level. The initial number of random patches used at the lower resolution level was 10. Computation of DRRs and the Grad-NCC similarity metric were performed on the GPU. The remainder of the similarity metrics were parallelized CPU implementations. All registration trials were computed with dual Intel Xeon E5-2690 v2 CPUs and a single NVIDIA GeForce GTX TITAN Black GPU.

3.2   Simulation Study Results

Fourteen registration trials were discarded, corresponding to initialization offsets greater than 20° or 100 mm. Single-tailed Mann-Whitney U-Tests were performed to compare the errors of P-Grad-NCC-Pr and the remaining methods. Acceptance of the alternative hypothesis indicated that the errors of P-Grad-NCC-Pr were drawn from a distribution with smaller median than the errors of the other method. A p-value threshold of 0.005 was used in each test.

The rotation and translation components of the initialization and registration errors are shown in Table 1. Each similarity metric performed well with respect to rotation, all with mean rotation error angles less than 1°, however the patched similarity metrics with forward projected weights had the smallest mean rotation errors. With respect to the total rotation angle error, there was no statistical difference between P-Grad-NCC, P-Grad-NCC-Pr, and P-Grad-NCC-Pr-R, however significantly larger errors were indicated for Grad-NCC and P-Grad-NCC-Var. Most translation error was found in the depth direction (Z). The patched similarity metrics achieved the best performance with respect to mean translation errors. No statistical differences were indicated for the total translation errors of P-Grad-NCC, P-Grad-NCC-Pr, and P-Grad-NCC-Pr-R. Grad-NCC and P-Grad-NCC-Var both had statistically larger total translation errors than P-Grad-NCC-Pr.

Landmark triangulation errors are summarized in Table 2. Grouping all landmarks together, P-Grad-NCC-Pr and P-Grad-NCC-Pr-R had the smallest mean errors and were not significantly different. Considering individual landmarks except the GSN, P-Grad-NCC-Pr and P-Grad-NCC-Pr-R had the smallest mean errors. The only landmark for which a non-forward projected method did not have a significantly larger result was the GSN. ASIS and AIIS errors were larger than errors of the remaining landmarks. We believe this is due to inconsistent misalignments of the anterior iliac spine (AIS) across the views used for

Table 1. Rotation/translation offsets from ground truth. Rotation units are degrees and translation units are mm. Statistically significant results are indicated with ∗.

Component		Initialization	Grad-NCC	P-Grad-NCC	P-Grad-NCC-Var	P-Grad-NCC-Pr	P-Grad-NCC-Pr-R
Rot.	Total	$2.0 \pm 1.2*$	$0.6 \pm 0.5*$	0.4 ± 0.8	$0.7 \pm 0.9*$	0.4 ± 0.7	0.4 ± 0.7
	X	$1.1 \pm 1.0*$	$0.3 \pm 0.5*$	$0.3 \pm 0.6*$	$0.4 \pm 0.7*$	0.3 ± 0.6	0.3 ± 0.6
	Y	1.1 ± 0.9	$0.4 \pm 0.4*$	$0.2 \pm 0.5*$	$0.3 \pm 0.5*$	0.2 ± 0.4	0.2 ± 0.4
	Z	0.9 ± 0.8	0.2 ± 0.2	0.1 ± 0.3	0.2 ± 0.4	0.1 ± 0.2	0.1 ± 0.2
Trans.	Total	$13.5 \pm 10.9*$	$3.5 \pm 4.6*$	2.6 ± 5.0	$4.0 \pm 6.4*$	2.3 ± 4.6	2.3 ± 4.6
	X	$1.0 \pm 1.2*$	0.4 ± 0.5	0.3 ± 0.7	0.5 ± 0.9	0.2 ± 0.6	0.2 ± 0.6
	Y	$1.1 \pm 1.0*$	0.6 ± 0.7	$0.4 \pm 0.7*$	$0.7 \pm 0.9*$	0.4 ± 0.6	0.4 ± 0.6
	Z	$13.3 \pm 10.9*$	3.3 ± 4.6	2.5 ± 5.0	3.8 ± 6.4	2.2 ± 4.6	2.2 ± 4.6

Table 2. Landmark triangulation errors from ground truth for initialization and each similarity metric. Units are mm. Statistically significant results are indicated with ∗.

Landmark	Initialization	Grad-NCC	P-Grad-NCC	P-Grad-NCC-Var	P-Grad-NCC-Pr	P-Grad-NCC-Pr-R
FH	$6.1 \pm 6.3*$	$1.9 \pm 5.5*$	$1.6 \pm 5.3*$	$2.4 \pm 5.8*$	1.6 ± 5.6	1.6 ± 5.8
ASIS	$13.0 \pm 11.7*$	$4.7 \pm 8.5*$	$3.2 \pm 8.7*$	$3.7 \pm 8.7*$	2.9 ± 8.8	2.9 ± 8.8
AIIS	$9.5 \pm 9.2*$	$3.6 \pm 7.3*$	$2.5 \pm 7.4*$	$3.1 \pm 7.5*$	2.3 ± 7.6	2.3 ± 7.7
GSN	$5.5 \pm 4.1*$	$1.5 \pm 1.2*$	0.9 ± 1.7	$1.4 \pm 1.9*$	1.0 ± 2.0	1.0 ± 2.0
IOF	$4.1 \pm 3.1*$	$1.6 \pm 1.7*$	$1.1 \pm 2.1*$	$2.3 \pm 3.4*$	0.9 ± 1.9	0.9 ± 1.9
SPS	$4.0 \pm 3.0*$	$4.8 \pm 2.8*$	$2.0 \pm 1.8*$	$3.8 \pm 3.2*$	1.6 ± 1.5	1.6 ± 1.4
Combined	$7.0 \pm 7.7*$	$3.0 \pm 5.5*$	$1.9 \pm 5.4*$	$2.8 \pm 5.7*$	1.7 ± 5.5	1.7 ± 5.5

triangulation. Compared to the rami of the ischium and pubis, the AIS is oriented parallel to the viewing directions, causing AIS image features to have less influence on image similarity than features associated with the ischium and pubis.

The mean registration runtimes, in seconds, were 2.5 ± 0.5, 8.0 ± 0.8, 7.9 ± 0.9, 8.4 ± 2.5, 6.9 ± 3.0, for Grad-NCC, P-Grad-NCC, P-Grad-NCC-Var, P-Grad-NCC-Pr, P-Grad-NCC-Pr-R, respectively. Using random subsets of patches yields a speedup while not sacrificing performance.

4   Discussion and Conclusion

Accurate registration of the fractured pelvis during PAO is an essential component of an X-Ray navigation system for osteotomes and fragment relocations. Through simulation, we have demonstrated the feasibility of a pelvis registration which is robust to the mismatch between the preoperative pelvis model and the intraoperative fractured pelvis. Patch weightings are updated during each optimization iteration, resulting in significantly improved registration and triangulation performance compared with two existing methods. Using random subsets of patches when iteratively updating weights was shown to have equivalent performance to using all patches and also have shorter runtimes.

We believe that a careful GPU implementation of P-Grad-NCC-Pr-R should have runtimes on par, or quicker than, the runtimes of Grad-NCC. The most significant speedup could be obtained by limiting DRR computation to only pixels used by the similarity metric. At each iteration, the CMA-ES optimization evaluates a large number of objective functions, each requiring a DRR. A population size of 100 was used, resulting in $3,686,400$ pixels per iteration. In contrast, a maximum of $121,000$ pixels are required when using ten 11×11 patches; a reduction of 97% in the number of pixels. We originally used a fixed number of random patches for P-Grad-NCC-Pr-R, however this resulted in poor convergence and excessive runtimes. Analysis should be conducted to determine the optimal growth factor, and why a growth factor is necessary. Preoperative annotation and planning is time consuming, however this process may be automated by registering the preoperative CT to a statistical model. We plan to perform validation studies against fluoroscopy from cadavers which have undergone PAO.

References

1. Murphy, S.B., Ganz, R., Müller, M.: The prognosis in untreated dysplasia of the hip. A study of radiographic factors that predict the outcome. J. Bone Joint Surg. Am. **77**(7), 985–989 (1995)
2. Ganz, R., Klaue, K., Vinh, T.S., Mast, J.W.: A new periacetabular osteotomy for the treatment of hip dysplasias technique and preliminary results. Clin. Orthop. Relat. Res. **232**, 26–36 (1988)
3. Troelsen, A.: Surgical advances in periacetabular osteotomy for treatment of hip dysplasia in adults. Acta Orthop. **80**(sup332), 1–33 (2009)
4. Langlotz, F., Bächler, R., Berlemann, U., Nolte, L.P., Ganz, R.: Computer assistance for pelvic osteotomies. Clin. Orthop. Relat. Res. **354**, 92–102 (1998)
5. Murphy, R.J., Armiger, R.S., Lepistö, J., Mears, S.C., Taylor, R.H., Armand, M.: Development of a biomechanical guidance system for periacetabular osteotomy. Int J Comput Assist Radiol Surg **10**(4), 497–508 (2015)
6. Liu, L., et al.: Periacetabular osteotomy through the pararectus approach: technical feasibility and control of fragment mobility by a validated surgical navigation system in a cadaver experiment. Int Orthop **40**(7), 1389–1396 (2016)
7. Troelsen, A., Elmengaard, B., Søballe, K.: A new minimally invasive transsartorial approach for periacetabular osteotomy. J. Bone Joint Surg. Am. **90**(3), 493–498 (2008)
8. Markelj, P., Tomaževič, D., Likar, B., Pernuš, F.: A review of 3D/2D registration methods for image-guided interventions. Med. Image Anal. **16**(3), 642–661 (2012)
9. Gong, R.H., Stewart, J., Abolmaesumi, P.: Multiple-object 2-D-3-D registration for noninvasive pose identification of fracture fragments. IEEE Trans. Biomed. Eng. **58**(6), 1592–1601 (2011)
10. Joskowicz, L., Milgrom, C., Simkin, A., Tockus, L., Yaniv, Z.: FRACAS: a system for computer-aided image-guided long bone fracture surgery. Comput. Aided Surg. **3**(6), 271–288 (1998)
11. Knaan, D., Joskowicz, L.: Effective intensity-based 2D/3D rigid registration between fluoroscopic X-Ray and CT. In: Ellis, R.E., Peters, T.M. (eds.) MICCAI 2003. LNCS, vol. 2878, pp. 351–358. Springer, Heidelberg (2003). https://doi.org/10.1007/978-3-540-39899-8_44
12. Otake, Y., et al.: Intraoperative image-based multi-view 2D/3D registration for image-guided orthopaedic surgery: incorporation of fiducial-based C-arm tracking and GPU-acceleration. IEEE Trans. Med. Imag. **31**(4), 948–962 (2012)

13. Krčah, M., Székely, G., Blanc, R.: Fully automatic and fast segmentation of the femur bone from 3D-CT images with no shape prior. In: Proceedings of IEEE International Symposium on Biomedical Imaging, pp. 2087–2090 (2011)
14. Markelj, P., Likar, B., Pernuš, F.: Standardized evaluation methodology for 3D/2D registration based on the visible human data set. Med. Phys. **37**(9), 4643–4647 (2010)

.

A Mixed Reality Guidance System for Robot Assisted Laparoscopic Radical Prostatectomy

Abhishek Kolagunda[1(✉)], Scott Sorensen[1], Sherif Mehralivand[2],
Philip Saponaro[1], Wayne Treible[1], Baris Turkbey[2], Peter Pinto[2],
Peter Choyke[2], and Chandra Kambhamettu[1]

[1] University of Delaware, Newark, USA
abhi@udel.edu
[2] National Institute of Health, Bethesda, USA

Abstract. Robotic surgery with preoperative imaging data for planning have become increasingly common for surgical treatment of patients. For surgeons using robotic surgical platforms, maintaining spatial awareness of the anatomical structures in the surgical area is key for good outcomes. We propose a Mixed Reality system which allows surgeons to visualize and interact with aligned anatomical models extracted from preoperative imagery as well as the in vivo imagery from the stereo laparoscope. To develop this system, we have employed techniques to 3D reconstruct stereo laparoscope images, model 3D shape of the anatomical structures from preoperative MRI stack and align the two 3D surfaces. The application we have developed allows surgeons to visualize occluded and obscured organ boundaries as well as other important anatomy that is not visible through the laparoscope alone, facilitating better spatial awareness during surgery. The system was deployed in 9 robot assisted laparoscopic prostatectomy procedures as part of a feasibility study.

Keywords: Mixed reality · AR · VR · Robot assisted prostatectomy

1 Introduction

Robotic assisted laparoscopic surgery carried out from platforms such as the da Vinci surgical system has been widely used to treat patients. This treatment approach uses preoperative imaging for diagnosis and planning purposes. Experts in [19] emphasize that surgery is spatial manipulation, and that a system which can combine information from multiple modalities and present it in way that gives surgeons the best spatial awareness possible would be very useful. Surgeons report using preoperative imaging for surgical planning, to build a mental map of the anatomical structures. They then constantly refer to it during surgery by merging, in their mind, the current laparoscopic view and the preoperative information to make critical decisions. Our interactions with the surgeons performing

© Springer Nature Switzerland AG 2018
D. Stoyanov et al. (Eds.): OR 2.0/CARE/CLIP/ISIC 2018, LNCS 11041, pp. 164–174, 2018.
https://doi.org/10.1007/978-3-030-01201-4_18

Robot Assisted Laparoscopic Prostatectomy (RALP) revealed that pinpointing the interface of the prostate with the neurovascular bundle can be very challenging. Recognizing the ideal point of incision in the prostate-vesical junction is a difficult but critical task especially in the presence of prostate cancer at the prostatic base, or a median prostatic lobe that is outside the direct field of view. During RALP procedure, a surgeon might have to periodically step away from the robot's console and consult the preoperative MRI data to plan their next course of actions. This involves the surgeons scrolling through MRI stacks on a 2D monitor provided by picture archiving and communication (PAC) system in order to spatially orient their current position with respect to the prostate, tumor and other critical anatomy. To expedite this process and present the preoperative information to the surgeons in a more effective way, we have developed a Mixed Reality system for assisting laparoscopic radical prostatectomy.

Cohen et al. conducted a user study which indicated that augmenting preoperative data onto the surgeon's view during RALP is useful [3] at key stages of the procedure. Augmented Reality (AR) systems that combine pre-operative and intra-operative information by overlaying virtual pre-operative objects on real intra-operative scenes have received significant attention from researchers as a tool to assist surgical procedures, specially robotic assisted procedures [5,10,20]. Alignment of pre-operative and intra-operative data which forms a very critical part of such AR systems are usually prone to errors and thus can be misleading or distracting. While augmenting surface features of the organ would still be useful, visualizing the features under the surface of the organ is still challenging, and with an augmented reality system the surgeon is still limited to only a few viewing angles (defined by the position of the laparoscope) of the aligned, augmented imagery. Virtual Reality (VR) systems have been typically used to run simulation for training surgeons for robotic surgery (MDVT-Mimic da Vinci Trainer) [12,15]. VR has also been used to spectate as well as for remote guidance (VIPAR) [17] during robotic surgical procedures for training and education purposes. It has also been used as a tool to view 3D pre-operative data for diagnosis and planning purposes. While VR provides an effective framework to view and explore pre-operative data, it does not fuse pre-operative and intra-operative data thus limiting its applicability during surgery. Keeping these limitations of AR and VR in mind we have developed a Mixed Reality (MR) system which is intended to be used during surgery to guide the procedure. It is designed to supplement or replace the 2D monitors used by the surgeons periodically during the procedure for consulting pre-operative data to asses their current state and plan future actions. Augmenting the intra-operative data into the virtual environment with pre-operative data presents all the required information is the same space. The system also provides enhanced visualization and interactive abilities.

2 System Components

The proposed MR system for RALP has the following modules: **Shape Modeling**, **Stereo Reconstruction**, **Shape Registration** and **Interactive Visualization**.

Shape Modeling Module: 3D rendering and registration of the shape extracted from MRI data requires a dense and complete surface. Preoperative MRI image stacks are semi-automatically labeled by experts, giving us a series of 3D contours with low resolution in the Z-direction of the stack, but these are neither dense nor complete surfaces. To facilitate visualization and registration we model patient specific prostate shape using the hybrid shape model proposed in [13] which is a combination of Extended Superquadrics (ESQ) and Radial Basis interpolation Function (RBF). Fitting the model involves first estimating parameters of the ESQ and then using the residual error to solve for the RBF parameters. Once the model is fit, the points on the surface of the shape satisfy the equation

$$F(x, y, z)^{\frac{\epsilon_1}{2}} + G(x, y, z) = 1. \ Where, \tag{1}$$

$$F(x, y, z) = \left[\left(\frac{|x|}{a} \right)^{2/\epsilon_2} + \left(\frac{|y|}{b} \right)^{2/e2} \right]^{\epsilon_2/\epsilon_1} + \left(\frac{|z|}{c} \right)^{2/\epsilon_1} \quad and \tag{2}$$

$$G(x, y, z) = \sum_{j=1}^{N} w_j \lambda(d_j). \tag{3}$$

$G(x, y, z)$ corresponds to the RBF where λ is a Gaussian with compact support, d_j is the cosine distance of (x, y, z) from the jth RBF center, w_j is a weight associated with j^{th} RBF center. $F(x, y, z)$ corresponds to the ESQ and its parameters include size parameters (a, b, and c), and exponents (ϵ_1 and ϵ_2) which are cubic spline interpolation functions. To reconstruct the shape from the shape model parameters, we use geodesic domes based on an icosahedron that generate approximately uniformly spaced points on a sphere. These points are first projected onto the ESQ and then scaled using the RBF function. Given the points on a geodesic dome D, they are used to reconstruct the shape S as shown below.

$$S = \frac{D}{F(D)^{\frac{\epsilon_1}{2}}} \cdot (1 - G(D)). \tag{4}$$

The geodesic dome also gives us the triangular faces for constructing the mesh. The point resolution of the reconstructed shape is controlled by the dome frequency. This representation allows us to model the 3D shape of annotated MRI imagery, and quickly generate a meshed surface and point cloud of desired resolution for rendering and registration respectively.

The hybrid shape model was used to model the glands and organs but it was not best suited for vascular structures. For vascular structures like the Neuro-Vascular bundle we employ Iso-surface fitting and Poisson surface interpolation [11] to reconstruct the entire 3D surface from labeled contours. We construct a uniformly sampled 3D volume of size $L \times B \times D$ where L and B are the height and width of the MRI stack and D is the number of labeled 3D contours. The value at a voxel in the volume is set as 0 if it lies within the contour else set as the distance to the nearest in-plane contour point. An Isosurface is fit to this volume, normals are estimated at the contour points, the contour points along with their normals are transformed from image space to metric space and finally Poisson surface reconstruction is performed to recover the dense 3D surface mesh for visualization.

Stereo Reconstruction Module: The da Vinci surgical system uses a high resolution stereoscopic laparoscope which captures two images at 1280×1024 resolution. This allows for 3D reconstruction using stereo reconstruction methods. The stereo laparoscope is calibrated using Zhang's calibration method [22]. We follow the traditional shape from calibrated stereo pipeline [8], using semi-global block matching algorithm [9] for computing stereo disparity from rectified images. The reconstructed point cloud is noisy and has errors. We place a depth threshold to eliminate distant points reconstructed erroneously, then we use DBSCAN [6] to find dense clusters to remove noise and erroneous points. The processed point cloud is used as the target shape to register the preoperative shape. For visualization, we perform Delaunay triangulation of the reconstructed points in the image space to define a triangular mesh. The dense reconstructed points from stereo are connected using the computed triangular mesh, triangles that are too large or are too narrow and elongated are removed as these might correspond to discontinuities in depth. This allows us to render the stereo model as mesh with texture corresponding to the input image frames.

Shape Registration Module: To help surgeons spatially orient themselves to the surgical area, we align the shape from MRI to the surface of the prostate as seen through the laparoscope. This allows surgeons to visualize the position of the tumor and the spatial relation to other critical organs around the prostate. There have been different approaches to align preoperative data to laparoscopic data. The imaging modalities are pre-calibrated and the laparoscopic camera tracked to initially align and maintain alignment [7,21]. In these approaches, tracking can be error prone due to large camera motion and deformations of the organs. Point correspondences between preoperative and live images are used to find the transformation for alignment [16]. The lack of correspondences, occlusions and noise affects the robustness of such methods. Fiducial markers can be used for correspondences [18]. In [21], multi-modal registration technique is used. Imaging modality such as the 3D ultrasound is used in which identifying the prostate boundary is relatively easy. The two modalities are calibrated with each other, and the live camera is tracked to maintain alignment. Using fiducial markers and imaging modalities such as the 3D ultrasound might not be preferred during the surgery as they are intrusive. Su et al. [20] use manual initial alignment followed by ICP [1,2] based refinement using manually marked or automatically detected key points on the surface of the organ. This approach requires identifying key points used for alignment. In our case, when the surgeon is using the system, the anatomical structures are no longer being manipulated, and there are no active deformations of the organ that needs to be tracked. So we use the landmark free registration approach proposed in [14], which we found to work better than ICP for our data. This method requires no additional equipments, no known correspondences, and is robust to outliers and small scale non-rigid deformations. The method uses fuzzy correspondences to solve for the transformation that maximizes the overlap between the two shapes. Since the method is designed to work for point clouds, the implicit form of the shape from MRI is used to generate uniformly spaced points on the surface of the prostate. The transformation is initialized using prior knowledge of the scene; the surgeon's view of the prostate, using the standard laparoscope placement for RALP, has the apex at the top, the bladder at the bottom and the rectum behind the prostate. Once registered, the shape from MRI and the shape from stereo can be visualized in the interactive mixed reality system.

Visualization Module: We have used the Unreal Engine 4 to develop an interactive application. Within the application surgeons can view the current reconstructed stereo view, the MRI shape, and stereo shape registered to the MRI shape. Meshes are rendered using different material properties to emphasize organ differences. The prostate is rendered as a wire-frame, giving it a readily identifiable 3D shape, but also to create a form of transparency that allows the surgeon to see occluded surfaces of other organs. Other organs are rendered in contrasting colors, with specular and diffuse components to allow users to intuitively understand the 3D shape. The textured stereo model is rendered using purely emissive color so artificial shadows and shading are not a problem. The Unreal engine supports a wide variety of hardware including major head mounted device (HMD) for visualization, and supports motion controls. This means our application allows the surgeon to hold the models and manipulate it using intuitive motion controls for grabbing and manipulating. If the surgeons think that the shape alignment is incorrect they can also manually align them in the mixed reality application. The application supports standing and room scale interface, allowing surgeons to lean, physically walk around, or virtually teleport using motion controls. This allows for novel viewing points that can help the surgeons to visualize patient specific anatomy better.

3 System Evaluation

In this section we will discuss our evaluation approach for the proposed system. This includes performance evaluation, user evaluation, and a feasibility test performed by deploying the system during 9 RALP procedures. A recording system was developed that can connect to the stereo DVI output ports of the da Vinci surgical system. We have selected individual stereo pairs of key portions of the 9 procedures for our evaluation.

Shape Representation Module: The shape model is fit to MRI data offline before the procedure begins. We fit the shape model to points extracted from MRI data. A model with 294 parameters took, on average, 7.5 s to fit to the 3D points with an average error of 0.36 mm.

Stereo Reconstruction Module: We evaluated the stereo reconstruction module by reconstructing 24 video sequences of 12 frames each. The disparity range for semi global block matching algorithm was set to $[-160, 160]$. Stereo reconstruction of the laparoscope image pair, meshing of the reconstructed point cloud and noise removal takes, on average, took 10.6 s to run per frame. An image pair produces approximately 10000 to 20000 points with about 20000 to 40000 triangular faces. We only reconstruct every 5th pixel in the image which still gives us a dense enough mesh for visualization.

Shape Registration Module: We evaluated the registration scheme on data from total 9 patients. The shape registration module takes, on average, 21.5 s to align the stereo reconstructed model to the shape model from MRI. The registration process is a hierarchical approach which starts with a low resolution model of the point clouds and moves to progressively higher resolutions. We run the registration method with 2 levels of hierarchy. This was sufficient since the initialization, based on the prior knowledge of the scene, leads to good registration. For registration we used points on the stereo shape that were reconstructed from the central 40% of the image as these points mostly corresponded to the prostate. To measure the accuracy of the registration scheme, we use the cloud compare utility [4] to measure distances between the reconstructed prostate points and the aligned prostate surface from MRI. The mean error of registration was 1.45 mm. Figure 1 shows sample histogram of registration errors for one of the patients data.

Fig. 1. Shape registration accuracy: shown from left to right are, aligned prostate regions from stereo and MRI, points from stereo prostate shape color-mapped based on the distance to the prostate surface from MRI, and histogram showing the distribution of distances.

Visualization Module: Performance in mixed reality is critical as drops in frame rate can lead to nausea, and user discomfort. The shape model and stereo reconstruction can both be tuned to modify the density of the models allowing us to choose for higher quality or less computational load. We have settled on 125,000 polygons for our application, as this allows us consistent frame rate with dense looking models. Our application supports both the Oculus Rift CV1 with touch controls and the HTC Vive, and allows for standing and room-scale on both platforms. The application maintains a consistent 90 frames per second on the visualization platform, which is the maximum supported frame rate for both the Oculus Rift and the Vive. This frame rate maximizes user comfort and none of the experts reported motion sickness or any other discomfort.

User Evaluation: We presented the application to a group of 7 experts which included surgeons and radiologists. Each user was given a few minutes to move around and explore the mixed reality space and interact with the models. After having an opportunity to experiment and view the application, they were given a survey asking about their experience and preferences. After experiencing our system, every expert who was polled liked the application and felt that they could better orient themselves spatially. Many pointed out anatomical features unique to the patient that would influence how they proceed. While the system automatically aligned pre-operative and intra-operative shapes, the ability to manually align the models quickly using intuitive motion controls was also deemed useful (Fig. 2).

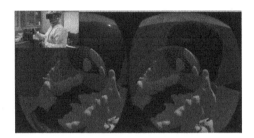

Fig. 2. A screen shot showing a surgeon interacting with the system.

Feasibility Test: The system described above was deployed during 9 RALP procedures. To our knowledge this was the first time ever such a system was used during the procedure. The imaging platform was connected to the da Vinci surgical robot through the passive DVI output ports to collect and process stereo images from the laparoscope. The Visualization platform was set up in one of the corners, away from the surgical table and close to the robot's console. The setup did not interfere with the procedure or the functioning of the robot. The stereo laparoscopes were calibrated prior to being used in the surgery. Pre-operative, segmented MRI (axial with resolution of $0.23 \times 0.23 \times 3$ mm) data was provided to us 1–5 days prior to the procedure. 3D shape of the anatomical structures were reconstructed from the labeled contours and were available for visualization before the surgery. During surgery, when the surgeon found the need to consult pre-operative data, he requested for it. Our system, then captured the current view of the surgery, performed stereo reconstruction, ran shape alignment, and then loaded the models into the mixed reality application. Once ready the surgeon interacted with the models in the virtual space to plan his/her next course of actions. During the course of a procedure, a surgeon typically used our system 4 times: (i) Before the surgery, he/she interacted with the 3D anatomical models extracted from pre-operative MRI to build a plan for the surgery. (ii) When the prostate was first visible, to re-confirm the spatial relation between critical anatomical structures. (iii) Prior to bladder neck sparing, to visualize the interface between the prostate and the bladder before separating the bladder from the prostate. (iv) Prior to apical dissection, which involves separating the prostate from the urethra. Our system took approximately 3 minutes from the time of initiating stereo image capture to being able to view the models in virtual space. This includes the time spent verifying the outputs of each module before visualizing them. The system, when run end-to-end takes less than a minute from capture to visualization. The surgeons spent approximately a minute using the application each time, during the surgery. They stated that it was easy for them to use the system and the turnaround time was quicker than anticipated. The surgeons stated that, the tool helped visualize the spatial relation between anatomical structures and orient better during the surgery.

4 Results and Discussion

Procedures in all 9 deployments of the system were successfully completed without any complications. Our system integrated into the current work-flow of the surgery by replacing/augmenting the 2D monitors and mouse interface of the PAC system with a full immersive and interactive 3D visualization that assists surgeons during surgery. The alignment of the 3D models lets them quickly localize spatially within the surgical area seen through the laparoscope and strategize on how to move forward with the procedure. The alignment proposed by our system was deemed correct for 7 patients, one of them was slightly mis-aligned which they had to correct manually and one of them had failed alignment due to inaccuracy in stereo reconstruction caused by blood/fat lodging on one of the camera's lens. During the feasibility study, on multiple occasions, the surgeon explained how the system helped him make a quick decision on the approach to take, which would not have been possible for him to do without our system. For example, in one of the cases the surgeon conducted a wider excision of the Neuro-Vascular bundles (NVB) based on the information he saw using our system that the lesion had invaded the NVB (see Fig. 3). Similarly, in another case, based on the information the surgeon saw in our system he conducted wider excision of the bladder neck (see Fig. 4). Both these pieces of information were not clear when looking at the MRI stack and the laparoscopic images separately.

One of the major criticisms of the system was that it required an external HMD and motion controllers to visualize and interact with the models. The surgeons stated that it would be more convenient if the visualization and the interaction can be done at the robot's console.

We see the advantages of using our system being two-fold. One, it helps improve patient health and two, it is a convenience for the surgeons performing the procedure. While a broader randomized study is required to evaluate the effectiveness of the system in improving patient health, the results from the feasibility study indicate that such a system would help surgeons make decisions during the procedure thus being a convenience tool. This is encouraging to continue developing and improving the system.

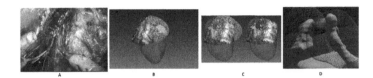

Fig. 3. (A): Surgeon's view before nerve sparing. Marked by letter N is the NVB and by letter P is the prostate gland. (B): Intra-operative and Pre-operative models aligned (White mesh: prostate, Pink: rectum). (C): Different view of the aligned models (Yellow: NVB Black: tumor). It can be seen that the tumor is extending into the NVB. (D): A close up of the model as seen in the HMD by the surgeon (Blue: urethra, Magenta: prostate, Yellow: NVB, Black: Tumor, Beige: seminal vesicle and in Pink: rectum). (Color figure online)

Fig. 4. From left to right: (1) Surgeon's view before bladder neck sparing. (2) aligned pre-operative and intra-operative models. (Magenta: prostate, Green: bladder). (3–4) Different views of pre-operative models showing tumor extending into bladder (Gray: Tumor). (Color figure online)

5   Conclusion and Future Work

We have developed a system which fuses pre-operative and intra-operative image data and presents it in a virtual 3D space for visualization and interaction using HMD and motion controllers to surgeons performing RALP. Through a feasibility study we have shown that the system could help improve spatial awareness during surgery and also help in making decisions at key stages of the procedure. To our knowledge this was the first time that such a system was deployed during RALP. Moving forward we are working towards developing a system that can integrate the visualization and interaction module into the surgical robot's console. We also wish to study the effectiveness of the system in long term patient outcome.

Acknowledgments. We would like to thank Kai Hammerich, Kaitlin Cobb, Vladimir Valera Romero, Jonathan Bloom, Gustavo Pena Lagrave, Vikram Sabarwal, Samuel Gold, Graham Hale, Kareem Rayn, Stephanie Harmon, Clayton Smith, Marcin Czarniecki and Bradford J. Wood of the National Institute of Health, Bethesda, MD, USA. They have provided valuable inputs and assistance during the development and testing of our system.

References

1. Besl, P.J., McKay, H.D.: A method for registration of 3-D shapes. IEEE Trans. Pattern Anal. Mach. Intell. **14**(2), 239–256 (1992). https://doi.org/10.1109/34. 121791
2. Chen, Y., Medioni, G.G.: Object modelling by registration of multiple range images. Image Vision Comput. **10**(3), 145–155 (1992)
3. Cohen, D., et al.: Augmented reality image guidance in minimally invasive prostatectomy. In: Madabhushi, A., Dowling, J., Yan, P., Fenster, A., Abolmaesumi, P., Hata, N. (eds.) Prostate Cancer Imaging 2010. LNCS, vol. 6367, pp. 101–110. Springer, Heidelberg (2010). https://doi.org/10.1007/978-3-642-15989-3_12
4. EDF R&D, T.P.: Cloudcompare (version 2.5.5.2)[gpl software] (2014). http://www.cloudcompare.org/
5. Edgcumbe, P., Singla, R., Pratt, P., Schneider, C., Nguan, C., Rohling, R.: Augmented reality imaging for robot-assisted partial nephrectomy surgery. In: Zheng, G., Liao, H., Jannin, P., Cattin, P., Lee, S.-L. (eds.) MIAR 2016. LNCS, vol. 9805, pp. 139–150. Springer, Cham (2016). https://doi.org/10.1007/978-3-319-43775-0_13
6. Ester, M., Kriegel, H.P., Sander, J., Xu, X., et al.: A density-based algorithm for discovering clusters in large spatial databases with noise. In: Kdd, vol. 96, pp. 226–231 (1996)
7. Gao, Q., et al.: Modeling of the bony pelvis from mri using a multi-atlas AE-SDM for registration and tracking in image-guided robotic prostatectomy. Comput. Med. Imaging Graph. **37**(2), 183–194 (2013)
8. Hartley, R., Zisserman, A.: Multiple View Geometry in Computer Vision. Cambridge University Press (2003)
9. Hirschmuller, H.: Stereo processing by semiglobal matching and mutual information. IEEE Trans. Pattern Anal. Mach. Intell. **30**(2), 328–341 (2008)
10. Hughes-Hallett, A., et al.: Augmented reality partial nephrectomy: examining the current status and future perspectives. Urology **83**(2), 266–273 (2014). https://doi.org/10.1016/j.urology.2013.08.049, http://www.sciencedirect.com/science/article/pii/S0090429513011333
11. Kazhdan, M., Hoppe, H.: Screened poisson surface reconstruction. ACM Trans. Graph. (ToG) **32**(3), 29 (2013)
12. Kenney, P.A., Wszolek, M.F., Gould, J.J., Libertino, J.A., Moinzadeh, A.: Face, content, and construct validity of DV-trainer, a novel virtual reality simulator for robotic surgery. Urology **73**(6), 1288–1292 (2009)
13. Kolagunda, A., Lu, G., Kambhamettu, C.: Hierarchical hybrid shape representation for medical shapes. In: BMVC, pp. 74–1 (2015)
14. Kolagunda, A., Sorensen, S., Saponaro, P., Treible, W., Kambhamettu, C.: Robust shape registration using fuzzy correspondences. arXiv preprint arXiv:1702.05664 (2017)
15. Perrenot, C., et al.: The virtual reality simulator DV-trainer is a valid assessment tool for robotic surgical skills. Surg. Endosc. **26**(9), 2587–2593 (2012). https://doi.org/10.1007/s00464-012-2237-0, http://dx.doi.org/10.1007/s00464-012-2237-0
16. Pratt, P., et al.: An effective visualisation and registration system for image-guided robotic partial nephrectomy. J. Robot. Surg. **6**(1), 23–31 (2012)
17. Shenai, M.B., et al.: Virtual interactive presence and augmented reality (VIPAR) for remote surgical assistance. Oper. Neurosurg. **68**, ons200–ons207 (2011)

18. Simpfendörfer, T., Baumhauer, M., Müller, M., Gutt, C.N., Meinzer, H.P., Rass-weiler, J.J., Guven, S., Teber, D.: Augmented reality visualization during laparo-scopic radical prostatectomy. J. Endourol. **25**(12), 1841–1845 (2011)
19. Solis, M.: New frontiers in robotic surgery: the latest high-tech surgical tools allow for superhuman sensing and more. IEEE Pulse **7**(6), 51–55 (2016). https://doi.org/10.1109/MPUL.2016.2606470
20. Su, L.M., Vagvolgyi, B.P., Agarwal, R., Reiley, C.E., Taylor, R.H., Hager, G.D.: Augmented reality during robot-assisted laparoscopic partial nephrectomy: toward real-time 3D-CT to stereoscopic video registration. Urology **73**(4), 896–900 (2009)
21. Ukimura, O., Gill, I.S.: Imaging-assisted endoscopic surgery: Cleveland clinic expe-rience. J. Endourol. **22**(4), 803–810 (2008)
22. Zhang, Z.: A flexible new technique for camera calibration. IEEE Trans. Pattern Anal. Mach. Intell. **22**(11), 1330–1334 (2000)

Fusion of Microelectrode Neuronal Recordings and MRI Landmarks for Automatic Atlas Fitting in Deep Brain Stimulation Surgery

Eduard Bakštein[1,2]([✉]), Tomáš Sieger[1,3], Filip Růžička[3], Daniel Novák[1], and Robert Jech[3]

[1] Department of Cybernetics, Faculty of Electrical Engineering,
Czech Technical University in Prague, Prague, Czech Republic
eduard.bakstein@fel.cvut.cz
[2] National Institute of Mental Health, Klecany, Czech Republic
[3] Department of Neurology and Center of Clinical Neuroscience,
First Faculty of Medicine, Charles University and General University Hospital,
Prague, Czech Republic
http://neuro.felk.cvut.cz/

Abstract. The deep brain stimulation (DBS) is a symptomatic treatment technique used mainly for movement disorders, consisting of chronic electrical stimulation of subcortical structures. To achieve very precise electrode implantation, which is necessary for a good clinical outcome, many surgical teams use electrophysiological recording around the assumed target, planned in pre-operative MRI images. In our previous work, we developed a probabilistic model to fit a 3D anatomical atlas of the subthalamic nucleus to the recorded microelectrode activity in Parkinson's disease (PD) patients. In this paper, we extend the model to incorporate characteristic landmarks of the target nucleus, manually annotated in pre-operative MRI data. We validate the approach on a set of 27 exploration five-electrode trajectories from 15 PD patients. The results show that such combined approach may lead to a vast improvement in optimization reliability, while maintaining good fit to the electrophysiology data. The combination of electrophysiology and MRI-based data thus provides a promising approach for compensating brain shift, occuring during the surgery and achieving accurate localization of recording sites in DBS surgery.

Keywords: Deep brain stimulation · Anatomical atlas fitting
Microelectrode recordings · Magnetic resonance imaging
Subthalamic nucleus

© Springer Nature Switzerland AG 2018
D. Stoyanov et al. (Eds.): OR 2.0/CARE/CLIP/ISIC 2018, LNCS 11041, pp. 175–183, 2018.
https://doi.org/10.1007/978-3-030-01201-4_19

1   Introduction

The deep brain stimulation (DBS) is a well established treatment method for late-stage Parkinson's disease (PD), essential tremor, dystonia and other movement disorders. It consists of surgical placement of a permanent stimulation electrode into subcortical structures and chronic electrical stimulation using a stimulator implanted commonly in the chest cavity. In order to achieve a high level of symptom suppression with low side-effects, a highly accurate positioning of the stimulation contact is necessary, yet challenging. In case of the DBS for PD, which is the main focus of this study, the most common target – the subthalamic nucleus (STN) – is around 10 mm long along its longest axis and has a relatively low contrast in pre-operative MRI scans (see Fig. 1). Moreover, the optimal stimulation target is even smaller and lies in the dorsolareral motory subregion of the STN.

A typical implantation procedure starts with a pre-operative MRI scanning, which is used for target nucleus localization and surgical planning. In order to mitigate brain shift and other inaccuracies, occurring during the surgery, most surgical teams then employ intra-operative microelectrode recording (MER) of electrophysiological activity in the vicinity of the planned target, using typically up to five parallel microelectrodes. In clinical practice, the individual MER signals are evaluated manually by a neurologist and the target nucleus is identified based on a characteristic firing pattern.

Over previous years, researchers have suggested several automatic classification methods for the MER signals, based most commonly on signal power and spectral properties of the MER, some of which got recently included into clinical software tools for microexploration [1,2]. Despite the apparent benefits these methods may have for implantation efficiency, they provide no spatial mapping of the electrophysiological findings or explicit MER localization within the nucleus, necessary for both clinical and research applications.

In our recent study [3], we presented a probabilistic model, which allows mapping of an anatomical STN atlas to the recorded multi-electrode MER directly and thus provides MER classification and localization at the same time. However, due to the inherent anisotropy and low spatial distribution of the MER (we used a common "Ben-gun" setting with 5 parallel MER trajectories, spaced 2 mm apart in a cruciform configuration, with signals recorded at steps of 0.5 mm), the MER data provide accurate information about size of the STN along the axis of the electrodes around the planned target but provide substantially less information about the shape of the STN in other anatomical directions.

In this paper, we investigate the possibilities of fusion of our previous model with additional information obtained from the pre-operative MRI imagery, by combining atlas rotation and scaling based on pre-operative MRI landmarks with additional position refinement and brain shift estimation using the MER data. We validate the properties of the extended models on a set of 27 multielectrode trajectories from 15 PD patients. As both approaches are not without limitations, we also outline the possibility to perform a complete fusion of MRI and MER data to estimate the patient-specific stn shape, as well as the brain shift directly at the same time.

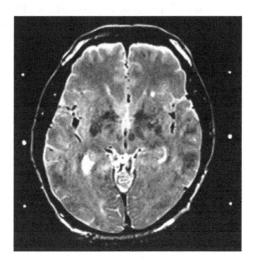

Fig. 1. Illustration of STN size and contrast in an axial slice of pre-operative T2-weighted MRI image: STN contour (red, right hemisphere) and characteristic hypointensity (green circle, left hemisphere) (Color figure online)

2   Methods

2.1   Common Definitions

Throughout this text, we use transformation vector r with 9 degrees of freedom to transform a 3D surface-based atlas into patient-specific coordinates.

$$r = [t, s, \gamma], \tag{1}$$

where $t = [t_x, t_y, t_z]$ is the translation, $s = [s_x, s_y, s_z]$ scaling and $\gamma = [\gamma_x, \gamma_y, \gamma_z]$ rotation along/around the x (medial $\rightarrow$ lateral), y (posterior $\rightarrow$ anterior) and z (ventral $\rightarrow$ dorsal) axis. We use the 3D STN atlas from [4] in a form of standard 3D triangular mesh but any surface-based STN atlas can be used as well. As a reference, we use a set of 12 characteristic STN landmark points (plus the anterior and posterior commissure: AC and PC) as in [5], which were identified by an experienced neurologist on the atlas, as well as on pre-operative MRI data of each patient.

The MER recordings are represented in the feature vector $x = \{x_1, ..., x_N\}$, recorded at corresponding spatial locations $L = \{l_1, ..., l_N\}$. The vector x consists of a single feature, the normalized signal root-mean-square of the whole MER signal (NRMS) as in [6]. For the purposes of validation, we use manual annotation of each MER signal as STN or non-STN, done by an experienced neurologist during the surgery.

2.2   Imaging-Only Method (allPoints)

As a reference, we use a method based solely on pre-operative MRI data and STN landmark points annotated therein, the *allPoints*. This method uses 12 characteristic landmarks on the STN boundaries, defined previously in [5] and coordinates of the anterior and posterior commissure. The method then finds a full 9-DOF transformation to minimize the least-square distance between the characteristic points on the atlas and in given patient's manually annotated MRI data.

2.3   Basic Electrophysiology-Only Model (nrmsCon)

This model forms the basis for the extended models below and has been presented in our previous paper [3]. Simply put, the model shifts, scales and rotates and the 3D atlas around the MER recording sites in a way that the high NRMS values are encapsulated in the STN atlas volume and the low NRMS values are excluded (owing to the higher neuron density and thus higher NRMS values inside of the STN).

In more formal terms, model assumes different distribution of NRMS values observed inside and outside of the STN (*emission probabilities*, modeled using separate log-normal distributions), and fuzzy boundaries of the STN atlas (*membership probabilities* modeled using a logistic function). These parameters form together the parameter vector $\boldsymbol{\Theta}$, which is estimated from training data. In order to fit the atlas to MER recordings of a particular patient (NRMS values $\boldsymbol{x}$ measured at locations $\boldsymbol{L}$), the model finds parameters $\boldsymbol{r}^*$, which maximize the likelihood, defined as:

$$\boldsymbol{r}^* = arg\max_{\boldsymbol{r}} \mathcal{L}(\boldsymbol{r}|\{\boldsymbol{x},\boldsymbol{L}\},\boldsymbol{\Theta}) = arg\max_{\boldsymbol{r}} p(\{\boldsymbol{x},\boldsymbol{L}\}|\boldsymbol{r},\boldsymbol{\Theta}) \tag{2}$$

where the probability of a single observation $\{x_i, l_i\}$ being in state s is given by the product of the *emission probability* and *membership probabilities*

$$p(\{x_i, l_i \in s\}|\boldsymbol{r},\boldsymbol{\Theta}) = p(x_i|l_i \in s, \boldsymbol{r},\boldsymbol{\Theta}) \cdot p(l_i \in s|\boldsymbol{r},\boldsymbol{\Theta}) \tag{3}$$

The joint probability for a single observation is then computed as a summation over both states possible states (*IN*side and *OUT*side the STN):

$$p(\{x_i, l_i\}|\boldsymbol{r},\boldsymbol{\Theta}) = p(\{x_i, l_i \in IN\}|\boldsymbol{r},\boldsymbol{\Theta}) + p(\{x_i, l_i \in OUT\}|\boldsymbol{r},\boldsymbol{\Theta}) \tag{4}$$

To compute the joint probability of the whole observation sequence of N MER, we naïvely assume conditional independence given model parameters and compute the joint probability as:

$$p(\{\boldsymbol{x},\boldsymbol{L}\}|\boldsymbol{r},\boldsymbol{\Theta}) = \prod_{i=1}^{N} p(\{x_i, l_i\}|\boldsymbol{r},\boldsymbol{\Theta}) \tag{5}$$

The maximum shift is constrained to $\pm 5\,\mathrm{mm}$ in any direction, maximum scaling to $\pm 25\%$ in each direction and rotation maximum $\pm 15°$ around each axis, the model is thus abbreviated *nrmsCon*. For more details on model structure and fitting, please refer to the aforementioned publication [3] or the thesis [7].

2.4   The Proposed Combined Model (nrmsBrainShift)

We introduce the following way to fuse the electrophysiology-based model with prior information about STN size and rotation, contained in the pre-operative MRI landmarks: In the first step, the *allPoints* landmark-based transformation is used to compute atlas scaling and rotation. Subsequently, the MER-based model described above is used to estimate the translation parameters t, and thus to estimate the brain shift. The model is also capable of additional modification of the scaling and rotation parameters, which are regularized. The probability density function for all observations from Eq. (5), is modified as follows:

$$p(\{\boldsymbol{x}, \boldsymbol{L}\}|\boldsymbol{r}, \hat{\boldsymbol{\Theta}}) = \prod_{i=1}^{N} p(\{x_i, l_i\}|\boldsymbol{r}, \hat{\boldsymbol{\Theta}}) \cdot \prod_{m \in \{s, \gamma\}} p(r_m|\hat{\boldsymbol{\Theta}})^w, \qquad (6)$$

where the additional term $p(r_m|\hat{\boldsymbol{\Theta}})$ penalizes deviation from the initial *allPoints* scaling and rotation, using likelihood of the normal distribution ($p(r_m|\hat{\boldsymbol{\Theta}}) = 1/\sqrt{2\pi\sigma_m^2} \cdot exp(-\frac{(x-r_m)^2}{2\sigma_m^2})$), centered at the initial value of given parameter r_m, with standard deviation σ_m estimated from the training data and stored in the extended parameter vector $\hat{\boldsymbol{\Theta}}$. The exponent w represents a weighting parameter, which can be used to set the trade-off between MER-based ($w \to 0$) and MRI-based ($w \to \infty$) fitting. We evaluated the results for $w \in \{0, 0.01, 0.025, 0.05, 0.1, 0.25, 0.5, 1\}$.

2.5   Performance Evaluation

In order to estimate the out of sample performance of the proposed method and due to the relatively small sample size (in terms of whole patient sets), we employed the leave one subject out (LOSO) procedure. In each iteration we kept one subject's data (maximum two 5-electrode trajectories for bi-laterally implanted patients) for model fitting and evaluation, while all other data were used to obtain the parameters $\boldsymbol{\Theta}$.

To compute performance metrics, we use two approaches:

(i) **Machine-learning metrics** where we count the number of STN MER recordings (according to expert MER labels), correctly encapsulated in the atlas volume at the final position (true positives), or falsely excluded from the atlas volume (false negatives). True negatives and false positives are computed analogously from the non-STN labeled MERs. Standard performance measures are calculated: sensitivity, specificity and accuracy.

(ii) **Evaluation of transformation parameters**, obtained from the tested model, compared to least-squares transformation of the atlas to the STN landmark points in the pre-operative MRI data of given patient (see the *allPoints* method below). Here, we assume that the pre-operative data provides accurate information about the rotation and scaling of the atlas, but does not provide a good estimate of the translation vector t due to the non-negligible brain-shift.

3 Results and Discussion

3.1 Collected Data

For validation of the method, we use a dataset from 27 explorations in 15 PD patients with complete 3D information and another 9 explorations from 4 patients without information on spatial recording locations, used in the training phase to estimate Θ (or $\hat{\Theta}$) only. But was excluded from validation. Altogether, we used 175 electrode trajectories and 4538 recorded MER signals from 19 PD patients.

Table 1. Classification results (LOSO validation-set)

Method	w	Accuracy	Sensitivity	Specificity
		Mean (sd)	Mean (sd)	Mean (sd)
allPoints		78.7 (8.7)%	44.6 (19.8)%	92.3 (4.9)%
nrmsCon		88.0 (5.3)%	68.3 (14.6)%	95.6 (5.4)%
nrmsBrainShift	0	88.3 (5.4)%	69.8 (14.1)%	95.5 (5.6)%
	0,1	86.6 (5.4)%	60.7 (15.0)%	96.6 (3.2)%
	1	86.4 (5.7)%	60.6 (15.1)%	96.4 (3.4)%

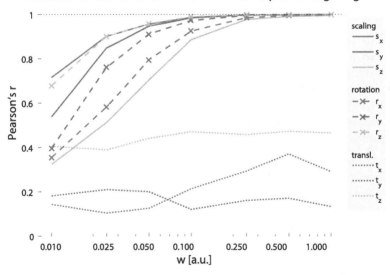

Fig. 2. Evaluation of the dependency of the proposed *nrmsBrainShift* method on the weighting parameter sigma, by computing Pearson's correlation coefficient for each transformation parameter with the reference *allPoints* method for varying values of the weighting coefficient w. Note that the translation parameters t_x, t_y, t_z are not penalized and are thus unaffected by the value of w.

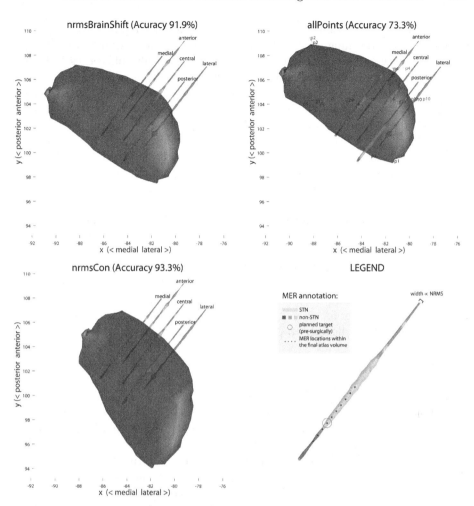

Fig. 3. Examples of model fit using the proposed *nrmsBrainShift* method (left), fusing electrophysiology data with MRI landmarks, the MRI-landmark-only *allPoints* method (center) and the electrophysiology-only *nrmsCon* (right) on data from patient No. 5 (right STN). The final STN atlas position after fitting is shown in purple, width of the five microelectrode trajectory cylinders denotes the NRMS value, while colors denote manual labels: STN in yellow, non-STN in grey. MER positions inside the resulting model are denoted by black points, planned target by red o. The *nrmsBrainShift* method provides an anatomically more reasonable fit at the cost of slightly lower accuracy. (Color figure online)

3.2   Fitting Results

The classification results on validation data is shown in Table 1. Although the electrophysiology-based *nrmsCon* achieves much better fit to the electrophysiology data, than the MRI-based *allPoints* method, there was almost no correlation of the scaling and rotation parameters with the reference *allPoints* method. As we assume the prevailing source of inaccuracy during surgery to be due to displacement, rather than deformation, we expected the only differences in terms of shift/translation. On the presented dataset, the *nrmsCon* model achieved the pre-set optimization constraints (min/max scaling and rotation) in 47 cases, which accounted for more than 30% of the fits (and 19 out of 27 trajectories). The method apparently leads to overfitting, providing good classification at the cost of diverging from anatomically reasonable transformation.

In contrast, the newly proposed combined *nrmsBrainShift* technique achieved only slightly lower classification accuracy, while maintaining reasonable transformation - a fact illustrated also in the Fig. 2.

The impact of the weighting coefficient on divergence from anatomically relevant location is illustrated in Fig. 3. While high values of w lead to a highly constrained fit, where the only changes are in the translation parameters, low values of w lead to more flexible fit to the MER data at the cost of lower veracity of the transformation. Comparing the properties to the Table 1, it is clear that increasing w towards one leads to only a minor drop in classification accuracy, and a more marked drop in sensitivity. Overall, the sensitivity is the most problematic parameter for all methods, which is likely due to the inability of the model to adapt more flexibly to patient-specific STN shapes.

4   Conclusion

While the previously published electrophysiology-only *nrmsCon* model [3] proved electrophysiology-based fitting feasible, a subsequent detailed investigation revealed strong overfitting with too harsh model transformation, leading to unlikely results.

Fortunately, the proposed model using the pre-operative landmarks to initialize (and potentially constrain) the fitting, achieves comparable accuracy - i.e. ability to correctly contain STN-labeled MER locations - while maintaining anatomically accurate scaling and rotation. The main drawback of the method is thus in the necessity to identify the 12 landmark points in pre-operative data. We believe, that similar probabilistic framework could be used for direct automatic fusion of pre-operative MRI data, which would eliminate the need for the manual landmark labelling and increase the ability of the model to adapt to inter-individual differences in STN shape.

Overall, the fusion of pre-operative MRI data with electrophysiology provides a promising option for increasing accuracy of electrode localization both intra-operatively, as well as during offline evaluation in research studies on DBS mechanisms and STN physiology.

Acknowledgement. The work presented in this paper was supported by the Czech Science Foundation (GACR), under grant no. 16-13323S and by the Ministry of Education Youth and Sports, under NPU I program Nr. LO1611. The work of Daniel Novak was supported by the Research Center for Informatics project no. CZ.02.1.01/0.0/0.0/16_019/0000765.

References

1. Zaidel, A., Spivak, A., Shpigelman, L., Bergman, H., Israel, Z.: Delimiting subterritories of the human subthalamic nucleus by means of microelectrode recordings and a Hidden Markov Model. Mov. Disord. **24**(12), 1785–1793 (2009)
2. Thompson, J.A., et al.: Semi-automated application for estimating subthalamic nucleus boundaries and optimal target selection for deep brain stimulation implantation surgery. J. Neurosurg. 1–10 (2018, in press)
3. Bakštein, E., Sieger, T., Novák, D., Růžička, F., Jech, R.: Automated Atlas fitting for deep brain stimulation surgery based on microelectrode neuronal recordings. In: Proceedings of the World Congress on Medical Physics and Biomedical Engineering 2018, pp. 105–111 (2019)
4. Krauth, A., Blanc, R., Poveda, A., Jeanmonod, D., Morel, A., Szekely, G.: A mean three-dimensional atlas of the human thalamus: generation from multiple histological data. NeuroImage **49**(3), 2053–2062 (2010)
5. Sieger, T., et al.: Distinct populations of neurons respond to emotional valence and arousal in the human subthalamic nucleus. Proc. Nat. Acad. Sci. U.S.A. **112**(10), 3116–3121 (2015)
6. Moran, A., Bar-Gad, I., Bergman, H., Israel, Z.: Real-time refinement of subthalamic nucleus targeting using Bayesian decision-making on the root mean square measure. Mov. Disord. **21**(9), 1425–1431 (2006)
7. Bakstein, E.: Deep brain recordings in Parkinson's disease: processing, analysis and fusion with anatomical models. Doctoral thesis, Czech Technical University in Prague (2016)

Preoperative Planning and Simulation Framework for Twin-to-Twin Transfusion Syndrome Fetal Surgery

Jordina Torrents-Barrena[1](✉), Rocío López-Velazco[1], Narcís Masoller[2],
Brenda Valenzuela-Alcaraz[2], Eduard Gratacós[2], Elisenda Eixarch[2],
Mario Ceresa[1], and Miguel Ángel González Ballester[1,3]

[1] BCN MedTech, Universitat Pompeu Fabra, Barcelona, Spain
jordina.torrents@upf.edu

[2] Fetal i+D Medicine Research Center, BCNatal - Center for Maternal-Fetal
and Neonatal Medicine (Hospital Clínic and Hospital Sant Joan de Déu),
Institut Clínic de Ginecologia, Obstetricia i Neonatologia, Institut d'Investigacions
Biomèdiques August Pi i Sunyer, Universitat de Barcelona, and CIBER-ER,
Barcelona, Spain

[3] ICREA, Barcelona, Spain

Abstract. Twin-to-twin transfusion syndrome (TTTS) is a complication of monochorionic twin pregnancies in which arteriovenous vascular communications in the shared placenta lead to blood transfer between the fetuses. Selective fetoscopic laser photocoagulation of abnormal blood vessel connections has become the most effective treatment. Preoperative planning is thus an essential prerequisite to increase survival rates for severe TTTS. In this work, we present the very first TTTS fetal surgery planning and simulation framework. The placenta is segmented in both magnetic resonance imaging (MRI) and 3D ultrasound (US) via novel 3D convolutional neural networks. Likewise, the umbilical cord is extracted in MRI using 3D convolutional long short-term memory units. The detection of the placenta vascular tree is carried out through a curvature-based corner detector in MRI, and the Modified Spatial Kernelized Fuzzy C-Means with a Markov random field refinement in 3D US. The proposed TTTS planning software integrates all aforementioned algorithms to explore the intrauterine environment by simulating the fetoscope camera, determine the correct entry point, train doctors' movements ahead of surgery, and consequently, improve the success rate and reduce the operation time. The promising results indicate potential of our TTTS planner and simulator for further assessment on clinical real surgeries.

Keywords: Twin-to-twin transfusion syndrome
Fetal surgical planning and simulation · MITK
Computer vision · Deep learning

Equally contributing authors: Jordina Torrents-Barrena implemented the novel research algorithms, and Rocío López-Velazco designed and developed the framework.

D. Stoyanov et al. (Eds.): OR 2.0/CARE/CLIP/ISIC 2018, LNCS 11041, pp. 184–193, 2018.
https://doi.org/10.1007/978-3-030-01201-4_20

1   Introduction

Twin-to-twin transfusion syndrome (TTTS) is a rare and fatal condition that affects around 10–15% of monochorionic twin pregnancies between 16–26 weeks of gestation. This syndrome is caused by the presence of small anastomoses in the placenta vasculature that let the twins exchange an unbalanced blood flow [1]. The most effective treatment of severe TTTS is fetoscopic laser photo-coagulation and it consists in closing blood vessels connecting the twins. Nevertheless, in up to 33% of operated pregnancies, some inter-twin vascular connections remain open causing a recurrence of the TTTS [1].

TTTS surgery is very complex and risky because of several constraints to the fetal clinical setting. Firstly, the placenta position, size and shape greatly varies between pregnancies. Secondly, there is a tiny space to move the fetoscope and the field-of-view is limited. Thirdly, the exact localization of the vessels to coagulate is usually not known ahead of surgery [2]. If the surgeon is not able to reach and coagulate all the anastomoses, reentry in a different point is not allowed (*i.e.*, one-shot procedure), as it is associated with high mortality [1]. Hence, the choice of the entry point is the most critical factor of the intervention as it directly affects the fetoscope maneuverability and the possibility to reach all the anastomoses.

Prenatal evaluation of placental abnormalities is mainly performed by Ultrasound (US) B-scan and Doppler images. US allows fast assessment of the fetus and appears to be safe when following clinical guidelines. TTTS diagnosis can also benefit from fetal magnetic resonance imaging (MRI), which offers outstanding visualization of both the fetal anatomy and its tissue characterization. However, it has limited availability and does not provide complete real-time imaging although dynamic sequences can be acquired [3]. The registration and fusion of MRI with real-time US can therefore be of interest in prenatal diagnosis of targeted anastomoses during the laser ablation therapy.

Related Work. The work proposed by [4] illustrated the feasibility of planning the TTTS preoperative phase with MRI and computerized volume rendering. Authors studied and rendered the anatomy of each amniotic cavity and fetus, the umbilical cord insertions and the location of the inter-twin membrane in relation to the port placement. The optimum port entry point was calculated, as well as the length and angle required to reach the target region. However, authors did not implement a user-specific application to provide real functionality and visualization. Also, they did not segment the placenta vasculature which plays a key role in TTTS fetal surgery. The presented study was not validated quantitatively as the 3D reconstructions were performed almost manually.

Contribution. In this paper we present the first TTTS planning software oriented to clinical use. Novel computer vision and deep learning algorithms are integrated to create a 3D model of the womb including the placenta and its vascular tree, and the umbilical cord of both twins, extracted from MRI and 3D US. The fetoscope entry point is estimated taking into account the cord insertions located on the placenta surface. Our framework is also capable to simulate the movements of the fetoscope and the camera visualization to explore the entire placenta volume. Therefore, our TTTS planning software can aid fetal surgeons to know more about the intrauterine environment (*i.e.,* placental vascular tree, boundary between the vascular hemispheres), determine a suitable entry point, train the fetoscope movements before the intraoperative phase, and consequently, successfully improve the performance rate and reduce the surgery time.

2   Methods

The TTTS surgical outcome depends greatly on choosing the right entry point so that all the anastomoses can be individuated and properly coagulated. To plan the ideal insertion point, we developed an application to load MRI and 3D US images and create a personalized 3D model of the mother uterus. It also provides tools to explore the best entry point and simulate the surgeons' fetoscope movements, calculating the probability that all the targets can be favorably reached. The following subsections describe our software (see Fig. 1).

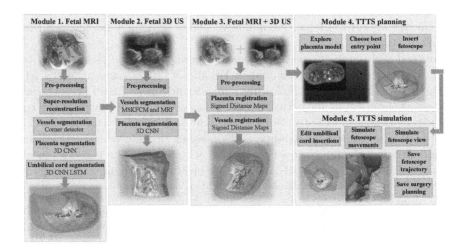

Fig. 1. Modules of our TTTS preoperative planning and simulation framework.

Module 1. Fetal MRI. The acquisition of 3D MRI is challenging in fetal setting because maternal respiratory motion and fetal movements cause motion artifacts between individual slices. To reduce this effect, we acquire several stacks for the whole womb in axial, sagittal and coronal views. Those stacks are resampled to $0.75 \times 0.75 \times 3.5\,mm^3$, normalized, denoised and fused together using a super-resolution reconstruction method [5].

Once the MRI is reconstructed a 3D Convolutional Neural Network (CNN) [6] to automatically segment the placenta is defined as follows:

$$f(\left[\mathbf{v}, \{s^{(j)}\}_{j \in A}\right]; \theta) = f_{out} \circ f_L \circ ... \circ f_2 \circ f_1 \circ f(\left[\mathbf{v}, \{s^{(j)}\}_{j \in A}\right]; \theta_1), \quad (1)$$

where ∘ denotes the composition operator, θ represents the CNN parameters, and the output is a binary value indicating whether the voxel belongs to the placenta or not. Each network layer in Eq. 1 contains a set of filters, with each filter being defined by:

$$\mathbf{x}(l+1) = f_l(\mathbf{x}(l); \theta_l) = \sigma(\mathbf{W}_l^\top \mathbf{x}(l) + \beta_l), \tag{2}$$

where $\sigma(.)$ represents a non-linearity, $\mathbf{W}_l$ and β_l denote the weight and bias parameter, and $\mathbf{x}(1) = \left[\mathbf{v}, \{s^{(j)}\}_{j \in A}\right]$. The last layer L of the model in Eq. 1 produces a response $\mathbf{x}(L+1)$, which is the input for $f_{out}(.)$ that contains two output nodes, where layers L and out are fully-connected. The training of the model minimizes the binary cross entropy loss.

Small vessels are also quite difficult to recognize in MRI scans, because the size of their lumen is close to the spatial resolution limit of the images. We apply the corner definition (*i.e.*, high intensity variations in all directions due to the amniotic fluid and the placenta texture) to efficiently recognize peripheral vessels, since they appear as dark and non-tubular areas attached to the placenta surface [6]. To detect corners, our method finds the extrema of the Gaussian curvature, which is the product of the minimum and maximum values of the local curvature estimated from the following partial derivatives [7]:

$$K = \frac{I_x^2(I_{yy}I_{zz} - I_{yz}^2) + 2I_xI_{xz}(I_yI_{yz} - I_zI_{yy}) + cycl.(x, y, z)}{I_x^2 + I_y^2 + I_z^2}, \tag{3}$$

where I_u and I_{uv} denote the first and second partial derivative w.r.t u and $u, v \in \{x, y, z\}$, respectively, of image $I(x, y, z)$, and *cycl. (x, y, z)* stands for a cyclic permutation of the coordinates.

To extract the umbilical cord a 3D CNN similar to [8] and Eq. 1 is also implemented. The motivation behind the addition of a Long Short-Term Memory (LSTM) recurrent model is to explore the spatial dependences across adjacent MRI slices and learn image features that capture the global (and intricate) anatomical structure of the umbilical cord. Hence, three main phases define our recurrent network: a down-sampling step, a recurrent component and an up-sampling step. The former deploys four convolutional layers with 5^3 volumetric kernels followed by a rectified linear unit (ReLU) and 2^3 max-pooling operations. The recurrent mechanism extracts global features that capture the spatial changes of the MRI slices and compensates the max-pooling reduction. The last up-sampled stage is based on four convolutional layers followed by ReLU and several feature map concatenation modules (that combines both the up-sample layer output and the parallel feature extraction). The final segmentation is obtained by a soft-max function.

Module 2. Fetal 3D US. The US volumes are down-sampled to $128 \times 128 \times 64$, in which the central part (more information) is preserved.

We also adopt a 3D CNN architecture [9] to segment the placenta. The down-sampling path operates at different resolutions via three convolutional layers with 5^3 kernels and PReLu non-linearities. The up-sampling path enlarges the spatial resolution of the feature maps to gather and assemble information. Residual functions are employed to gather fine details and improve the model convergence. The final output is converted to a binary segmentation using a soft-max function. A multiple refinement is subsequently applied to reduce the false positives. An automatic thresholding is computed as the mean of the voxel values in the original US weighted by its gradient image. Afterwards, a morphological closing operation eliminates isolated dark voxels to refine the placental boundary. A 2D slice-by-slice filter is employed to detect and remove unconnected structures associated to smallest non-placenta regions.

Regarding the placental vascular tree, three different classes are considered to fully describe the intrauterine environment. The darkest voxels stand for blood vessels, placenta cavities, amniotic fluid and acoustic shadows. The gray voxels apply to the various mother and fetus tissues. Finally, the brightest voxels correspond to bone and gases. The goal is to identify the structures linked to the darkest voxels to further extract the peripheral blood vessels only. The unsupervised classification is automatically done via the Modified Spatial Kernelized Fuzzy C-Means (MSKFCM) [10]. We initialize three MSKFCM centroids using a Kd-tree based K-means estimator. Each mean represents the statistical distribution of intensity values in the voxels associated to different uterus tissues. To refine the resulting fuzzy segmentation, a maximum a posteriori Markov random field (MRF) [11] is employed. The Mahalanobis distance is iteratively updated to measure the distance between each voxel in the original US to a set of known classes provided by the MSKFCM labeled image. The initial MSKFCM mask is provided as MRF input to guarantee an accurate segmentation of the vessels.

Module 3. Fetal MRI + 3D US. Registration of fetal MRI and 3D US is challenging due to several factors such as the choice of a suitable similarity measure (*i.e.*, the relationship between MRI and US intensities is difficult to express), the artefacts existent in US acquisitions (*i.e.*, acoustic shadows, attenuation and reverberations), among others.

To overcome some of these issues, we directly register the output segmentation mask of the placenta in MRI and 3D US. Once the placenta is aligned, we employ the same transformation to register the placenta vasculature. Because of its large field-of-view we select the MRI image modality as fixed volume and the 3D US as moving volume. More specifically, we employ a *Danielsson* mapping [12] to compute the signed distance field for the placenta output segmentation mask in MRI. Such filter returns: (1) a signed distance map with the approximation to the euclidean distance, (2) a voronoi partition, and (3) a vector map relating the current voxel with the closest point of the closest object to this voxel. Afterwards, the same mapping is performed on the 3D US mask of the placenta. A BSpline transformation is subsequently computed to register both image modalities (the mask and the original image for placenta). Finally, identical transformations are applied for the placental vasculature co-registration.

Module 4. TTTS Planning. Once the personalized model of the patient is obtained, we provide several functionalities to virtually place the fetoscope into the mother's womb. The fetal MRI was clinically selected as the most relevant image modality to plan the surgery due to its large anatomical field-of-view.

A fetoscope mesh was previously generated via 3DSlicer[1] using the plug-in IGT-CreateModels. The original direction of this mesh is named $d_{original} = (0, 0, -1) = (d_{ox}, d_{oy}, d_{oz})$, and its length $meshLength$.

A multi-planar widget initializes the axial, sagittal and coronal views and the 3D model. The clinician places two points in an axial slice: the entry (p_{entry}) and target (p_{target}) points. Both points create a new directional vector named $d_{planning}$ (see Eq. 4). Following 3D classical linear algebra, we apply a rotation transform to place the mesh following $d_{planning}$.

$$d_{planning} = p_{entry} - p_{target} = (d_{px}, d_{py}, d_{pz}) \tag{4}$$

At this point, we need to solve a system of equations where the rotation axis and the angle α are both unknown variables. The rotation axis is calculated by the cross product of $d_{original}$ and $d_{planning}$ (see Eq. 5):

$$d_{original} \times d_{planning} = |d_{original}| \cdot |d_{planning}| \cdot \sin\alpha = \begin{bmatrix} x & y & z \\ d_{ox} & d_{oy} & d_{oz} \\ d_{px} & d_{py} & d_{pz} \end{bmatrix} \tag{5}$$

where the rotation angle can be isolated as $\alpha = \dfrac{\arccos\left[\dfrac{(d_{px} \cdot d_{ox} + d_{py} \cdot d_{oy} + d_{pz} \cdot d_{oz})}{\sqrt{(d_{px}^2 + d_{py}^2 + d_{pz}^2)}}\right]}{\frac{\pi}{180}}$.

Afterwards, the mesh is translated to $p_{target} - d_{planning} \times meshLength$, so that the tip of the fetoscope reaches the destination point. At this point, it is essential to know the anatomical constraints (i.e., range of movement of the fetoscope) derived from the insertion point of the fetoscope into the uterus. The rotation point is finally computed automatically from the intersection between the vector $d_{planning}$ and the uterus mesh through an oriented bounding box (OBB) tree [13]. The rotation point will be used in the simulation module.

Furthermore, the interface of this module gives the clinician the opportunity to eliminate and edit both the p_{entry} and p_{target} points.

Module 5. TTTS Simulation. The fetoscope insertion is simulated using two different 3D render windows (see Fig. 4). One allows the clinician to explore the registered 3D model being the main reference space. The other offers an intrauterine visualization provided by the virtual camera located at the tip of the fetoscope mesh. The simulation reproduces a real clinical intervention.

The aforementioned virtual environment is implemented in VTK[2]. A new *vtkRenderWindow* interactor is deployed in the second render window to enable the mouse navigation. By clicking the left button of the mouse, the interactor captures its position on the display, and returns a rotation transform that will move the fetoscope mesh to the desired direction.

More specifically, the proposed method takes into account three references: the center of the VTK render window, the clicked point and the rotation point

---

[1] 3DSlicer: https://www.slicer.org.
[2] The Visualization Toolkit (VTK): https://www.vtk.org.

(see Fig. 2). These points located on the display are converted to world coordinates into the 3D scene. These world coordinates allow us to compute iteratively the rotation needed to move the fetoscope in the scene. We take advantage of the previous Eqs. 4 and 5 to calculate this transform, where $\boldsymbol{d}_{original} = \boldsymbol{d}_{center}$ and $\boldsymbol{d}_{planning} = \boldsymbol{d}_{mouse\_clicked}$.

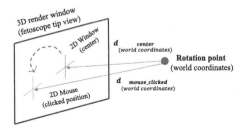

Fig. 2. Simulation scheme to show the computation of the fetoscope rotation.

In addition, the simulation interface offers the following functionalities: (1) show the range of movement of the fetoscope using a virtual cone, (2) highlight the area of the placenta that can be reached from the planned insertion point, (3) record the trajectory of the fetoscope, (4) show or hide the umbilical cord insertions on the placenta surface, and (5) save the TTTS surgical planning.

3   Experimental Results

Database. An in-house database provided by the Hospital Clínic de Barcelona was used according with its Ethical Research Committee and the current legislation. MRI and 3D US scanning of 12 monochorionic twin pregnancies between 25–37 gestational weeks were collected using a *Siemens MAGNETOM Aera 1.5T* (Fat Saturated (FS): 1.5, Echo Time (TE): 98 ms and Repetition Time (TR): 1200 ms). Each fetus had several MRI volumetric data in different views (axial, sagittal and coronal) with slice dimension 256×208, slice thickness 3.5 mm, and voxel spacing 1.4^2 mm^2. The 3D US scanning were collected using a GE Voluson E10 (GE Healthcare, Milwaukee, WI, USA) with a curved electronic matrix 4D probe transducer.

Programming Environment. The software uses proven open source technology such as VTK, ITK[3], MITK[4], and Qt[5]. Supplementary programming languages (*i.e.*, C++, Python and Bash Shell scripting) and libraries (*i.e.*, Tensorflow[6]) are also used to implement the aforementioned segmentation and registration algorithms. The experimentation was executed on an Intel Core i7 2.60 GHz, 16 GB of RAM with Fedora 24 and a NVIDIA GeForce GTX Titan X.

---

[3] The Insight Segmentation & Registration Toolkit (ITK): https://itk.org.
[4] The Medical Imaging Interaction Toolkit (MITK): http://mitk.org/wiki/MITK.
[5] Qt framework: https://www.qt.io.
[6] Tensorflow library: https://www.tensorflow.org.

Experiments. Module 1 and 2 are quantitatively tested using the following metrics (see Table 1): Dice and Jaccard coefficients, Area under ROC (AUC), Sensitivity, and Specificity. A heterogeneous set of images from different placenta positions and twin pregnancies is used to cover a real clinical environment.

Results are accurate (see Table 1) although some regions inside the uterus (*i.e.*, fetal tissues) possess a texture similar to that of the placenta and for this reason some non-placenta pixels are misclassified. There is room for further improvement in the case of blood vessels extraction. The color Doppler modality has been a great support to validate 3D US placental vasculature segmentation. So far, the MRI/3D US registration assessment has been done clinically by taking advantage of the surgeons' anatomical knowledge. More work is required to accurately fuse the registered vessels.

Table 1. Performance measures (*i.e.*, Dice, Jaccard, AUC, Sensitivity and Specificity) for placenta, vessels and umbilical cord segmentation methods from MRI and 3D US.

Modality	Segmentation	Dice	Jaccard	AUC	Sensitivity	Specificity
MRI	Placenta	0.75 ± 0.11	0.63 ± 0.07	0.80 ± 0.08	0.67 ± 0.12	1.0
	Vessels	0.85 ± 0.06	0.73 ± 0.10	0.88 ± 0.06	0.77 ± 0.10	1.0
	Umbilical cord	0.79 ± 0.03	0.71 ± 0.02	0.82 ± 0.07	0.71 ± 0.03	0.86 ± 0.05
3D US	Placenta	0.88 ± 0.07	0.79 ± 0.10	0.94 ± 0.03	0.90 ± 0.07	0.98 ± 0.02
	Vessels	0.79 ± 0.05	0.66 ± 0.08	0.84 ± 0.03	0.73 ± 0.07	0.99

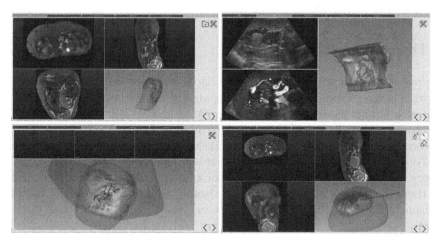

Fig. 3. User interface of the proposed TTTS planning and simulation software (*from left to right* and *up to down*): (1) Module 1: Fetal MRI, (2) Module 2: Fetal 3D US, (3) Module 3: Fetal MRI + 3D US, and (4) Module 4: TTTS planning.

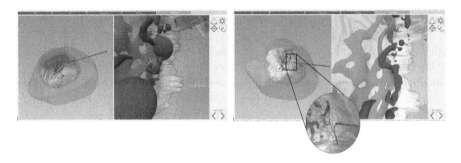

Fig. 4. User interface of Module 5 (*from left to right*): (1) reference and fetoscope camera scenes with both umbilical cord insertions (purple), and (2) reference and fetoscope camera scenes with cone illumination and fetoscope trajectory (black). (Color figure online)

Figures 3 and 4 show the interface and tools of the proposed TTTS surgical planning and simulation framework. We performed a usability trial with a post-test questionnaire to gauge what doctors think about our application. Two different expert surgeons successfully tested the software and reported clinical feedback. Both agreed on the clear visualization of the 3D anatomical models, as well as the comfortable user-experience provided by the current functionalities. Nevertheless, they agreed on the importance of simulating the laser burn to know exactly the already coagulated vessels. A fixed orientation of the uterus in all tabs with respect to the patients' position was also required to avoid a reference-free navigation.

4   Discussion and Conclusion

We present the first TTTS surgery planning and simulation software. State-of-the-art computer vision and deep learning algorithms are integrated together to generate a full 3D model of the womb from MRI and 3D US. The movements of the fetoscope and the camera visualization used to examine the mother uterus are also simulated through an intuitive and easy-to-use user interface. Hence, the main objective of the presented application is to enable doctors ahead of TTTS surgery by knowing the correct entry point of the fetoscope, the movements and the estimation of an approximate trajectory that will traverse the vascular hemisphere. In short, this software aims to increase the success rate and survival of both twins.

The proposed framework is validated on a set of 12 (monochorionic) twin pregnancies between 25–37 weeks of gestation. Dice coefficients of 0.75 ± 0.11, 0.85 ± 0.06 and 0.79 ± 0.03 are achieved for placenta, vessels and umbilical cord segmentation from MRI, respectively. Similarly, Dice coefficients of 0.88 ± 0.07 and 0.79 ± 0.05 are obtained for placenta and its vasculature from 3D US, respectively. Nevertheless, there is room for further improvement. Although

MRI/3D US placenta registration is assessed under anatomy experience of doctors, the fidelity of the resulting 3D model needs to be improved. In near future, we will investigate how the current simulation module can mimic the laser ablation of placental vessels as well as the fetoscope motion constraints in order to be as realistic as possible. In addition, several 3D reference markers regarding the patients' position and orientation are required to improve the user experience. We are also planning to move soon in the clinical evaluation phase.

Acknowledgments. This work was supported by CELLEX Foundation and the Google Women Techmakers scholarship awarded to Jordina Torrents-Barrena. Also this work was funded by the Spanish Ministry of Economy and Competitiveness under the María de Maeztu Units of Excellence Programme [MDM-2015-0502].

References

1. Papanna, R., et al.: Histologic changes of the fetal membranes after fetoscopic laser surgery for twin-twin transfusion syndrome. Pediatr. Res. **78**, 247–255 (2015)
2. Pratt, R., Deprest, J., Vercauteren, T., Ourselin, S., David, A.L.: Computer-assisted surgical planning and intraoperative guidance in fetal surgery: a systematic review. Prenat. Diagn. **35**, 1159–1166 (2015)
3. Luo, J., et al.: In vivo quantification of placental insufficiency by BOLD MRI: a human study. Sci. Rep. **7**(3713), 1–10 (2017)
4. Luks, F.I., Carr, S.R., Ponte, B., Rogg, J.M., Tracy Jr., T.F.: Preoperative planning with magnetic resonance imaging and computerized volume rendering in twin-to-twin transfusion syndrome. Am. J. Obstet. Gynecol. **185**(1), 216–219 (2001)
5. Kuklisova-Murgasova, M., Quaghebeur, G., Rutherford, M.A., Hajnal, J.V., Schnabel, J.A.: Reconstruction of fetal brain MRI with intensity matching and complete outlier removal. Med. Image Anal. **16**, 1550–1564 (2012)
6. Ceresa, M., et al.: Surgical planning system for twin-to-twin transfusion syndrome fetal surgery. In: Proceedings of the 31st International Conference on Computer Assisted Radiology and Surgery, pp. S100–S101 (2017)
7. Monga, O., Benayoun, S.: Using partial derivatives of 3D images to extract typical surface features. Comput. Vis. Image Underst. **660**, 171–189 (1995)
8. Torrents-Barrena, J., et al.: LSTM fully convolutional neural networks for umbilical cord segmentation in TTTS foetal surgery planning. In: Proceedings of the 32nd International Conference on Computer Assisted Radiology and Surgery (2018)
9. Milletari, F., Navab, N., Ahmadi, S.-A.: V-Net: fully convolutional neural networks for volumetric medical image segmentation. In: Proceedings of the 4th International Conference on 3D Vision, pp. 565–571 (2016)
10. Castro, A., Boveda, C., Arcay, B.: Comparison of various fuzzy clustering algorithms in the detection of ROI in lung CT and a modified kernelized spatial fuzzy c-means algorithm. In: Proceedings of the 10th Information Technology and Applications in Biomedicine (2010)
11. Moussouris, J.: Gibbs and Markov random systems with constraints. J. Stat. Phys. **10**(1), 11–33 (1974)
12. Danielsson, P.-E.: Euclidean distance mapping. Comput. Graph. Image Process. **14**(3), 227–248 (1980)
13. Gottschalk, S., Lin, M.C., Manocha, D.: OBBTree: a hierarchical structure for rapid interference detection. In: Proceedings of the ACM SIGGRAPH Conference on Computer Graphics, pp. 171–180 (1996)

Automatic Teeth Segmentation in Cephalometric X-Ray Images Using a Coupled Shape Model

Andreas Wirtz[1,2(✉)], Johannes Wambach[1], and Stefan Wesarg[1,2]

[1] Fraunhofer IGD, Fraunhoferstr. 5, 64283 Darmstadt, Germany
{Andreas.Wirtz,Stefan.Wesarg}@igd.fraunhofer.de
[2] Interactive Graphics Systems Group, TU Darmstadt, 64283 Darmstadt, Germany

Abstract. Cephalometric analysis is an important tool used by dentists for diagnosis and treatment of patients. Tools that could automate this time consuming task would be of great assistance. In order to provide the dentist with such tools, a robust and accurate identification of the necessary landmarks is required. However, poor image quality of lateral cephalograms like low contrast or noise as well as duplicate structures resulting from the way these images are acquired make this task difficult. In this paper, a fully automatic approach for teeth segmentation is presented that aims to support the identification of dental landmarks. A 2-D coupled shape model is used to capture the statistical knowledge about the teeth's shape variation and spatial relation to enable a robust segmentation despite poor image quality. 14 individual teeth are segmented and labeled using gradient image features and the quality of the generated results is compared to manually created gold-standard segmentations. Experimental results on a set of 14 test images show promising results with a DICE overlap of 77.2% and precision and recall values of 82.3% and 75.4%, respectively.

Keywords: Coupled shape model · Automatic segmentation
Cephalometric dental X-ray image

1 Introduction

Radiographic images are a common tool used for diagnosis in dentistry. They support the dentist in identifying many teeth related problems. Caries, infections and bone abnormalities would be hard or impossible to detect during visual inspection only. This allows the dentist to choose the optimal treatment plan for the patient. There exist two categories of dental radiographic images: intra-oral and extra-oral [9]. Intra-oral images are obtained inside the patient's mouth and only show specific regions of the set of teeth or individual teeth. They are mostly used to get more detailed information. Extra-oral images like cephalograms or

D. Stoyanov et al. (Eds.): OR 2.0/CARE/CLIP/ISIC 2018, LNCS 11041, pp. 194–203, 2018.
https://doi.org/10.1007/978-3-030-01201-4_21

panoramic radiographs capture the entire teeth region as well as the surrounding areas and provide fundamental information about the teeth of a patient.

Cephalometric analysis aims to extract this fundamental information from lateral cephalometric images. Therefore, several different landmark positions on soft tissue, dental or bony structures have been defined and identified in the image. The type and number of landmarks varies between different analysis methods (e.g. Steiner, Schwarz, Ricketts). Linear and angular measurements are computed based on the relative position of these landmarks. Figure 1 shows an example for a cephalometric analysis using different landmarks.

Several methods for automatic landmark detection in lateral cephalograms have been proposed in the past. In 2014[1] and 2015[2], Wang et al. [9] organized two Grand Challenges at the International Symposium on Biomedical Imaging (ISBI) on this topic and compared the performance of state-of-the-art methods. The best results were achieved by approaches utilizing Random Forests for classifying the intensity appearance of different landmarks while exploiting the spatial relations between landmarks using statistical shape models. Lindner et al. [6] presented a fully automatic landmarks annotation (FALA) where Random Forest regression-voting is used for both the detection of the skull and the localization of individual landmarks. Recently, Arik et al. [1] employed a convolutional neural network to detect landmarks and a statistical shape model to refine the landmark potions.

Despite all these efforts, the detection of these landmarks is still done manually or semi-automatically in the clinical context which is a very time consuming process [6]. Moreover, most of the presented approaches rely on the publicly available dataset from the ISBI 2015 Grand Challenge [9] which is composed of 400 images and features 19 landmarks positions. However, these 19 landmarks only include two dental landmarks, namely the incisal edge of the maxillary and mandibular central incisor (upper and lower incisal incision). Other dental landmarks like the root tip of the central incisors, the tip of the mesiobuccal cusp of the first molar or the posterior point of occlusion are not included and therefore not covered by these approaches.

To fill this gap, we propose an approach for fully-automatic teeth segmentation in these lateral cephalograms. To the best of our knowledge, there does not exist any other automatic segmentation method for teeth in cephalometric radiographs. The generated segmentations can later be used to support the identification of the dental landmarks by directly using the detected teeth contours of the corresponding teeth. Furthermore, the model could be extended to include more structures like bones or skin to further support the identification of additional landmarks and increase the robustness of the detection. Teeth segmentation in cephalograms is a challenging task. The lateral cephalogram is a projection of the patients skull onto a 2-D image plane from a lateral position which results in overlapping structures. This is especially evident in the teeth region. Asymmetries between the teeth on the left and right hemisphere

---

[1] http://www-o.ntust.edu.tw/~cweiwang/celph/.

[2] http://www-o.ntust.edu.tw/~cweiwang/ISBI2015/challenge1/.

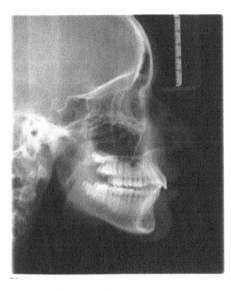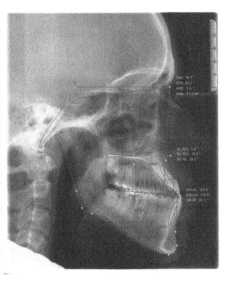

Fig. 1. An example of a lateral cephalogram (left) and the result of a manual cephalometric analysis (right).

of the patients like shape variations or different spatial configurations as well as variations in the head position of the patient during image acquisition result in duplicate structures. Like other radiographs, cephalograms also suffer from intensity variations, noise or low contrast.

To overcome these challenges, in this paper an approach for the automatic segmentation of teeth in lateral cephalometric radiographs using a coupled-shape model is presented. 14 individual teeth (excluding wisdom teeth) are segmented and labeled using a coupled shape model approach based on [10]. The 2-D coupled model combines the statistical knowledge about the shape of each tooth with information about their spatial relation. This combination of gradient image features (bottom-up information) with a priori statistical knowledge about the shape and position of the teeth (top-down information) leads to a more robust segmentation process [7], especially in case of poor image quality or unreliable image features. However, when local search algorithms like active shape models are used to find suitable image features, statistical models highly depend on a good initialization [4]. To solve this problem, we present a pre-processing step that will compute the required parameters like position and scale for the initialization of the model. The initialized model is then adapted to the cephalometric images using a step-wise adaptation process.

2   Methods

2-D Coupled Shape Model. The presented segmentation method is based on a coupled shape model consisting of individual deformable model items which are

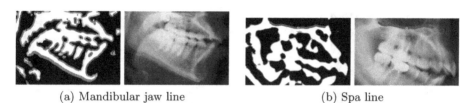

(a) Mandibular jaw line   (b) Spa line

Fig. 2. Extraction of the two lines used for the approximation of the orientation of the occlusal plane. The left image in (a) and (b) depicts the contours found in the binary image. The colors indicate different line segments after contour splitting. The thick green and red line represent the detected jaw-line and spa-line, respectively. (Color figure online)

coupled by their spatial relation. It has already been successfully used on 3-D CT images in order to segment different structures in the head & neck area [8] and for teeth segmentation in 2-D panoramic radiographs, where it was combined with a convolutional neural network to handle the initialization [10]. The individual 2-D deformable model items are represented as statistical shape models and are generated using a point distribution model (PDM) [2] and principal component analysis (PCA). The contour of an individual item is hereby represented by 100 landmark points in form of the 2-dimensional pixel coordinates. During PCA, only the principal components describing 95% of the shape variation are kept. Additionally, each individual item also contains its relative position in relation to the center of mass of the complete model, described by an affine 2-D transformation. The coupled model is then created by combining all individual items, each one containing its shape information and its relative position. For more details about the 2-D coupled shape model, please refer to [10].

The coupled shape model used in this approach contains 14 individual teeth, namely the central and lateral incisors, the canine, first and second pre-molar and first and second molar, both maxillary and mandibular for the right hemisphere of the patient. The reason for only using the teeth of one hemisphere of the patient and not the complete set of 28 teeth is the lateral position the image is captured from. The teeth on both hemispheres will by roughly superimposed onto each other during image acquisition. However, the teeth are never perfectly superimposed but rather sightly shifted (mostly in horizontal direction), resulting in duplicated structures with a high overlap. Since the value and direction of the shift between the two hemispheres are arbitrary for each individual image, no meaningful statistical information will be gained by using the full set of 28 teeth. Wisdom teeth have not been included in the model due to the limited amount of training data available. The coupled model was trained based on a set of 14 manually annotated lateral cephalometric images.

Model Initialization. A robust initialization of the mean model in terms of position and scale is required in order to adapt the model to the image features and segment the teeth successfully. Estimates for both of these values are computed from the input image. Additionally, the orientation of the occlusal plane is

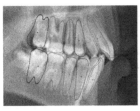 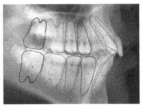 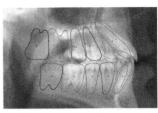

(a) Successful init.   (b) Successful init.   (c) Failed initialization

Fig. 3. Results of the automatic initialization process which estimates position, rotation and scale of the mean model. In example (c) the scale estimation was incorrect.

estimated and considered during model initialization. As a first step, histogram equalization and normalization are applied to the input image to ensure a similar brightness and contrast among all images. Then, several references are extracted from the image.

The estimation of the orientation of the occlusal plane is based on the mandibular jaw line and a line close to the anterior nasal spine (spa). Both are extracted from a binarized version of the input image using a contour segmentation based on the detection of zero crossings of the Laplacian of Gaussian (Log) (cf. Grau et al. [3]). The set of closed contours is split into parts based on the curvature of individual line fragments. The sought-after lines can then be extracted based on their length and orientation (see Fig. 2). The orientation of the occlusal plane is approximated by the orientation of the bisecting-line of those two lines.

The initial position of the mean model is determined by finding the tip of the central incisors. The region of interest (RoI) is restricted using the previously detected lines. After applying a binary thresholding (Otsu) to the RoI, predefined starting positions are used to analyze the contour of the binary mask and detect the target points. A rough approximation of these tip points is sufficient for a good initial model position. In order to estimate the scale factor for the initialization, the size of individual teeth in the input image is approximated. A reference line is defined using the previously determined position of the incisors as an anchor point in combination with the approximated orientation of the occlusal plane. Individual teeth are then separated similar to the approach of Jain and Chen [5]. Integral projection is used to compute the sum of pixel values along lines perpendicular to the reference line. The 'gaps' between teeth can be detected by analyzing these sum for local minima. After removing outliers, the scale factor for the initialization is computed by comparing the detected distances to the known distances of the mean model.

Model Adaptation. After the initializing the model in terms of position, rotation and scale, the model is adapted to the input image. The adaptation is done by minimizing an energy functional:

$$E(f,t) = E_{ext}(f,t) + \lambda E_{int}(f) \tag{1}$$

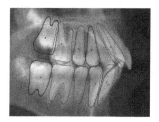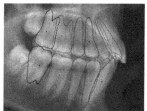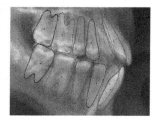

Fig. 4. Three examples of successful segmentation results.

Hereby, E_{ext} is the external energy which is responsible for ensuring that the contour of model items moves in the direction of strong image features. E_{int} is the internal energy which restricts the model to stay within or close to the learned configuration space. t stands for the transformation describing the global position of the model and f for the vector describing the configuration of the coupled model. A gradient descent optimizer is used for the optimization process. The transformation parameters t are optimized first, and then the configuration and transformation parameters f, t are optimized jointly. Please refer to [10] and [8] for more information.

A multi-step approach is used to adapt the model to the image features which are gradient features computed on the input image. Thereby, the size of the set of model items which are actively adapted to the input image is progressively increased. This is done to ensure the best possible overlap between a model item and the corresponding teeth in the image before adapting the respective model item. All model items which are not actively matched to image features are only passively modified through the learned statistical information. Initially, only the incisors are adapted since they are used for the model initialization and therefore always have a good overlap. The teeth farther away from the incisors (e.g. molars) might, at that point, not match as good, depending on the patient's configuration of the teeth (cf. Fig. 3(b)). By adapting these teeth during a later adaptation step, they have already been (passively) moved closer to their correct position and more reliable image features can be found. Starting from the central incisors, a new category of teeth (i.e. lateral incisor, canine, first pre-molar, and so on) is added after each adaptation step until the complete set of teeth is actively adapted. The final step of the adaptation process is a refinement step. Here, the contour of the individual teeth is only adpated based on the gradient features and no longer restricted by the statistical information. The final segmentation result of each individual tooth is stored as a binary image.

3   Experiments and Results

The presented fully-automatic segmentation approach has been evaluated on a separate test set of 14 manually annotated cephalometric images (referred to as gold-standard segmentations). These 14 images were not part of the training set.

Table 1. The mean plus standard deviation, minimum and maximum values for different metrics used for comparing the segmentation results of the 12 successful cases to manually created gold-standard segmentations.

	Precision	Recall	Accuracy	Specificity	F-score	DICE
Mean	0.823	0.754	0.813	0.852	0.782	0.772
Std. Dev.	±0.058	±0.070	±0.038	±0.029	±0.057	±0.057
Min.	0.683	0.728	0.754	0.795	0.688	0.679
Max.	0.912	0.914	0.862	0.912	0.848	0.840

The test images have a resolution of either 1800×2148 pixels or 1935×2400 pixels. As a first step, it was visually inspected if the model was positioned, rotated and scaled correctly by the automatic initialization process since the quality of the final segmentation highly depends on a good initialization. Visual inspection was used because the multi-step adaptation approach only requires a good overlap of certain structures. The initial position was considered to be correct, if the incisor teeth of the mean model are overlapping with the incisor teeth in the input image. This was the case for all 14 test cases. The rotation of the model was regarded as correct if the orientation of the occlusal plane of the initialized mean model and the orientation of the occlusal plane of the teeth in the image are roughly the same. This was also true for all 14 test instances. The scale estimate was considered to be correct if the size of the scaled mean model roughly matches the size of the set of teeth in the input images. This estimation was sufficiently accurate for 12 out of the 14 test cases. For the two failed cases, the initial size of the model was too large. While the incisor teeth are still positioned correctly, the molar teeth are far away from their intended position. Even with the multi-step adaptation process, the model was unable to segment the teeth successfully in these cases. Figure 3 shows two correct and a failed initialization. The incorrect scale factor was caused by an incorrect separation of the teeth based on the integral projection, i.e. some teeth were not separated at all. Therefore, the reference values extracted from the image were too large, resulting in a too big scale factor for the model.

The final teeth segmentations of the 12 cases with a successful initialization have been compared to manually created gold-standard segmentations and evaluated in terms of the following metrics: precision, recall, accuracy, specificity, f-score and dice overlap. Since both specificity and accuracy consider the amount of background-pixels that have been correctly labeled as background (true-negatives), the evaluation needs to be restricted to a smaller region to retrieve meaningful results. Therefore, the evaluation is only performed on the minimum bounding box that covers both automatic- and gold-standard segmentation. The metric values for an individual test instance are computed by first calculating the values for each tooth separately. Then, these values are averaged over all teeth in that test instance. Finally, the average is computed over the remaining 12 instances. Table 1 shows the average metric values as well as minimum

Table 2. Average metric values for individual teeth of the lower jaw. Tooth number correspond to the following teeth: 1 = second molar, 2 = first molar, 3 = second premolar, 4 = first premolar, 5 = canine, 6 = lateral incisor, 7 = central incisor.

	tooth_1	tooth_2	tooth_3	tooth_4	tooth_5	tooth_6	tooth_7
Precision	0.855	0.896	0.940	0.828	0.774	0.825	0.780
Sensitivity	0.823	0.855	0.790	0.761	0.754	0.683	0.636
Accuracy	0.824	0.864	0.859	0.796	0.805	0.845	0.821
Specificity	0.822	0.874	0.946	0.847	0.845	0.930	0.915
F-score	0.837	0.874	0.854	0.785	0.758	0.746	0.695
Dice	0.829	0.865	0.846	0.776	0.747	0.736	0.686

Table 3. Average metric values for individual teeth of the upper jaw. Tooth number correspond to the following teeth: 1 = second molar, 2 = first molar, 3 = second premolar, 4 = first premolar, 5 = canine, 6 = lateral incisor, 7 = central incisor.

	tooth_1	tooth_2	tooth_3	tooth_4	tooth_5	tooth_6	tooth_7
Precision	0.819	0.787	0.903	0.877	0.829	0.767	0.647
Sensitivity	0.712	0.821	0.844	0.805	0.776	0.679	0.613
Accuracy	0.765	0.767	0.846	0.807	0.806	0.820	0.760
Specificity	0.830	0.706	0.849	0.807	0.836	0.894	0.833
F-score	0.757	0.798	0.871	0.836	0.797	0.717	0.623
Dice	0.749	0.788	0.860	0.825	0.786	0.707	0.611

and maximum values for each category. Exemplary segmentation results are depicted in Fig. 4.

The metric values for individual teeth of the upper provided in Table 3, the ones for the lower jaw are provided in Table 2.

4   Discussion

The presented approach uses a coupled shape model to segment teeth in lateral cephalograms. The statistical knowledge about the shape and spatial configuration of the teeth is useful to handle the challenges of cephalometric images, like overlapping structures, noise low and contrast. Instead of only relying on image information, the a prior knowledge about the teeth helps to guide the search for suitable image features. The proposed initialization process provides robust estimates in terms of model placement and rotation. Only the scale estimation leaves room for improvement as it failed in 2 out of 14 cases, making a successful adaptation impossible. To the best of our knowledge, this is the first approach that successfully performs automatic teeth segmentation in lateral cephalograms.

Wisdom teeth have not been included in the model at the moment. There exists a high variation in their position and shape in between individual patients and not all patients have some or all wisdom teeth. With the limited amount data available, a meaningful shape model and estimate of their spatial position could not be computed. Wisdom teeth can be added in a future version of the model when sufficient training data is available.

From experience with other data modalities, we know that the approach is able to handle missing teeth, if the space originally occupied by the missing tooth is present. In that case, the mean shape model of the corresponding tooth can be placed into the gap and subsequent teeth can be positioned correctly. However, subsequent teeth will be labeled incorrectly if the gap is too small or no longer present. In the current test set, no patient was missing any teeth except for wisdom teeth. Overall, the presented approach provides promising segmentation results on a test set of 14 images.

Based on the segmentation result, a robust identification of dental landmarks for the cephalometric analysis should be possible. Moreover, many of the references extracted from the image for the model initialization can also be used to identify other landmarks. The statistical model can furthermore easily be extended to include additional structures like skin and bones to further improve the robustness of the segmentation and provide references for even more cephalometric landmarks.

5   Conclusion and Future Work

In this paper an automatic model-based approach for teeth segmentation in lateral cephalograms was presented. It provides a robust segmentation of the teeth and is an good basis for identifying dental landmarks for cephalometric analysis. Out of a set of 14 test images, 12 could be segmented successfully. For the 2 unsuccessful cases, the initialization of the model failed due to incorrect scale estimation. The achieved average DICE overlap is 77.2%. Average precision and recall values are 82.3% and 75.4%, respectively.

Future work includes increasing the robustness of the scale estimation for initialization and improving the segmentation accuracy. The amount of training data could be extended based on the data from the 2015 ISBI Grand Challenge on cephalometric landmark detection. However, manual labeling of all these images would be required. Most importantly, the approach is to be extended to identify the dental landmarks based on the segmentations and potentially other landmarks as well.

Acknowledgements. We thank Dr. Jan H. Willmann, University Hospital of Düsseldorf for providing the cephalometric images used in this work.

References

1. Arik, S., Ibragimov, B., Xing, L.: Fully automated quantitative cephalometry using convolutional neural networks. J. Med. Imaging **4**, 1–11 (2017)
2. Cootes, T.F., Taylor, C.J., Cooper, D.H., Graham, J.: Training models of shape from sets of examples. In: Hogg, D., Boyle, R. (eds.) BMVC92, pp. 9–18. Springer, London (1992). https://doi.org/10.1007/978-1-4471-3201-1_2
3. Grau, V., Alcaiz, M., Juan, M., Monserrat, C., Knoll, C.: Automatic localization of cephalometric landmarks. J. Biomed. Inform. **34**(3), 146–156 (2001)
4. Heimann, T., Meinzer, H.P.: Statistical shape models for 3D medical image segmentation: a review. Med. Image Anal. **13**(4), 543–563 (2009)
5. Jain, A.K., Chen, H.: Matching of dental X-ray images for human identification. Pattern Recognit. **37**(7), 1519–1532 (2004)
6. Lindner, C., Wang, C.W., Huang, C.T., Li, C.H., Chang, S.W., Cootes, T.F.: Fully automatic system for accurate localisation and analysis of cephalometric landmarks in lateral cephalograms. Sci. Rep. **6**, 33581 (2016)
7. McInerney, T., Terzopoulos, D.: Deformable models in medical image analysis: a survey. Med. Image Anal. **1**(2), 91–108 (1996)
8. Steger, S., Jung, F., Wesarg, S.: Personalized articulated atlas with a dynamic adaptation strategy for bone segmentation in CT or CT/MR head and neck images. In: Medical Imaging 2014: Image Processing. vol. 9034, p. 90341I. International Society for Optics and Photonics (2014)
9. Wang, C.W., et al.: A benchmark for comparison of dental radiography analysis algorithms. Med. Image Anal. **31**, 63–76 (2016)
10. Wirtz, A., Mirashi, S.G., Wesarg, S.: Automatic teeth segmentation in panoramic X-ray images using a coupled shape model in combination with a neural network (2018, accepted for publication at MICCAI 2018)

Fully-Automated Analysis of Body Composition from CT in Cancer Patients Using Convolutional Neural Networks

Christopher P. Bridge[1(✉)], Michael Rosenthal[2], Bradley Wright[1],
Gopal Kotecha[1], Florian Fintelmann[3], Fabian Troschel[3], Nityanand Miskin[2],
Khanant Desai[2], William Wrobel[2], Ana Babic[4], Natalia Khalaf[2],
Lauren Brais[4], Marisa Welch[4], Caitlin Zellers[4], Neil Tenenholtz[1],
Mark Michalski[1], Brian Wolpin[4], and Katherine Andriole[1]

[1] MGH and BWH Center for Clinical Data Science, Boston, USA
cbridge@partners.org
[2] Brigham and Women's Hospital, Boston, USA
[3] Massachusetts General Hospital, Boston, USA
[4] Dana-Farber Cancer Institute, Boston, USA

Abstract. The amounts of muscle and fat in a person's body, known as body composition, are correlated with cancer risks, cancer survival, and cardiovascular risk. The current gold standard for measuring body composition requires time-consuming manual segmentation of CT images by an expert reader. In this work, we describe a two-step process to fully automate the analysis of CT body composition using a DenseNet to select the CT slice and U-Net to perform segmentation. We train and test our methods on independent cohorts. Our results show Dice scores $(0.95-0.98)$ and correlation coefficients $(R = 0.99)$ that are favorable compared to human readers. These results suggest that fully automated body composition analysis is feasible, which could enable both clinical use and large-scale population studies.

1 Introduction

Body composition (the amounts of fat and muscle in the body) is associated with important outcomes like cancer risk and survival [8,12]. The standard for analysis of body composition is to manually segment the body compartments through a single computed tomography (CT) image at the level of the third lumbar vertebra (L3) [12]. This approach was shown to strongly correlate with whole-body assessments [14,15]. Slice selection and manual segmentation by an expert analyst require over 20 min per scan in our experience. This time-intensive method has limited the feasibility of population-scale research on body composition.

C. P. Bridge and M. Rosenthal—Equal contribution

© Springer Nature Switzerland AG 2018
D. Stoyanov et al. (Eds.): OR 2.0/CARE/CLIP/ISIC 2018, LNCS 11041, pp. 204–213, 2018.
https://doi.org/10.1007/978-3-030-01201-4_22

In this paper, we propose a fully automated method to estimate a patient's body composition from an abdominal CT scan and validate the method across two large scale and diverse datasets. Although automated methods may enable the analysis of muscle and fat distributions across entire abdominal scans, in this work we seek to replicate the gold standard manual approach by segmenting a single CT slice.

Our method therefore breaks the problem of analyzing a CT series down into two steps. First, a convolutional neural network (CNN) model is used to identify a slice at the L3 level, as described in Sect. 3.2. Next, the chosen slice is passed to a segmentation model (Sect. 3.3) to estimate the cross-sectional areas of muscle, subcutaneous fat, and visceral fat. See Fig. 1 for an overview of the workflow.

We demonstrate on a large and diverse dataset that efficient, repeatable and accurate automatic body composition analysis is possible from routinely-acquired CT images (Sect. 4).

2 Related Work

A number of previous works [5–7,10,11] have demonstrated automated methods to segment body fat and/or muscle from axial CT images. Typically these have depended on handcrafted procedures. In this work, we take a different approach using deep learning methods trained on expert-annotated data.

Of particular note is the work of Popuri et al. [11] who use a finite element model (FEM) based approach to segmentation regularised by a statistical deformation model (SDM) prior and achieve high accuracy on a large and diverse dataset, but assume pre-selected slices at the L3 and T4 (thoracic) levels. They also demonstrate segmentation of muscle and fat, but do not make the clinically significant distinction between visceral fat and subcutaneous fat.

Lee et al. [7] previously demonstrated quantification of muscle tissue from single L3 slices using fully convolutional networks. We improve upon this work by using more modern segmentation architectures, resulting in better performance, and add the ability to segment visceral and subcutaneous fat in order to provide a more comprehensive assessment of body composition. Furthermore we add a slice-selection step to allow the model to operate on entire CT series without any human intervention, opening up the potential for large-scale cohort analysis.

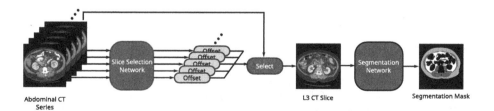

Fig. 1. Overview of the body composition workflow

Belharbi et al. [1] perform slice selection using convolutional neural networks and use a regression approach on the maximum intensity projection (MIP) image. We adopt a similar approach and show that the preprocessing to find the MIP is unnecessary and regression based on a single axial slice is highly accurate.

3   Methodology

3.1   Cohorts

The training cohort (Dataset A) used in this study is composed of 595 CT scans from subjects with biopsy-proven pancreatic adenocarcinoma who were treated at any of several collaborating centers (Brigham and Women's Hospital, Dana-Farber Cancer Institute, and others). Our group has previously used this cohort to demonstrate that body composition, as determined through manual segmentation through the L3 vertebral body, is associated with overall survival in patients with pancreatic adenocarcinoma [2], and that muscle area is associated with outcomes in critical care patients [3]. Scan parameters, the use of intravenous and oral contrast, and imaging hardware varied widely across the cohort. All scans were reviewed by a radiologist and a representative slice through L3 was selected. The three body compartments were manually segmented by trained image analysts using Slice-O-Matic software (Tomovision, Canada). Standard attenuation constraints were used: -29 to 150 HU for muscle and -190 to -30 HU for fat [12]. All segmentations were reviewed and corrected by a board-certified radiologist (MR). Dataset A was randomly divided into 412 training, 94 validation and 89 segmentation test series.

The testing cohort (Dataset B) is composed of 534 CT scans from subjects with lymphoma treated at a single institution (Massachusetts General Hospital). Scan parameters and imaging hardware varied across the cohort. Slice selection and manual segmentation were performed by a trained image analyst and revised by a board-certified radiologist (FF). Of the total number of series, 512, 473, and 514 series had manual segmentations for muscle, subcutaneous fat, and visceral fat respectively. Segmentation in this cohort used the same attenuation constraints but was performed in Osirix (Pixmeo, Geneva). This dataset was used to test the full body composition estimation framework.

3.2   Slice Selection Model

The first step in our method is to automatically identify a slice at the L3 level from the full CT volume to be passed on to the segmentation model. We pose this problem as a slice-wise regression problem, which operates on each slice of the volume independently, followed by post-processing to choose a single slice.

This allows us to use a more efficient 2D network model and allows us to work on a per DICOM image basis, reducing network complexity and avoiding the need to deal with series with different slice spacings, whilst still considering a slice's local context in the selection process. The model takes as input a 2D CT slice, downsampled to a 256×256 image, and learns to predict a single continuous-valued output representing the offset of that slice from the L3 region in the craniocaudal direction. Instead of directly predicting this offset, we find it advantageous to saturate this value into the range 0 to 1 using a sigmoid function, such that the model learns to focus its discriminatory capability within the area around the L3 region. If we define the z-coordinate of a slice as its location along the craniocaudal axis (the 'Slice Location' field in the DICOM metadata) and the z-coordinate of the L3 slice in that series is known to be z_{L3} then the model learns to predict the regression target $r(z)$ where,

$$r(z) = \frac{1}{1 + e^{-\tau(z - z_{L3})}} \tag{1}$$

and τ is a free parameter defining the size of the region of interest. Based on preliminary experiments, we found $\tau = 20\,\mathrm{mm}$ to be a suitable value.

We experimented with variations on two state-of-the-art CNN architectures: ResNeXt [16] and DenseNet [4]. Each of these architectures has recently achieved excellent performance on large-scale image classification tasks and is designed to overcome common problems with training very deep neural networks by introducing skip connections to allow gradients to propagate more directly back to earlier layers of the network. To adapt the architectures for regression, we replace the final fully-connected layer and softmax activation with a fully-connected layer with a single output unit and a sigmoid activation function in order to output a number in the range 0 to 1. We then apply a mean absolute error loss between this output and the regression target $r(z)$.

Since these architectures were originally developed for the task of multi-class natural image classification on very large-scale datasets, we experiment with various aspects of the architecture in order to find the optimal design for our purposes. The model architectures are shown in Fig. 2. For the ResNeXt architecture, we experiment with the initial feature width, f, and the cardinality, C, of the grouped convolution layers. For the DenseNet architecture we experiment with the number of layers b in each dense block and the 'growth rate' k, which is the number of features added by each convolutional layer.

At test time, the full series is passed into the model as a sequence of individual slices. The predicted offsets are placed into an array using the known slice ordering, and the values are smoothed using a small Gaussian kernel ($\sigma = 2$ slices) in order to incoporate local context. Then the location where this smoothed signal crosses 0.5 (corresponding to $z - z_{L3} = 0$ during training) is chosen as the L3 slice. If there are multiple such locations, the slice closest to the head is chosen.

3.3   Tissue Segmentation Model

Once a slice has been selected according to the slice selection model (Sect. 3.2), the full 512×512 slice is passed to a segmentation model for body composition analysis. The segmentation network is based on a U-Net model [13],

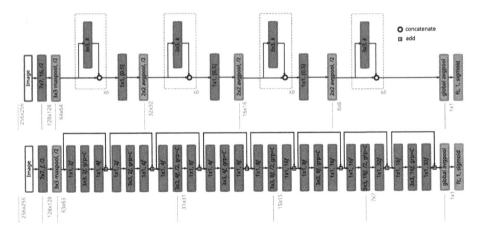

Fig. 2. Schematics of networks: *below* ResNeXt, *above* DenseNet. Red blocks indicate convolutional layers described by their kernel dimensions and number of output features. All convolutional layers are followed by a batch normalization layer followed by a rectified linear unit (ReLU) activation. Green blocks represent pooling layers. '/2' indicates that the conv/pool layer has a stride of 2, otherwise the stride is 1. In the ResNeXt model 'grp= C', indicates that the layer is a grouped convolution layer with a cardinality of C. In the DenseNet transition blocks '[0.5]' indicates that the number of output features is half the number of input features (a compression factor of 0.5). (Color figure online)

which has previously proved highly effective in a number of biomedical image segmentation tasks. We add batch normalization before each activation and change the loss function of the network to be a soft Dice maximization loss [9] in order to deal with class imbalances between three tissue classes and the background class. The full loss function is defined as the sum of the three soft Dice losses for the three non-background classes (muscle, visceral fat, and subcutaneous fat), i.e.

$$
L = - \sum_{c=1}^{3} \left(\frac{2 \sum_{i=0}^{N} p_{i,c} \, q_{i,c} + \epsilon}{\sum_{i=0}^{N} p_{i,c} + \sum_{i=0}^{N} q_{i,c} + \epsilon} \right) \tag{2}
$$

where $p_{i,c} \in [0, 1]$ is the predicted probablility (softmax output) of pixel i belonging to class c and $q_{i,c} \in \{0, 1\}$ is the ground truth label for pixel i (1 if pixel i belongs to class c, otherwise 0). ϵ is a small constant that avoids divide-by-zero problems, and was set to 1 in all experiments.

We experiment with different numbers of downsampling/upsampling modules in the architecture, d, the number of convolutional layers per module, l, and the initial number of features in the network f.

3.4   Training Details

All models were trained from scratch using the Keras deep learning library with the Tensorflow backend on Nvidia V100 or P100 GPU hardware. Input image intensities were windowed at train and test time to match the standard viewing range with the center at 40 HU and a width of 400 HU, and then normalized into the range 0–255. For all models, the Adam optimizer was used with a batch size of 16 images and the training images (and segmentation masks in the case of the segmentation model) were augmented during training by applying small random translations of up to 0.05 times the image size in both the horizontal and vertical directions, drawn from a uniform distribution, and also small rotations of up to 5° in either direction, also drawn from a uniform distribution.

For the slice selection models, training lasted for 75 epochs with the learning rate initially set to 0.001 and reduced by a factor of 10 at $\frac{1}{2}$ and $\frac{3}{4}$ of the way through the training process. Every slice from the training set series was used as a single training sample along with its known $r(z)$ value.

For the segmentation model, training lasted for 100 epochs and the learning rate was initially set to 0.1 with the same decay schedule. The L3 images from the test set series were used along with their manual segmentation masks.

4   Experiments and Results

4.1   Model Selection

The different model architectures were evaluated through their performance on the validation subset of Dataset A. These results are shown in Table 1. It can be seen that the performance of the ResNeXt and DenseNet models is broadly similar, and that in both cases relatively small models can achieve high accuracy. It is worth noting that the DenseNet models are typically far smaller (in terms of number of parameters) than the ResNeXt models. For this reason, we chose the DenseNet model with $l = 12$, $k = 12$ as the final slice selection model.

It can also be seen that the hyperparameters of the U-Net segmentation model do not significantly effect the results, but there is a weak trend that deeper models with more downsampling and upsampling modules achieve a higher accuracy, probably reflecting the increased capacity of the network to capture global context. Accordingly, we selected the U-Net model with $d = 5$, $l = 1$, $f = 16$ as the segmentation model for further experiments.

4.2   Test Results

Results for the segmentation step in isolation using the selected models on the test partition of Dataset A are shown in Table 2. The Dice similarity coefficient (DSC) is used to measure the difference between the automatic segmentation and the manual ground truth. Our results improve upon those of Lee et al. [7], who had an average DSC of 0.93 for muscle, suggesting that the additional representational power of the U-Net and the more informative three-class training labels were effective at improving network accuracy. Additionally, our results improve upon those of Popuri et al. [11] who achieved Jaccard indices of 0.904 for muscle, and 0.912 for fat (visceral and subcutaneous as a single class) which correspond to DSC values of 0.950 and 0.954.

Table 1. Model selection results for the two tasks on the validation partition of Dataset A. *Above* slice selection using mean absolute error loss, *below* segmentation using the Dice loss (a perfect overlap between all three classes would have a loss of 3).

Architecture	ResNeXt						DenseNet								
f	16	32	64	16	32	64	-	-	-	-	-	-	-	-	-
C	1	1	1	32	32	32	-	-	-	-	-	-	-	-	-
b	-	-	-	-	-	-	6	6	6	12	12	12	18	18	18
k	-	-	-	-	-	-	12	18	24	12	18	24	12	18	24
Loss ($\times 10^{-2}$)	2.62	2.38	2.64	2.48	**2.25**	2.53	2.67	3.04	2.68	2.28	2.64	2.75	2.66	2.62	2.31

Architecture	U-Net											
d	4	4	4	4	4	4	5	5	5	5	6	6
f	16	16	16	32	32	32	16	16	16	32	16	16
l	1	2	3	1	2	3	1	2	3	1	1	2
Loss	2.937	2.935	2.941	2.939	2.942	2.934	**2.944**	2.938	2.938	2.942	2.937	2.942

The full validation was then performed on Dataset B treating the two models as a single process that takes in a full abdominal CT series and produces estimates of body composition in terms of square cross-sectional area of muscle, subcutaneous fat, and visceral fat. In this case, the DSC is not an appropriate measure because the segmentation may be performed on a different slice from the ground truth mask. Table 2 compares the accuracy of the different tissue types and Fig. 3 shows some example outputs.

The mean absolute localization error on the Dataset B test set was 9.4 mm, which lies within the range of the L3 vertebra on the majority of patients.

The slice selection model takes approximately 0.5 s to 1.0 s per series to run on our Nvidia V100 GPU hardware, with a further 0.02 s to 0.025 s for the segmentation model. This compares to the times reported in [11] of 0.60 s for the segmentation step alone on a CPU (although our model does make use of GPU hardware). This makes our approach suitable for use for large scale cohort studies and deployment within a clinical environment (Fig. 4).

Table 2. Test results on unseen data. *Above* Segmentation results on the test partition of Dataset A, *below* body composition estimation on Dataset B.

Tissue	Muscle	Subc. Fat	Visc. Fat
Mean DSC	0.968	0.984	0.954
Std. Dev. of DSC	0.034	0.021	0.100

Tissue	Muscle	Subc. Fat	Visc. Fat
Mean Absolute Error (cm^2)	4.3	10.9	7.9
Mean Absolute Percentage Error (%)	3.1	5.9	6.5
Correlation Coefficient	0.986	0.986	0.994

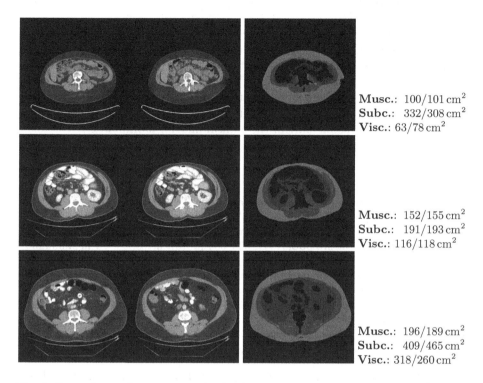

Musc.: $100/101\,\text{cm}^2$
Subc.: $332/308\,\text{cm}^2$
Visc.: $63/78\,\text{cm}^2$

Musc.: $152/155\,\text{cm}^2$
Subc.: $191/193\,\text{cm}^2$
Visc.: $116/118\,\text{cm}^2$

Musc.: $196/189\,\text{cm}^2$
Subc.: $409/465\,\text{cm}^2$
Visc.: $318/260\,\text{cm}^2$

Fig. 3. Example results on two randomly-chosen series from the test dataset (Dataset B) and one with poor subcutaneous and visceral fat prediction (third row): *left* manually selected L3 slice, *center* L3 slice chosen by slice selection model, *right* automatically segmented slice showing muscle (red), subcutaneous fat (green) and visceral fat (blue). Areas given in the fourth column are estimated/true values. (Color figure online)

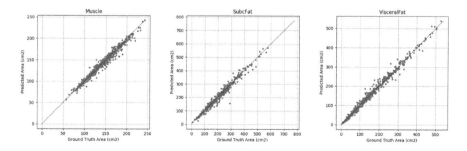

Fig. 4. Scatter plots of predicted tissue area versus ground truth tissue area for the three tissue types in Dataset B. Black dashed line indicates perfect prediction ($y = x$).

5   Conclusions

We have demonstrated that a two-stage convolutional neural network model can estimate the abdominal muscle and fat areas on abdominal CT scans with high accuracy. We demonstrate higher segmentation accuracy and faster computation times than the current state of the art. These findings could enable population-scale research on metabolism by dramatically decreasing the costs associated with this type of analysis. This could ultimately make routine assessment of body composition a feasible part of the clinical imaging workflow.

References

1. Belharbi, S.: Spotting L3 slice in CT scans using deep convolutional network and transfer learning. Comput. Biol. Med. **87**, 95–103 (2017)
2. Danai, L.V., et al.: Altered exocrine function can drive adipose wasting in early pancreatic cancer. Nature **558**(7711), 600–604 (2018). https://www.ncbi.nlm.nih.gov/pubmed/29925948
3. Foldyna, B., et al.: Computed tomography-based fat and muscle characteristics are associated with mortality after transcatheter aortic valve replacement. J. Cardiovasc. Comput. Tomogr. **12**(3), 223–228 (2018). http://www.sciencedirect.com/science/article/pii/S1934592518300571
4. Huang, G., Liu, Z., van der Maaten, L., Weinberger, K.Q.: Densely connected convolutional networks. In: Proceedings of the IEEE Conference on Computer Vision and Pattern Recognition (2017)
5. Kim, J.Y., et al.: Computerized automated quantification of subcutaneous and visceral adipose tissue from computed tomography scans: development and validation study. JMIR Med. Inform. **4**(1), e2 (2016)
6. Kullberg, J., et al.: Automated analysis of liver fat, muscle and adipose tissue distribution from CT suitable for large-scale studies. Sci. Rep. **7**(1), 10425 (2017)
7. Lee, H., et al.: Pixel-level deep segmentation: artificial intelligence quantifies muscle on computed tomography for body morphometric analysis. J. Digit. Imaging **30**(4), 487–498 (2017)
8. Martin, L., et al.: Cancer cachexia in the age of obesity: skeletal muscle depletion is a powerful prognostic factor, independent of body mass index. J. Clin. Oncol. **31**(12), 1539–47 (2013)
9. Milletari, F., Navab, N., Ahmadi, S.A.: V-net: fully convolutional neural networks for volumetric medical image segmentation. In: 2016 Fourth International Conference on 3D Vision (3DV), pp. 565–571, October 2016
10. Parikh, A.M., et al.: Development and validation of a rapid and robust method to determine visceral adipose tissue volume using computed tomography images. PLoS ONE **12**(8), e0183515 (2017)
11. Popuri, K., Cobzas, D., Esfandiari, N., Baracos, V., Jägersand, M.: Body composition assessment in axial CT images using FEM-based automatic segmentation of skeletal muscle. IEEE Trans. Med. Imaging **35**(2), 512–520 (2016)
12. Prado, C.M., et al.: Prevalence and clinical implications of sarcopenic obesity in patients with solid tumours of the respiratory and gastrointestinal tracts: a population-based study. Lancet Oncol. **9**(7), 629–35 (2008)

13. Ronneberger, O., Fischer, P., Brox, T.: U-Net: convolutional networks for biomedical image segmentation. In: Navab, N., Hornegger, J., Wells, W.M., Frangi, A.F. (eds.) MICCAI 2015. LNCS, vol. 9351, pp. 234–241. Springer, Cham (2015). https://doi.org/10.1007/978-3-319-24574-4_28

14. Shen, W., et al.: Total body skeletal muscle and adipose tissue volumes: estimation from a single abdominal cross-sectional image. J. Appl. Physiol. **97**(6), 2333–2338 (2004)

15. Shen, W., et al.: Visceral adipose tissue: relations between single-slice areas and total volume. Am. J. Clin. Nutr. **80**(2), 271–278 (2004)

16. Xie, S., Girshick, R., Dollar, P., Tu, Z., He, K.: Aggregated residual transformations for deep neural networks. In: The IEEE Conference on Computer Vision and Pattern Recognition (CVPR), July 2017

Image-Based Bronchial Anatomy Codification for Biopsy Guiding in Video Bronchoscopy

Esmitt Ramírez[1]([✉])([iD]), Carles Sánchez[1]([iD]), Agnés Borràs[1]([iD]),
Marta Diez-Ferrer[2]([iD]), Antoni Rosell[2]([iD]), and Debora Gil[1]([iD])

[1] Computer Vision Center, Autonomous University of Barcelona,
08193 Barcelona, Spain
{esmitt.ramirez,csanchez,agnesba,debora}@cvc.uab.es
[2] Bellvitge University Hospital, L'Hospitalet de Llobregat, 08907 Barcelona, Spain
{marta.diez,arosell}@bellvitgehospital.cat

Abstract. Bronchoscopy examinations allow biopsy of pulmonary nodules with minimum risk for the patient. Even for experienced bronchoscopists, it is difficult to guide the bronchoscope to most distal lesions and obtain an accurate diagnosis. This paper presents an image-based codification of the bronchial anatomy for bronchoscopy biopsy guiding. The 3D anatomy of each patient is codified as a binary tree with nodes representing bronchial levels and edges labeled using their position on images projecting the 3D anatomy from a set of branching points. The paths from the root to leaves provide a codification of navigation routes with spatially consistent labels according to the anatomy observes in video bronchoscopy explorations. We evaluate our labeling approach as a guiding system in terms of the number of bronchial levels correctly codified, also in the number of labels-based instructions correctly supplied, using generalized mixed models and computer-generated data. Results obtained for three independent observers prove the consistency and reproducibility of our guiding system. We trust that our codification based on viewer's projection might be used as a foundation for the navigation process in Virtual Bronchoscopy systems.

Keywords: Biopsy guiding · Bronchoscopy · Lung biopsy
Intervention guiding · Airway codification

1 Introduction

Suspicious pulmonary nodules might be diagnosed with a histopathologic analysis on a sample of biopsy tissue, which can be extracted in minimally invasive bronchoscopic examinations. A main restraint of flexible bronchoscopy is the difficulty to determine the best pathway to peripheral lesions. According to [1], physician's accuracy at defining proper 3D routes is only on the order of 40%

© Springer Nature Switzerland AG 2018
D. Stoyanov et al. (Eds.): OR 2.0/CARE/CLIP/ISIC 2018, LNCS 11041, pp. 214–222, 2018.
https://doi.org/10.1007/978-3-030-01201-4_23

for ROIs located near airways at fourth generation or less, with errors beginning as early as second generation.

Despite recent advances, a few novel endoscopy techniques seem to increase diagnostic yield to 70–80% and still radiate the patient. The diagnostic yield could be improved by reducing the radiation and costs and with the support of imaging technologies which may better guide the physician to the target lesion.

Virtual bronchoscopic (VB) systems [2] are used to reconstruct computed tomography (CT) data into three-dimensional representations of the tracheobronchial tree. VB systems allow for pairing virtual and real-time bronchoscopy, being useful for guiding ultrathin bronchoscopes and other devices in diagnostic interventions [3]. During exploration, indicating the planned path on the current intra-operative video could increase the intervention efficiency whereas reducing radiation to clinical staff. To accurately guide the operator across the planned path, assisted navigation, such as electromagnetic [4], radial probe ultrasound [5] or image-based virtual bronchoscopic navigation [6,7], should identify in intra-operative videos the different airway levels that VB follows.

According to Khan [3], the main advantage of virtual bronchoscopic navigation (VBN) whether electromagnetic navigation or radial probe ultrasound is its lower cost including consumables. Furthermore, during the procedure, VBN might provide information on the airways in cases where video bronchoscopic frames do not display the tracheobronchial tree due to either blood, mucus or airway swelling. The main disadvantage of VBN is the lack to capture the real-time information about both 3D position and directional guidance from the operator point of view [3]. The codification of patient's airways 3D anatomy includes a labeling of the bronchial levels traversed across the navigation path. This can help the operator to identify the path to follow and, as consequence, to improve VBN intra-operative guidance.

The codification of patient's airways 3D anatomy is a main point in the development of a computer-assisted system for diagnosis, treatment planning, and follow-up of pulmonary diseases. Several works are concerned with the codification and matching for improving registration of 3D scans in assessment of obstructive pulmonary diseases. Airways 3D anatomy is usually described as a graph using the bifurcations and end-points of the segmentation skeleton [8]. The variability across acquisitions and patients, as well as, imperfections in segmentation and skeletonization introduce missing and spurious branches that hamper further matching and labelling of the constructed graphs. Usual solutions include pruning of small skeleton branches [9] or tree-matching strategies able to cope with topological changes [10,11].

Concerning airways labeling, this process is mainly restricted to anatomical names identified by matching unlabeled airway trees to atlas-based labeled models. Even for methods successfully handling topological changes of the airway tree [12], anatomical labeling in human airway trees is well defined up to the segmental level. This restricts the number of labels to 20–32 bronchial segments [10], is a major inconvenience for distal navigation in biopsy guiding. A recent work [13] proved the feasibility of labeling at sub-segmental levels using spatial 3D information of branches.

In this paper, we present a graph-based codification of airways for guiding bronchoscopy interventions in lung cancer biopsy procedures. Contrasting other approaches, we use a graph structure to prune bifurcations introduced by imperfections in the segmentation and skeletonization. Our proposal uses geometrical aspects (i.e. branching levels) of the segmentation skeleton to obtain an appropriate codification for guiding. Also, we label the airways using their position in 2D images (quadrant-based approach), projected from the perspective of the viewer which is obtained from virtual VB explorations. As far as we know, this is the first work using virtual explorations to label airways according to their position in video-bronchoscopy 2D frames. We provide a sub-segmental personalized labeling to generate intuitive routing instructions for physicians.

2   Codification of Airways Navigation Paths

A navigation path across airways can be given by the sequence of the navigated bronchial levels labeled in such a way that the branch to follow is identified into intra-operative bronchoscopy videos. The complete structure of all bronchial levels is represented using a graph with nodes. This structure is defined by bronchial levels and edges labeled according to the position that bronchi would have in bronchoscopic explorations.

Airways are tubular structures with their geometry determined by the centerline given by bronchi lumen center. The airways centerlines correspond to the skeleton of segmented volumes, and they allow the construction of a tree-based structure on bronchi branching. The skeleton of a segmented volume is encoded using the Kerschnitzki et al. [14] approach, where a graph represents its branching geometry using nodes and edges. For instance, this approach was previously used to segment airways amongst match CT-videos bronchial structure with encoded airways, using landmarks in the anatomical structure [15,16].

The nodes of the graph correspond to the skeleton branching points and its edges represent branch connectivity. The Depth-First Search (DFS) algorithm considers the trachea as the root node, and it allows directs the graph to depth levels; this allows associate a level for each of its nodes to define a binary rooted tree structure. DFS also defines the relationship parent/children each time a bronchi branch is found, being the bifurcations before skeleton end-points the leaves of the tree. This parent/children relationship lets encoding the tree structure using two adjacency matrices, see Fig. 1, for fast computing of graph operations (e.g. cycle detection, graph matching, maximum flow, and others). The first matrix represents the node tree connectivity in a binary matrix, and the second one is a matrix of 3D segments that keeps the list of 3D skeleton points (i.e. $(x, y, z) \in R^3$) that connect each pair of adjacent nodes. Each position in the matrix of 3D segments is composed by a list of equally spaced points.

Skeleton false branches that not belong at bronchial anatomy, introduce extra nodes in the graph structure that hinder the codification of bronchial levels. These branches correspond to intermediate nodes of first order (i.e. with only one child), in the adjacency matrix connecting two nodes, namely v_i, v_j, of different order (either a leaf or a node of order two). Intermediate nodes are deleted from the two adjacency matrices removing their rows and columns, and updating the position i, j with the adjacency information and the list of skeleton points connecting v_i, v_j.

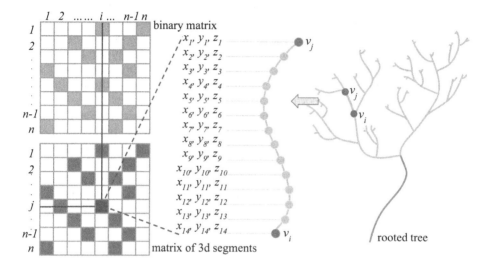

Fig. 1. Binary and segments matrices codifying airway anatomy as rooted tree. The colored positions in both matrices, represent the parent/children relationship.

A navigation route is defined as a node sequence $v_{k0}, v_{k1}, \ldots v_{kj-1}, v_{kj}$, connecting a leaf node (v_{kj}) with the root (v_{k0}). A final navigation path inside the segmented volume is the collection of skeleton 3D points extracted from the matrix of 3D segments by considering the entrances given by $(k0, k1), \ldots, (kj - 1, kj)$. To provide an edge labeling consistent with intra-operative visual information, a navigation route was simulated. This route is created across the segmented volume and projects the segmented 3D geometry at each traversed bronchial level to obtain a collection of virtual images of the intra-operative path. The position of the projected bronchi in such virtual images provides our edge labeling for intuitive routing.

Then, in a navigation route, to each pair of consecutive nodes, v_{k-1}, v_k, a camera is placed in one of the skeleton points at a given distance d_k from the end node v_k. This distance permits capture the complete border of lumen's border for bifurcations. Next, the camera target point is set to v_k, and the up vector is accumulated during path traversal (i.e roll axis) using the Frenet-Serret frame. Also, the camera field of view is set to 120° to ensure full visibility of geometry in virtual frames. Accordingly, d_k varies on each segment being set to $0.2 \times dist(v_{k-1}, v_k)$. The scene projected at each level is given by the following simplified representation of the essential bronchial 3D structure. We project two lines from v_k to its children nodes v_{k+1}^1 and v_{k+1}^2, called $S1$ and $S2$ respectively.

This allows a clear identification of the lines in virtual images, each projected line has a different primary color, red and green. Thus, each line is codified in a different RGB channel.

To label each projected line, the virtual image is split into four quadrants centered at the projected position of v_k. Since quadrants represent the spatial distribution of airway lumens in bronchoscopic frames during traversal of bronchial levels, each projected segment will be labeled according to the quadrant it belongs to. Then for each point of the projected segment, the position of the quadrant they belong to is computed. For this, the mode and average values are considered. The mode indicates the predominant quadrant where each segment belongs. When two or three segments lie on the same quadrant, they are counterclockwise ordered according to their average.

The labeling process is described in the visual scheme shown in Fig. 2. Figure shows an outline of airways and a navigation path with its branching nodes labeled. The figure also displays a camera positioned at distance d_k from the node v_k, and the segments $S1$, $S2$ colored in red and green respectively. The rectangular images show the simplified scene projected over the complete airway anatomy. The most left image is split into four colored quadrants: Q_1 = red, Q_2 = green, Q_3 = yellow, Q_4 = blue, to illustrate that $S1$ lies in Q_1 and $S2$ in Q_2.

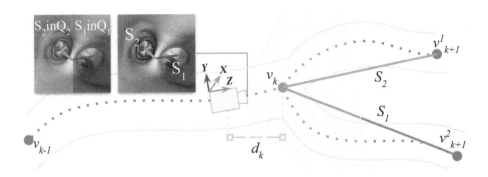

Fig. 2. Edge Labelling Procedure: the camera captures an image at distance d_k from the v_k, projecting lines to children at level $k + 1$. Image is split into quadrants to label line segments S_1, S_2. (Color figure online)

Using edge labels, navigation paths are encoded with a set of spatial instructions specified by the labels of the edges linking path nodes, Q_1-Q_3-Q_1-Q_2-Q_4. This agrees to route a path with instructions (up/right/left/down at every branch) which are natural for physicians [17]. Such instructions mean "at first bifurcation take the first quadrant, after the third, . . . , and so on". Since these instructions are not intuitive to follow during an intervention, we replace quadrant names for upper-right, upper-left, lower-left and lower-right indicating each quadrant in a more natural language.

3   Experiments and Discussion

The capabilities of our labeling for bronchoscopy guiding were evaluated, mainly focus in two aspects: identification of the bronchial levels traversed, and validation of bronchi orientation in projected images as intuitive instructions for distal routing. To do so, a set of virtual explorations on CT volumes using an interactive simulation platform developed in Unity were developed.

For each CT-scan of a patient, four virtual explorations were generated, covering the four main lobes: left and right upper lobes, noted LUL, RUL, and left and right lower lobes, noted LLL, RLL. These paths were performed using the central navigation without rotation around the scope. For each path, a sequence of intuitive instructions (upper-left, upper-right, down-left, down-right) was extracted using our method. These instructions were validated by three experts who tried to reproduce the path in the simulation platform using the instructions supplied at each level detected by the graph. Experts were asked to identify instructions not corresponding to an actual branching level to define a false level rate (FLR). At each bifurcation where an expert could not reproduce the route previously simulated, was also recorded to define a false instruction rate (FIR).

Data were managed and evaluated through generalized mixed models using software R version 3.2.5. For each quality score (FLR, FIR), a different Poisson model was adjusted to include the segmental lobe as a factor. Moreover, a random subject effect to account for intra-individual variability among cases and a random effect to model inter-observer variability:

$$log(FIRijk) = \beta_0 + \beta_1 Lobe + Pat_i + Obs_j + \epsilon_{ijk}$$
$$log(FLRijk) = \beta_0 + \beta_1 Lobe + Pat_i + Obs_j + \epsilon_{ijk}$$

for $Pat_i \sim N(0, \sigma_{Pat})$ denoting the random effect that models intra-patient variability, $Obs_j \sim N(0, \sigma_{Obs})$ the random effect for inter-observer variability and $Lobe$ (with values LUL, RUL, LLL, RLL) for the grouping factor of the four segmental lobes considered. Model assumptions were validated by means of residual analysis and influential values. The model coefficients, p values and 95% confidence interval (CI) for significance in main effects were also computed. The CIs values were back transformed to the original scale for their interpretation. Furthermore, a p value < 0.05 was considered statistically significant.

For our tests, ten cases were considered with paths reaching between the sixth and twelfth bronchial level. Descriptive statistics, for instance, the average and standard deviation (SD), also the model adjustment for both, FLR and FIR as percentage way, are shown in Table 1. There are not any significant differences across lung lobes for the rate of false detected levels with average overall values in the range 3 ± 7. Nevertheless, the lower left lung lobe has a significantly worse (p-val < 0.01) rate of false instructions with CIs equal to $(5.2, 20.6)\%$.

The increase in the FIR value for the lower left lung lobe is mainly due to the confusing instructions at the third generation, just after the LUL-LLL branching point. Although the 3D geometry around the third generation presents two branching points (thus, two levels), they are not appreciated in the projected

Table 1. Models for FLR and FIR.

FLR (%)	Descriptive mean	SD	Model coeff	p-val	CI	FIR (%)	Descriptive mean	SD	Model coeff	p-val	CI
RLL	0.0	0.0	1	-	(0.0,1.6)		2.8	4.6	1	-	(0.6, 5.2)
LLL	3.3	7.2	0.5	0.33	(0.0, 3.4)		13	11.7	1.3	<0.01	(5.2, 20.6)
RUL	1.8	3.5	0.4	0.4	(0.0, 3.0)		1.7	4.0	-0.35	0.06	(0.1, 3.4)
LUL	7.0	12.4	1.0	0.07	(0.0, 6.0)		6.4	8.7	0.64	0.08	(2.2, 10.5)

images due to a short distance between them. In fact, in projected images, the LLL lumen is not visually identified and three airway lumens that correspond to the projection of LLL next generation are visible. Therefore, from the point of view of the operator, there are three possible airways to follow at the same level, while for our codification there are two consecutive levels with two airways each.

Figure 3 illustrates this phenomenon. Whereas the 3D structure in front of the camera contains the segments $v_k \rightarrow v_{k+1}^1$ and $v_k \rightarrow v_{k+1}^2$ as well as v_{k+1}^1 children segments $v_{k+1}^1 \rightarrow v_{k+2}^1$ and $v_{k+1}^1 \rightarrow v_{k+2}^2$, its projection shown in the right image only shows lumens corresponding to v_{k+1}^2, v_{k+2}^1, v_{k+2}^2. This visual artifact also occurs in intra-operative videos as the top image illustrates. The image shows a frame extracted at the same position from an exploration performed on the patient, which is used to generate the simulated image shown below.

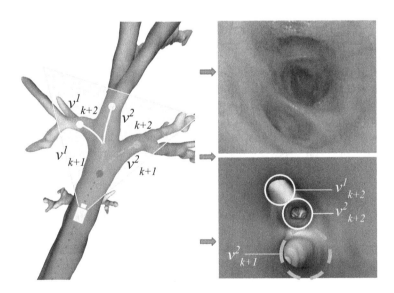

Fig. 3. System failure at spatially close bifurcations, where projections skip one of them and show three possible airways to follow.

4   Conclusions

We have introduced a codification of the bronchial anatomy, for biopsy guiding based on a symbolic representation of each patient's airway anatomy as a binary rooted tree. Tree nodes represent the bronchial levels, and their edges are labeled according to the position of bronchi in virtual video bronchoscopy. This provides to physicians intuitive instructions during biopsy guiding.

Experiments on data simulating different routes to each pulmonary lobe allow the validation of our approach as a system for supplying instructions in biopsy guiding (with the successful average guiding of $94.7\% \pm 9.1\%$ in the cases). Also, we might correctly codify up to the tenth generation, forward of that, our segmentation approach needs some improvements. The statistical analysis detected a bias in instructions for the left lower lobe introduced by the spatially close consecutive levels, which are visualized as a single level with three lumens in the projected images. In such cases, the system should issue a single instruction instead of two. To avoid this phenomenon, the tree codification may be merged consecutive levels into a single level, considering the branching point distance).

Although this is an off-line validation with simulated data, we might conclude that a guiding system based on bronchi orientation in 2D projections is feasible and simple enough, and it might be easily deployed in operating rooms with low costs. The integration of this approach into an interactive navigation support system is currently under development [18], and we have the confidence to compare it with the LungPoint system in a near future.

Acknowledgments. This work was supported by Catalan, Spanish and European projects DPI2015-65286-R, 2014-SGR-1470, CERCA Programme/Generalitat de Catalunya. Also, the first author holds the fellowship number BES-2016-078042 granted by the Ministry of Economy, Industry and Competitiveness, Spain. A Titan X Pascal was used for this research, donated by NVIDIA. Debora Gil is part of the Serra Hunter programme.

References

1. Dolina, M.Y., et al.: interbronchoscopist variability in endobronchial path selection: a simulation study. Chest **133**(4), 897–905 (2008)
2. Reynisson, P.J., et al.: Navigated bronchoscopy: a technical review. J. Bronchol. Interv. Pulmonol. **21**(3), 242–264 (2014)
3. Khan, K.A., Nardelli, P., Jaeger, A., O'Shea, C., Cantillon-Murphy, P., Kennedy, M.P.: Navigational bronchoscopy for early lung cancer: a road to therapy. Adv. Therapy **33**(4), 580–596 (2016)
4. Khandhar, S.J., et al.: Electromagnetic navigation bronchoscopy to access lung lesions in 1,000 subjects: first results of the prospective, multicenter NAVIGATE study. BMC Pulm. Med. **17**(1), 59 (2017)
5. Ikezawa, Y., et al: Usefulness of endobronchial ultrasonography with a guide sheath and virtual bronchoscopic navigation for ground-glass opacity lesions. Ann. Thoracic Surg. **103**(2), 470–475 (2017)

6. Asano, F., et al.: Virtual bronchoscopic navigation without X-ray fluoroscopy to diagnose peripheral pulmonary lesions: a randomized trial. BMC Pulm. Med. **17**(184), 12 (2017)

7. Eberhardt, R., Kahn, N., Gompelmann, D., Schumann, M., Heussel, C.P., Herth, F.J.: LungPoint-a new approach to peripheral lesions. J. Thorac. Oncol. **5**(10), 1559–1563 (2010)

8. Florez Valencia, L., Morales Pinzón, A., Richard, J.-C., Hernandez Hoyos, M., Orkisz, M.: Simultaneous skeletonization and graph description of airway trees in 3D CT images. In: XXVème Colloque GRETSI, Lyon, France, September 2015

9. Gómez Betancur, D.A., et al.: Airway segmentation, skeletonization, and tree matching to improve registration of 3D CT images with large opacities in the lungs. In: International Conference on Computer Vision and Graphics (ICCVG), vol. 9972, pp. 395–407 (2016)

10. Pinzón, A.M., Hoyos, M.H., Richard, J.C., Flórez-Valencia, L., Orkisz, M.: A tree-matching algorithm: Application to airways in CT images of subjects with the acute respiratory distress syndrome. Med. Image Anal. **35**, 101–115 (2017)

11. Bauer, C., Eberlein, M., Beichel, R.R.: Airway tree reconstruction in expiration chest CT scans facilitated by information transfer from corresponding inspiration scans. Med. Phys. **43**, 1312–1323 (2016)

12. Feragen, A., et al.: Geodesic atlas-based labeling of anatomical trees: application and evaluation on airways extracted from CT. IEEE Trans. Med. Imaging **34**(6), 1212–1226 (2015)

13. Tschirren, J., Vidal, C., Baron, B., Raffy, P., Hoffman, E.A.: Fully automated labeling of sub-segmental airways in human airway trees. 46:PA758, September 2015

14. Kerschnitzki, M., et al.: Architecture of the osteocyte network correlates with bone material quality. J. Bone Miner. Res. Off. J. Am. Soc. Bone Miner. Res. **28**(8), 1837–1845 (2013)

15. Oyarzun Laura, C., et al. (eds.): CLIP 2015. LNCS, vol. 9401. Springer, Cham (2016). https://doi.org/10.1007/978-3-319-31808-0

16. Sánchez, C., Esteban-Lansaque, A., Borras, A., Diez-Ferrer, M., Rosell, A., Gil, D.: Towards a videobronchoscopy localization system from airway centre tracking. In: 12th International Conference on Computer Vision Theory and Applications (VISAPP), pp. 352–359 (2017)

17. Bronchoscopy International. What is Bronchoscopy Step-by-Step (2018). https://bronchoscopy.org

18. Ramírez, E., et al.: BronchoX: Bronchoscopy Exploration Software for Biopsy Intervention Planning. Healthcare Technology Letters (2018). https://doi.org/10.1007/978-3-319-31808-0

Clinical Implementation of DeepVoxNet for Auto-Delineation of Organs at Risk in Head and Neck Cancer Patients in Radiotherapy

Siri Willems[1](✉), Wouter Crijns[3], Agustina La Greca Saint-Esteven[1], Julie Van Der Veen[2], David Robben[1], Tom Depuydt[2,3], Sandra Nuyts[2,3], Karin Haustermans[2,3], and Frederik Maes[1]

[1] Medical Image Computing (ESAT/PSI), KU Leuven, Leuven, Belgium
siri.willems@kuleuven.be
[2] Laboratory of Experimental Radiotherapy, Department of Oncology, KU Leuven – University of Leuven, Herestraat 49, 3000 Leuven, Belgium
[3] Department of Radiation Oncology, University Hospitals Leuven, Herestraat 49, 3000 Leuven, Belgium

Abstract. Delineation of organs at risk (OAR) on CT images is a crucial step in the planning of radiotherapy treatment. Manual delineation is time-consuming and high interrater variability is observed within and across radiotherapy centers. Automated delineation of OAR is fast and can lead to more consistent treatment plans. We developed an auto-delineation tool based on a 3D convolutional neural network (CNN) to automatically delineate 16 OAR structures in head and neck cancer (HNC) patients. The CNN was trained off-line using 70 previously collected patient datasets and implemented to be available on-line in clinical routine practice. The tool was applied prospectively for delineation of 20 consecutive new HNC cases within the department of Radiation Oncology, with subsequent manual editing and approval of the contours by the clinical expert. Validation based on the automatically proposed and edited contours shows that the auto-delineation tool is able to achieve highly accurate segmentation results for most OAR. As a result, 3D delineation time is reduced to less than 19 min on average (about 1 min/structure), compared to usually 1 h or more without auto-delineation tool.

Keywords: Auto-delineation · Deep convolutional neural network
Deep learning · Organs at risk · Radiotherapy

1 Introduction

Cancer is a major disease worldwide with head and neck cancers (HNC) among the most common cancers in Europe [1,20]. State of the art treatment of patients

© Springer Nature Switzerland AG 2018
D. Stoyanov et al. (Eds.): OR 2.0/CARE/CLIP/ISIC 2018, LNCS 11041, pp. 223–232, 2018.
https://doi.org/10.1007/978-3-030-01201-4_24

diagnosed with HNC often involves external beam radiotherapy (RT). Treatment planning systems (TPS) are used in radiotherapy to determine an optimal treatment plan for each patient. Precise delivery of ionizing radiation to the tumor increases probability of local tumor control while maximally sparing healthy tissue in order to avoid treatment complications.

Accurate delineation of target volumes and OAR on the planning CT is required to ensure proper plan and dose optimization. In clinical practice, the delineation is performed manually by radiation oncologists (RO) based on published guidelines and is time consuming [12]. The delineation strongly depends on experience level, knowledge and preferences of a RO, leading to high intra- and interobserver variability [2]. Consequently, the induced variations may affect the final treatment plan [2,14]. Automatic delineation can improve accuracy, consistency and reproducibility of contours leading to more consistent treatment plans within and across radiotherapy centers [12,19].

Atlas-based models are widely used to automatically segment OAR in HNC [4,12,19]. Prior knowledge is incorporated in the form of atlases, which are registered to the target image using deformable image registration techniques [12].

Recently, machine learning approaches, in particular deep learning based on convolutional neural networks (CNN), proved their success in many computer vision tasks such as object detection [5], semantic segmentation [11] and classification [8,10,18] and are becoming a state-of-the-art approach in medical imaging as well (e.g. [7,16]), including RT planning (e.g. [13]). For HNC in particular, Ibragimov et al. [6] developed a convolutional neural network extended with Markov random fields for segmentation of OAR in HNC patients. Men et al. [12] published a deep deconvolutional network focusing on the auto-delineation of the target volumes in HNC patients. Cardenas et al. [3] used convolutional neural networks for delineation of high risk oropharyngeal target volumes.

To investigate the clinical potential of CNN-based auto-delineation, we developed and implemented such a tool and integrated it within the conventional planning workflow within the department of Radiation Oncology of UZ Leuven. The tool is applied on-line, i.e. results are available to the radiation oncologist within few minutes after invoking the tool at the start of the planning procedure. The tool generates delineations of multiple (up to 16) organs at once, including: brainstem, spinal cord, parotid glands, submandibular glands, mandible, oral cavity, left and right cochlea, supraglottic and glottic larynx, upper esophagus and pharyngeal constrictor muscles (PCM). The auto-delineation results are imported in the planning system and visually inspected and edited as needed by the clinical expert. We report on our initial clinical experience with a quantitative and qualitative evaluation of the tool based on clinical feedback for 20 actual planning cases. Auto-delineated contours are generally well perceived by the radiation oncologists and reduce overall delineation time drastically. Due to the generic nature of the underlying CNN, the implementation is easily extendable to other organs.

2   Materials and Methods

2.1   Data Acquisition

The dataset used for training of the CNN consist of planning CT images of 70 patients and their OAR delineations. All patients were diagnosed with a tumor in head and neck region and received RT treatment. All CT images were acquired using the same clinical protocol on the same CT scanner in our institute (Somatom Sensation Open, Siemens Healthcare, Forchheim Germany). During CT acquisition, all patients were immobilized in treatment position using a thermoplastic mask. The auto-delineation tool is validated on planning CT images of 20 new HNC patients, which were consecutively acquired in clinical practice between April and May 2018. The auto-delineation tool was prospectively applied to these new cases to assess both the performance of the underlying 3D CNN and the impact on the RT planning workflow in daily routine clinical practice. Two patients received right parotidectomy, one patient left parotidectomy and four patients total laryngectomy before RT treatment, which means that the right (left) parotid resp. upper esophagus, inferior pharyngeal constrictor muscle and larynx were surgically removed and were consequently not present in the planning CT image of the patient.

2.2   3D Convolutional Neural Network: DeepVoxNet

A 3D convolutional neural network (DeepVoxNet) based on previous work from Kamnitsas et al. [7], is developed to automatically segment OAR in HNC for RT treatment planning. This end-to-end automated delineation network predicts a class label for each voxel present in a CT image [15]. CT images are normalized and resampled to a voxel size of $1 \times 1 \times 3\,\mathrm{mm}^3$ as a preprocessing step. Data augmentation is performed by introducing Gaussian noise and randomly flipping images. For computational efficiency, a patch based approach ($19 \times 19 \times 13$ voxels) is used in which multiple voxels are predicted at once. The network has four inputs (instead of two in [7]) that receive subvolumes of the image at different resolutions. Each input is followed by 10 convolutional layers and is then upsampled to the original resolution. The output of these four pathways are concatenated in the feature dimension and followed by two final convolutional layers and the classification layer. This multi-scale approach allows the network to consider both fine details in the immediate neighborhood as more coarse information in a wider environment when making a prediction. The parametric ReLU is used as activation function. Adam optimizer and dropout were used during training. As postprocessing steps, connected component analysis and smoothing are performed using MeVisLab modules (version 2.7.1).

2.3   Implementation

The auto-delineation tool using the proposed CNN and postprocessing steps, is deployed for testing in clinical practice within the Radiation Oncology department of UZ Leuven. New HNC planning cases follow the automated delineation protocol, which is summarized in Fig. 1. A patient's planning CT is transferred to the Medical Image Research Center using a DICOM server (OsiriX [17]) followed by auto-delineation of the OAR using the online auto-delineation tool running on a GPU server. The auto-delineation tool is built using MeVisLab (version 2.7.1) and combines three different steps. First, preprocessing is performed by normalising the CT image and resampling it to a voxel size of $1 \times 1 \times 3\,\mathrm{mm}^3$. Consequently, contours of all OAR are predicted using DeepVoxNet followed by connected component analysis and smoothing as postprocessing steps. The final contours are transferred to the Radiation Oncology department in DICOM format and imported into the TPS (Eclipse, Varian Medical Systems, Palo Alto, CA, USA). If necessary the structures are corrected by a junior RO and thereafter approved by a senior RO. Corrected contours are transferred back to the Medical Image Research Center and extra clinical feedback on delineation quality and efficiency is collected. Plan and dose optimizations are performed using the standard clinical workflow. This clinical implementation allows us to gather feedback fast and efficiently to further improve auto-delineations of OAR.

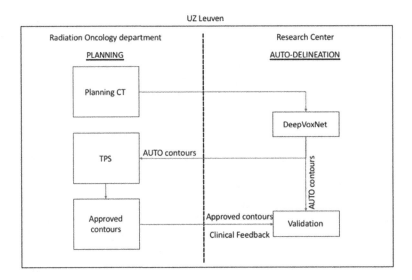

Fig. 1. Overview of clinical implementation.

2.4   Validation Process

Both a quantitative and qualitative validation is performed to assess the performance of the auto-delineation tool as well as its impact on the clinical workflow. Quantitative analysis is achieved using three similarity measures calculated in 3D including: Dice similarity coefficient (DSC), Hausdorff distance (H) and average symmetric surface distance (ASSD), which each determine the similarity between auto-delineated structures and the approved structures. Moreover, the RO recorded the time necessary to correct auto-delineated structures for each patient.

A qualitative validation is performed based on clinical assessment. The RO classifies the 3D delineation of each structure for each patient as 'good', 'adequate' or 'insufficient' depending on the perceived performance of the auto-delineation and the amount of extent of the manual corrections.

3   Validation Results

3.1   Quantitative Validation

Quantitative validation results reported in DSC (%), H (mm) and ASSD (mm) are summarized in Figs. 2, 3 and Table 1. The DSC values show diverse results for different anatomical structures. Brainstem, mandible, oral cavity, parotid glands, submandibular glands and spinal cord show highly accurate delineations on average, with mandible receiving the highest average DSC of 95.9% and the submandibular gland the lowest average DSC of 78.8%. Intraclass variations are rather low, which means that DeepVoxNet is able to consistently delineate the same structure. In contrast, higher intraclass variations are noticed for cochleae, pharyngeal constrictor muscles (PCM), larynx and the upper esophagus, with DSC values ranging from 0% to 100%. Cochleae are small structures and usually consist of one or two slices on the planning CT, such that even small corrections can have a large impact on DSC, resulting in a lower average DSC for the cochleae. Both the left and the right cochlea were once not recognized by the network and consequently not delineated, which explains the DSC value of 0%. The delineation results for pharyngeal constrictor muscles perform approximately the same as reported in literature [9]. Although some good auto-delineations of PCM, glottic and supraglottic larynx are obtained, leading to DSC values above 80%, the network fails to achieve accurate segmentation results when the tumor is located close to the PCM, glottic and supraglottic larynx. Moreover the transition between the PCM or glottic and supraglottic larynx are the most challenging parts to achieve high accuracy.

The average symmetric surface distance (ASSD) is below 3 mm for all structures except for the upper esophagus (7.81 mm) and the oral cavity (10.07 mm). The mandible, cochleae, spinal cord, brainstem and the right submandibular gland are the structures with the least corrections, resulting in an ASSD of less than 1 mm. Same trends are observed when evaluating Hausdorff distances. The ASSD and H highlight the influence of volume on DSC values. Although both cochleae reached lower average DSC with high intraclass variations, the cochleae achieved the best performance on ASSD scores compared to other structures.

The upper esophagus shows poor results on all three similarity measures with an average DSC of only 36.4% and Hausdorf distance of more than 3.6 cm. This can be explained by the fact that the training set only contains delineations of the upper part of the esophagus, hence labeled as 'upper esophagus' in Figs. 2 and 3. However, when correcting the auto-delineations, the RO extended the delineation of the upper esophagus caudally for some patients due to a lower located tumor, which explains the lower averaged similarity measures for the structure.

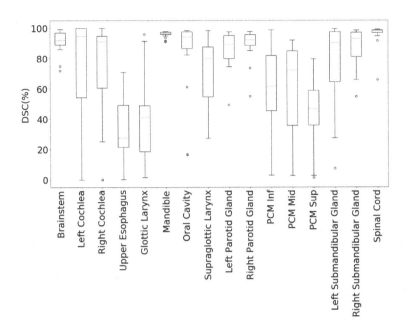

Fig. 2. DSC results of auto-delineations vs. corrected contours for various organs at risk (left axis).

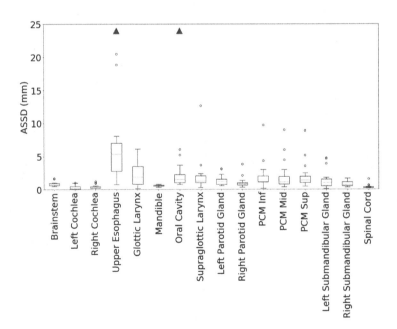

Fig. 3. ASSD for auto-delineations vs. corrected contours. Triangles represent outliers above 25 mm (see text for explanation)

Figure 4 visualizes correction time per patient, recorded by the RO for correcting all the OAR delineations of a specific patient, with on average about 290 2D contours per patient. The average correction time recorded by the RO is 15 min, which is less than one minute for each 3D structure. The proposed auto-delineation tool predicts 3D contours in less than 4 min using a GPU server. This drastically decreases overall delineation time to about 19 min from approximately 45–120 min, measured in our institute.

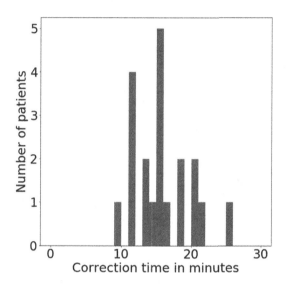

Fig. 4. Correction time recorded by the RO necessary to correct all the OAR for each patient separately

3.2 Qualitative Validation

The auto-delineated structures are overall well perceived in clinical practice, Fig. 5. Mandible, brainstem, cochleae and spinal cord are perceived as 'good' for more than 80% of the cases, which is in line with the results from the quantitative validation. Every organ is more classified as 'good' than as 'insufficient' except for the upper pharyngeal constrictor muscle. The delineation of this structure needed in general more corrections, which is also observed in the quantitative validation. The upper esophagus however, scored remarkably well on the clinical score although the quantitative results are rather poor. Although the esophagus was not fully delineated, the auto-delineation of the upper part of the structure was well perceived in clinical practice.

Table 1. Results of auto-delineation reporting volume in ml, Average Symmetric Surface Distance (ASSD) in mm, Hausdorff Distance (H) in mm and Dice Similarity Coefficient (DSC_D) in % for each organ seperately. The results are compared with the largest dice similarity coefficient for auto-delineation algorithms (DSC_L) and interrater variability (DSC_I) reported in literature in the last two columns.

Organ	V (ml)	H (mm)	ASSD (mm)	DSC_D (%)	DSC_L (%)	DSC_I (%)
Brainstem	21.67	6.52	0.84	91.5	81.0 [9]	83.0 [19]
Left cochlea	0.04	1.64	0.34	75.4	69.0 [9]	37.0 [19]
Right cochlea	0.06	1.66	0.41	73.1	63.0 [9]	36.0 [19]
Upper esophagus	8.60	35.8	7.66	34.8	-	87.1 [14]
Glottic larynx	2.32	11.14	2.40	39.4	-	49.0 [19]
Mandible	42.71	6.48	0.60	95.9	89.5 [6]	-
Oral cavity	83.97	23.18	10.07	83.5	-	-
Supraglottic larynx	9.83	11.09	2.22	71.2	-	60.0 [19]
Left parotis	22.06	11.27	1.35	86.3	79.0 [9]	76.1 [14]
Right parotis	20.75	10.06	1.05	89.7	79.0 [9]	76.5 [14]
PharConsInf	2.72	9.62	1.98	57.9	66.0 [9]	50.0 [19]
PharConsMid	2.59	12.65	1.99	60.9	57.0 [9]	50.0 [19]
PharConsSup	4.55	14.74	2.05	46.1	36.0 [9]	44.0 [19]
Left submandibular	5.83	7.72	1.47	78.8	69.7 [6]	-
Right submandibular	5.87	5.54	0.83	87.7	73.0 [6]	-
Spinal cord	11.26	4.26	0.39	95.9	87.0 [6]	79.5 [14]

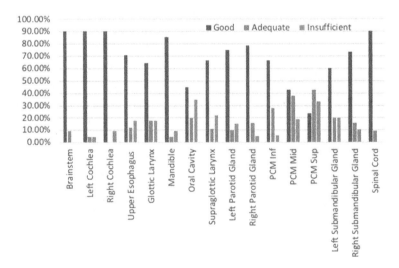

Fig. 5. Clinical assessment of the RO reported in percentage of 3D contours for which segmentation performance was perceived as "good", "adequate" or "insufficient".

4 Discussion and Conclusion

We developed an online auto-delineation tool for organs at risk in HNC patients in the context of RT treatment planning. The auto-delineation tool, based on 3D CNN (DeepVoxNet) is deployed in clinical practice to evaluate the performance of auto-delineations and to asses the impact on the clinical workflow.

Manual delineations are sensitive to interrater variability, leading to inconsistent treatment plans. Dice similarity coefficients of interrater variability published in literature are summarized in Table 1 [14,19]. A high interrater variability is observed for smaller organs such as: cochleae, upper esophagus, supraglottic larynx and PCM. The inter observer variability stresses the difficulty of automatic delineations of the OAR. Segmentation results of organs at risk using both atlas-based methods and deep learning, have been reported in literature [4,19] DeepVoxNet [15] is able to provide better segmentation results for organs at risk in head and neck patients compared to results published in literature (Table 1). Ibragimov et al. [6] was the first to propose a convolutional neural network for auto-delineations of OAR in HNC patients. Our results reported in DSC, tend to exceed the results of [6].

Our initial experience shows that in general, only small corrections are necessary for clinical acceptance of auto-delineated contours for most of the structures. The largest corrections for clinical acceptance are observed for the upper esophagus and glottic area while mandible needed the least corrections. Moreover the automated workflow is less time consuming, reducing the delineation time to 19 min in total compared to 45 min–120 min if manually delineated.

References

1. Borras, J.M., et al.: How many new cancer patients in Europe will require radiotherapy by 2025? An ESTRO-HERO analysis. Radiother. Oncol. **119**, 5–11 (2016)
2. Brouwer, C.L., Steenbakkers, R.J.H.M., Heuvel, E.V.D., Duppen, J.C., Navran, A.: 3D variation in delineation of head and neck organs at risk. Radiat. Oncol. 7–32 (2012)
3. Cardenas, C.E., et al.: Deep learning algorithm for auto-delineation of high-risk oropharyngeal clinical target volumes with built-in dice similarity coefficient parameter optimization function. Int. J. Radiat. Oncol. Biol. Phys. **101**(2), 468–478 (2018)
4. Fortunati, V., et al.: Tissue segmentation of head and neck CT images for treatment planning: a multiatlas approach combined with intensity modeling. Med. Phys. **40**(7), 071905 (2013)
5. Girshick, R., Donahue, J., Darrell, T., Malik, J.: Rich feature hierarchies for accurate object detection and semantic segmentation. In: Proceedings of the IEEE Computer Society Conference on Computer Vision and Pattern Recognition, pp. 580–587, June 2014
6. Ibragimov, B., Xing, L.: Segmentation of organs-at-risks in head and neck CT images using convolutional neural networks. Med. Phys. **44**(2), 547–557 (2017)
7. Kamnitsas, K., et al.: Efficient multi-scale 3D CNN with fully connected CRF for accurate brain lesion segmentation. Med. Image Anal. **36**, 61–78 (2017)

8. Krizhevsky, A., Sulskever, I., Hinton, G.E.: ImageNet classification with deep convolutional neural networks. In: Advances in Neural Information and Processing Systems (NIPS), vol. 60(6), pp. 84–90 (2012)

9. La Macchia, M., et al.: Systematic evaluation of three different commercial software solutions for automatic segmentation for adaptive therapy in head-and-neck, prostate and pleural cancer. Radiat. Oncol. **7**(1), 1 (2012)

10. Litjens, G., et al.: A survey on deep learning in medical image analysis. Med. Image Anal. **42**, 60–88 (2017)

11. Long, J., Shelhamer, E., Darrell, T.: Fully convolutional networks for semantic segmentation. In: Proceedings of the IEEE Computer Society Conference on Computer Vision and Pattern Recognition, 7–12 June 2015, pp. 3431–3440 (2015)

12. Men, K., et al.: Deep deconvolutional neural network for target segmentation of nasopharyngeal cancer in planning computed tomography images. Front. Oncol. **7**, 315 (2017)

13. Men, K., Dai, J., Li, Y.: Automatic segmentation of the clinical target volume and organs at risk in the planning CT for rectal cancer using deep dilated convolutional neural networks. Med. Phys. **44**(12), 6377–6389 (2017)

14. Nelms, B.E., Tomé, W.A., Robinson, G., Wheeler, J.: Variations in the contouring of organs at risk: test case from a patient with oropharyngeal cancer. Int. J. Radiat. Oncol. Biol. Phys. **82**(1), 368–378 (2012)

15. Robben, D., Bertels, J., Willems, S., Vandermeulen, D., Maes, F., Suetens, P.: DeepVoxNet: voxel-wise prediction of 3D images. Technical report, KU Leuven/ESAT/PSI, 1801, June 2018

16. Ronneberger, O., Fischer, P., Brox, T.: U-Net: convolutional networks for biomedical image segmentation. In: Navab, N., Hornegger, J., Wells, W.M., Frangi, A.F. (eds.) MICCAI 2015. LNCS, vol. 9351, pp. 234–241. Springer, Cham (2015). https://doi.org/10.1007/978-3-319-24574-4_28

17. Rosset, A., Spadola, L., Ratib, O.: OsiriX: an open-source software for navigating in multidimensional DICOM images. J. Digit. Imaging **17**(3), 205–216 (2004)

18. Sermanet, P., Eigen, D., Zhang, X., Mathieu, M., Fergus, R., Lecun, Y.: OverFeat: integrated recognition, localization and detection using convolutional networks (2014)

19. Tao, C.J., et al.: Multi-subject atlas-based auto-segmentation reduces interobserver variation and improves dosimetric parameter consistency for organs at risk in nasopharyngeal carcinoma: a multi-institution clinical study. Radiother. Oncol. **115**(3), 407–411 (2015)

20. Torre, L., Siegel, R., Ward, E., Jemal, A.: Global cancer incidence and mortality rates and trends - an update. Cancer Epidemiol. Biomark. Prev. **25**(1), 16–27 (2016)

Proceedings of the Third International Skin Imaging Collaboration Workshop (ISIC 2018)

Deeply Supervised Rotation Equivariant Network for Lesion Segmentation in Dermoscopy Images

Xiaomeng Li[(✉)], Lequan Yu, Chi-Wing Fu, and Pheng-Ann Heng

Department of Computer Science and Engineering,
The Chinese University of Hong Kong, Shatin, Hong Kong
xmli@cse.cuhk.edu.hk

Abstract. Automatic lesion segmentation in dermoscopy images is an essential step for computer-aided diagnosis of melanoma. The dermoscopy images exhibits rotational and reflectional symmetry, however, this geometric property has not been encoded in the state-of-the-art convolutional neural networks based skin lesion segmentation methods. In this paper, we present a deeply supervised rotation equivariant network for skin lesion segmentation by extending the recent group rotation equivariant network. Specifically, we propose the G-upsampling and G-projection operations to adapt the rotation equivariant classification network for our skin lesion segmentation problem. To further increase the performance, we integrate the deep supervision scheme into our proposed rotation equivariant segmentation architecture. The whole framework is equivariant to input transformations, including rotation and reflection, which improves the network efficiency and thus contributes to the segmentation performance. We extensively evaluate our method on the ISIC 2017 skin lesion challenge dataset. The experimental results show that our rotation equivariant networks consistently excel the regular counterparts with the same model complexity under different experimental settings. Our best model also outperforms the state-of-the-art challenging methods, which further demonstrate the effectiveness of our proposed deeply supervised rotation equivariant segmentation network.

1 Introduction

Skin cancer has become the most prevalent cancer in the United States [12], and melanoma is the most deadly form of skin cancer, leading to over 9,000 deaths in the Unite States in 2017 [13]. A common technique used by dermatologists for diagnosing skin diseases is the dermoscopy, which enables observation by enhancing the visual effect of pigmented skin lesions. Lesion segmentation in dermoscopy images is an essential component in the diagnosis of skin diseases. However, segmenting skin lesions by dermatologists is time-consuming and error-prone to inter- and intra-observer variabilities. Moreover, due to the growing shortage of dermatologists per capita, the automatic lesion segmentation in dermoscopy images would be beneficial to more people [8]. Convolutional

© Springer Nature Switzerland AG 2018
D. Stoyanov et al. (Eds.): OR 2.0/CARE/CLIP/ISIC 2018, LNCS 11041, pp. 235–243, 2018.
https://doi.org/10.1007/978-3-030-01201-4_25

neural networks (CNNs) have proven to be very powerful models for a board array of image recognition tasks. In the domain of skin lesion segmentation, all leading methods adopted CNN-based methods [2,16,17]. For example, Yuan et al. [17] proposed a deep convolutional neural network (DCNN), trained it with multiple color spaces, and achieved the best performance in the ISIC 2017 skin lesion segmentation challenge. Yu et al. [16] explored the network depth property and proposed a deep residual network with more than 50 layers for automatic skin lesion segmentation.

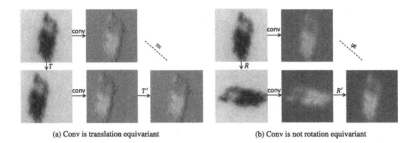

(a) Conv is translation equivariant   (b) Conv is not rotation equivariant

Fig. 1. Convolution layer is translation equivariant (a); but convolution is not rotation equivariant (Zoom in to see the detailed comparison), as shown in (b).

The success of these CNN-based models can be partially attributed to the effectiveness of weights sharing in the convolution layer, where the translation equivariance is preserved. To be specific, translating a layer's input produces the corresponding translation in the layer's output. As shown in Fig. 1(a), shifting the input of the convolution leads to the predictable shifting in the output. This translation equivariance property of convolution is effective in most perception tasks, where the same weights can be used to encode the local spatial pattern and reduce the model parameter to avoid overfitting. Unlike natural images, dermoscopy images exhibit not only translation symmetry but also rotation and flipping symmetry as well. However, if one rotates the convolution input, the generated output does not necessarily rotate in a predictable manner, as shown in Fig. 1(b). Previous works utilized data augmentation technique like rotation and flipping, to encourage the network to learn rotation and flipping covariance. Even though this strategy could regularize the network to learn the equivariance on the training set, there is no guarantee that the equivariance property will generalize to other images. Moreover, forcing the network to learn the redundant knowledge introduced by different data transformations would reduce the model efficiency. Specifically, with the same level of model complexity, the regular CNN needs to learns not only the discriminative features but only the input rotations and reflections. Furthermore, comparing with natural images, the biomedical images are scarce and more difficult to obtain, and it is highly demanded to design an efficient network to improve the model efficiency.

We consider to improve the network efficiency by encoding the rotation and flipping equivariance into the network, in which the network preserves the equivariance inherent without relying on data augmentation. Recently, there are some works have made significant progress for rotation equivariant networks [6,10]. Cohen et al. [6] explored rotation and reflection equivariant inherent network for classification problems, where the feature learned in the G space exhibits rotation equivariance. In this paper, we propose a deeply supervised rotation equivariant network by extending G-CNN [6] for skin lesion segmentation. Our network encodes the translation, rotation and flipping symmetry of dermoscopy images, and thus improves the skin lesion segmentation performance. Specifically, we design the G-upsampling layer and the G-projection layer for the segmentation task with the G-convolution layer. The G-upsampling layer upsamples the features in the G space and the G-projection layer performs average pooling over the rotation dimension and then projects features from the G space to $\mathbb{Z}$ space, making the whole network rotation equivariant. To better stabilize the learning processing of the proposed network, we also integrated the deep supervision [4,9] in our network to further improve the performance. Compared with the plain convolution neural networks, our network enjoys a substantially higher degree of weight sharing, and increases the expressive capacity of the network without increasing the number of parameters. We extensively evaluate our method on the ISIC 2017 skin lesion segmentation challenge. The results demonstrate the efficiency of our proposed rotation equivariant segmentation network, and our method outperforms other state-of-the-art methods on the challenging dataset. Several works [1,14,15] also explore the rotation equivariant network in the biomedical image domain. However, our work further explores the equivariant segmentation networks with deep supervision scheme [4,9] for automatic lesion segmentation in dermoscopy images.

2   Method

In this section, we first introduce the concept of group equivariant convolution (G-convolution), and then describe the proposed G-upsampling and G-projection layers for the segmentation task. Finally we present our proposed deeply supervised rotation equivariant framework.

2.1   G-convolution

The regular first convolution layer is a function that maps the input to feature maps with K channels $f : \mathbb{Z}^2 \to \mathbb{R}^K$. The function can be described as Eq. 1.

$$[f * \varphi](x) = \sum_{y \in \mathbb{Z}^2} \sum_k f_k(y)\varphi_k(x - y), \tag{1}$$

where φ_k denotes the convolution kernel.

To encode rotation equivariance in the network, Cohen et al. [6] proposed to conduct convolution on groups, where the group $p4$ consists of all compositions of translations and rotations by $90°$ about any center of rotation in the grid, and

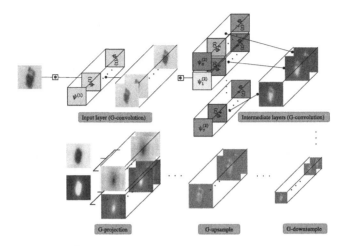

Fig. 2. The illustration of the G-convolution, G-upsampling and G-projection operation. Except the G-projection layer, we only show 1 channel in all other layers to simplify the illustration.

the group $p4m$ additionally includes reflections. Specifically, for the input layer, the $(\mathbb{Z}^2 \to G)$ convolution is defined as

$$[f * \varphi](g) = \sum_{y \in \mathbb{Z}^2} \sum_k f_k(y) \varphi_k(g^{-1}y), \tag{2}$$

where g is a transformation in the predefined group $p4$ or $p4m$. Then, in the following layers, feature maps and filters are both functions on G and the $(G \to G)$ convolution can be described as

$$[f * \varphi](g) = \sum_{h \in G} \sum_k f_k(h) \varphi_k(g^{-1}h) \tag{3}$$

2.2 G-upsampling and G-projection for Segmentation Problem

In the segmentation problem, the down-sampled feature maps need to be upsampled in the G space for pixel-level prediction, and thus we design the G-upsampling layer. The convention upsampling layer performs upsample operation for feature maps at the spatial dimension. In the G space, the G-upsampling layer performs upsample operation over all eight rotations (for group $p4m$) at each spatial position, as shown in Fig. 2.

To enable the equivariant network to produce final score maps for skin lesion segmentation, we also define the $(G - \mathbb{Z}^2)$ projection layer.

$$f_k(y) = \frac{1}{|G|} \sum_G (f_k(h)), \tag{4}$$

where $|G|$ denotes the number of element in group G. For example, it equals to 4 for group $p4$ and 8 for group $p4m$. With the G-upsampling layer and the G-projection layer, we can design a segmentation network, which is equivariant to the input symmetric transformations.

2.3 Deeply Supervised G-FCNs

The deeply supervised rotation equivariant network is based on the ResNet34 [7] architecture, where we replace the convolution layer, upsampling layer to the G-convolution, G-upsampling and G-projection layers. As shown in Fig. 3, we use three 2×2 G-upsampling layers and one G-projection layer following the feature maps generated by ResNet34. We also adopt the U-net like long-skip connections to preserve the low-level features. The deep supervision mechanism is performed by upsampling at three different spatial resolution of features, and the final result is the weighted combination of three segmentation predictions. Since all the elements in the network are equivariant to 90° rotation and reflection of the input, the whole framework also preserves the rotation equivariant property. In other words, if one clock-wise rotates the input image 90°, the network output will rotate in the same manner. Readers can find more details about the network architecture from our code[1].

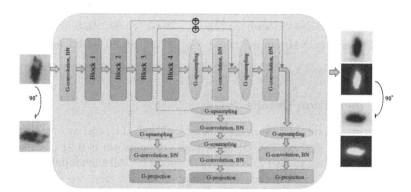

Fig. 3. The framework of our proposed rotation equivariant network for skin lesion segmentation. The network is based on ResNet34 backbone, and is integrated with deep supervision and U-Net connections. All the regular operations are replaced to G-convolution, G-upsampling, and G-projection operations. The whole architecture is equivariant to input symmetric transformation. In other words, if one rotate the input for 90°, then the prediction score would rotate in the same way. Note that we omit the pooling operation, ReLU activations to simplify the illustration.

---

[1] https://github.com/xmengli999/Deeply-Supervised-Rotation-Equivariant-Network-for-Lesion-Segmentation.

3   Experiments and Results

3.1   Dataset and Evaluation Metrics

We evaluate our method on the dataset of ISIC 2017 skin lesion segmentation challenge [5], which consists of a training set with 2000 annotated dermoscopic images, a validation set with 150 images, and a testing set with 600 images. The image size ranges from 540×722 to 4499×6748. To keep balance between segmentation performance and computational cost, we first resize all the images to 224×224 using bicubic interpolation. For evaluation metric, we follow the challenge instructions to employ five evaluation metrics, including jaccard index (JA), dice coefficient (DI), pixel-wise accuracy (AC), sensitivity (SE) and specificity (SP). Note that the final rank is determined according to JA in the ISIC 2017 skin lesion segmentation challenge.

Table 1. Ablation study of the deeply supervised rotation equivariant network.

Model	No. of para	Evaluation metrics				
		JA	DI	AC	SE	SP
ResnetFCN34*	22.8M	71.27	80.21	91.39	78.31	96.78
(RE)-ResnetFCN34*	22.8M	74.54	83.27	92.58	81.05	**97.59**
DS-U-ResnetFCN34*	23.2M	74.38	83.06	92.51	82.52	97.14
(RE)-DS-U-ResnetFCN34* (ours)	23.2M	76.65	85.00	93.27	84.61	96.80
(RE)-DS-U-ResnetFCN34 (ours)	23.5M	**77.23**	**85.60**	**93.55**	**85.40**	97.15

3.2   Implementation Details

All the experiments were implemented using PyTorch [11], and were trained with stochastic gradient descent (SGD) algorithm (momentum is 0.9) from scratch. The learning rate is set to 0.01 and decays at epoch 60. All the models are trained for 70 epochs. As for experiments with the plain convolution, we employed data augmentation like 90° rotation and flipping. The main loss function and the deep supervision branches are trained with cross entropy loss. The weights for main loss and deep supervision are 0.7, 0.2 and 0.1 respectively.

3.3   Ablation Study

Table 1 shows the segmentation performance on the test dataset with different configurations. ResnetFCN34* refers to the FCN-based Resnet34 network, while (RE)-ResnetFCN34* and DS-U-ResnetFCN34* are the rotation equivariant and deeply supervised with long range U-Net connections counterparts, respectively. The * denotes that we remove the first pooling layer from the original Resnet34 network, following the setting in [6]. Note that all the rotation equivariant networks are performed with group $p4m$ [6]. To analyze the effectiveness of rotation equivariant network fairly, all the comparison are performed with the same model complexity. Specifically, compared with the original filter numbers in Resnet34, the number of filters is divided by roughly $\sqrt{8}$ in each G-convolution layer.

From the comparison in Table 1, we can see that the rotation equivariant network largely excels the plain counterpart, with 3.27% improvement on JA. The deeply supervised version also improve the JA performance significantly. When integrate the deep supervision with U-Net connections into the rotation equivariant network ((RE)-DS-U-ResnetFCN34*), we can further improve the segmentation performance (2.27% on JA). To better adapt the network for our skin lesion segmentation task, we replace the first pooling layer of ResnetFCN34 with a G-convolution with stride of 2 and denoted the deeply supervised rotation equivariant version as (RE)-DS-U-ResnetFCN34. It is observed that (RE)-DS-U-ResnetFCN34 achieves the best performance on the all evaluation metrics excepting for SP, demonstrating the superiority and effectiveness of rotation equivariant networks under same level of model complexity.

Table 2. Comparison with state-of-the-art methods on the ISIC 2017 test dataset.

Team	JA	DI	AC	SE	SP
Our Method	**0.772**	**0.856**	**0.936**	**0.854**	0.972
Yuan and Lo [17]	0.765	0.849	0.934	0.825	0.975
Berseth [2]	0.762	0.847	0.932	0.820	0.978
Bi et al. [3]	0.760	0.844	0.934	0.802	**0.985**
RECOD	0.754	0.839	0.931	0.817	0.970
Jer	0.752	0.837	0.930	0.813	0.976
NedMos	0.749	0.839	0.930	0.810	0.981
INESC	0.735	0.824	0.922	0.813	0.968
Shenzhen U (Lee)	0.718	0.810	0.922	0.789	0.975

3.4   Comparison with Other Methods

We compare our result with state-of-the-art results on the ISIC 2017 testing dataset. There are totally 21 submissions and the top results are listed in Table 2. Yuan et al. [17] trained a CNN network with multiple color spaces and achieves the best performance on the skin lesion segmentation challenge. Our best model, trained from scratch on the single RGB color space, outperforms other state-of-the-arts in the test dataset of the ISIC challenge. This comparison validates the effectiveness of our proposed deeply supervised rotation equivariant network in the skin lesion segmentation task.

4   Conclusion

In this paper, we present a deeply supervised rotation equivariant segmentation network for skin lesion segmentation by utilizing the recent findings on rotation equivariant CNNs. We design the G-upsampling and G-projection layers to enable our network for the segmentation task, and introduce the deep supervision mechanism to improve performance. Our network encodes the rotation and reflection symmetry of dermoscopy images, and significantly improves the skin lesion segmentation performance. Our method has achieved the best performance on the ISIC 2017 skin lesion segmentation challenge dataset. Future works include the extension of equivariance to arbitrary rotation and scaling.

Acknowledgments. The work described in this paper was supported by a grant from the Research Grants Council of the Hong Kong Special Administrative Region (Project no. GRF 14225616) and a grant from Hong Kong Innovation and Technology Commission (Project no. ITS/426/17FP). We special thank Dr. Taco Cohen for fruitful discussions, kindly help and encouragement in our exploration.

References

1. Bekkers, E.J., Lafarge, M.W., Veta, M., Eppenhof, K.A., Pluim, J.P.: Roto-translation covariant convolutional networks for medical image analysis. arXiv preprint arXiv:1804.03393 (2018)
2. Berseth, M.: ISIC 2017-skin lesion analysis towards melanoma detection. arXiv preprint arXiv:1703.00523 (2017)
3. Bi, L., Kim, J., Ahn, E., Feng, D.: Automatic skin lesion analysis using large-scale dermoscopy images and deep residual networks. arXiv preprint arXiv:1703.04197 (2017)
4. Chen, H., Qi, X., Yu, L., Heng, P.A.: DCAN: deep contour-aware networks for accurate gland segmentation. In: Proceedings of the IEEE conference on Computer Vision and Pattern Recognition, pp. 2487–2496 (2016)
5. Codella, N.C., Gutman, D., Celebi, M.E., et al.: Skin lesion analysis toward melanoma detection: a challenge at the 2017 international symposium on biomedical imaging (ISBI), hosted by the international skin imaging collaboration (ISIC). arXiv preprint arXiv:1710.05006 (2017)
6. Cohen, T., Welling, M.: Group equivariant convolutional networks. In: International Conference on Machine Learning, pp. 2990–2999 (2016)
7. He, K., Zhang, X., Ren, S., Sun, J.: Deep residual learning for image recognition. In: Proceedings of the IEEE Conference on Computer Vision and Pattern Recognition, pp. 770–778 (2016)
8. Kimball, A.B., Resneck, J.S.: The us dermatology workforce: a specialty remains in shortage. J. Am. Acad. Dermatol. **59**(5), 741–745 (2008)
9. Lee, C.Y., Xie, S., Gallagher, P., Zhang, Z., Tu, Z.: Deeply-supervised nets. In: Artificial Intelligence and Statistics, pp. 562–570 (2015)
10. Marcos, D., Volpi, M., Komodakis, N., Tuia, D.: Rotation equivariant vector field networks. In: 2017 IEEE International Conference on Computer Vision (ICCV), pp. 5058–5067. IEEE (2017)
11. Paszke, A., et al.: Automatic differentiation in PyTorch (2017)
12. Rogers, H.W., Weinstock, M.A., Feldman, S.R., Coldiron, B.M.: Incidence estimate of nonmelanoma skin cancer (keratinocyte carcinomas) in the us population, 2012. JAMA Dermatol. **151**(10), 1081–1086 (2015)
13. Siegel, R.L., Miller, K.D., Jemal, A.: Cancer statistics, 2017. CA Cancer J. Clin. **67**(1), 7–30 (2017). https://doi.org/10.3322/caac.21387

14. Veeling, B.S., Linmans, J., Winkens, J., Cohen, T., Welling, M.: Rotation equivariant CNNs for digital pathology. arXiv preprint arXiv:1806.03962 (2018)
15. Winkens, J., Linmans, J., Veeling, B.S., Cohen, T.S., Welling, M.: Improved semantic segmentation for histopathology using rotation equivariant convolutional networks. Med. Imaging Deep Learn. 330–341 (2018)
16. Yu, L., Chen, H., Dou, Q., Qin, J., Heng, P.A.: Automated melanoma recognition in dermoscopy images via very deep residual networks. IEEE Trans. Med. Imaging **36**(4), 994–1004 (2017)
17. Yuan, Y., Lo, Y.C.: Improving dermoscopic image segmentation with enhanced convolutional-deconvolutional networks. IEEE J. Biomed. Health Inform. (2017). https://doi.org/10.1109/JBHI.2017.2787487

Skin Image Analysis for Erythema Migrans Detection and Automated Lyme Disease Referral

P. Burlina[1(✉)], N. Joshi[1], E. Ng[3], S. Billings[1], A. Rebman[2], and J. Aucott[2]

[1] Applied Physics Laboratory, The Johns Hopkins University, Baltimore, USA
pburlina@hotmail.com
[2] Department of Rheumatology, The Johns Hopkins University, Baltimore, USA
[3] Department of Dermatology, The Johns Hopkins University, Baltimore, USA

Abstract. This study develops approaches for the automated referral of individuals with Lyme disease using erythema migrans rash (EM) images with clinical-grade or 'in the wild' characteristics. We develop a pre-screener using a Deep Convolutional Neural Network (DCNN) that classifies EM vs. other conditions, including either control/unaffected skin, or skin presenting with other confuser lesions. We test and report performance metrics for the proposed approach on this dataset including Cohen's Kappa coefficient, area under the receiver operating characteristic (ROC) curve (AUC), accuracy, sensitivity, specificity. The machine classification yields accuracy (and error margin) of 93.04% (1.49), AUC of 0.9504 (0.0156), and Kappa of 0.7549 (0.0586), which is a significant improvement over previously published state-of-the-art methods. Results also suggest substantial agreement between machine and expert clinician annotated gold standard images. The DCNN model developed for this skin classifier is made publicly available and can potentially be used by others for transfer learning to other types of skin lesion classification models including those for skin cancer.

1 Introduction

This study aims to leverage deep learning (DL) and DCNNs [1–6, 8, 19, 20] for prescreening of Lyme disease [9–15]. Lyme disease is the most common vector-borne disease in the United States, with over 300,000 new cases annually. *Borrelia burgdorferi* is the causative bacterial agent of Lyme disease, and it is transmitted through the bite of an infected tick into the skin of the affected individual. Infection progresses through three stages, advancing from skin-limited disease to disseminated disease affecting the nervous, cardiac, and rheumatologic systems. In the majority of cases, the initial skin infection is manifested by a round or oval red skin lesion called erythema migrans (EM), which is a direct result of bacterial infection of the skin and marks the first stage of Lyme disease. Treatment with oral antibiotics is highly effective in early, uncomplicated cases. Therefore, recognition of EM is crucial to early diagnosis and treatment, and ultimately, prevention of potentially devastating long-term complications.

© Springer Nature Switzerland AG 2018
D. Stoyanov et al. (Eds.): OR 2.0/CARE/CLIP/ISIC 2018, LNCS 11041, pp. 244–251, 2018.
https://doi.org/10.1007/978-3-030-01201-4_26

Erythema migrans typically occurs 1 to 3 weeks after the initial tick bite and expands centrifugally by as much as a centimeter per day. Classically, the lesion will also display central clearing as it expands, leading to the hallmark bull's-eye rash of Lyme disease. However, many individuals will not display this finding and the majority of individuals are unable to recall a tick bite, making early diagnosis challenging. EM usually persists for weeks during which its visual recognition is the primary basis for the clinical diagnosis of early Lyme disease. Following this early period, untreated EM usually disappears or progresses to disseminated disease through the spread of infection through the bloodstream. Diagnosis of early Lyme disease is usually made based on clinical signs and symptoms and history of potential exposure to ticks, due to the lack of reliable serologic blood testing early in the disease course [9, 10]. Blood tests are insensitive during the early phase of infection and are not recommended because of the high false negative rate at the time of initial EM presentation. Only 25 to 40% will have positive results during the acute phase of infection. Direct detection of bacteria in blood or biopsy samples can be performed, but are generally unavailable in non-research settings and not practical due to the time required for results [11].

The clinical diagnosis of early Lyme disease and EM is still a challenge. This is because EM may take on a variety of appearances besides the characteristic ring-within-a-ring, or bull's-eye rash. The majority (80%) of EM lesions in the US lack the central clearing [13] of the stereotypical bull's eye lesion and appear uniformly red or bluish red (Fig. 1). Thus, they are often mistaken for a spider bite or bruise. A small percentage (4–8%) of skin lesions have a small central blister, which may lead to the incorrect diagnosis of shingles (herpes zoster) [14]. Approximately 20% of patients have multiple skin lesions arising from the spread of infection through the bloodstream, which often have an atypical appearance. Atypical skin lesions are often misdiagnosed, which results in delayed diagnosis and treatment and increases risk of long-term complications.

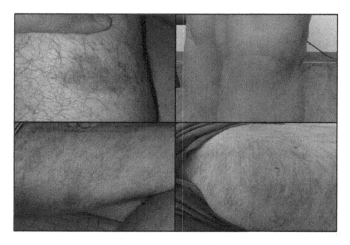

Fig. 1. Examples of EM with atypical (top) and classic bull's-eye (bottom) presentations. (sources: left: https://commons.wikimedia.org/wiki/Category:Erythema_migrans; right: JHU)

Previous studies have shown that the general population does not correctly identify EM skin lesions that lack the classic bull's-eye appearance and misidentify this condition approximately 80% of the time. As 80% of skin lesions do not have the bull's eye appearance [15], this means that approximately 60% of all EM lesions may be misdiagnosed by patients (80% of 80%). Machine-based prescreening of skin lesions associated with Lyme disease has the potential to identify a high percentage of both typical and atypical lesions, thereby decreasing the incidence of misdiagnosis of early Lyme disease.

Prior to 2012 and the demonstration of significant improvement in object recognition performance on ImageNet via the use of DCNNs (AlexNet [4]), object classification in computer vision was largely based on applying traditional classifiers to hand-engineered image features [18]. DCNNs have replaced these approaches for both computer vision and medical imaging tasks (e.g. [1, 2]), and recently, they have been successfully used for performing a number of medical imaging diagnostics, including identifying skin cancer [12]. To the best of our knowledge, however, Lyme disease detection from skin lesions has only been addressed thus far using classical ML approaches [16].

This study aims to expand on prior state of the art with the following novel and salient contributions: (a) we develop a novel, carefully clinician-annotated dataset called Lyme1600, which includes over 1600 images with several types of fine-grained annotations for skin lesions, mostly focused on EM, but also including other confuser lesions and clear/unaffected cases; this dataset size is over two orders of magnitude larger than prior non-public datasets previously studied (such as [16] having 143 images), and (b) we develop a baseline DCNN approach that achieves a significant performance improvement over prior state of the art, and demonstrates substantial agreement with human clinician annotations. We make the DCNN model for this classifier publicly available; it can potentially be used by others for fine tuning and transfer learning for addressing classification of other types of skin affects including skin cancer lesions.

2   Methods

Problem Statement: We pose the problem as a 2-class classification problem, classifying images into patients that have EM (Lyme disease) vs. individuals that have no skin lesions or another skin condition, including confounding skin lesions. The main confusers that are considered in this second class include cases of herpes zoster (HZ), also known as shingles. HZ was used as the principal confuser with the rationale that the main application envisioned here is a pre-screening tool, possibly implemented as a smartphone application, that could help individuals self-identify and screen lesions suspicious for Lyme disease. An acute onset rash, such as HZ, might prompt an individual to suspect Lyme disease and seek medical attention. This application is targeted towards such individuals for whom such a tool would provide a means of disambiguation.

Data: As an annotated, and publicly available dataset for the study of machine pre-screening of Lyme disease and EM is not available and as there is a paucity of clinical images having the associated consent and approval required for use in this research, an image dataset was created using publicly available images extracted from the web. This strategy was motivated by a recent study [12] on skin cancer where online images were also successfully leveraged—after careful annotation—for generating DL classification models of referable skin cancers. The online images of skin lesions leveraged in this study principally include EM, herpes zoster, other non-Lyme skin lesions, and normal skin. Such images were mined from online sources, after which clinicians (J.A., A.R., and E.N.) were tasked with carefully annotating the images based on the visual appearance and the estimated size of the skin lesions. Clinicians were asked to do a whole image classification first using a high level labeling of the pathology, followed by a fine grained annotation that included the type of specific EM that was present (e.g. simple vs. diffuse). Additional curation steps included a machine-based removal of full or near duplicates, followed by human assessment for the presence of duplicates and the removal of inappropriate images. Following this, a subset of images was selected to include images with moderate to high probability of depicting EM or herpes zoster (and other confounding skin lesions). Images with a low probability of EM or HZ diagnosis were excluded from the dataset. In the end, a 2-class partitioning of those images into affected (C0) and unaffected (C1) classes was performed (Table 1).

DL Approach: Recent advances in DL performance have been realized via a number of factors including the development of large labeled datasets, the availability of markedly increased computational power via graphic processing units, and various algorithmic improvements. DCNNs, used here, form feature representations at increased levels of abstraction via multiple layers of processing [1, 2] and solve discriminative problems (e.g. classification). Here, a DCNN takes a skin image as input and produces proba-bilities that the image belong to one of several specific classes of pathologies (EM vs. no EM here) as output. Our study uses the ResNet50 [8] DCNN architecture. ResNet was originally conceived as a means of producing deeper networks and include specific design patterns such as bottleneck and skip connections that make the output of upstream layer directly available to downstream layers. Our implementation used the Keras and TensorFlow frameworks. We used transfer learning and fine-tuned the original ResNet50 weights using the skin classification problem addressed herein. We used stochastic gradient descent with Nesterov momentum = 0.9 for training, with initial learning rate set to 1E-3. The training scheme used an early stopping approach, which terminates training after 10 epochs of no improvement of the validation accuracy. We used a categorical cross entropy loss function. Dynamic learning rate scheduling was also used, in which we multiplied the learning rate by 0.5 when the training loss did not improve for 10 epochs. A batch size of 32 was used. Data augmentation was used and included horizontal flipping, blurring, sharpening, and changes to saturation, brightness, contrast, and color balance. We are making the DCNN model, with trained weights, available at https://github.com/neil454/lyme-1600-model.

N-Fold Validation: The datasets were further subdivided into training and testing subsets. We used a K-fold cross-validation method, with K = 5, where four folds were employed for training and one fold was used for testing (with rotation of the folds for 5 runs). One training fold was further equally subdivided into two parts, with one used for validation and stopping conditions. In sum, the train/validation/test partition distribution was 70%/10%20%, respectively.

Performance Metrics: The performance metrics used in this study included accuracy, F1, sensitivity, specificity, PPV (Positive predicted value), NPV, (Negative predicted value) and kappa score, which discounts chance agreement [7]. Since any classifier trades off between sensitivity and specificity, to compare methods, we used ROC (receiver operating characteristic) curves, showing detection probability (sensitivity) vs. false alarm rate (100% - specificity) and AUC (area under curve) was computed.

3 Results

Results of experiments are shown for applying the above method to the data partitioned using 5-fold cross validation. Table 1 shows the class partitions, Table 2 the resulting metrics, and Fig. 2 the resulting ROC curve. Results show promising accuracy of 93.04%. The ROC curve shows that one can operate with 90% sensitivity and above while having a specificity ranging in the 75% to 85% range, a tradeoff which suggests a potential for deployment as a pre-screener. Kappa score of 0.7549 also demonstrates substantial agreement with the human-annotated gold standard.

Table 1. Class balancing and characteristic table

Class	Number of samples
C0: control, unaffected, and confuser lesions including herpes zoster	1387
C1: erythema migrans	308

Table 2. Performance metrics for five-fold cross validation

Metric	Value	Standard deviation
Accuracy	93.04	1.49
Sensitivity/Recall	75.66	7.28
Specificity	96.90	0.48
PPV/Precision	84.35	2.79
NPV	94.73	1.51
Kappa	0.7549	0.0586
Positive Likelihood	24.94	4.72
Negative Likelihood	0.25	0.076
F1 Score	0.7967	0.0502
AUC	0.9504	0.0156
Confusion matrix	|1344 43| |75 233|	

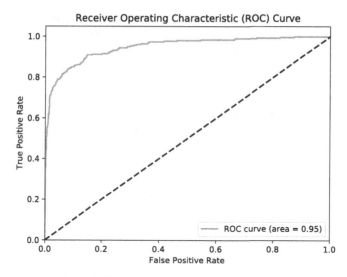

Fig. 2. ROC curve for the proposed pre-screener

4 Discussion

Data sets of EM rashes with annotation for research or teaching purposes are not currently widely available. Only one large study of EM rash characteristics in the United States from 2002 has been done. Physician review of images in that dataset reported an unexpected diversity in the appearance of EM lesions, with only 10% of lesions having the classic central clearing and ring-within-a-ring target appearance [17]. The photos of EM lesions from that study had not been analyzed further using computerized approaches. To our knowledge, only one other study of computer-assisted detection of EM has been reported in the literature [16]. That study [16] used machine learning methods including boosting, SVM, naïve Bayes, and neural nets (but not DL) applied on hand-designed image features, and was tested with a smaller dataset of 143 EM rash images. Reported accuracies ranged from 69.23% to 80.42%. These results are a testimony to the difficulty in addressing the problem of how to discern between the varied presentations of the EM lesions. By comparison, our results, performed on a much larger dataset, and images taken 'in the wild', show notable enhancements in performance.

Because of the lack of publicly available labeled datasets for EM ML studies, the use of photographs from online image banks was made necessary in this study in order to obtain an adequate number of images, particularly as we addressed a less common condition such as erythema migrans. In doing so, our work followed the approach of a recently published high-impact study investigating detection of skin cancer using DCNNs [12], which also exploited online images to produce a curated training dataset and corresponding model. While our dataset is still being developed with new types of confounding pathologies and lesions such as tinea corporis, our goal is to release it in the future once the study has completed procuring all examples of confusing lesions and all annotation has been done. In the meantime, we are making the classification model available online.

One limitation of the current dataset includes the fact that individuals with dark skin are underrepresented. In addition, certain characteristics inherent to online images, such as variability in viewpoint/angle, lighting, and photo resolution, made the problem more challenging. At annotation time, the inability to verify the skin lesion through inspection at different angles or magnification in order to estimate the size of the skin lesion in some cases was an issue. However, images for which there was significant ambiguity or uncertainty in diagnosis due to these factors were excluded. We were also limited in our ability to verify diagnoses through corroborating clinical and laboratory data. However, this limitation is mitigated by the fact that diagnosis of both EM and the principal confuser considered here, HZ, are primarily clinical—that is, the diagnosis of these conditions relies primarily on visual inspection and suspicion. There is no universally accepted "gold standard" diagnostic test for Lyme disease given the variable reliability of serologic testing and the impractical nature of culture identification of the organism in the clinical setting. Meanwhile, the gold standard for diagnosis of herpes zoster consists of PCR or culture detection of varicella zoster virus from skin lesions, but this is usually not performed for diagnosis given the characteristic clinical appearance and symptoms associated with the rash.

In sum, considering all of the elements above, our study was able to substantially advance the state of the art in automated Lyme prescreening with DL models that have significant promise for clinical deployment as pre-screeners. Such an application would prove to be of great utility given the challenges of diagnosing Lyme disease at an early stage when treatment is effective and can prevent the otherwise serious long-term complications associated with advanced Lyme disease. Based on our results, an application using DL is likely more sensitive than patient self-assessment and may even be more accurate than diagnosis by a general non-specialist physician, who would ordinarily serve as the screening gatekeeper for acute onset rashes such as EM. Given the frequent under-diagnosis of EM, the use of automated detection would be beneficial by increasing the number of patients who seek further medical assessment for EM rashes and minimizing the number of cases that go unevaluated and undiagnosed, with an expected positive effect on patient morbidity. Future work will involve studying multi-class problems such as also trying to separately identify the HZ and other confounding classes, which may lead to improved performance for the 2-class EM problem.

5   Conclusion

We make several contributions to automated EM and Lyme disease detection: we develop the first carefully clinician-annotated large dataset for the study of ML-based diagnostics of Lyme disease, including cases of affected, confuser, and control images. We propose a pre-screener for EM using DCNNs that shows substantial agreement with expert human clinician gold standard annotations and make this model publicly available.

References

1. Goodfellow, I., Bengio, Y., Courville, A., Bengio, Y.: Deep Learning. MIT Press, Cambridge (2016)
2. LeCun, Y., Bengio, Y., Hinton, G.: Deep learning. Nature **521**, 436–444 (2015)
3. Girshick, R., Donahue, J., Darrell, T., Malik, J.: Rich feature hierarchies for accurate object detection and semantic segmentation. In: IEEE Computer Vision and Pattern Recognition (2014)
4. Krizhevsky, A., Sutskever, I., Hinton, G.: Imagenet classification with deep convolutional neural networks. In: Advances in Neural Information Processing Systems (2012)
5. Simonyan, K., Zisserman, A.: Very deep convolutional networks for large-scale image recognition. arXiv (2014)
6. Szegedy, C., et al.: Going deeper with convolutions. In: IEEE Computer Vision and Pattern Recognition (2015)
7. Landis, J.R., Koch, G.G.: The measurement of observer agreement for categorical data. Biometrics **33**, 159–174 (1977)
8. He, K., et al.: Deep residual learning for image recognition. In: IEEE Computer Vision and Pattern Recognition (2016)
9. Bhate, C., Schwartz, R.: Lyme disease. Part I. Advances and perspectives. J. Am. Acad. Dermatol. **64**, 619–636 (2011)
10. Bhate, C., Schwartz, R.: Lyme disease. Part II. Management and prevention. J. Am. Acad. Dermatol. **64**, 639–653 (2011)
11. Shapiro, E.: Lyme disease. N. Engl. J. Med. **370**, 1724–1731 (2014)
12. Esteva, A., et al.: Dermatologist-level classification of skin cancer with deep neural networks. Nature **542**, 115–118 (2017)
13. Tibbles, C.D., Edlow, J.A.: Does this patient have Erythema Migrans? JAMA **298**, 1159–1160 (2007)
14. Mazori, D.R., Orme, C.M., Mir, A., Meehan, S.A., Neimann, A.L.: Vesicular erythema migrans: an atypical and easily misdiagnosed form of Lyme disease. Dermatol. Online J. **21** (8) (2015)
15. Aucott, J.N., Crowder, L.A., Yedlin, V., Kortte, K.B. : Bull's-eye and nontarget skin lesions of Lyme disease: an internet survey of identification of erythema migrans. Dermatol. Res. Pract. **2012** (2012)
16. Čuk, E., et al.: Supervised visual system for recognition of erythema migrans, an early skin manifestation of Lyme borreliosis. Strojniški vestnik-J. Mech. Eng. **60**, 115–123 (2014)
17. Smith, R.P., Schoen, R.T., Rahn, D.W.: Clinical characterization and treatment outcomes of early Lyme disease in patients with microbiologically confirmed erythema migrans. Ann. Inter. Med. **136**, 421–428 (2002)
18. Kankanahalli, S., Burlina, P.M., Wolfson, Y., Freund, D.E., Bressler, N.M.: Automated classification of severity of age-related macular degeneration from fundus photographs. Invest. Ophthalmol. Vis. Sci. **54**, 1789–1796 (2013)
19. Burlina, P., et al.: Comparing humans and deep learning performance for grading AMD: a study in using universal deep features and transfer learning for automated AMD analysis. Comput. Biol. Med. **82**, 80–86 (2017)
20. Burlina, P.M., et al.: Automated grading of age-related macular degeneration from color fundus images using deep convolutional neural networks. JAMA Ophthalmol. **135**, 1170–1176 (2017)

Severity Assessment of Psoriatic Plaques Using Deep CNN Based Ordinal Classification

Anabik Pal[1]([✉]), Akshay Chaturvedi[1], Utpal Garain[1], Aditi Chandra[2], Raghunath Chatterjee[2], and Swapan Senapati[3]

[1] CVPR Unit, Indian Statistical Unit, Kolkata 700108, West Bengal, India
`anabik_r@isical.ac.in`
[2] Human Genetics Unit, Indian Statistical Unit, Kolkata 700108, West Bengal, India
[3] Consultant Dermatologist, Uttarpara, Hooghly 712258, West Bengal, India

Abstract. Development of computer-aided diagnosis (CAD) tool for severity assessment of psoriatic plaques is important to assist the dermatologists to overcome the human limitation. In this paper, a pioneering attempt is made to build a Convolutional Neural Network (CNN) model to classify a skin image with respect to its severity class. However, the commonly used loss functions like categorical cross entropy and mean square error ignores the underlying ordinal class relationships (distance between predicted and actual class) which are important for the present problem. In this paper, the Earth Mover's Distance based loss function is proposed for training CNN since it takes into account the corresponding ordinal class relationships. Separate CNNs are trained for severity scoring corresponding to three plaque characteristics- erythema (redness), scaling (silveryness) and induration (elevation). Mean accuracy (MA), mean absolute error (MAE) and Kendall's τ_b are used for performance evaluation. The experimental result shows that the proposed ordinal classification technique outperforms the traditional approaches.

Keywords: Psoriasis image · Psoriatic plaque · Erythema · Scaling Induration · Convolutional Neural Network · Ordinal loss · Dataset

1 Introduction

Psoriasis is a chronic, immune-mediated, relapsing, inflammatory skin disease and usually associated with itch. The prevalence of psoriasis varies 1%–12% among different populations worldwide [1]. This disease develops when the immune system mistakes a normal skin cell for a pathogen and sends out faulty signals that cause overproduction of new skin cells. This disease can be diagnosed by visual and haptic inspection. The visual changes of outer skin surface due to this disease include development of elevated red scaly dry patches with well-demarcated borders on the skin surface. However, the shape, size, color and

© Springer Nature Switzerland AG 2018
D. Stoyanov et al. (Eds.): OR 2.0/CARE/CLIP/ISIC 2018, LNCS 11041, pp. 252–259, 2018.
https://doi.org/10.1007/978-3-030-01201-4_27

distribution of these patches vary. In dermatology, these patches are termed as psoriatic plaque [13].

No drug is available yet to cure psoriasis completely but the severity can be controlled by suitable drug doses. As the drug response varies among different patients thus development of reliable severity assessment procedure is required to decide the type and dose of the drugs as well as measure disease progress and drug's efficacy. Dermatologists use Psoriasis Area Severity Index (PASI) [5] for estimating severity. PASI considers two major aspects of the disease: ratio of body surface area affected by this disease and the severity of the plaques formed on the skin surface. The severity of the plaque is determined by the visual disorder formed on the affected skin regions. Three different aspects are considered for severity of the plaques: degree of redness or erythema, thickness or induration and scaling or desquamation. All aspects are scored with a value between $0-4$. Table 1 contains a sample image for every severity class.

Table 1. Visualization of psoriasis plaques with different severity scores.

Severity Factor	Absent (0)	Mild (1)	Moderate (2)	Severe (3)	Very Severe (4)
Erythema (Redness)					
Scaling (Silvery-ness)					
Induration (Elevation)					

The severity factors are determined by the dermatologists in an eye estimation technique. The severity assessment procedure suffers from both inter- and intra-observer variability. Hence, development of an automated and robust system for severity assessment of psoriatic plaque is necessary for clinical studies. Some approaches have already been proposed for automatic scoring of scaling [2] and erythema [4,6,7,12]. In [14], an image based system is also proposed to compute the aggregated severity score according to plaque characteristics. In [11], an attempt has been made to assess the erythema, scaling and induration scores from psoriatic plaque images. However, all of these approaches consider the present severity grading task as an image classification problem but fail to capture the underlying ordinal relationship among the severity labels. This motivates us to develop CNN based ordinal classifiers for severity assessment of psoriatic plaques.

To summarize, the key contributions of this paper are: (i) a pioneering attempt towards developing a deep convolutional neural network based ordinal classifier for predicting severity score of psoriatic plaque, (ii) a new loss function is used for training a CNN which can capture the ordinal relationship among the class labels, (iii) two pre-trained CNN models (namely, ResNet-50 and Mobile Net) trained on imagenet dataset are fine-tuned to develop the severity assessment classifiers, and finally, (iv) the performance of the proposed CNN is compared with several baselines.

2 Methodology

2.1 Convolutional Neural Network

Nowadays, Convolutional Neural Network (CNN) is widely used for image classification tasks as it relieves the researchers from designing hand-engineered feature descriptors and automatically develops powerful mathematical models directly from the training images. These models are made up of multiple processing units and each processing unit consists of trainable weights and biases. In the training phase, the network parameters are updated by comparing the distribution of predicted class labels with the actual class labels of the training images. A brief description of the traditional categorical cross entropy (CCE) loss and the mean square error (MSE) loss functions are given below.

Suppose, for a C-class ($C > 2$) single-label image classification problem, the ground truth of a particular image is given by a binary vector G of length C such that $G_i = 1$ whenever $i = k$ and 0 otherwise. The output of the CNN is a probability distribution P of length C such that its ith entry (P_i) represents the predicted probability of the ith class. Now the definition of CCE loss and the MSE loss are given in Eqs. 1 and 2.

$$\mathcal{L}_{CCE} = -\sum_{i=1}^{C} G_i \, ln(P_i) \tag{1}$$

$$\mathcal{L}_{MSE} = \sum_{i=1}^{C} (P_i - G_i)^2 \tag{2}$$

2.2 Ordinal Classification and Limitation of CCE and MSE Loss

In the present severity assessment task, there exists an ordinal relationship among the severity grades. Suppose, the actual and predicted severity score of a misclassified image is K and K_1 respectively. Then, we would prefer the classifier to have the least possible absolute difference $|K - K_1|$. But it can be seen from Eqs. 1 and 2, CCE and MSE loss ignores this relationship since CCE only considers the probability of the correct class and MSE is invariant to permutation of probabilities of incorrect classes.

2.3   Proposed Loss Function

Motivated from [9], for the present classification task, we used the Earth Mover's Distance (EMD) based loss function. Let X_i^{CDF} denote the ith element of the cumulative distribution of X then the loss function is as follows:

$$\mathcal{L}_{EMD} = \sum_{i=1}^{C} (P_i^{CDF} - G_i^{CDF})^2$$

$$= \sum_{i=1}^{C} (\sum_{j=1}^{i} P_j - \sum_{j=1}^{i} G_j)^2$$

$$= \underbrace{\sum_{i=1}^{k-1} \left(\sum_{j=1}^{i} P_j \right)^2}_{\mathcal{A}} + \underbrace{\sum_{i=k}^{C} \left(\sum_{j=1}^{i} P_j - 1 \right)^2}_{\mathcal{B}} \qquad (3)$$

where k is the correct class. According to Eq. 3, when $i < k$, increasing the value of P_i increases the value of $\mathcal{A}$ whereas when $i \geq k$, increasing the value of P_i decreases the value of $\mathcal{B}$. Since, in $\mathcal{A}$, P_i occurs $(k - i)$ times hence, the value of $\mathcal{L}_{EMD}$ increases as $|i - k|$ increases. Similarly, in $\mathcal{B}$, for $i \geq k$, P_i occurs $(C - i)$ times hence, the value of $\mathcal{L}_{EMD}$ increases as $|i - k|$ increases. Thus the proposed loss function trains the network in such a way that the class label farthest from actual class gets less probability.

3   Experimental Setup

Dataset: In this research, an image dataset of seven hundred seven (707) psoriatic plaque images having expert annotated severity scores for erythema, scaling and induration is used. This dataset is built by cropping sub-images from a dataset of psoriasis images collected from 80 patients. The original images are collected in an uncontrolled environment by layman photographers with different view angle, distance, lighting condition and varying background. Apart from photographic limitation and skin color tone variation, the presence of several artefacts like hair, wrinkle etc. make the severity assessment task challenging.

Network: As the data volume is small, the training of a Convolutional Neural Network (CNN) from scratch does not produce satisfactory performance. Fine-tuning of pre-trained network is opted for the present classification task. Two pre-trained networks ResNet-50 [8] and Mobile Net [10] trained on imagenet dataset are considered for fine-tuning. ResNet-50 is chosen due to its impressive performance on imagenet classification. The mobile net is chosen as it contains comparatively fewer parameters but produces good performance on imagenet classification.

Training: In this paper, the performance of the developed system is reported on the basis of 7-fold cross validation. The model is trained with stochastic gradient descent optimizer using a batch size of 4 images, momentum of 0.9, weight decay of 10^{-6} and with the learning rate of 0.001. For every fold, the network is trained 10 times and the trained model which ends with minimal loss is chosen for prediction of test images. Horizontal and vertical flipping augmentation is used for improving the generalization ability of the classifiers.

Baselines: In this paper, the performance of the CNN trained with proposed ordinal loss minimization is compared with four baselines. First two CNNs are trained with traditional categorical cross entropy (**CNN$_{\text{CCE}}$**) and mean-square error (**CNN$_{\text{MSE}}$**) loss minimization. In the third approach (**CNN$_{\text{Regr}}$**), the severity scores are projected into C equal partitions in $[0, 1]$ and the CNN is trained in such a way that the ith class ($i = 1, 2, ...C$) image outputs a value in $[\frac{i-1}{C}, \frac{i}{C}]$. The last approach is the decomposition (**CNN$_{\text{Decomp}}$**) of the C class classification problem into $C - 1$ binary classification problems where the ith classifier predicts whether an image has classification label more than i or not. Then these trained classifiers are used to predict class labels of the test images. It is worth mentioning that the binary CNNs are trained with binary cross-entropy loss minimization. Among all considered baselines, only the last two classifiers can capture the ordinal relationship among the labels.

Performance Evaluation Metrics: The performance of the trained CNN is measured with three different evaluation metrics- (i) Mean Accuracy (MA), (ii) Mean Absolute Error (MAE) and (iii) Kendall's τ_b. The value of MA lies in $[0, 1]$ and a higher value represents better performance. A lower value of MAE represents better performance. On the other hand, Kendall's τ_b measures the association or rank correlation between two measured quantities. The τ_b value lies in $[-1, +1]$, where, $+1$ is the maximum agreement between the prediction and the ground truth class labelling, 0 represents no correlation between them and -1 represents maximum disagreement. MAE and Kendall's τ_b are used since MA ignores the ordinal relationship between predicted and actual class for a misclassified image.

Suppose, there are N test images having a discrete class label in $[1, C]$. Let Y_i^p, Y_i^g represent the predicted and the ground-truth class label of the ith test image respectively. Then the mathematical expressions of these metrics are shown in Eqs. 4, 5, 6.

$$MA = \frac{1}{N}\sum_{i=1}^{N}\delta(Y_i^g, Y_i^p); \qquad \delta(x, y) = \begin{cases} 1, & \text{if } x = y \\ 0, & \text{otherwise.} \end{cases} \qquad (4)$$

$$MAE = \frac{1}{N}\sum_{i=1}^{N}|Y_i^g - Y_i^p| \qquad (5)$$

$$\tau_b = \frac{\sum_{i,j=1}^{N}\hat{C}_{i,j}C_{i,j}}{\sqrt{\sum_{i,j=1}^{N}\hat{C}_{i,j}^2 \sum_{i,j=1}^{N}C_{i,j}^2}}, \text{where}$$

$$\hat{C}_{ij} = \begin{cases} 1, & \text{if } Y_i^p > Y_j^p \\ -1, & \text{if } Y_i^p < Y_j^p \\ 0, & \text{otherwise.} \end{cases} \qquad C_{ij} = \begin{cases} 1, & \text{if } Y_i^g > Y_j^g \\ -1, & \text{if } Y_i^g < Y_j^g \\ 0, & \text{otherwise.} \end{cases} \qquad (6)$$

4 Results and Discussion

The average performance (metrics described in Sect. 3) of Mobile Net and ResNet-50 for erythema, scaling and induration scoring using considered approaches are listed in Table 2. According to Table 2, the performance of the chosen networks trained with proposed loss function outperforms the same network trained with CCE or MSE loss minimization. However, the networks trained with CCE and MSE loss minimization produce comparable performance. We receive poor performance when the CNN is trained for regression (Regr) output. This justifies the fact that the sensitivity of this method towards presence of noise in test images affects the performance badly. So, this approach is unsuitable for the present task. On the other hand, binary decomposition approach outperforms the CNN models trained with CCE and MSE loss minimization. However, in most cases, this approach is beaten by the proposed method. Obviously, the success of the binary decomposition approach depends on the robustness of all decomposed classifiers and a weak classifier may affect the whole classification scheme adversely. According to Table 2, among all considered approaches, the best performance is achieved when ResNet-50 is fine-tuned with EMD loss minimization. Some images in our dataset along with their actual and predicted severity scores with respect to erythema, scaling and induration predicted by the best models are given in Fig. 1.

Table 2. Experimental Result

	Method	Erythema			Scaling			Induration		
		MA (%)	MAE	τ_b	MA (%)	MAE	τ_b	MA (%)	MAE	τ_b
MobileNet	CNN_{MSE}	57.14	0.521	0.763	57.28	0.523	0.775	59.97	0.443	0.757
	CNN_{CCE}	57.57	0.501	0.779	57.14	0.502	0.790	58.84	0.457	0.748
	CNN_{Regr}	47.52	0.605	0.737	45.54	0.634	0.734	55.45	0.504	0.721
	CNN_{Decomp}	56.01	0.508	0.777	58.84	**0.471**	**0.804**	**60.54**	**0.431**	**0.766**
	Proposed	**59.69**	**0.488**	**0.781**	**59.26**	0.478	0.800	60.11	0.446	0.758
ResNet-50	CNN_{MSE}	58.27	0.478	0.791	58.56	0.487	0.790	58.84	0.444	0.764
	CNN_{CCE}	59.26	0.467	0.796	59.83	0.457	0.809	61.39	0.410	0.772
	CNN_{Regr}	45.97	0.632	0.728	43.71	0.655	0.729	48.23	0.581	0.686
	CNN_{Decomp}	58.56	0.474	0.792	59.83	0.465	0.803	62.52	0.409	0.775
	Proposed	**61.10**	**0.440**	**0.812**	**62.66**	**0.430**	**0.820**	**63.51**	**0.390**	**0.782**

The psoriasis image dataset developed for [11] is reused in our research. In [11], the best models for erythema and induration were obtained from the AlexNet based MTL network and for scaling it was from the AlexNet based

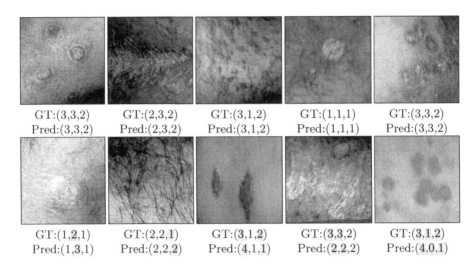

| GT:(3,3,2) | GT:(2,3,2) | GT:(3,1,2) | GT:(1,1,1) | GT:(3,3,2) |
| Pred:(3,3,2) | Pred:(2,3,2) | Pred:(3,1,2) | Pred:(1,1,1) | Pred:(3,3,2) |

| GT:(1,2,1) | GT:(2,2,1) | GT:(3,1,2) | GT:(3,3,2) | GT:(3,1,2) |
| Pred:(1,3,1) | Pred:(2,2,2) | Pred:(4,1,1) | Pred:(2,2,2) | Pred:(4,0,1) |

Fig. 1. Psoriasis images and their ground-truthed (GT) and Predicted (Pred) severity scores achieved from the best classifiers. The scores are given in (Erythema, Scaling, Induration). The errors are highlighted in yellow. (Color figure online)

STL network. The performance was evaluated with average correct classification accuracy, without and with ± 1 tolerance[1], combined average classification accuracy[2] without and with ± 1 tolerance (see footnote 1). In Table 3, the first row contains the previous best result and the second row contains the result produced by our best model. According to Table 3, our model redefines the current state of the art.

Table 3. Comparison with the state of the art. WoT refers **without t**olerance and WT refers **w**i**t**h **t**olerance.

Method	Individual Mean Accuracy						Overall Mean Accuracy	
	Erythema		Scaling		Induration			
	WoT	$WT(\pm 1)$	WoT	$WT(\pm 1)$	WoT	$WT(\pm 1)$	WoT	$WT(\pm 1)$
[11]	60.68	93.64	58.98	94.77	61.10	93.78	27.58	86.28
Our	**61.10**	**95.47**	**62.66**	**95.19**	**63.51**	**97.45**	**28.43**	**89.11**

5   Conclusion

A novel loss function is designed to make CNN suitable for ordinal classification and used for automatic severity assessment of psoriatic plaques. The use of such

---

[1] Maximum deviation of predicted scores for an image lies in $[-1, 1]$.
[2] Erythema, scaling and induration all scores are correct.

loss function is a pioneering attempt. The proposed learning scheme successfully improves the classification performance. Specifically, improvement of MAE and τ_b in comparison to the considered baselines justifies the advantage of training a CNN with ordinal loss minimization. The proposed loss minimization in CNN training can be employed for other image based severity prediction from medical images, age group estimation from face images [3] etc.

References

1. Chandran, V., Raychaudhuri, S.P.: Geoepidemiology and environmental factors of psoriasis and psoriatic arthritis. J. Autoimmun. **34**(3), J314–J321 (2010)
2. Delgado, D., Ersbøll, B., Carstensen, J.M.: An image based system to automatically and objectively score the degree of redness and scaling in psoriasis lesions. In: Proceedings fra den 13. Danske Konference i, p. 130 (2004)
3. Escalera, S., et al.: Chalearn looking at people 2015: apparent age and cultural event recognition datasets and results. In: 2015 IEEE International Conference on Computer Vision Workshop (ICCVW), pp. 243–251, December 2015
4. Fadzil, M.H.A., Ihtatho, D.: Modeling psoriasis lesion colour for PASI erythema scoring. In: International Symposium on Information Technology, ITSim 2008, vol. 2, pp. 1–6. IEEE (2008)
5. Fredriksson, T., Pettersson, U.: Severe psoriasiseoral therapy with a new retinoid. Dermatologica **157**, 238–244 (1978)
6. Gupta, M.D., Srinivasa, S., Madhukara, J., Antony, M.: Random forest based erythema grading for psoriasis. In: 2015 IEEE 12th International Symposium on Biomedical Imaging (ISBI), pp. 819–823, April 2015
7. Hani, A.F.M., Prakasa, E., Nugroho, H., Asirvadam, V.S.: Implementation of fuzzy c-means clustering for psoriasis assessment on lesion erythema. In: 2012 IEEE Symposium on Industrial Electronics and Applications (ISIEA), pp. 331–335. IEEE (2012)
8. He, K., Zhang, X., Ren, S., Sun, J.: Deep residual learning for image recognition. In: The IEEE Conference on Computer Vision and Pattern Recognition (CVPR), June 2016
9. Hou, L., Yu, C.-P., Samaras, D.: Squared earth mover's distance-based loss for training deep neural networks. arXiv preprint arXiv:1611.05916 (2016)
10. Howard, A.G., et al.: Mobilenets: efficient convolutional neural networks for mobile vision applications. CoRR, abs/1704.04861 (2017)
11. Pal, A., Chaturvedi, A., Garain, U., Chandra, A., Chatterjee, R.: Severity grading of psoriatic plaques using deep CNN based multi-task learning. In: 23rd International Conference on Pattern Recognition (ICPR 2016), December 2016
12. Raina, A., Hennessy, R., Rains, M., Allred, J., Diven, D., Markey, M.K.: Objective measurement of erythema in psoriasis using digital color photography with color calibration. In: 2014 36th Annual International Conference of the IEEE Engineering in Medicine and Biology Society (EMBC), pp. 3333–3336, August 2014
13. Roenigk, H.H.: Psoriasis Basic and Clinical Dermatology. Informa Healthcare (1998)
14. Shrivastava, V.K., Londhe, N.D., Sonawane, R.S., Suri, J.S.: A novel approach to multiclass psoriasis disease risk stratification: machine learning paradigm. Biomed. Signal Process. Control. **28**, 27–40 (2016)

Generating Highly Realistic Images of Skin Lesions with GANs

Christoph Baur[1]([✉]), Shadi Albarqouni[1], and Nassir Navab[1,2]

[1] Computer Aided Medical Procedures (CAMP), TU Munich, Munich, Germany
c.baur@tum.de
[2] Whiting School of Engineering, Johns Hopkins University, Baltimore, USA

Abstract. As many other machine learning driven medical image analysis tasks, skin image analysis suffers from a chronic lack of labeled data and skewed class distributions, which poses problems for the training of robust and well-generalizing models. The ability to synthesize realistic looking images of skin lesions could act as a reliever for the aforementioned problems. Generative Adversarial Networks (GANs) have been successfully used to synthesize realistically looking medical images, however limited to low resolution, whereas machine learning models for challenging tasks such as skin lesion segmentation or classification benefit from much higher resolution data. In this work, we successfully synthesize realistically looking images of skin lesions with GANs at such high resolution. Therefore, we utilize the concept of progressive growing, which we both quantitatively and qualitatively compare to other GAN architectures such as the DCGAN and the LAPGAN. Our results show that with the help of progressive growing, we can synthesize highly realistic dermoscopic images of skin lesions that even expert dermatologists find hard to distinguish from real ones.

1 Introduction

Just like for many other medical fields, the problems of data scarcity and class imbalance are also apparent for machine learning driven skin image analysis. In the ISIC2018 challenge, the provided dataset comprises only 10,000 labeled training samples, and the class distribution is heavily skewed among the seven categories of skin lesions, due to the rare nature of some pathologies. In order to tackle the problem of limited training data, state-of-the-art approaches for skin lesion classification and segmentation rely on heavy data augmentation [9,18] or webly supervised learning [11]. As an alternative, synthetic images could open up new ways to deal with these problems. Generative Adversarial Networks (GANs) [5] have shown outstanding results for this task. In the computer vision community, GANs have been successfully used for the generation of realistically looking images of indoor and outdoor scenery [3,13], faces [13] or handwritten digits [5]. Some conditional variants [10] have also set the new state-of-the-art in the realms of super-resolution [8] and image-to-image translation [6]. A few of

© Springer Nature Switzerland AG 2018
D. Stoyanov et al. (Eds.): OR 2.0/CARE/CLIP/ISIC 2018, LNCS 11041, pp. 260–267, 2018.
https://doi.org/10.1007/978-3-030-01201-4_28

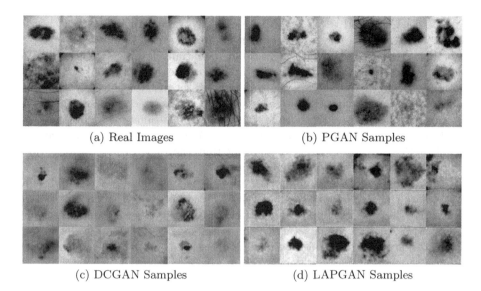

(a) Real Images   (b) PGAN Samples

(c) DCGAN Samples   (d) LAPGAN Samples

Fig. 1. Samples generated with the different models.

these successes have been translated to the medical domain, with applications for cross-modality image synthesis [16], CT image denoising [17] and for the pure synthesis of biological images [12], PET images [2], and OCT patches [14]. First successful attempts for medical data augmentation using GANs have been made in [1,4], however at a level of small patches.

In contrast to many other medical classification problems, skin lesion segmentation and classification models often utilize ImageNet-pretrained models, meaning that these rely on input data with resolutions of 224×224 px or higher. For image synthesis, this implies that higher resolution images need to be generated without trading off realism. Thoroughly engineered, unconditional architectures such as DCGAN [13] or LAPGAN [3] have proven to work well for high quality image synthesis from noise, however at fairly low resolution. Conditional approaches [15] have shown that both high quality and high resolution image synthesis up to 2048×1024 px is possible when mapping from semantic labelmaps to synthetic images with a hierarchy of conditional GANs, however this setting requires well structured input into the generator. Recently, progressive growing of GANs (PGAN) [7] has shown outstanding results for realistic image synthesis of faces at resolutions up to 1024×1024 px, without the need for any conditioning.

Contribution. In this work, we synthesize skin lesion images at sufficiently high resolution while ensuring high quality and realism. For our experiments, we utilize dermoscopic images of benign and malignant skin lesions provided by the ISIC2018 challenge[1]. For data synthesis, we employ the PGAN and compare

---

[1] https://challenge2018.isic-archive.com/.

it to the DCGAN and the LAPGAN. As PGANs can natively only synthesize images whose size is a power of 2, we aim for a target resolution of 256×256 px, such that State-of-the-Art classifiers could potentially leverage the samples. A quantitative comparison of the image statistics of the synthetic and real images shows that the PGAN matches the training dataset distribution very well, and visual exploration further corroborates its superiority over the other approaches in terms of sample diversity, sharpness and artifacts. Ultimately, we evaluate the quality of the PGAN samples in a user study involving 3 expert dermatologists as well 5 Deep Learning experts, showing that the experts have a hard time distinguishing between real and fake images.

The remainder of this manuscript is organized as follows: We first briefly recapitulate the GAN framework as well as the different GAN concepts before we describe the experimental setup. Afterwards, we introduce the dataset, evaluation metrics, provide a quantitative comparison of the aforementioned concepts for skin lesion synthesis and the results of our user study. We conclude this paper with a discussion and an outlook on future work.

2   Skin Lesion Synthesis

2.1   Generative Adversarial Networks

The original GAN framework consists of a pair of adversarial networks: A generator network G tries to transform random noise $z \sim p_z$ from a prior distribution p_z (usually a standard normal distribution) to realistically looking images $G(z) \sim p_{fake}$. At the same time, a discriminator network D aims to classify well between samples coming from the real training data distribution $x \sim p_{real}$ and fake samples $G(z)$ generated by the generator. By utilizing the feedback of the discriminator, the generator G can be adjusted such that its samples are more likely to fool the discriminator in its classification task, ultimately teaching the generator to approximate the training dataset distribution. Mathematically speaking, the networks play a two-player minimax game against each other:

$$\min_{G} \max_{D} V(D, G) = \mathbb{E}_{x \sim p_{real}(x)}[log(D(x))] + \mathbb{E}_{z \sim p_z(z)}[1 - log(D(G(z)))] \quad (1)$$

In consequence, as D and G are updated in an alternating fashion, the discriminator D becomes better in distinguishing between real and fake samples while the generator G learns to produce even more realistic samples.

In this work, we employ three different GAN concepts for the task of high resolution skin lesion synthesis, namely the DCGAN, the LAPGAN and finally the very recent PGAN. An overview of the setup is given in Fig. 2.

The DCGAN architecture is a popular and well engineered convolutional GAN that is fairly stable to train and has proven to yield high quality results at a resolution of 64×64 px. The architecture is carefully designed with concepts such as leaky ReLu activations to avoid sparse gradients and a specific weight initialization to allow for a robust training.

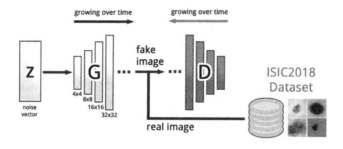

Fig. 2. An overview of the PGAN employed for skin lesion synthesis.

The LAPGAN is a generative image synthesis framework inspired by the concept of Laplacian pyramids. In essence, it consists of a hierarchy of GANs, where the first generator G_0 is trained to synthesize low-resolution images from noise. Successive generators G_i are targeted to map from lower-resolution images of the previous generator G_{i-1} to residual images, which have to be added to the upsampled, input in order to obtain compelling higher resolution images.

The PGAN utilizes the idea of progressive growing [7] to facilitate high resolution image synthesis from noise at unprecedented levels of quality and realism. Opposed to the LAPGAN, the PGAN consists only of a single generator and a discriminator, which both start as small networks which grow in depth and model complexity during training (see Fig. 2). Gradually, the output-resolution of the generator and the input-resolution to the discriminator are simultaneously ramped up, leading to a very stable training behavior and very realistic, synthetic images at resolutions up to 1024×1024 px.

3   Experiments and Results

In the first part of our experiments, we train a PGAN, and to prove its superiority over other concepts, also a DCGAN and a LAPGAN for skin lesion synthesis at a resolution of 256×256 px. In succession, we investigate the properties of the synthetic samples both quantitatively and qualitatively. In the second part of our experiments, we conduct a user study to verify the realism of the generated images.

3.1   Dataset

For our experiments, we utilize the ISIC2018 dataset consisting of 10,000 dermoscopic images of both benign and malignant skin lesions (see Fig. 1a). The megapixel dermoscopic images are center cropped to square size and downsampled to 256×256 px. No data augmentation or pre-processing was applied.

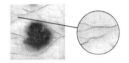

Fig. 3. Artifacts produced by the different models. DCGAN samples show characteristic checkerboard patterns (left), LAPGAN produces high frequency artifacts (middle), whereas PGAN has only problems synthesizing hair (right).

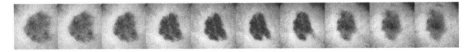

Fig. 4. Walking along the visual manifold of synthetic PGAN samples.

3.2 Evaluation Metrics

A variety of methods have been proposed for evaluating the performance of GANs in capturing data distributions and for judging the quality of synthesized images. In order to evaluate visual fidelity, numerous works utilized either crowdsourcing or expert user studies. We also conduct such a user study to rate the realism of our synthetic images. In addition, we discuss visual fidelity of the generated images with a focus on diversity, realism, sharpness and artifacts. For quantitatively judging sample realism, the Sliced Wasserstein Distance (SWD) has recently shown to be a reasonably good metric for approximately comparing image distributions [7], thus we also make use of it.

3.3 Image Synthesis

We trained a PGAN as described in [7] from all 10,000 images, as well as a DCGAN and a LAPGAN. The PGAN has been trained for 3M iterations, until the SWD between the synthetic samples and the training dataset did not decrease noticeably any further. For a valid comparison, the LAPGAN and DCGAN were also trained for the same amount of iterations.

Per model, we then generate 10,000 synthetic images and compare their distribution to the real data by means of the SWD (see Table 1). Since the SWD constitutes an approximation, we also compute the SWD between the real data and itself to obtain a lower bound. In comparison, the lowest SWD is clearly obtained with the PGAN samples, whereas the DCGAN and LAPGAN perform considerably, but equally worse. This is also reflected by a visual exploration of the samples (see Fig. 1 for a comparison of samples generated with the different models). The DCGAN samples are prone to checkerboard artifacts (Fig. 3, left) and can thus easily be identified as fake. The LAPGAN samples (Fig. 3, middle) seem more realistic and diverse, but close inspection shows a vast amount of high frequency artifacts, which again, negatively impact realism of these samples. The PGAN samples (Fig. 3, right) seem highly realistic, alone filamentary structures such as hair raise suspicion.

Table 1. Sliced Wasserstein Distances (SWDs) between the real and generated samples from different models. Closest to the lower bound (i.e. SWD between real images and themselves) is the PGAN, whereas the distribution of DCGAN and LAPGAN samples differs considerably from the real one.

Lower bound	PGAN vs Real	DCGAN vs Real	LAPGAN vs Real
4.3360	**20.0197**	94.71508	96.68380

Table 2. Confusion matrix coefficients, Accuracy, TPR & TNR per voter.

	DLE1	DLE2	DLE3	DLE4	DLE5	ED1	ED2	ED3
TP	50	30	36	26	26	27	35	29
FP	26	10	9	16	20	11	18	17
FN	0	20	14	24	24	23	15	21
TN	4	20	21	14	10	19	12	13
ACC	0.675	0.625	0.712	0.500	0.450	0.575	0.587	0.525
TPR	1.000	0.600	0.720	0.520	0.520	0.540	0.700	0.580
TNR	0.133	0.666	0.700	0.466	0.333	0.633	0.400	0.433

Exploring the Visual Manifold. Since the PGAN samples look so compelling, there might be a chance that the model memorized the training dataset. Therefore, we explore the manifold of synthetic samples. The smooth transitions among samples provide clear evidence that memorization did not occur (see Fig. 4).

3.4   Visual Turing Test

In order to juge realism of the generated images, we conduct a so-called Visual Turing Test (VTT) involving 3 expert dermatologists (ED) and 5 deep-learning experts (DLE). Each participant is asked to classify the same random mix of generated and real images as being either real (class 1) or fake (class 0). The DLEs are familiar with common GAN artifacts and are thus expected to be skilled to identify unplausible generated images, even though they do not have experience in judging actual skin lesion images. On the other hand, the EDs are not aware of these deep-learning induced image artifacts, but instead know about the gamut of possible skin lesion phenotypes.

Using the PGAN, we first generate 30 synthetic images, which are then mixed with 50 randomly chosen images from the real training dataset. In the VTT, we present each participant with these 80 images in random order and let him/her classify. The performances of all the participants in terms of the TPR (how many real images have been identified as real), the FPR (how many fake images have ben classified as real) and the Accuracy are reported in Fig. 5a. Performance statistics among EDs and DLEs are provided in Fig. 5b), and the complete user study details can be found in Table 2. Interestingly, the classification accuracy is slightly lower for the EDs than for the DLEs. Overall, the accuracy is just slightly

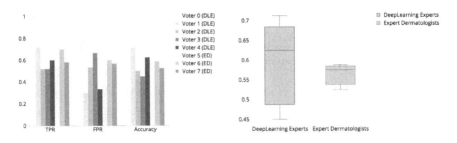

(a) TPR, FPR and Accuracies of all the voters, color coded by expert type.

(b) Boxplots for the classification accuracies of DLEs (left) and EDs (right).

Fig. 5. Visual Turing Test results

above 50%, implying that the experts can distinguish between real and fake just slightly better than chance. Thereby, not all fakes have been mistaken as real (on average 56%), but on average 42% of the real images have also mistakingly be identified as fake. All in all, none of the participants is able to reliably distinguish the fake samples from real ones, leading to the conclusion that these synthetic samples are in fact highly realistic.

4   Discussion and Conclusion

We have shown that with the help of PGANs, we are able to generate extremely realistic dermoscopic images, which carves open new opportunities to tackle the problems of data scarcity and class imbalance. Yet, it is unclear to which extent these synthetic data provide additional information to supervised deep learning models. In fact, a variety of questions need to be answered, such as (i) whether there is an information gain in the synthetic samples over the actual training dataset, (ii) if the gain is higher than using standard data augmentation and (iii) how many training images are in fact required to obtain reliable generative models. Noteworthy, we trained the PGAN ignoring the presence of different classes. For generating images along with class information, one would need to leverage labeled data and effectively train a single model per class. Further, the synthetic images are not always perfect. In particular, the methodology has to be enhanced to account for filamentary structures. In future work, we aim to perform large scale experiments and strive to answer these question.

Overall, we have shown that we can synthesize images of skin lesions at yet unprecedented levels of realism. In fact, the level of realism is so high such that experts from both the medical and the deep-learning fields were not able to reliably distinguish real images from generated ones. This leaves us confident that such synthetic data can be leveraged for new data augmentation approaches.

References

1. Antoniou, A., Storkey, A., Edwards, H.: Data augmentation generative adversarial networks. arXiv preprint arXiv:1711.04340 (2017)
2. Bi, L., Kim, J., Kumar, A., Feng, D., Fulham, M.: Synthesis of Positron Emission Tomography (PET) images via multi-channel Generative Adversarial Networks (GANs). In: Cardoso, M.J., et al. (eds.) CMMI/SWITCH/RAMBO -2017. LNCS, vol. 10555, pp. 43–51. Springer, Cham (2017). https://doi.org/10.1007/978-3-319-67564-0_5
3. Denton, E.L., Chintala, S., Fergus, R., et al.: Deep generative image models using a Laplacian pyramid of adversarial networks. In: NIPS, pp. 1486–1494 (2015)
4. Frid-Adar, M., Klang, E., Amitai, M., Goldberger, J., Greenspan, H.: Synthetic data augmentation using gan for improved liver lesion classification. In: ISBI, pp. 289–293 (2018)
5. Goodfellow, I., et al.: Generative adversarial nets. In: NIPS, pp. 2672–2680 (2014)
6. Isola, P., Zhu, J.Y., Zhou, T., Efros, A.A.: Image-to-image translation with conditional adversarial networks. In: CVPR, pp. 5967–5976, July 2017
7. Karras, T., Aila, T., Laine, S., Lehtinen, J.: Progressive growing of GANs for improved quality, stability, and variation. In: ICLR (2018)
8. Ledig, C., et al.: Photo-realistic single image super-resolution using a generative adversarial network. In: CVPR, pp. 105–114 (2017)
9. Matsunaga, K., Hamada, A., Minagawa, A., Koga, H.: Image classification of melanoma, nevus and seborrheic keratosis by deep neural network ensemble. arXiv preprint arXiv:1703.03108 (2017)
10. Mirza, M., Osindero, S.: Conditional generative adversarial nets. arXiv preprint arXiv:1411.1784 (2014)
11. Navarro, F., Conjeti, S., Tombari, F., Navab, N.: Webly supervised learning for skin lesion classification. arXiv preprint arXiv:1804.00177 (2018)
12. Osokin, A., Chessel, A., Carazo-Salas, R.E., Vaggi, F.: GANs for biological image synthesis. In: ICCV, pp. 2252–2261 (2017)
13. Radford, A., Metz, L., Chintala, S.: Unsupervised representation learning with deep convolutional generative adversarial networks. CoRR abs/1511.06434 (2015)
14. Schlegl, T., Seeböck, P., Waldstein, S.M., Schmidt-Erfurth, U., Langs, G.: Unsupervised anomaly detection with generative adversarial networks to guide marker discovery. In: Niethammer, M., et al. (eds.) IPMI 2017. LNCS, vol. 10265, pp. 146–157. Springer, Cham (2017). https://doi.org/10.1007/978-3-319-59050-9_12
15. Wang, T.C., Liu, M.Y., Zhu, J.Y., Tao, A., Kautz, J., Catanzaro, B.: High-resolution image synthesis and semantic manipulation with conditional GANs. In: CVPR, June 2018
16. Wolterink, J.M., Dinkla, A.M., Savenije, M.H.F., Seevinck, P.R., van den Berg, C.A.T., Išgum, I.: Deep MR to CT synthesis using unpaired data. In: Tsaftaris, S.A., Gooya, A., Frangi, A.F., Prince, J.L. (eds.) SASHIMI 2017. LNCS, vol. 10557, pp. 14–23. Springer, Cham (2017). https://doi.org/10.1007/978-3-319-68127-6_2
17. Yang, Q., et al.: Low-dose CT image denoising using a generative adversarial network with wasserstein distance and perceptual loss. IEEE Trans. Med. Imaging **37**(6), 1348–1357 (2018)
18. Yu, L., Chen, H., Dou, Q., Qin, J., Heng, P.A.: Automated melanoma recognition in dermoscopy images via very deep residual networks. IEEE Trans. Med. Imaging **36**(4), 994–1004 (2017)

A Hyperspectral Dermoscopy Dataset for Melanoma Detection

Yanyang Gu[1]([✉]), Yi-Ping Partridge[2], and Jun Zhou[1]

[1] School of Information and Communication Technology, Griffith University,
Nathan, Australia
`yanyang.gu@griffithuni.edu.au`
[2] Kalowen Skin Cancer Clinic, Caloundra, Australia
`dpp60@hotmail.com`

Abstract. Melanoma is the most fatal type of skin cancer. Non-invasive melanoma detection is crucial for preliminary screening and early diagnosis. Among various image based techniques, hyperspectral imaging is a tool with great potential for melanoma detection since it provides highly detailed spectral information beyond the human vision capability. However, so far no hyperspectral image dataset has been published, although some pilot methods have been studied. In this paper, we introduce a hyperspectral dermoscopy image dataset for melanoma detection. This dataset consists of 330 hyperspectral images with 16 spectral bands each in the visible wavelength, containing images of melanoma, dysplastic nevus, and other types, all histopathologically validated. To build a baseline for melanoma detection, we evaluate several classification methods on the dataset.

Keywords: Skin cancer · Melanoma · Hyperspectral imaging
Dermoscopy · Dataset

1 Introduction

Skin cancer accounts for the most common among all newly diagnosed cancers in Australia and in USA [1,2]. The Cancer Council Australia estimated that two in three Australians will be diagnosed with skin cancer by the time they are 70 years old [1]. Skin cancer can be classified as melanoma and non-melanoma. Melanoma is the most deadly type of all skin cancers [1], although it is not the most prevalent type.

An early screening of melanoma can greatly increase the chance of cure. During the diagnosis process, dermoscopy has been widely used to provide a detailed and magnified view of skin. However, it is still a challenging problem to overcome the subjectivity of dermatologists in differentiating melanoma from benign pigmented lesions, as melanoma shows great similarity with nevus, solar lentigo etc. Although experienced clinicians can make initial screening, histology of biopsy is the only confident way of final diagnosis. This, however, is often restricted

© Springer Nature Switzerland AG 2018
D. Stoyanov et al. (Eds.): OR 2.0/CARE/CLIP/ISIC 2018, LNCS 11041, pp. 268–276, 2018.
https://doi.org/10.1007/978-3-030-01201-4_29

by the available resources. Therefore, an early computer aided screening of skin cancer is of high interest to help dermatologists to make the diagnosis objective and to increase the speed and accuracy of pre-diagnosis.

Existing computer aided systems for melanoma detection are mainly developed based on clinicians' visual assessment methods, such as the ABCD (asymmetry, border, color, dimension) rules [3]. In many cases, the early decision also combines existence of subtle features, such as irregular streaks [4], pigment network [5], and blue-white veil [6] etc. In more recent, deep learning based methods have been proposed so as to avoid development of hand crafted features [7–10], which has demonstrated state-of-the-art detection performance.

Traditional imaging systems normally capture color or grayscale images in the visible wavelengths. They do not have the capability of detecting fine changes of skins with respect to the light wavelength change. Hyperspectral imaging is a technique that combines both spatial information provided by conventional imaging system and spectral information of imaging spectroscopy. Comparing with traditional imaging system, besides characterising the spatial distribution of pigmented skin lesion, hyperspectral imaging provides the potential of measuring concentration of melanin and hemoglobin molecular by analysing reflectance spectra. Therefore, this technology gradually attracts the attention in skin related medical imaging [13], such as burn characterization [14] and gunshot assessment [15]. A melanoma mouse model was build on hyperspectral imaging [18], which shows the potential of diagnostic improvements. Hyperspectral melanoma images were analysed by Zherdeva et al. [16], with band selection method proposed to select the most informative wavelength for cancer detection [17]. Nagaoka et al. proposed a melanoma discrimination index method using hyperspectral data in the visible to near infrared wavelength range [19], which achieved high sensitivity on a small dataset.

Most existing hyperspectral imaging systems are expensive and not portable. Some of them use line-scan hyperspectral cameras, which are slow in image acquisition. These have generated a lot of hurdles in clinical operation and producing a public hyperspectral skin image dataset for research purpose. In this paper, we introduce a hyperspectral dermoscopy imaging dataset captured using a portable real-time imaging system. The dataset contains 330 dermoscopy images which are all histology verified, including 85 melanomas, 175 dysplastic nevi and 70 other pigmented lesions (solar lentigo, IEC, nevi and Seborrheic Keratosis). Each image has 16 bands, covering the wavelength from 465 nm to 630 nm. We also provide bounding boxes on melanocytic human skin lesions to support the training and evaluation of melanoma detection methods.

The rest of the paper is organised as follows. We present the dataset and its statistics in Sect. 2. The baseline detection approach and experimental results are given in Sect. 3. Finally, conclusions are drawn in Sect. 4.

2 Hyperspectral Dermoscopy Dataset

This section introduces the imaging system and how to calibration of captured images. It also provides basic data analysis on different skin images.

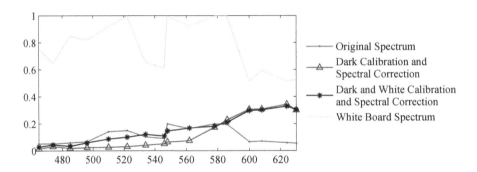

Fig. 1. Spectral responses at a pixel on original and calibrated images.

2.1   Imaging System and Calibration

The main hardware of the image system includes a portable device and an Ximea MQ022HG-IM-SM4X4-VIS camera. The portable devices consists of a Raspberry PI, a 7 in. touch screen, an 8G Raspberry PI compatible MicroSD card, and a set of nickel–metal hydride batteries, all sealed in a box. Together with the portable device, the camera can be put on top of dermatoscope to capture magnified image of skin lesion. The dermatoscope provides visible light from LED, with which the Ximea camera is capable of capturing hyperspectral images of 16 bands from 465 nm to 630 nm. Each band image is constituted of approximately 512 × 272 pixels. The Ximea camera is only 32 grams in weight and can capture hyperspectral images at up to 170 cubes per second. The camera is operated using a lab developed software which allows image capture and management.

Each captured image consists of 1024 × 2048 pixels arranged in 256 × 512 blocks of spatial information. Each block contains 4 rows and 4 columns of grayscale values, corresponding to spectral information from 16 wavelength-indexed bands. Therefore, each image can be converted into a 256 × 512 × 16 data cube, which is later processed with dark and white calibration as well as camera based spectral correction. In dark calibration step, we deducted a dark image (captured with lens cap on) from the captured image. For white calibration, we normalised the image with the mean of the selected region from a white calibration board. Finally, we performed spectral calibration, which multiplies the image with a correction matrix corresponding to the sensitivity function associated with the CMOS sensor of the camera. The three preprocessing steps can be formulated as:

$$I = \frac{I_o - I_b}{I_w - I_b} C \tag{1}$$

where I_o is the original data cube converted from the raw image, I_b is the black reference data cube, I_w is the white reference data cube which is obtained by capturing image of the white calibration board under the dermatoscope, and C is a 16 × 16 correction matrix which is related to the camera. Figure 1 shows the comparison of a sample spectral response after different operations of calibration.

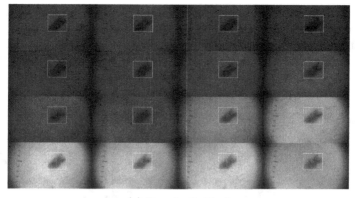

(a) Dysplastic Nevi

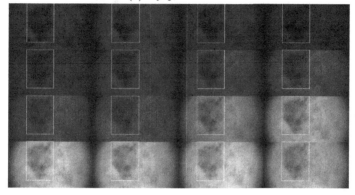

(b) Melanoma

Fig. 2. Band images of two samples.

2.2 Data Collection and Basic Spectral Analysis

The collection of this hyperspectral dermoscopy image dataset is a joint collaboration between our research team and a local Skin Cancer Clinic. Before the data collection, we went through an ethics approval, so only the clinic staff can get in contact with the patients and get their consent. All patient's privacy information are protected without being released to people other than the clinic. The clinic doctor helped to collect the images with the developed portable hyperspectral imaging device and a dermatoscope of 10 times of magnification. All images were captured before biopsy which were later taken to pathologists for final diagnosis. Then, all the images were labeled according to diagnosis reports. The first stage data collection started from 6th January, 2017 and ended on 18th February, 2018.

In total 330 hyperspectral dermoscopy images with good quality were selected to build the dataset. These include 80 melanoma images, 180 dysplastic nevus images and 70 other images for solar lentigo, IEC, nevi and Seborrheic Keratosis.

We manually labelled the legion regions using bounding boxes. Two dysplastic nevi and melanoma data samples with bounding boxes are illustrated in Fig. 2. We also show in Fig. 3 some sample images of each lesion class in the dataset, including melanoma, solar lentigo, IEC, dysplastic nevi, nevi and Seborrheic Keratosis.

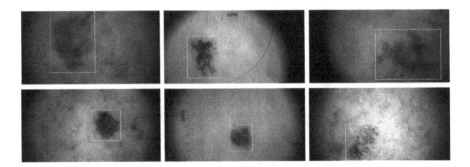

Fig. 3. Sample images in the dataset (the 11th band). First row from left to right: melanoma, solar lentigo and IEC. Second row from left to right: dysplastic nevi, nevi and Seborrheic Keratosis.

To compare the spectral responses of typical targets in the captured image, we plot sample responses of melanoma (green plus sign), dysplastic nevus (red dots), hair (blue stars) and normal skin (cyan triangles) in Fig. 4. Among all the spectra, normal skin shows the highest intensities, as it is inherently lighter than other lesions. Intensities of hair, dysplastic nevus and melanoma are roughly in the same level of intensity, although hair spectrum is slightly less steady than the other two. Moreover, we notice that cancer/non-cancer spectra are close to each other, which implies effective spectral-spatial analysis methods shall be developed to distinguish them.

3   Baseline Method

To validate the feasibility of the proposed dataset, we developed a sparse coding method [20,21] to classify the images in the hyperspectral dataset, and compared the results with those obtained on RGB images of the same scene. The RGB images were generated from the hyperspectral images by sampling band images at 630 nm, 546 nm and 465 nm, which roughly correspond to the centers of the red (610–700 nm), green (500–570 nm), and blue (450–500 nm) wavelength ranges [22].

The baseline method has three main steps. First, we randomly sampled spectral responses from the labelled bounding boxes in the training images. The bounded image is evenly divided into grids, with half of the points in each grid used to produce a sparse dictionary. Then sparse codes were calculated on each

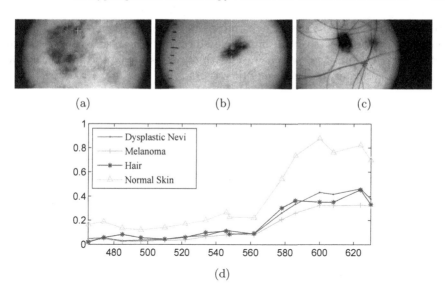

(a)   (b)   (c)

(d)

Fig. 4. Different regions and their spectral responses. (a) Melanoma. (b) Nevus and normal skin. (c) Hair. (d) Corresponding spectral responses. (Color figure online)

image followed by max pooling to convert the image into a vector. Finally, the vectorised images were used to train a multi-class SVM classifier. Please note that this baseline method is purely based on spectral analysis. In RGB image classification, we used the same SVM classifier, but adopted local binary patterns [23] for feature extraction. In the experiments, we randomly sampled 60 images from each class as training samples, and used the rest images as the testing samples. The random split of training and testing sets were done for five times with the mean and standard deviation of the results reported.

3.1 Experimental Results

We use sensitivity (ratio between true positive and all positive cases) and specificity (ratio between true negative and all negative cases) to evaluate the performance of our sparse coding method. Since melanoma is considered as the true case, all correctly predicted melanoma samples are true positive, while all wrongly predicted other cases are false negative. In the classification, we tried both three-class (melanoma VS dysplastic nevi VS Other type) and two-class (melanoma VS dysplastic Nevi) settings.

The result comparison is given in Table 1. It can be seen that the performance of classification based on hyperspectral images is much better than that from RGB images. This proves that spectral information is useful for melanoma detection. Moreover, all 2-class classification results are better than 3-class classification. Standard deviations of all 3-class classification results are high, due to the large variation and the small size of the third class, namely the other type. We also tested the case when the size of the lesion is added as an additional feature for hyperspectral image classification. The results show that the performance is improved, which implies that size is an important feature for differentiating melanoma from the other types.

Table 1. Comparison of classification performance.

Image type	Feature	Classes	SE %	STD %	SP %	STD %
Hyperspectral	Sparse codes	3	69.33	19.82	72.95	1.74
Hyperspectral	Sparse codes	2	84.00	7.60	72.10	6.00
Hyperspectral	Sparse codes + size	3	77.33	14.61	73.61	1.00
Hyperspectral	Sparse codes + size	2	80.00	6.67	80.70	6.91
Hyperspectral	Size	3	76.55	3.87	66.67	19.44
Hyperspectral	Size	2	82.63	2.00	68.00	8.69
RGB	LBP	3	55.44	3.99	46.09	10.91
RGB	LBP	2	64.56	2.82	62.67	18.62

4   Conclusion

We have presented a hyperspectral imaging dataset of 330 histology verified skin lesion images. The images in the dataset are calibrated and with lesion regions provided using bounding boxes. This dataset provides a foundation for further research on hyperspectral imaging techniques and its usefulness in early screening of skin cancers using image based approaches, namely wavelength analysis. The experimental results on a baseline approach show that pure spectral analysis is not sufficient to reliably detect melanoma. More effective spectral-spatial data analysis approach and advanced classification approaches are yet to be developed. In the future, we will also continue to explore and collaborate with skin cancer clinics for more data collection.

References

1. Cancer Council Australia. https://www.cancer.org.au/about-cancer/types-of-cancer/skin-cancer.html. Accessed 2 May 2018
2. America Cancer Society. https://www.cancer.org/cancer/skin-cancer.html. Accessed 30 July 2018
3. Rastgoo, M., Garcia, R., Morel, O., Marzani, F.: Automatic differentiation of melanoma from dysplastic nevi. Comput. Med. Imaging Graph. **43**, 44–52 (2015)
4. Sadeghi, M., Lee, T.K., McLean, D., Lui, H., Atkins, M.S.: Detection and analysis of irregular streaks in dermoscopic images of skin lesions. IEEE Trans. Med. Imaging **32**(5), 849–861 (2013)
5. Sadeghi, M., Razmara, M., Lee, T.K., Atkins, M.S.: A novel method for detection of pigment network in dermoscopic images using graphs. Comput. Med. Imaging Graph. **35**(2), 137–143 (2011)

6. Madooei, A., Drew, M.S., Sadeghi, M., Atkins, M.S.: Automatic detection of blue-white veil by discrete colour matching in dermoscopy images. In: Mori, K., Sakuma, I., Sato, Y., Barillot, C., Navab, N. (eds.) MICCAI 2013. LNCS, vol. 8151, pp. 453–460. Springer, Heidelberg (2013). https://doi.org/10.1007/978-3-642-40760-4_57

7. Codella, N., Cai, J., Abedini, M., Garnavi, R., Halpern, A., Smith, J.R.: Deep learning, sparse coding, and SVM for melanoma recognition in dermoscopy images. In: Zhou, L., Wang, L., Wang, Q., Shi, Y. (eds.) MLMI 2015. LNCS, vol. 9352, pp. 118–126. Springer, Cham (2015). https://doi.org/10.1007/978-3-319-24888-2_15

8. Yu, L., Chen, H., Dou, Q., Qin, J., Heng, P.A.: Automated melanoma recognition in dermoscopy images via very deep residual networks. IEEE Trans. Med. Imaging **36**(4), 994–1004 (2017)

9. Xie, F., Fan, H., Li, Y., Jiang, Z., Meng, R., Bovik, A.: Melanoma classification on dermoscopy images using a neural network ensemble model. IEEE Trans. Med. Imaging **36**(3), 849–858 (2017)

10. Esteva, A., et al.: Dermatologist-level classification of skin cancer with deep neural networks. Nature **542**(7639), 115 (2017)

11. Chang, I.: Hyperspectral Imaging: Techniques for Spectral Detection and Classification. Springer, New York (2003). https://doi.org/10.1007/978-1-4419-9170-6

12. Wei, X., Liu, F., Qiu, Z., Shao, Y., He, Y.: Ripeness classification of astringent persimmon using hyperspectral imaging technique. Food Bioprocess Technol. **7**(5), 1371–1380 (2014)

13. Lu, G., Fei, B.: Medical hyperspectral imaging: a review. J. Biomed. Opt. **19**(1), 010901 (2014)

14. Calin, M.A., Parasca, S.V., Savastru, R., Manea, D.: Characterization of burns using hyperspectral imaging technique-a preliminary study. Burns **41**(1), 118–124 (2015)

15. Kersh, K.L., Childers, J.M., Justice, D., Karim, G.: Detection of gunshot residue on dark-colored clothing prior to chemical analysis. J. Forensic Sci. **59**(3), 754–762 (2014)

16. Zherdeva, L.A., Bratchenko, I.A., Myakinin, O.O., Moryatov, A.A., Kozlov, S.V., Zakharov, V.P.: In vivo hyperspectral imaging and differentiation of skin cancer. In: Optics in Health Care and Biomedical Optics VII, vol. 10024, p. 100244G. International Society for Optics and Photonics (2016)

17. Quinzan, I., Sotoca, J.M., Latorre-Carmona, P., Pla, F., Garcia-Sevilla, P., Boldo, E.: Band selection in spectral imaging for non-invasive melanoma diagnosis. Biomed. Opt. Express **4**(4), 514–519 (2013)

18. Tsapras, A., et al.: Hyperspectral imaging and spectral classification for assisting in vivo diagnosis of melanoma precursors: preliminary results obtained from mice. In: IEEE International Conference on Imaging Systems and Techniques, pp. 379–383 (2016)

19. Nagaoka, T., Nakamura, A., Kiyohara, Y., Sota, T.: Melanoma screening system using hyperspectral imager attached to imaging fiberscope. In: Annual International Conference of the IEEE Engineering in Medicine and Biology Society, pp. 3728–3731 (2012)

20. Cai, D., Bao, H., He, X.: Sparse concept coding for visual analysis. In: IEEE Conference on Computer Vision and Pattern Recognition, pp. 2905–2910 (2011)

21. Yang, J., Yu, K., Gong, Y., Huang, T.: Linear spatial pyramid matching using sparse coding for image classification. In: IEEE Conference on Computer Vision and Pattern Recognition, pp. 1794–1801 (2009)

22. Su, H., Du, Q., Du, P.: Hyperspectral image visualization using band selection. IEEE J. Sel. Top. Appl. Earth Obs. Remote. Sens. **7**(6), 2647–2658 (2014)
23. Guo, Z., Zhang, L., Zhang, D.: A completed modeling of local binary pattern operator for texture classification. IEEE Trans. Image Process. **19**(6), 1657–1663 (2010)

A Deep Residual Architecture for Skin Lesion Segmentation

G. M. Venkatesh[(✉)], Y. G. Naresh, Suzanne Little, and Noel E. O'Connor

Insight Centre for Data Analytics-DCU, Dublin City University, Dublin, Ireland
{venkatesh.gurummunirathnam,naresh.yarlapati,suzanne.little,
noel.oconnor}@insight-centre.org

Abstract. In this paper, we propose an automatic approach to skin lesion region segmentation based on a deep learning architecture with multi-scale residual connections. The architecture of the proposed model is based on UNet [22] with residual connections to maximise the learning capability and performance of the network. The information lost in the encoder stages due to the max-pooling layer at each level is preserved through the multi-scale residual connections. To corroborate the efficacy of the proposed model, extensive experiments are conducted on the ISIC 2017 challenge dataset without using any external dermatologic image set. An extensive comparative analysis is presented with contemporary methodologies to highlight the promising performance of the proposed methodology.

Keywords: Skin lesion · FCNs · Residual connection · U-Net

1 Introduction

Medical imaging is an emerging and successful tool increasingly employed in precision medicine. It aids in making a medical decision for providing appropriate and optimal therapies to an individual patient. Skin Cancer is one such disease which can be identified through medical imaging using dermoscopic techniques. There are many types of skins cancers, but we can broadly put them in to two general categories viz., Non melanoma and Melanoma. Non-melanoma cancers are unlikely to spread to other parts of the body but Melanoma is likely to spread to other parts of the body and is known to be aggressive cancer. Malignant Melanoma is a cutaneous disease. It affects the melanin producing cells known as melanocytes. Melanoma is likely to be fatal, it has caused more deaths than any other type of skin disease [18]. The dermoscopic acquisition of a skin image targets segmentation into two regions: lesion and normal skin. The affected part of an organ or a tissue due to a disease or an injury is generally termed as lesion. Efficient and accurate segmentation of the lesion region in dermoscopic images aids in classification of various skin diseases. Furthermore, the severity of the diseases can be predicted through various grading techniques which result in

© Springer Nature Switzerland AG 2018
D. Stoyanov et al. (Eds.): OR 2.0/CARE/CLIP/ISIC 2018, LNCS 11041, pp. 277–284, 2018.
https://doi.org/10.1007/978-3-030-01201-4_30

early identification of a skin disease which plays a vital role in the treatment and cure of the disease.

2   Literature

In the existing literature, several attempts have been made to develop a more robust and efficient segmentation of the lesion region in dermoscopic and non-dermoscopic clinical images. The methods for skin lesion segmentation can be segregated into the following categories [8] viz., thresholding, active contours, region merging methods [13] and deep learning architectures. Some methods [7,16] have been proposed on non-dermoscopic images which address skin lesion segmentation based on colour features and textural properties respectively. The method in [15] addresses the illumination effects and artifacts. These methods apply post processing steps for refining the segmentation results. In [19], a deep convolutional neural network (CNN) has been proposed which combines both local texture and global structure information to predict a label for each pixel for segmentation of the lesion region. In [11], an automated system for skin lesion region segmentation has been proposed to classify each pixel based on pertinent geometrical, textural and colour features which are selected using Ant Colony Optimization (ACO). The complementary strengths of a saliency and Bayesian framework are applied to distinguish the shape and boundaries of the lesion region and background in [2]. In [23], an unsupervised methodology based on the wavelet lattice, shift and scale parameters of wavelets has been proposed for the segmentation of skin lesion regions in dermoscopic images. In [6], image-wise supervised learning is proposed to derive a probabilistic map for automated seed selection and multi-scale super-pixel based cellular automata to acquire structural information for skin lesion region segmentation. A Guassian membership function is applied for image fuzzification and to quantify each pixel for skin segmentation [12].

Despite several methods being available for segmentation of lesion region in images of skin diseases, there is still scope for exploring new models, which are efficient and provide better segmentation. Thus, in this work, we propose a deep residual architecture inspired by UNet [22] for skin lesion segmentation. The rest of this paper is organized as follows: Sect. 3 elaborates the proposed model for the segmentation of skin lesion region. Section 4 gives the experimental analysis and comparative analysis. Section 5 gives a conclusion.

3   Proposed Method

The proposed methodology for automatic skin lesion region segmentation using deep learning architecture is shown in Fig. 1. The architecture is inspired from UNet [22] and residual network [17]. The input to the network is RGBH (Red, Green, Blue and Hue planes respectively) of a dermoscopic image and the output is binary segmented image with white and Black pixels representing the affected skin and non-affected regions respectively. There are four important components in the proposed network. The first is construction of a multi-scale [14] image pyramid input which makes the network scale invariant. The second is a U-shape convolutional network, to learn a vivid hierarchical representation. The third is to incorporates residual learning to preserve spatial and contextual information from the preceding layers. The residual connections are used at two levels. Firstly, at each step of the contracting (encoder) and expansive (decoder) path of the U-Net and another short connection between the multi-scale input and expansive (encoder) path of respective step. The information lost in the encoder stages due to the max-pooling layer at each level is preserved through the multi-scale residual connection. Finally, a layer with binary cross-entropy loss function based on Jaccard index [3] is included for classification of pixels.

3.1   Multi-scale Input Layer

The proposed method has similar architecture to the methodology in [14] for constructing the multi-scale input by using an average pooling layer to downsample the images naturally and construct a multi-scale input in the encoder path. These scaled input layers are used to increase the network width of decoder path and also as a shortcut connection to the encoder path to increase the network width of the decoder path.

3.2   Network Structure

U-Net [22] is an efficient fully convolutional network which has been proposed for biomedical image segmentation. The proposed architecture adopts similar architecture consisting of two blocks placed in U-shape as shown in Fig. 1. The block with green color (Fig. 2(a)) represents the residual downsampling block and the red color (Fig. 2(b)) represents residual upsampling block. A 2×2 max-pooling operation with stride 2 for downsampling is used and at each stage number of feature channels chosen in the proposed architecture are shown in Fig. 1. The left side path consist of repeated residual downsampling block (henceforth referred as resDownBlock) which are connected to the corresponding residual upsampling block (henceforth referred as resUpBlock). This connection is shown with dotted lines in Fig. 1 similar to U-Net, where the feature maps of resDownBlock is concatenated to the corresponding resUpBlock. Along with the u-connection, there are also short connections between the Multi-scale input at each step of the U-Net with the corresponding resUpBlock by convolving the scaled input with 3×3 convolution which avoids convergence on a local optimal solution and thus helps the network to achieve good performance in complex image segmentation.

3.3   Residual-Down-sampling Block(resDownBlock)

The structure of resDownBlock consists of two 3×3 convolutions, each followed by a rectified linear unit (ReLU). A shortcut connection of the input layer is added with the output feature-maps of the second convolution layer before passing to the ReLU as shown in Fig. 2(a). Batch Normalization is adopted between

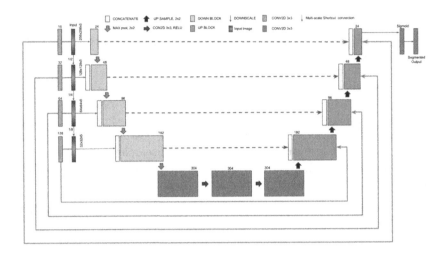

Fig. 1. Proposed architecture of Multi-Scale Residual UNet

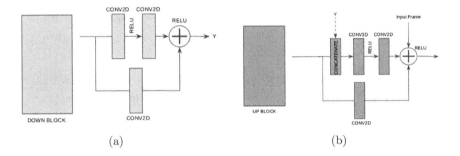

Fig. 2. (a) Details of resDownBlock, (b) Details of resUpBlock (Color figure online)

convolutional layer and rectified linear units layer as well as during the shortcut connection. The max-pooling layer in the resDownBlock has a kernel size of 2×2 and a stride of 2. Excluding the initial resDownBlock in the encoder path all other resDownBLocks receives the concatenated output feature-maps from the preceding block with the scaled input.

3.4 Residual-Up-sampling Block(resUpBlock)

The structure of resUpBlock consists of two 3×3 convolutional layers, each followed by a rectified linear unit (ReLU) and a shortcut connection of the input layer is added with the output feature-maps of second convolution layer along with the shortcut connection of the scaled input image before passing to the ReLU as shown in Fig. 2(b). There is a Concatenation layer, which concatenates the upsampled feature-maps from previous block with the feature-maps of resDownblock. According to the architecture, the resolution of resDownBlocks output should match with the resUpBlock's input for adding the upsampling layer in the beginning of each block. Batch Normalization is adopted between convolutional layer and rectified linear units layer similarly as mentioned in the above section.

4 Experiments

In order to evalute the efficacy of the proposed model, experiments have been conducted on the **ISIC 2017 Challenge** [10] official dataset. The dataset consists of dermoscopic images with 2000 training, 150 validation and 600 test samples respectively. The proposed network is implemented using the Keras neural network API [9] with Tensorflow backend [1] and trained on a single GPU (GeForce GTX TITAN X, 12 GB RAM). The network is optimized by Adam optimizer [20] with an initial learning rate of 0.001. For increasing the number of samples during the training phase, we have used standard geometrical (linear) data augmentation techniques, namely rotation($-45°$ to $+45°$), horizontal and vertical flipping, translation and scaling (-10% to $+10\%$)) of the input image. We choose 256×256 square images with batch size of 4 samples. The number of learning steps at each epoch is set to 1000. We have exploited RGB and HSI color space model for deriving RGBH (Red, Blue, Green and Hue Channels of dermoscopic images) as input data to the network to capture the color variations in the data. Figure 3 presents the lesion region segmentation for few test samples with overlay of segmentation results. The overlay consists of differentiations viz., blue, green and red overlays representing false negatives, true positives and false positives respectively. It is evident that the proposed model effectively captures the lesion region without any post-processing steps.

To evaluate the performance of the segmentation, we have use Accuracy (AC), Jaccard Index (JA), Dice coefficient (DI), Sensitivity (SE) and Specificity (SP). Consider β_{tp}, β_{tn}, β_{fp} and β_{fn} which represent the number of true positive, true negative, false positive and false negative respectively. All the above mentioned metrics are computed using Eqs. (1)–(5):

$$Accuracy(AC) = \frac{\beta_{tp} + \beta_{tn}}{\beta_{tp} + \beta_{tn} + \beta_{fp} + \beta_{fn}} \tag{1}$$

$$Sensitivity(SE) = \frac{\beta_{tp}}{\beta_{tp} + \beta_{fn}} \tag{2}$$

$$Dice\ coefficient(DI) = \frac{2 * \beta_{tp}}{2 * \beta_{tp} + \beta_{fp} + \beta_{fn}} \tag{3}$$

$$Specificity(SP) = \frac{\beta_{tn}}{\beta_{tp} + \beta_{fn}} \tag{4}$$

$$JaccardIndex(JA) = \frac{\beta_{tp}}{\beta_{tp} + \beta_{fp} + \beta_{fn}} \tag{5}$$

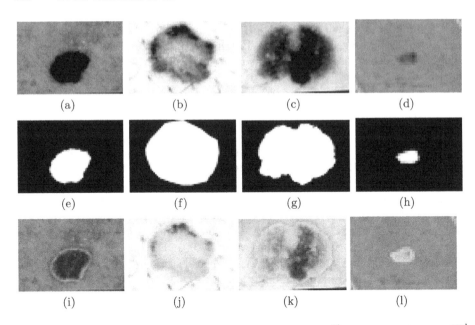

Fig. 3. The visual examples of lesion region segmentations, 1st row are test images, 2nd row corresponding ground truth images and 3rd are output of the segmented lession region (Color figure online)

Figure 4 presents the segmentation results of the proposed model compared to other methods in the literature by depicting number of test samples in each bin, where each bin in x-axis represents the Jaccard Index range, y-axis represents number of test samples. The results of our method is presented in Table 1. From Table 1, it is evident that the proposed method outperforms the other methods in terms of Accuracy, Dice Coefficient and Sensitivity. The results of our method is quite competitive for the ISIC 2017 dataset in comparison with the methods which have shown top performance in the literature.

Table 1. Comparison of Skin Lesion Segmentation on ISIC 2017.

Method	Accuracy	Dice Co-efficient	Jaccard Index	Sensitivity	Specificity
Yading Yuan [24]	0.934	0.849	**0.765**	0.825	0.975
Our Method	**0.936**	**0.856**	0.764	**0.83**	0.976
Matt Berseth [4]	0.932	0.847	0.762	0.82	0.978
popleyi [5]	0.934	0.844	0.76	0.802	**0.985**
Euijoon Ahn [5]	0.934	0.842	0.758	0.801	0.984
RECOD Titans [21]	0.931	0.839	0.754	0.817	0.97

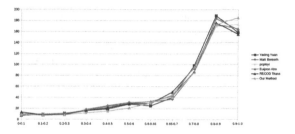

Fig. 4. Graphical representation of Jaccard Index on overall test set.

5   Conclusion

In this work, we have proposed a deep architecture for skin lesion segmentation termed as Multi-scale residual UNet. From the results in Fig. 3, it can be observed that the boundaries of lesion regions and the background are well separated and differentiable. Furthermore, the proposed model uses only ≈16M parameters when compared to other well known conventional deep architectures for various complex applications. To further improve the performance, in our future work visual saliency shall be explored in conjunction with deep features and post processing methods based on Conditional Random fields.

Acknowledgement. This publication has emanated from research conducted with the financial support of Science Foundation Ireland (SFI) under grant number SFI/12/RC/2289.

References

1. Abadi, M., et al.: Tensorflow: Large-scale machine learning on heterogeneous distributed systems. arXiv preprint arXiv:1603.04467 (2016)
2. Ahn, E., et al.: Saliency-based lesion segmentation via background detection in dermoscopic images. IEEE J. Biomed. Health Inf. **21**(6), 1685–1693 (2017)
3. Berman, M., Rannen Triki, A., Blaschko, M.B.: The lovász-softmax loss: a tractable surrogate for the optimization of the intersection-over-union measure in neural networks. In: Proceedings of the IEEE Conference on Computer Vision and Pattern Recognition, pp. 4413–4421 (2018)
4. Berseth, M.: ISIC 2017-skin lesion analysis towards melanoma detection. arXiv preprint arXiv:1703.00523 (2017)
5. Bi, L., Kim, J., Ahn, E., Feng, D.: Automatic skin lesion analysis using large-scale dermoscopy images and deep residual networks. arXiv preprint arXiv:1703.04197 (2017)
6. Bi, L., Kim, J., Ahn, E., Feng, D., Fulham, M.: Automated skin lesion segmentation via image-wise supervised learning and multi-scale superpixel based cellular automata. In: 2016 IEEE 13th International Symposium on Biomedical Imaging (ISBI), pp. 1059–1062. IEEE (2016)
7. Cavalcanti, P.G., Yari, Y., Scharcanski, J.: Pigmented skin lesion segmentation on macroscopic images. In: 2010 25th International Conference of Image and Vision Computing New Zealand (IVCNZ), pp. 1–7. IEEE (2010)

8. Celebi, M.E., Iyatomi, H., Schaefer, G., Stoecker, W.V.: Lesion border detection in dermoscopy images. Comput. Med. Imaging Graph. **33**(2), 148–153 (2009)
9. Chollet, F.: Keras (2017). https://github.com/fchollet/keras
10. Codella, N.C., et al.: Skin lesion analysis toward melanoma detection: a challenge at the 2017 International Symposium on Biomedical Imaging (ISBI), hosted by the International Skin Imaging Collaboration (ISIC). In: 2018 IEEE 15th International Symposium on Biomedical Imaging (ISBI 2018), pp. 168–172. IEEE (2018)
11. Dalila, F., Zohra, A., Reda, K., Hocine, C.: Segmentation and classification of melanoma and benign skin lesions. Optik-Int. J. Light Electron Optics **140**, 749–761 (2017)
12. Diniz, J.B., Cordeiro, F.R.: Automatic segmentation of melanoma in dermoscopy images using fuzzy numbers. In: 2017 IEEE 30th International Symposium on Computer-Based Medical Systems (CBMS), pp. 150–155. IEEE (2017)
13. Emre Celebi, M., et al.: Border detection in dermoscopy images using statistical region merging. Skin Res. Technol. **14**(3), 347–353 (2008)
14. Fu, H., Cheng, J., Xu, Y., Wong, D.W.K., Liu, J., Cao, X.: Joint optic disc and cup segmentation based on multi-label deep network and polar transformation. IEEE Trans. Med. Imaging (2018)
15. Glaister, J., Amelard, R., Wong, A., Clausi, D.A.: MSIM: multistage illumination modeling of dermatological photographs for illumination-corrected skin lesion analysis. IEEE Trans. Biomed. Eng. **60**(7), 1873–1883 (2013)
16. Glaister, J., Wong, A., Clausi, D.A.: Segmentation of skin lesions from digital images using joint statistical texture distinctiveness. IEEE Trans. Biomed. Eng. **61**(4), 1220–1230 (2014)
17. He, K., Zhang, X., Ren, S., Sun, J.: Deep residual learning for image recognition. In: Proceedings of the IEEE Conference on Computer Vision and Pattern Recognition, pp. 770–778 (2016)
18. Heath, M., Jaimes, N., Lemos, B., Mostaghimi, A., Wang, L.C., Peñas, P.F., Nghiem, P.: Clinical characteristics of merkel cell carcinoma at diagnosis in 195 patients: the AEIOU features. J. Am. Acad. Dermatol. **58**(3), 375–381 (2008)
19. Jafari, M.H., et al.: Skin lesion segmentation in clinical images using deep learning. In: 2016 23rd International Conference on Pattern Recognition (ICPR), pp. 337–342. IEEE (2016)
20. Kingma, D., Ba, J.: Adam: a method for stochastic optimization. arXiv preprint arXiv:1412.6980 (2014)
21. Menegola, A., Tavares, J., Fornaciali, M., Li, L.T., Avila, S., Valle, E.: Recod titans at ISIC challenge 2017. arXiv preprint arXiv:1703.04819 (2017)
22. Ronneberger, O., Fischer, P., Brox, T.: U-Net: convolutional networks for biomedical image segmentation. In: Navab, N., Hornegger, J., Wells, W.M., Frangi, A.F. (eds.) MICCAI 2015. LNCS, vol. 9351, pp. 234–241. Springer, Cham (2015). https://doi.org/10.1007/978-3-319-24574-4_28
23. Sadri, A.R., Zekri, M., Sadri, S., Gheissari, N., Mokhtari, M., Kolahdouzan, F.: Segmentation of dermoscopy images using wavelet networks. IEEE Trans. Biomed. Eng. **60**(4), 1134–1141 (2013)
24. Yuan, Y., Chao, M., Lo, Y.C.: Automatic skin lesion segmentation with fully convolutional-deconvolutional networks. arXiv preprint arXiv:1703.05165 (2017)

A Multi-task Framework for Skin Lesion Detection and Segmentation

Sulaiman Vesal[1(✉)], Shreyas Malakarjun Patil[1,2(✉)], Nishant Ravikumar[1],
and Andreas K. Maier[1]

[1] Pattern Recognition Lab, Friedrich-Alexander-Universität Erlangen-Nürnberg,
Erlangen, Germany
sulaiman.vesal@fau.de
[2] Department of Electrical Engineering, Indian Institute of Technology Jodhpur,
Karwar, Rajasthan, India
patil.3@iitj.ac.in

Abstract. Early detection and segmentation of skin lesions is crucial for timely diagnosis and treatment, necessary to improve the survival rate of patients. However, manual delineation is time consuming and subject to intra- and inter-observer variations among dermatologists. This underlines the need for an accurate and automatic approach to skin lesion segmentation. To tackle this issue, we propose a multi-task convolutional neural network (CNN) based, joint detection and segmentation framework, designed to initially localize the lesion and subsequently, segment it. A 'Faster region-based convolutional neural network' (Faster-RCNN) which comprises a region proposal network (RPN), is used to generate bounding boxes/region proposals, for lesion localization in each image. The proposed regions are subsequently refined using a softmax classifier and a bounding-box regressor. The refined bounding boxes are finally cropped and segmented using 'SkinNet', a modified version of U-Net. We trained and evaluated the performance of our network, using the ISBI 2017 challenge and the PH2 datasets, and compared it with the state-of-the-art, using the official test data released as part of the challenge for the former. Our approach outperformed others in terms of Dice coefficients (>0.93), Jaccard index (>0.88), accuracy (>0.96) and sensitivity (>0.95), across five-fold cross validation experiments.

1 Introduction

Recent trends indicate a growing number of skin cancer diagnoses worldwide, each year. In 2016, approximately 80,000 new cases of skin cancer were expected to be diagnosed, with 10,000 melanoma related deaths (the most aggressive form of skin cancer), in the USA alone [1]. Clinical screening and diagnosis typically involve examination by an expert dermatologist, followed by histopathological

---

S. Vesal and S. Malakarjun Patil contributed equally to this article.

© Springer Nature Switzerland AG 2018
D. Stoyanov et al. (Eds.): OR 2.0/CARE/CLIP/ISIC 2018, LNCS 11041, pp. 285–293, 2018.
https://doi.org/10.1007/978-3-030-01201-4_31

analysis of biopsies. These steps however, invariably suffer from high inter-rater and inter-center variability, and studies have shown that patient survival rates improve to over 95%, following early detection and diagnosis of melanomas. To reduce variability in the screening process, computer-aided-diagnosis (CAD) systems, which enable automatic detection, lesion segmentation and classification of dermoscopic images, in a manner robust to variability in image quality and lesion appearance, are essential.

Segmentation is an essential initial step, for CAD of skin lesions [2] and melanoma in particular. This is because melanoma is typically diagnosed based on the 'ABCD' criterion, which takes into account the shape-characteristics of lesions (such as diameter, asymmetry, border irregularity, etc.), together with appearance, or the 'seven-point checklist' [3]. Consequently, the quality of the initial segmentation is crucial to the subsequent evaluation of diagnostic metrics such as border irregularity and lesion diameter. Several deep learning-based approaches have been proposed, for skin lesion segmentation in recent years, for example - a multi-task CNN was formulated in [4], which simultaneously tackled lesion segmentation and two independent binary classification tasks; the winners of the ISBI 2016 skin lesion segmentation challenge [5], employed a fully convolutional residual network (FCRN), with more than 50 layers for segmentation and integrated it within a 2-stage framework for melanoma classification; and in [6], a multi-modal, multi-task CNN was designed, for the classification of the seven-point melanoma checklist criteria, and skin lesion diagnosis.

We proposed a CNN-based segmentation framework called 'SkinNet' [7] recently, to segment skin lesions in dermoscopic images automatically. The proposed CNN architecture was a modified version of the U-Net [8]. SkinNet employs dilated convolutions in the lowest layer of the encoder-branch, to provide a more global context for the features extracted in the image. Additionally, the model replaced the conventional convolution layers in both the encoder and decoder branches of U-Net, with dense convolution blocks, to better incorporate multi-scale image information.

In this paper, we propose a novel two-stage approach for skin lesion detection and segmentation where we first localize the lesion, and subsequently segment it. The recently developed 'faster region-based convolutional neural network' (Faster-RCNN) [9], a form of multi-task learning, is utilized for lesion localization. For each image, a number of bounding-boxes are initially generated by a region proposal network (RPN). Subsequently, each proposed region is jointly classified (as containing the object of interest or not) and refined using a softmax classifier, and a bounding-box regressor. Following refinement, the detected regions are cropped and segmented using SkinNet.

2   Methods

A fully automatic CAD system for analyzing dermoscopic images, must first be able to accurately localize, and segment the lesion, prior to classifying it into its sub-types. The framework devised in this study for skin lesion segmentation comprises, an initial localization step, using a network designed for object detection, followed by segmentation using a modified U-Net. The overall network was trained using the ISBI 2017 challenge (training) dataset [10].

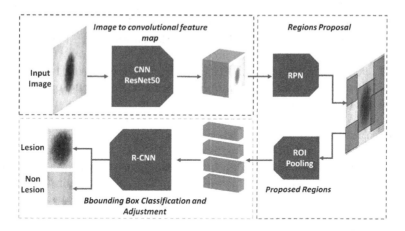

Fig. 1. Faster-RCNN architecture: Top left box represents the base network, box on the right represents the region proposal network (RPN) and the bottom left box represents the RCNN.

A network similar to the original Faster-RCNN was constructed for the initial task of lesion localization. The network's main components are summarized in Fig. 1. These include: (a) shared convolution layers (henceforth referred to as the base network) to extract both low- and high-level features from the input image; (b) a region proposal network (RPN) [9], which predicts anchor boxes and the probability that the predicted box contains a lesion; and (c) a region-based convolution network (RCNN) which refines the regions of interest (ROIs) generated in the preceding RPN step, by predicting the class (lesion present vs absent), and bounding box coordinates. Following localization, and selection of the refined regions, lesions were segmented within the estimated bounding boxes, using SkinNet. Henceforth, we refer to the combined localization and segmentation framework proposed in this study as, Faster-RCNN+SkinNet.

The Base Network: In order to extract discriminative features within the shared layers, we employed the pre-trained (on ImageNet) ResNet50 residual network [11]. The network was split into two parts, the first comprising the initial 87 layers was used as the base network, and the remaining layers were used for classification and regression in the final RCNN (refer to Fig. 1). The 87 layers were chosen based on experiments wherein, the number of layers of the base network were varied. Each trial was evaluated in terms of the Intersection-over-Union (IoU) of the bounding boxes predicted by the Faster-RCNN for each image, with respect to their ground truths, resulting in the chosen configuration.

Region Proposal Network: Following feature extraction, nine anchor boxes of various scales and aspect ratios were generated, centered on distinct, non-overlapping 3×3 patches of the feature map obtained from the base network, for each image. These anchors were generated at scales of $[128, 256, 512]$, and aspect ratios of $[1 : 1, 1 : 2, 2 : 1]$. The RPN was designed to predict the coordinates of these anchors for all patches, and their probability of containing a lesion. The similarity between the anchor boxes and the ground truth bounding boxes (generated using the training masks provided) was measured using IoU, and used to create references used by the RPN (as synthetic ground truths) to predict the probability of the anchors containing a lesion. These anchor boxes were labeled as positive, negative or neutral, based on IoU thresholds of 0.7 and 0.4, respectively. We ensured that the ground truth bounding boxes each had at least one corresponding positive anchor box, and if not, the neutral anchor box with the highest IoU was labeled positive. The RPN was implemented as a set of convolution layers, where each anchor box was first convolved with a 3×3 kernel, and subsequently, with five 1×1 kernels, resulting in five feature maps. Each of these feature maps in turn represent the coordinates of each anchor box, and its probability of containing a lesion. This process was repeated nine times, for each of the nine types of anchor boxes we considered, resulting in 9×5 feature maps that were predicted per image.

Classification and Bounding Box Regression: Classification of each region proposed by the RPN required feature maps of fixed sizes, as input to the RCNN. These were generated using region of interest (ROI) pooling. During ROI pooling, each feature map from the RPN was cropped and resized to $14 \times 14 \times 1024$ via bilinear interpolation. Next, max pooling with a 2×2 kernel was used, resulting in a final $7 \times 7 \times 1024$ feature map for each proposal. Finally, we used the remaining layers of the ResNet50 architecture (excluded in the base network), implemented as time-distributed layers, for the RCNN. Time-distributed convolution layers were used to avoid iterative classification and regression training and to accommodate the varied number of regions proposed per image, by the RPN. The RCNN subsequently classifies each proposal as lesion/non-lesion, and adjusts the bounding box coordinates to fit the lesion completely. Non-Maximum suppression with a threshold of 0.5 was used as a final step, to remove redundant bounding boxes.

Skin Lesion Segmentation: The final set of ROIs estimated for each image, using the Faster-RCNN based localization network, are subsequently, used as inputs for segmentation, by SkinNet [7] which we proposed in our recent studies. This segmentation network was designed to incorporate both local and global information, beneficial for any segmentation task. In segmentation networks such as the U-Net, the lowest level of the network connecting the encoder and decoder branches, has a small receptive field, which prevents the network from extracting features that capture non-local image information. We addressed this issue by using dilated convolution layers in the lowest part of the network. The encoded features are convolved with successively increasing dilation rates, which in turn, successively increases the size of the receptive field. The encoder and decoder

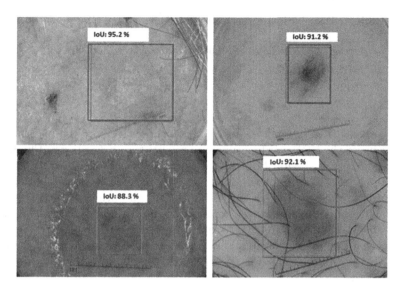

Fig. 2. Some examples of detected lesions and their respective IoU scores. The green and red bounding boxes represent the ground truth and predicted boxes, respectively. (Color figure online)

branches of SkinNet each comprise, three down- and up-sampling dense convolution blocks. These blocks incorporate multi-scale information through the use of dense convolution layers, where, the input to every layer is a concatenation of output feature maps, from all preceding convolution layers.

Losses: The losses used for RPN and RCNN classification are cross-entropy, and categorical cross-entropy, respectively. Mean squared error (MSE) was used as the regression loss in both the RPN and the RCNN. The ground truth for the bounding box regression was generated manually using the binary masks provided in the training dataset, for the ISBI 2017 challenge [10]. Many traditional segmentation networks employ cross-entropy [8] as a loss function. However, due to the small size of the lesion in dermoscopy images, cross-entropy is biased towards the background of the image. Consequently, for SkinNet, we used a dice coefficient loss function $\zeta(y, \hat{y}) = \zeta(y, \hat{y}) = 1 - \sum_k \frac{\sum_n y_{nk} \hat{y}_{nk}}{\sum_n y_{nk} + \sum_n \hat{y}_{nk}}$. The dice loss was chosen as experimental evidence suggested that it is less affected by class imbalances. Here, $\hat{y}_{nk}$ denotes the output of the model, where n represents the pixels and k the classes (i.e. background vs. lesion). The ground truth masks are one-hot encoded and denoted by y_{nk}. We take one minus the dice coefficient in order to constrain the loss to zero.

Training Procedure: A four-step training process for each batch was used in our approach. In the first step, we trained the RPN for a batch, generating numerous region proposals. Subsequently, the classification and bounding box regression branches of the RCNN were trained for the same batch. During both these steps, the weights of the base network were also fine tuned to enable the

Table 1. Distribution of the ISBI 2017 challenge and PH2 datasets.

Dataset	Training data	Validation data	Test data	Total
ISBI2017	2000	150	600	2750
PH2	-	-	200	200

network to learn task specific features. Next, the weights of the base network were frozen and the RPN was fine tuned, to predict the anchor boxes. Finally, the classification and regression branches of the RCNN were also fine tuned, once again keeping the weights of the base network fixed. The proposed detection method was trained for 100 epochs, using the Adam optimizer with a learning rate of 0.001. The model achieved an accuracy of 95.0% on the validation set (20% of the training set) and 94.0% on the test set (10% of the training set) respectively, for an overlap threshold of 0.9. Example outputs of lesion detection on test data are depicted in Fig. 2, which clearly highlight the high detection accuracy of the proposed approach.

3   Results and Discussion

Datasets: In order to evaluate the performance of our approach, we trained and tested it on two well-known public datasets, namely, the ISBI 2017 challenge dataset [10] and the PH2 [12] dataset. The former includes 2000 dermoscopic images and their corresponding lesion masks. These images are of various dimensions ranging from 1022×767 to 6688×4439. In addition to the training set, the organizers also provided a validation set comprising 150 images, and an additional test set with 600 images for final evaluation. The PH2 dataset contains 200 images, each 786×560 in size, and acquired at a magnification of $20\times$. We used these images purely as unseen data, to test the ability of our framework to generalize to images obtained from a different database. All images were resized to $512 \times 512 \times 3$. The number of images from both datasets used for training, validation and testing, are summarized in Table 1.

Evaluation Metrics: We used the metrics employed in the ISBI 2017 challenge, to evaluate segmentation performance, namely, Specificity (SP), Sensitivity (SE), Jaccard index (JI), Dice coefficient (DC) and Accuracy (AC), across five-fold cross validation experiments. Table 1 summarizes segmentation accuracy, evaluated using each of these metrics, for SkinNet and Faster-RCNN+SkinNet, on the ISBI 2017 test set and the PH2 data set. It also compares the achieved results with the state-of-the-art, which were trained and tested on the same data. For the ISBI 2017 test data, Faster-RCNN+SkinNet outperformed SkinNet and all other methods in terms of AC, DC, JI and SE. In particular, it achieved an average DC and JI score of 93.4% and 88%, respectively, which is significantly higher than all other methods. Visual assessment of the segmentation accuracy of Faster-RCNN+SkinNet relative to SkinNet, depicted in Fig. 3, confirms the superiority of the former relative to the latter. Furthermore, for the PH2

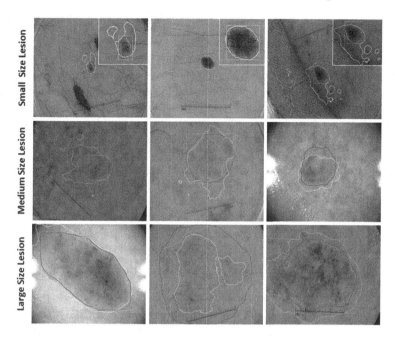

Fig. 3. Segmentation outputs using SkinNet and Faster-RCNN+SkinNet for different lesion sizes. The blue rectangle represents the detected bounding box. The green contour represents the ground truth segmentation, while the red and yellow represent the outputs of Faster-RCNN+SkinNet and SkinNet, respectively. (Color figure online)

Table 2. The segmentation accuracy results for different methods on ISBI 2017 challenge test data.

Datasets	Methods	AC	DC	JI	SE	SP
ISBI2017	Yuan et al. [13]	0.934	0.849	0.765	0.825	0.975
	SLSDeep [14]	0.936	0.878	0.782	0.816	0.983
	NCARG [15]	0.953	0.904	0.832	0.975	0.888
	FrCN [16]	0.956	0.896	0.813	0.890	0.974
	SkinNet	0.932	0.851	0.767	0.930	0.905
	Faster-RCNN+SkinNet	**0.968**	**0.934**	**0.880**	0.971	0.913
PH2	FrCN [16]	0.952	0.914	0.841	0.945	0.955
	Faster-RCNN+SkinNet	**0.964**	**0.946**	**0.899**	**0.952**	0.925

dataset, our method once again outperformed a state-of-the-art approach [16], in terms of AC, DC, JI and SE, highlighting its ability to generalize to images acquired from other databases. These results and comparisons, clearly outline the improvement in segmentation accuracy achieved by the proposed approach, relative to the state-of-the-art, and by extension, the benefit of formulating a multi-task learning approach, for skin lesion segmentation (Table 2).

4   Conclusion

The multi-task framework proposed in this study for joint lesion localization and segmentation, significantly outperformed the state-of-the-art, on two public test data sets. The results outline the significant benefits of object localization and multi-task learning, as auxiliaries to segmentation tasks. The proposed framework thus shows promise for the automatic analysis of skin lesions in dermoscopic images, for improved diagnosis and clinical decision support.

Acknowledgements. This study was partially supported by the project - BIG-THERA: Integrative 'Big Data Modeling' for the development of novel therapeutic approaches for breast cancer.

References

1. Siegel, R.L., Miller, K.D., Jemal, A.: Cancer statistics, 2016. CA Cancer J. Clin. **66**(1), 7–30 (2016)
2. Mirzaalian-Dastjerdi, H., Töpfer, D., Bangemann, M., Maier, A.: Detecting and measuring surface area of skin lesions. Bildverarbeitung für die Medizin 2018. I, pp. 29–34. Springer, Heidelberg (2018). https://doi.org/10.1007/978-3-662-56537-7_20
3. Jafari, M.H., et al.: Skin lesion segmentation in clinical images using deep learning. In: 2016 23rd International Conference on Pattern Recognition (ICPR), pp. 337–342. IEEE (2016)
4. Yang, X., Zeng, Z., Yeo, S.Y., Tan, C., Tey, H.L., Su, Y.: A novel multi-task deep learning model for skin lesion segmentation and classification. arXiv preprint arXiv:1703.01025 (2017)
5. Yu, L., Chen, H., Dou, Q., Qin, J., Heng, P.A.: Automated melanoma recognition in dermoscopy images via very deep residual networks. IEEE Trans. Med. Imaging **36**(4), 994–1004 (2017)
6. Kawahara, J., Daneshvar, S., Argenziano, G., Hamarneh, G.: 7-point checklist and skin lesion classification using multi-task multi-modal neural nets. IEEE J. Biomed. Health Inform. (2018)
7. Vesal, S., Ravikumar, N., Maier, A.: SkinNet: a deep learning framework for skin lesion segmentation (2018). Preprint https://arxiv.org/abs/1806.09522
8. Ronneberger, O., Fischer, P., Brox, T.: U-Net: convolutional networks for biomedical image segmentation. In: Navab, N., Hornegger, J., Wells, W.M., Frangi, A.F. (eds.) MICCAI 2015. LNCS, vol. 9351, pp. 234–241. Springer, Cham (2015). https://doi.org/10.1007/978-3-319-24574-4_28
9. Ren, S., He, K., Girshick, R., Sun, J.: Faster R-CNN: towards real-time object detection with region proposal networks. In: Advances in Neural Information Processing Systems, pp. 91–99 (2015)
10. Codella, N.C.F., et al.: Skin lesion analysis toward melanoma detection: a challenge at the 2017 international symposium on biomedical imaging (ISBI), hosted by the international skin imaging collaboration (ISIC). CoRR abs/1710.05006 (2017)
11. He, K., Zhang, X., Ren, S., Sun, J.: Deep residual learning for image recognition. In: Proceedings of the IEEE Conference on Computer Vision and Pattern Recognition, pp. 770–778 (2016)

12. Mendonça, T., Ferreira, P.M., Marques, J.S., Marcal, A.R., Rozeira, J.: PH^2 - a dermoscopic image database for research and benchmarking. In: 2013 35th Annual International Conference of the IEEE Engineering in Medicine and Biology Society (EMBC), pp. 5437–5440. IEEE (2013)

13. Yuan, Y., Chao, M., Lo, Y.C.: Automatic skin lesion segmentation using deep fully convolutional networks with Jaccard distance. IEEE Trans. Med. Imaging **36**(9), 1876–1886 (2017)

14. Kamal Sarker, M.M., et al.: SLSDeep: skin lesion segmentation based on dilated residual and pyramid pooling networks, eprint arXiv:1805.10241 (2018)

15. Guo, Y., Ashour, A.S., Smarandache, F.: A novel skin lesion detection approach using neutrosophic clustering and adaptive region growing in dermoscopy images. Symmetry **10**(4), 119 (2018)

16. Al-masni, M.A., Al-antari, M.A., Choi, M.T., Han, S.M., Kim, T.S.: Skin lesion segmentation in dermoscopy images via deep full resolution convolutional networks. Comput. Methods Programs Biomed. **162**, 221–231 (2018)

Skin Lesion Synthesis with Generative Adversarial Networks

Alceu Bissoto[1], Fábio Perez[2], Eduardo Valle[2], and Sandra Avila[1(✉)]

[1] RECOD Lab, IC, University of Campinas (Unicamp), Campinas, Brazil
`sandra@ic.unicamp.br`
[2] RECOD Lab, DCA, FEEC, University of Campinas (Unicamp), Campinas, Brazil

Abstract. Skin cancer is by far the most common type of cancer. Early detection is the key to increase the chances for successful treatment significantly. Currently, Deep Neural Networks are the state-of-the-art results on automated skin cancer classification. To push the results further, we need to address the lack of annotated data, which is expensive and require much effort from specialists. To bypass this problem, we propose using Generative Adversarial Networks for generating realistic synthetic skin lesion images. To the best of our knowledge, our results are the first to show visually-appealing synthetic images that comprise clinically-meaningful information.

Keywords: Skin cancer · Generative models · Deep learning

1 Introduction

Melanoma is the most dangerous form of skin cancer. It causes the most deaths, representing about 1% of all skin cancers in the United States[1]. The crucial point for treating melanoma is early detection. The estimated 5-year survival rate of diagnosed patients rises from 15%, if detected in its latest stage, to over 97%, if detected in its earliest stages [2].

Automated classification of skin lesions using images is a challenging task owing to the fine-grained variability in the appearance of skin lesions. Since the adoption of Deep Neural Networks (DNNs), the state of the art improved rapidly for skin cancer classification [6,7,15,19]. To push forward, we need to address the lack of annotated data, which is expensive and require much effort from specialists. To bypass this problem, we propose using Generative Adversarial Networks (GANs) [8] for generating realistic synthetic skin lesion images.

GANs aim to model the real image distribution by forcing the synthesized samples to be indistinguishable from real images. Built upon these generative models, many methods were proposed to generate synthetic images based

---

[1] http://www.cancer.net/cancer-types/melanoma/statistics.

D. Stoyanov et al. (Eds.): OR 2.0/CARE/CLIP/ISIC 2018, LNCS 11041, pp. 294–302, 2018.
https://doi.org/10.1007/978-3-030-01201-4_32

on GANs [10,16,17]. A drawback of GANs is the resolution of the synthetic images [20]. The vast majority of works is evaluated on low-resolution datasets such as CIFAR (32×32) and MNIST (28×28). However, for skin cancer classification, the images must have a higher level of detail (high resolution) to be able to display malignancy markers that differ a benign from a malignant skin lesion.

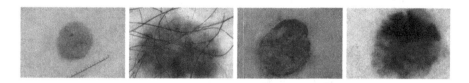

Fig. 1. Our approach successfully generates high-definition, visually-appealing, clinically-meaningful synthetic skin lesion images. All samples are synthetic. Details can be found in Sect. 2.

Very few works have shown promising results for high-resolution image generation. For example, Karras et al.'s [11] progressive training procedure generate celebrity faces up to 1024×1024 pixels. They start by feeding the network with low-resolution samples. Progressively, the network receives increasingly higher resolution training samples while amplifying the respective layers' influence to the output. In the same direction, Wang et al. [20] generate high-resolution images from semantic and instance maps. They propose to use multiple discriminators and generators that operate in different resolutions to evaluate fine-grained detail and global consistency of the synthetic samples. We investigate both networks for skin lesion synthesis, comparing the achieved results.

In this work, we propose a GAN-based method for generating high-definition, visually-appealing, and clinically-meaningful synthetic skin lesion images. To the best of our knowledge, this work is the first that successfully generates realistic skin lesion images (for illustration, see Fig. 1). To evaluate the relevance of synthetic images, we train a skin cancer classification network with synthetic and real images, reaching an improvement of 1% point. Our full implementation is available at https://github.com/alceubissoto/gan-skin-lesion.

2 Proposed Approach

Our aim is to generate high-resolution synthetic images of skin lesions with fine-grained detail. To explicitly teach the network the malignancy markers while incorporating the specificities of a lesion border, we feed these information directly to the network as input. Instead of generating the image from noise (usual procedure with GANs), we synthesize from a semantic label map (an image where each pixel value represents the object class) and an instance map (an image where the pixels combine information from its object class and its instance). Therefore, our problem of image synthesis specified to image-to-image translation.

2.1   GAN Architecture: The pix2pixHD Baseline

We employ Wang's et al. [20] pix2pixHD GAN, which improve the pix2pix network [10] (a conditional image-to-image translation GAN) by using a coarse-to-fine generator, a multi-scale discriminator architecture, and a robust adversarial learning objective function. The proposed enhancements allowed the network to work with high-resolution samples.

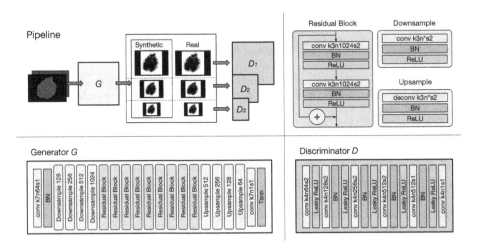

Fig. 2. Summary of the GAN architecture. In the bottom-left, we show the pipeline. We detail both discriminator and generator, and the blocks that compose them. We show the parameters for each convolutional layer: k is the kernel size; n is the number of channels; and s is the stride. The number that follows both Downsample and Upsample blocks are the numbers of channels.

For generating 1024×512 resolution images, we only take advantage of the Global generator from pix2pixHD. This generator's output resolution fits with the minimum common size of our dataset images. It is composed of a set of convolutional layers, followed by a set of residual blocks [9] and a set of deconvolutional layers.

To handle global and finer details, we employ three discriminators as Wang et al. [20]. Each of the three discriminators receives the same input in different resolutions. This way, for the second and third discriminator, the synthetic and real images are downsampled by 2 and 4 times respectively. Figure 2 summarizes the architecture of the GAN network.

The loss function incorporates the feature matching loss [17] to stabilize the training. It compares features of real and synthetic images from different layers of all discriminators. The generator learns to create samples that match these statistics of the real images at multiple scales. This way, the loss function is a combination of the conditional GAN loss, and feature matching loss.

2.2   Modeling Skin Lesion Knowledge

Modeling meaningful skin lesion knowledge is the crucial condition for synthesizing high-quality and high-resolution skin lesions images. In the following, we show how we model the skin lesion scenario into semantic and instance maps for image-to-image translation.

Semantic map [12] is an image where every pixel has the value of its object class and is commonly seen as a result of pixel-wise segmentation tasks.

To compose our semantic map, we propose using masks that show the presence of five malignancy markers and the same lesions' segmentation masks. The skin without lesion, the lesion without markers, and each malignancy marker are assigned a different label. To keep the aspect ratio of the lesions, while keeping the size of the input constant as the same of the original implementation by Wang et al. [20], we assign another label to the borders, which do not constitute the skin image.

Instance map [12] is an image where the pixels combine information from its object class and its instance. Every instance of the same class receives a different pixel value. When dealing with cars, people, and trees, this information is straightforward, but to structures within skin lesions, it is subjective.

To compose our instance maps, we take advantage of superpixels [1]. *Superpixels* group similar pixels creating visually meaningful instances. They are used in the process of annotation of the malignancy markers masks. First, the SLIC algorithm [1] is applied to the lesion image to create the superpixels. Then, specialists annotate each of the superpixels with the presence or absence of five malignancy markers. Therefore, superpixels are the perfect candidate to differentiate individuals within each class, since they are already in the annotation process as the minimum unit of a class. In Fig. 3 we show a lesion's semantic map, and its superpixels representing its instance map.

Next, we conduct experiments to analyze our synthetic images and compare the different approaches introduced to generate them.

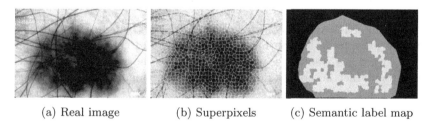

(a) Real image   (b) Superpixels   (c) Semantic label map

Fig. 3. A lesion's semantic map, and its superpixels representing its instance map. Note how superpixels change its shape next to hairs and capture information of the lesion borders, and interiors.

3   Experiments

In this section, we evaluate GAN-based approaches for generating synthetic skin lesion images: (1) DCGAN [16], (2) our conditional version of PGAN [11], and (3) our versions of pix2pixHD [20] using only semantic map, and (4) using semantic and instance maps. We choose DCGAN to represent low-resolution GANs because of its traditional architecture. Results for other low-resolution GANs do not show much of an improvement.

3.1   Datasets

For training and testing pix2pixHD, we need specific masks that show the presence or absence of clinically-meaningful skin lesion patterns (including pigment network, negative network, streaks, milia-like cysts, and globules). These masks are available from the training dataset of task 2 (2,594 images) of 2018 ISIC Challenge[2]. The same lesions' segmentation masks that are used to compose both semantic and instance maps were obtained from task 1 of 2018 ISIC Challenge. We split the data into train (2,346 images) and test (248 images). The test is used for generating images using masks the network has never seen before.

For training DCGAN and our version of PGAN, we use the following datasets: ISIC 2017 Challenge with 2,000 dermoscopic images [5], ISIC Archive with 13,000 dermoscopic images, Dermofit Image Library [4] with 1,300 images, and PH2 dataset [13] with 200 dermoscopic image.

For training the classification network, we only use the 'train' set (2,346 images). For testing, we use the Interactive Atlas of Dermoscopy [3] with 900 dermoscopic images (270 melanomas).

3.2   Experimental Setup

For pix2pixHD, DCGAN (official PyTorch implementation) and PGAN (except for the modifications listed below), we keep the default parameters of each implementation.

We modified PGAN by concatenating the label (benign or melanoma) in every layer except the last on both discriminator and generator. For training, we start with 4×4 resolution, always fading-in to the next resolution after 60 epochs, from which 30 epochs are used for stabilization. To generate images of resolution 256×256, we trained for 330 epochs. We ran all experiments using the original Theano version.

For skin lesion classification, we employ the network (Inception-v4 [18]) ranked first place for melanoma classification [14] at the ISIC 2017 Challenge. As Menegola et al. [14], we apply random vertical and horizontal flips, random rotations and color variations as data augmentation. Also we keep test augmentation with 50 replicas, but skip the meta-learning SVM.

---

[2] https://challenge2018.isic-archive.com.

3.3   Qualitative Evaluation

In Fig. 4 we visually compare the samples generated by GAN-based approaches.

DCGAN (Fig. 4a) is one of the most employed GAN architectures. We show that samples generated by DCGAN are far from the quality observed on our models. It lacks fine-grained detail, being inappropriate for generating high-resolution samples.

Despite the visual result for PGAN (Fig. 4b) is better than any other work we know of, it lacks cohesion, positioning malignancy markers without proper criteria. We cannot pixel-wise compare the PGAN result with the real image. This synthetic image was generated from noise and had no connection with the sampled real image, except it was part of the GAN's training set. But, we can compare the sharpness, the presence of malignancy markers and their fine-grained details.

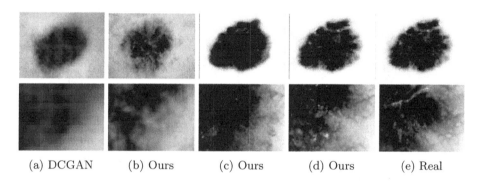

(a) DCGAN   (b) Ours   (c) Ours   (d) Ours   (e) Real

Fig. 4. Results for different GAN-based approaches: (a) DCGAN [16], (b) Our version of PGAN, (c) Our version of pix2pixHD using only semantic map, (d) Our version of pix2pixHD using both semantic and instance map, (e) Real image. In the first row, we present the full image while in the second we zoom-in to focus on the details.

When we feed the network with semantic label maps (Fig. 4c) that inform how to arrange the malignancy markers, the result improves remarkably. When combining both semantic and instance maps (Fig. 4d), we simplify the learning process, achieving the overall best visual result. The network learns patterns of the skin, and of the lesion itself.

3.4   Quantitative Evaluation

To evaluate the complete set of synthetic images, we train a skin classification network with real and synthetic training sets and compare the area under the ROC curve (AUC) when testing only with real images. We use three different synthetic images for this comparison: **Instance** are the samples generated using both semantic and instance maps with our version of pix2pixHD [20]; **Semantic** are the samples generated using only semantic label maps; **PGAN** are the samples generated using our conditional version of PGAN [11]. For statistical significance, we run each experiment 10 times.

For every individual set, we use 2,346 images, which is the size of our training set (containing semantic and instance maps) for pix2pixHD. For PGAN, there is not a limitation in the amount of samples we are able to generate, but we keep it the same maintaining the ratio between benign and malignant lesions. Our results are in Table 1. To verify statistical significance (comparing 'Real + Instance + PGAN' with other results), we include the p-value of a paired samples t-test. With a confidence of 95%, all differences were significant (p-value < 0.05).

Table 1. Performance comparison of real and synthetic training sets for a skin cancer classification network. We train the network 10 times with each set. The features present in the synthetic images are not only visually appealing but also contain meaningful information to correctly classify skin lesions.

Training data	AUC (%)	Training data size	p-value
Real	83.4 ± 0.9	2,346	2.5×10^{-3}
Instance	82.0 ± 0.7	2,346	2.8×10^{-5}
Semantic	78.1 ± 1.2	2,346	6.9×10^{-8}
PGAN	73.3 ± 1.5	2,346	2.3×10^{-9}
Real + Instance	82.8 ± 0.8	4,692	1.1×10^{-4}
Real + Semantic	82.6 ± 0.8	4,692	1.2×10^{-4}
Real + PGAN	83.7 ± 0.8	4,692	2.6×10^{-2}
Real + 2×PGAN	83.6 ± 1.0	7,038	2.0×10^{-2}
Real + Instance + PGAN	84.7 ± 0.5	7,038	–

The synthetic samples generated using instance maps are the best among the synthetics. The AUC follows the visual quality perceived.

The results for synthetic images confirm they contain features that characterize a lesion as malignant or benign. Even more, the results suggest the synthetic images contain features that are beyond the boundaries of the real images, which improves the classification network by an average of 1.3% point and keeps the network more stable.

To investigate the influence of the instance images over the achieved AUC for 'Real + Instance + PGAN', we replace the instance images with new PGAN samples ('Real + 2×PGAN'). Although both training sets have the same size, the result did not show improvements over its smaller version 'Real + PGAN'. Hence, the improvement over the AUC achieved suggests it is related with the variations the 'Instance' images carry, and not (only) by the size of the train dataset.

4   Conclusion

In this work, we propose GAN-based methods to generate realistic synthetic skin lesion images. We visually compare the results, showing high-resolution samples (up to 1024 × 512) that contain fine-grained details. Malignancy markers are present with coherent placement and sharpness which result in visually-appealing images. We employ a classification network to evaluate the specificities that characterize a malignant or benign lesion. The results show that the synthetic images carry this information, being appropriate for classification purposes.

Our pix2pixHD-based solution, however, requires annotated data to generate images. To overcome this limitation, we are working on different approaches to generate diversified images employing pix2pixHD without additional data: combining different lesions' semantic and instance masks, distorting existing real masks for creating new ones, or even employing GANs for the easier task of generating masks. Despite the method used, taking advantage of synthetic images for classification is promising.

Acknowledgments. We gratefully acknowledge NVIDIA for the donation of GPUs, Microsoft Azure for the GPU-powered cloud platform, and CCES/Unicamp (Center for Computational Engineering & Sciences) for the GPUs used in this work. A. Bissoto is funded by CNPq. E. Valle is partially funded by Google Research LATAM 2017, CNPq PQ-2 grant (311905/2017-0), and Universal grant (424958/2016-3). RECOD Lab. is partially supported by FAPESP, CNPq, and CAPES.

References

1. Achanta, R., Shaji, A., Smith, K., Lucchi, A., Fua, P., Süsstrunk, S.: SLIC superpixels. Technical report No. EPFL-REPORT-149300 (2010)
2. American Cancer Society: Survival rates for melanoma skin cancer, by stage (2016). www.cancer.org/cancer/melanoma-skin-cancer/detection-diagnosis-staging
3. Argenziano, G., et al.: Dermoscopy: a tutorial. EDRA, Medical Publishing & New Media, p. 16 (2002)
4. Ballerini, L., Fisher, R.B., Aldridge, B., Rees, J.: A color and texture based hierarchical K-NN approach to the classification of non-melanoma skin lesions. In: Celebi, M., Schaefer, G. (eds.) Color Medical Image Analysis. LNCVB, vol. 6, pp. 63–86. Springer, Dordrecht (2013). https://doi.org/10.1007/978-94-007-5389-1_4
5. Codella, N.C., Gutman, D., Celebi, M.E., Helba, B., Marchetti, M.A., et al.: Skin lesion analysis toward melanoma detection: a challenge at the 2017 International Symposium on Biomedical Imaging (ISBI), hosted by the International Skin Imaging Collaboration (ISIC). arXiv:1710.05006 (2017)
6. Esteva, A., et al.: Dermatologist-level classification of skin cancer with deep neural networks. Nature **542**(7639), 115–118 (2017)
7. Fornaciali, M., Carvalho, M., Bittencourt, F.V., Avila, S., Valle, E.: Towards automated melanoma screening: proper computer vision & reliable results. arXiv:1604.04024 (2016)
8. Goodfellow, I., et al.: Generative adversarial nets. In: NIPS (2014)
9. He, K., Zhang, X., Ren, S., Sun, J.: Deep residual learning for image recognition. In: IEEE CVPR (2016)
10. Isola, P., Zhu, J.Y., Zhou, T., Efros, A.A.: Image-to-image translation with conditional adversarial networks. In: IEEE CVPR (2017)
11. Karras, T., Aila, T., Laine, S., Lehtinen, J.: Progressive growing of GANs for improved quality, stability, and variation. In: ICLR (2018)

12. Lin, T.-Y., et al.: Microsoft COCO: common objects in context. In: Fleet, D., Pajdla, T., Schiele, B., Tuytelaars, T. (eds.) ECCV 2014. LNCS, vol. 8693, pp. 740–755. Springer, Cham (2014). https://doi.org/10.1007/978-3-319-10602-1_48

13. Mendonça, T., Ferreira, P., Marques, J., Marcal, A., Rozeira, J.: PH^2: a dermoscopic image database for research and benchmarking. In: IEEE EMBS (2013)

14. Menegola, A., Tavares, J., Fornaciali, M., Li, L.T., Avila, S., Valle, E.: RECOD titans at ISIC challenge 2017. arXiv:1703.04819 (2017)

15. Perez, F., Vasconcelos, C., Avila, S., Valle, E.: Data augmentation for skin lesion analysis. In: ISIC Skin Image Analysis Workshop (2018)

16. Radford, A., Metz, L., Chintala, S.: Unsupervised representation learning with deep convolutional generative adversarial networks. In: ICLR (2016)

17. Salimans, T., Goodfellow, I., Zaremba, W., Cheung, V., Radford, A., Chen, X.: Improved techniques for training GANs. In: NIPS (2016)

18. Szegedy, C., Ioffe, S., Vanhoucke, V., Alemi, A.A.: Inception-v4, inception-resnet and the impact of residual connections on learning. In: AAAI (2017)

19. Valle, E., et al.: Data, depth, and design: learning reliable models for melanoma screening. arXiv:1711.00441 (2018)

20. Wang, T.C., Liu, M.Y., Zhu, J.Y., Tao, A., Kautz, J., Catanzaro, B.: High-resolution image synthesis and semantic manipulation with conditional GANs. In: IEEE CVPR (2018)

Data Augmentation for Skin Lesion Analysis

Fábio Perez[1]([⊠]), Cristina Vasconcelos[2], Sandra Avila[3], and Eduardo Valle[1]([⊠])

[1] RECOD Lab., DCA, FEEC, University of Campinas (Unicamp), Campinas, Brazil
{fabiop,dovalle}@dca.fee.unicamp.br
[2] Computer Science Department, IC, Federal Fluminense University (UFF),
Niterói, Brazil
[3] RECOD Lab., IC, University of Campinas (Unicamp), Campinas, Brazil

Abstract. Deep learning models show remarkable results in automated skin lesion analysis. However, these models demand considerable amounts of data, while the availability of annotated skin lesion images is often limited. Data augmentation can expand the training dataset by transforming input images. In this work, we investigate the impact of 13 data augmentation scenarios for melanoma classification trained on three CNNs (Inception-v4, ResNet, and DenseNet). Scenarios include traditional color and geometric transforms, and more unusual augmentations such as elastic transforms, random erasing and a novel augmentation that mixes different lesions. We also explore the use of data augmentation at test-time and the impact of data augmentation on various dataset sizes. Our results confirm the importance of data augmentation in both training and testing and show that it can lead to more performance gains than obtaining new images. The best scenario results in an AUC of 0.882 for melanoma classification without using external data, outperforming the top-ranked submission (0.874) for the ISIC Challenge 2017, which was trained with additional data.

Keywords: Skin lesion analysis · Data augmentation · Deep learning

1 Introduction

Deep learning has achieved impressive results in computer vision tasks, including skin lesion analysis [4]. However, deep learning models are data-hungry, and collecting and annotating skin lesion images can be challenging.

In image classification tasks, knowledge transfer and data augmentation are regularly employed for small datasets. Knowledge transfer usually takes place by initially training a Convolutional Neural Network (CNN) in a large source dataset (e.g., ImageNet) and using its weights as a starting point for training in the smaller target dataset [10]. Data augmentation goal is to add new data points to the input space by modifying training images while preserving semantic information and target labels. Thus, it is used to reduce overfitting.

© Springer Nature Switzerland AG 2018
D. Stoyanov et al. (Eds.): OR 2.0/CARE/CLIP/ISIC 2018, LNCS 11041, pp. 303–311, 2018.
https://doi.org/10.1007/978-3-030-01201-4_33

In this work, we: (i) investigate the impact of applying diverse data augmentation techniques to three different CNN architectures (namely Inception-v4 [13], ResNet [5], and DenseNet [6]); (ii) investigate the impact of data augmentation on different dataset sizes; and (iii) evaluate the use of different data augmentation methods during test-time, aiming to reduce generalization error. We conducted the experiments on the ISIC Challenge 2017 dataset [3] for melanoma classification task.

2   Related Work

Data augmentation is broadly used in CNN architectures, such as AlexNet [8], Inception [7,13,14], ResNet [5], and DenseNet [6]. These architectures are trained on the ImageNet dataset , which contains millions of annotated images. Some examples of data augmentation techniques are color modifications and geometric transforms (rotation, scaling, random cropping).

Models can also benefit from data augmentation on test-time. Krizhevsky et al. [8] average the predictions on 10 patches (cropped from the center plus the four corners and then flipped) extracted from each test image. Szegedy et al. [14] report gains with a method that generates 144 patches by cropping images at different resolutions, when compared with the 10-crop method. These methods are commonly used in competitions to increase final performance but can be expensive for production.

Data augmentation is also extensively employed in skin lesion classification, a task that has much less available training data. Data augmentation is ubiquitous among top-ranked submissions in the ISIC Challenge 2017 [1,9,11].

Some works specifically explore data augmentation for skin lesion analysis [12,15,16]. Vasconcelos and Vasconcelos [16] report gains in performance by using data augmentation with geometric transforms (rotations by multiples of 90°; flips; lesion-preserving crops), PCA-based color augmentation, and specialist warping that preserves lesions symmetries and anti-symmetries. Valle et al. [15] highlight the importance of using data augmentation for both training and testing. They averaged the predictions for 50 augmented test samples. Pham et al. [12] compare the effects of data augmentation on classifiers (SVM, neural networks, and random forest) trained with features extracted with a pretrained Inception-v4. Their results indicate that using more samples in test data augmentation (100 vs. 50) increases the model's performance.

In this work, we further investigate the use of data augmentation for skin lesion analysis, by comparing: test techniques (testing on a single image; test data augmentation; and test cropping, commonly employed in CNN architectures for image classification); 13 different data augmentation scenarios, including a novel augmentation; and the effects of data augmentation on different dataset sizes.

3   Methodology

3.1   CNN Architectures

We evaluated every experiment on three very deep CNNs that are widely used in computer vision problems: Inception-v4 [13], ResNet-152 [5], and DenseNet-161 [6]. We chose these networks as they achieve increased depth with different design choices and represent the state of the art in image classification.

The Inception-v4 [13] architecture has modules that concatenate feature maps from parallel convolutional blocks, leading to increased width and depth. Residual Networks (ResNets) [5] use shortcut connections between layers, allowing even deeper networks. Densely Connected Networks (DenseNets) [6] concatenate the output of each layer to all subsequent layers inside a dense block, increasing the parameter efficiency and reducing overfitting.

Since we used the same optimization hyperparameters for the three networks, we do not intend to compare the numeric values alone, but rather compare big-picture results and trends.

3.2   Data Augmentation Techniques

We evaluated 13 data augmentation scenarios, comprising different image processing techniques, and some combinations of them. Table 1 describes the implementation details for each scenario. Figure 1 shows examples of all scenarios.

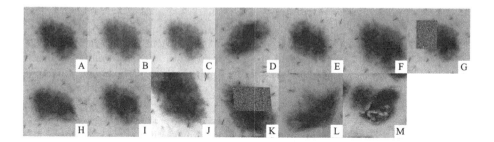

Fig. 1. Examples of augmentation scenarios, described in Table 1.

3.3   Training and Evaluation

We trained each network with Stochastic Gradient Descent (SGD) with a momentum factor 0.9, batch size of 32, starting learning rate 1e−3, reduced to 1e−4 after the 10th epoch. The training data was shuffled before each epoch. The networks were initialized with weights trained on the ImageNet dataset, and fine-tuned with the ISIC Challenge 2017 train dataset (2000 images) [3]. The experiments were implemented with PyTorch (pytorch.org). Augmentations were implemented with torchvision and imgaug (github.com/aleju/imgaug).

Table 1. Augmentation scenarios. Scenarios **J** to **M** represent augmentations compositions applied in the presented order.

ID	Name	Description
A	No Augmentation	No data augmentation. Only preprocess images, as described in Sect. 3.3
B	Saturation, Contrast, and Brightness	Modify saturation, contrast, and brightness by random factors sampled from an uniform distribution of $[0.7, 1.3]$, simulating changes in color due to camera settings and lesion characteristics
C	Saturation, Contrast, Brightness, and Hue	As described in B, but also shift the hue by a value sampled from an uniform distribution of $[-0.1, 0.1]$
D	Affine	Rotate the image by up to $90°$, shear by up to $20°$, and scale the area by $[0.8, 1.2]$. New pixels are filled symmetrically at edges. This can reproduce camera distortions and create new lesion shapes
E	Flips	Randomly flip the images horizontally and/or vertically
F	Random Crops	Randomly crop the original image. The crop has $0.4 - 1.0$ of the original area, and $3/4 - 4/3$ of the original aspect ratio
G	Random Erasing	Fill part of the image (area up to 30% of the original image) with random noise. The transformation is applied with a probability of 0.5. Implemented as described in [17]. The network may benefit from occlusion by learning to look for different lesion attributes
H	Elastic	Warp images with Thin Plate Splines (TPS). The warp is generated by defining the origins as an evenly-spaced 4×4 grid of points, and destinations as random points around the origins (by up to 10% of the image width on each direction). This can produce new lesion shapes while maintaining medical attributes
I	Lesion Mix	Mix two lesions, by inserting part of a foreground lesion (cut by its segmentation mask) into a background lesion. We apply Gaussian blur to the foreground lesion to avoid sharp edges, and equalize its color histogram with respect to the segmented background lesion. The resulting image is labeled as melanoma only if one of the two original lesions was labeled as melanoma. This can simulate clinical conditions with two lesions occur at the same location. We did not apply this transform at test-time
J	Basic Set	$F \to D \to E \to C$
K	Basic Set + Erasing	$F \to G \to D \to E \to C$
L	Basic Set + Elastic	$F \to D \to H \to E \to C$
M	Basic Set + Mix	$I \to F \to D \to E \to C$

All images were resized offline to a maximum width or height of 1024 pixels to avoid expensive resizing during training. On training, images were resized to the default input sizes for each network (224×224 for DenseNet and ResNet; 299×299 for Inception-v4), although larger sizes were possible due to global average pooling. Images were normalized (subtract from the mean and divide by the standard deviation) based on the ImageNet dataset, in which the networks were pretrained. Augmentations were randomly applied online during training.

We applied early stopping to interrupt the training, monitoring the AUC value for the ISIC Challenge 2017 official validation dataset (150 images) for each epoch. The AUC value was calculated by averaging the predictions for 16 randomly augmented copies of each validation image, by applying the same transforms used during training. The early stopping monitor interrupted the training when the validation AUC did not improve after 8 epochs. The final test AUC was calculated on the ISIC Challenge 2017 official test dataset (600 images) in three different ways: (i) inputting the original test images to the network; (ii) averaging the predictions for 64 randomly augmented copies of each test image; (iii) averaging the predictions for 144 patches produced by cropping each test image as described in [14]. The weights used for testing were selected from the best AUC in the validation dataset. The validation-time and test-time augmentations followed the same transforms as the training.

For every setup, we run 6 separate trainings to reduce the effects of randomness. We used Sacred (github.com/IDSIA/sacred) to organize all experiments.

To guarantee reproducibility, we provide the documented source code used in the experiments (github.com/fabioperez/skin-data-augmentation).

4   Results and Discussion

4.1   Augmentation on Training and Testing

In this section, we discuss the results of train and test data augmentation for the proposed scenarios. Figure 2 summarizes the results.

Scenario C (saturation, contrast, brightness, and hue) resulted in better AUC than scenario B (saturation, contrast, brightness) for all three networks. However, both color transforms performed worse than scenario A (no augmentation) with 144 crops on ResNet. Geometric transforms—affine (B), random crops (F), and elastic transformations (H)—had more consistent improvements among all three networks.

Random erasing (G) shows little improvements for Inception and DenseNet, but produce worse results than scenario A (no augmentation) with ResNet. Using 144 crops was better than test data augmentation, probably due to the destructive behavior of the method. When combined with other transformations (scenario K), random erasing reduced the test AUC in comparison with scenario J (basic set combining traditional augmentations).

Scenario H (elastic) shows promising results, but when applied with other common augmentation techniques (L) also performed worse than scenario J. This may occur due to deformations produced by the combined augmentation.

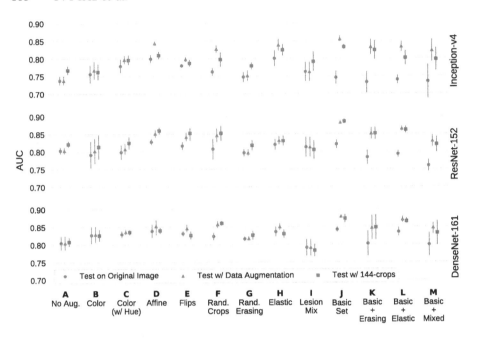

Fig. 2. Mean AUC values for augmentation scenarios. Each color and marker represent a prediction method: • original image; ▲ test-time data augmentation (64 images); ▥ 144 crops. Error bars represent the standard deviation for 6 runs. Values reported on ISIC Challenge 2017 test set. (Color figure online)

Lesion mix (I and M) had worse performances when compared to other augmentations, indicating that the generated images were not useful. We presume that the produced images were not able to preserve relevant features from both source lesions.

Scenario J (basic set) yields the best AUC values for all three networks: 0.854 for Inception-v4, 0.882 for ResNet, and 0.879 for DenseNet. The top-ranked submissions for melanoma classification scored 0.874 [11], 0.870 [1], 0.868 [9]. They used, respectively, 9640, 9600, and 3444 images for training. Our method achieved a higher AUC with ResNet and DenseNet without additional data. Scenario J also has the highest AUC for the validation set in all three networks.

For every scenario, averaging augmented samples or 144 crops resulted in better performance than predicting on the original image alone. Even when no data augmentation was employed during training, 144 crops significantly increased the AUC, indicating that the model can benefit from different representations of the input image.

For ResNet and DenseNet, 144 crops has similar results to using data augmentation on test-time. Considering that we used 64 augmented samples vs 144 crops, test data augmentation can lead to faster inference.

Particularly, Inception-v4 has a worse performance with 144 crops than with test data augmentation in most scenarios. This may indicate that Inception-v4 suffers from overfitting, considering that data augmentation produced similar patterns on both training and testing.

4.2   Impact of Data Augmentation on Different Dataset Sizes

We trained each network on random subsets of 1500, 1000, 500, 250, and 125 images of the original data to analyze the effects of having limited training data. We generated a random subset for each one of the 6 runs. Figure 3 summarizes the results.

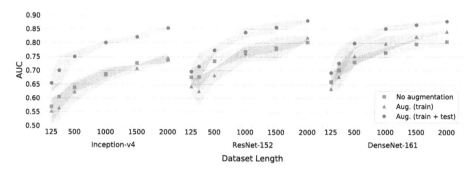

Fig. 3. Mean AUC values for different training dataset sizes, randomly sampled from the ISIC Challenge 2017 training dataset. Colors and markers represent the use of data augmentation: ■ no data augmentation; ▲ train data augmentation (scenario J); ● train and test data augmentation (scenario J, averaging each test image on 64 augmented samples). Bands represent the standard deviation for 6 runs. Values reported on ISIC Challenge 2017 test set. (Color figure online)

Applying data augmentation (scenario J) during both training and testing noticeably improved performance for datasets with 500 or more images. Data augmentation for training only worsened the results for very small data sizes (<500 images) and led to little or no improvement for other sizes, showing the importance of applying data augmentation during test-time.

The impact of data augmentation on Inception-v4 was more perceptible than on other networks, which may be caused by the regularizing properties of ResNet and DenseNet architectures. Training Inception-v4 with 500 images and data augmentation resulted in better performance than training with 1000, 1500 or 2000 images without augmentation. ResNet and DenseNet achieved a higher AUC with 1000 images and data augmentation than with 1500 and 2000 images without augmentation. This indicates that, in some cases, using data augmentation can be more effective than adding new training data. Nevertheless, employing data augmentation does not reduce the importance of adding new data, giving that the network can benefit from both.

5   Conclusion

The results highlight the positive impact of using data augmentation for training melanoma classification models. Moreover, models can also benefit from test data augmentation.

The best augmentation scenario (J), which combines geometric and color transformations, surpasses the top-ranked AUC values for the ISIC Challenge 2017 without any additional data. Fine-tuning hyperparameters and model ensembling may result in additional performance gains.

Lesion mix augmentation (scenarios I and M) have inferior results when compared with other scenarios. We implemented this augmentation through hand-crafted image processing techniques, which may not be appropriate for producing reliable images. More advanced approaches, such as Generative Adversarial Networks or other generative architectures [2], might lead to better results.

Acknowledgments. We gratefully acknowledge NVIDIA Corporation for the donation of GPUs and Microsoft Azure for the GPU-powered cloud platform used in this work. C. Vasconcelos and E. Valle are partially funded by Google Research LATAM 2017. E. Valle is also partially funded by CNPq PQ-2 grant (311905/2017-0) and Universal grant (424958/2016-3). RECOD Lab. is partially supported by diverse projects and grants from FAPESP, CNPq, and CAPES.

References

1. Bi, L., Kim, J., Ahn, E., Feng, D.: Automatic skin lesion analysis using large-scale dermoscopy images and deep residual networks. arXiv: 1703.04197 (2017)
2. Bissoto, A., Perez, F., Valle, E., Avila, S.: Skin lesion synthesis with generative adversarial networks. In: ISIC Skin Image Analysis Workshop (2018)
3. Codella, N.C.F., Gutman, D., Celebi, M.E., Helba, B., Marchetti, M.A., Dusza, S.W., et al.: Skin Lesion Analysis Toward Melanoma Detection: A Challenge at the 2017 International Symposium on Biomedical Imaging (ISBI), Hosted by the International Skin Imaging Collaboration (ISIC). arXiv: 1710.05006 (2017)
4. Fornaciali, M., Carvalho, M., Bittencourt, F.V., Avila, S., Valle, E.: Towards automated melanoma screening: Proper computer vision & reliable results. arXiv:1604.04024 (2016)
5. He, K., Zhang, X., Ren, S., Sun, J.: Deep residual learning for image recognition. In: IEEE CVPR, pp. 770–778 (2016)
6. Huang, G., Liu, Z., Weinberger, K.Q., van der Maaten, L.: Densely connected convolutional networks. In: IEEE CVPR (2017)
7. Ioffe, S., Szegedy, C.: Batch normalization: accelerating deep network training by reducing internal covariate shift. In: ICML, pp. 448–456 (2015)
8. Krizhevsky, A., Sutskever, I., Hinton, G.E.: ImageNet classification with deep convolutional neural networks. In: NIPS, pp. 1106–1114 (2012)
9. Matsunaga, K., Hamada, A., Minagawa, A., Koga, H.: Image classification of melanoma, nevus and seborrheic keratosis by deep neural network ensemble. arXiv: 1703.03108 (2017)
10. Menegola, A., Fornaciali, M., Pires, R., Bittencourt, F.V., Avila, S., Valle, E.: Knowledge transfer for melanoma screening with deep learning. In: ISBI (2017)

11. Menegola, A., Tavares, J., Fornaciali, M., Li, L.T., Avila, S., Valle, E.: RECOD titans at ISIC challenge 2017 (2017). arXiv: 1703.04819

12. Pham, T.C., Luong, C.M., Visani, M., Hoang, V.D.: Deep CNN and data augmentation for skin lesion classification. In: ACIIDS, pp. 573–582 (2018)

13. Szegedy, C., Ioffe, S., Vanhoucke, V., Alemi, A.A.: Inception-v4, Inception-ResNet and the impact of residual connections on learning. In: AAAI, vol. 4, p. 12 (2017)

14. Szegedy, C., et al.: Going deeper with convolutions. In: IEEE CVPR, pp. 1–9 (2015)

15. Valle, E., et al.: Data, depth, and design: learning reliable models for melanoma screening. arXiv: 1711.00441 (2017)

16. Vasconcelos, C.N., Vasconcelos, B.N.: Experiments using deep learning for dermoscopy image analysis. Pattern Recogn. Lett. (2017)

17. Zhong, Z., Zheng, L., Kang, G., Li, S., Yang, Y.: Random erasing data augmentation. arXiv:1708.04896 (2017)

A Structure-Aware Convolutional Neural Network for Skin Lesion Classification

Kevin Thandiackal[1,2](✉) and Orcun Goksel[1](✉)

[1] Computer-assisted Applications in Medicine, ETH Zurich, Zurich, Switzerland
{kevin.thandiackal,ogoksel}@vision.ee.ethz.ch
[2] IBM Research, Zurich, Switzerland

Abstract. Neural networks have emerged as a successful tool to solve end-to-end classification problems, potentially applicable in many diagnostic settings once trained with a sufficient number of existing annotations. Nevertheless, in such training it is often nontrivial to enter already available domain knowledge. We herein propose a simple approach of inputing any such information as additional layers to a network. This may then yield better performance by allowing for networks with fewer parameters that can be tuned with fewer annotations and with better generalization capabilities. This can also allow for interpretability of a deep network, by quantifying attribution to such additional inputs. We study this approach for the task of skin lesion classification, where we focus on prior knowledge in the form of pigment networks as they are known visual indicators of certain skin lesions, e.g. melanoma. We used a public dataset of dermoscopic images, where a low number of feature segmentations and a high number of classifications are provided in disjoint datasets. By including information from learned pigment network segmentations, the recall for malignant melanoma was seen to increase from 0.213 to 0.4. To help interpret the results, we also quantified the "attention" to pigment networks paid by the deep classifier both location- and channel-wise.

Keywords: Deep learning · Attention · Interpretability · Dermoscopy

1 Introduction

Skin cancer is one of the most prevalent types of cancer [1,2] and there is a growing need for accurate and scalable decision support systems for skin diseases. To assist doctors in making correct diagnoses, decision support systems can be trained on dermoscopic images, the same type of input data that dermatologists often use for an initial assessment.

The International Skin Imaging Collaboration (ISIC) [7,10] provides public datasets of dermoscopic images and organizes challenges where state-of-the-art (SoA) methods in this field can compete. These datasets allow researchers to design data-driven systems for the detection of skin diseases. Although in recent

© Springer Nature Switzerland AG 2018
D. Stoyanov et al. (Eds.): OR 2.0/CARE/CLIP/ISIC 2018, LNCS 11041, pp. 312–319, 2018.
https://doi.org/10.1007/978-3-030-01201-4_34

years high accuracy has been achieved with different Deep Learning approaches [7,9,10], most methods do not provide a mechanism to make use of prior medical knowledge.

In this work, we present a novel approach that tackles this issue. We aim at leveraging the predictive power of a deep convolutional neural network (CNN) while providing functionalities to understand which factors influence the network's prediction. We further quantify the *attention* that the trained classifier pays to each feature channel and image location, as a means to demonstrate our conclusions.

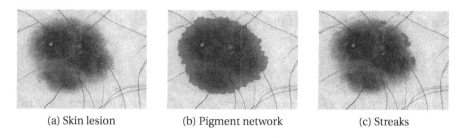

(a) Skin lesion   (b) Pigment network   (c) Streaks

Fig. 1. Annotation of dermascopic structures overlaid on images [7].

Related Work. Esteva et al. recently presented a CNN-based approach that outperformed certified dermatologists at differentiating benign and malignant lesions [9]. They used transfer learning and a disease partitioning algorithm for the generation of optimal training classes. They further computed saliency maps that highlight the importance of every pixel for the final prediction. However, the saliency maps provide only little interpretable information, such as the fact that the network mainly focuses on pixels belonging to the lesion rather than on the background.

Codella et al. used a mixture of hand-coded features and features extracted by deep CNNs to achieve SoA results on the dataset of the ISBI 2016 "Skin Lesion Analysis Towards Melanoma Detection" challenge [6,10]. Despite leveraging color features and shape descriptors for lesions, their approach does not facilitate an intuitive way of understanding the system's predictions.

The extensive work of López-Labraca et al. [13] is closely related to our approach. They employed sophisticated, hand-crafted filters to detect relevant dermoscopic structures (see Fig. 1). For a given lesion image, malignancy scores of different dermoscopic structures were computed and then combined to form a single diagnosis (malignant or benign). The authors were able to generate comprehensive reports containing the final diagnosis and the detected structures along with their respective malignancy scores. Nonetheless, their proposed approach requires extensive feature engineering and, in contrast to deep learning methods, is limited to features that are already known to dermatologists.

Building on the same idea, González-Díaz presented a method that used dermoscopic structures in combination with ResNet50, a deep residual network [8,11]. An input image was fed into a segmentation network that produced probability maps of eight different dermoscopic structures. These maps were then used to modulate the latent representation of the input image at a hidden layer in the ResNet50. Using this CNN-based method, González-Díaz achieved the best score for the detection of seborrheic keratosis in the ISBI 2017 "Skin Lesion Analysis Towards Melanoma Detection" challenge [7]. However, despite making use of known dermoscopic structures, this method does not provide interpretable information as the work of López-Labraca et al., where hand-crafted features were employed [13]. Furthermore, it is unclear to what extent the segmentations of the dermoscopic structures influence the final diagnosis.

2   Methods

Overview. Our method consists of two stages. Given an input image of a skin lesion, we first employ a segmentation network (SN) to detect dermoscopic structures that dermatologists consider to be important for disease classification (see Fig. 1). We focus on pigment networks as they are known indicators for malignant melanoma and benign nevi. Furthermore, they are the dermoscopic structures that are segmented with the highest confidence by our SN. In a second stage, the output of the network is stacked on top of the existing RGB channels of the original image, and then the resulting four-channel input is used to train a classifier network (CN) for each considered type of disease.

Additionally, we introduce two measures of attention given by the classifier network, namely the *channel-wise* and *location-wise* attention. These measures allow us to quantify how much attention the classifier is paying to the provided dermoscopic structure compared to the rest of the input data.

Material and Dataset. For the detection of pigment networks, we trained our SN with the dataset provided by the ISBI 2017 "Skin Lesion Analysis Towards Melanoma Detection" challenge [7]. It consists of 2000 training images and 600 testing images with superpixel level annotations of different types of dermoscopic structures, one of which is the pigment network. Every image is labeled with one of three classes: Melanoma, nevus, or seborrheic keratosis.

For the disease classification task, we trained our CN on the datasets released for the "ISIC 2018: Skin Lesion Analysis Towards Melanoma Detection" challenge [7,17]. It comprises 10,015 images belonging to one of seven classes: melanoma, melanocytic nevus, basal cell carcinoma, actinic keratosis, benign keratosis, dermatofibroma, or vascular lesion. For simplicity, we will from now on call the datasets *DS2017* and *DS2018*, respectively.

Methodology Overview. Since the images exhibit varying dimensions, they were resized to 224 × 224 pixels. Both datasets were augmented with random rotations of 90°, 180° and 270°, as well as vertical and horizontal flips. The algorithms for pigment network segmentation SN and disease classification CN were implemented in Tensorflow [3], both by extending the code provided by [5].

Detection of Pigment Networks. The detection task was formulated as a pixel-wise binary segmentation problem with a foreground and a background class. Due to the large class imbalance by background pixels, we reduced the original training set to a subset containing only those images where a pigment network was annotated. Note that this may result in a biased segmenter SN because it has been trained to always detect a pigment network somewhere in the image. Nevertheless, the subsequent disease classifier CN still sees the actual image and may choose to ignore this segmented area, if that does not facilitate the classification. Accordingly, our motivation was to have an (over-)sensitive SN, in order to let the subsequent CN decide how much importance to give to the allegedly-detected pigment network. Although such a two-step approach can be argued to potentially be inferior to an end-to-end solution, the former allows us to facilitate *dedicated datasets* and train *targeted models*, giving us more control over each step.

For SN, we employed a shallow U-Net [14] that outputs probability maps for the occurrence of pigment networks. To further alleviate the problem of background dominance, the Sørensen-Dice coefficient was used as loss function.

Disease Classification. We evaluated two types of classifiers: (*i*) ResNet50 (with 50 layers) pre-trained with images from the 2014 ImageNet Large Scale Visual Recognition Challenge [15], and (*ii*) the shallower ResNet18 (with 18 layers) proposed by He et al. [11], which we trained from scratch.

Fig. 2. Input images and their corresponding attribution maps (red = positive contribution, blue = negative contribution). (Color figure online)

Attention. Our attention measures are based on so-called *attribution* methods. Given a deep CNN with input $x = [x_1, ..., x_N] \in \mathbb{R}^N$ and output $f(x) = [f_1(x), ..., f_C(x)] \in \mathbb{R}^C$, attribution methods compute the contribution $R_{i,c}$ of every input pixel x_i to a specific target neuron f_c. Different types of attribution methods have been proposed in the past, such as the perturbation- and gradient-based approaches [4]. We herein employed a simple method of *input* × *partial-derivative* [16], which is fast and worked for generating successful *attribution maps* for our purposes (see Fig. 2). This metric defines attribution component $R_{i,c}$ of an input pixel x_i to a target neuron f_c as follows:

$$R_{i,c} := x_i \cdot \frac{\partial f_c(x)}{\partial x_i}. \tag{1}$$

Based on (1) we propose two quantities to measure the attention that a CNN pays to each input channel and image location.

Channel-wise attention (A_c) is defined as the ratio of contribution from a particular structure channel c to the contributions of all K channels:

$$A_c := \frac{\sum_{i=1}^{N} R_{i,c}^2}{\sum_{k=1}^{K} \sum_{i=1}^{N} R_{i,k}^2}. \qquad (2)$$

Location-wise attention (A_L) captures the local attention in the image space, again as a ratio. The numerator contains the contributions of all channels except for the dermoscopic structure channel c. The contributions are weighted with p, the local probability of the dermoscopic structure; and the denominator contains the corresponding unweighted contributions:

$$A_L := \frac{\sum_{i=1}^{N} p_i \cdot \sum_{k=1}^{K-1} R_{i,k}^2}{\sum_{k=1}^{K-1} \sum_{i=1}^{N} R_{i,k}^2}. \qquad (3)$$

We used the implementation of Ancona et al.[1] to compute the contribution values and to generate the attribution maps.

3   Results and Discussion

Segmentation. Examples for segmentations of pigment networks are depicted in Fig. 3. We trained and tested on DS2017 because at the moment of this writing, SoA results for DS2018 are not yet publicly available for comparison. As seen in Table 1, our pigment network segmentation results are not as accurate but comparable to the SoA results by Kawahara & Hamarneh from the ISBI 2017 "Skin Lesion Analysis Towards Melanoma Detection" challenge [7] in dermoscopic structure segmentation [12]. Note that our goal herein was not to perfect the SN stage, but rather to investigate if and how any information that SN provides can be further used in classification.

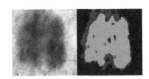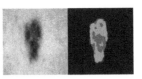

Fig. 3. Input images and segmented pigment networks (green = true positives, red = false positives, black = true negatives, blue = false negatives) (Color figure online)

Classification. For the classification experiments, we used the DS2018 training set and applied an 80%-10%-10%-split into training, validation and test set. Table 2 and 3 show the classification scores of ResNet18 and ResNet50 with and without additional pigment network channel.

---

[1] DeepExplain repository 24 May 2018: https://github.com/marcoancona/DeepExplain.

Table 1. Evaluation scores for the segmentation of pigment networks

Method	ROC AUC	Accuracy	Recall	Specificity
Kawahara and Hamarneh [12]	0.945	0.951	0.803	0.956
U-Net	0.914	0.901	0.786	0.904

For ResNet18, the ROC AUC values do not change significantly when the pigment network channel is added. Despite a slight overall decrease in ROC AUC values, Table 3 shows that the F1-score for the crucial melanoma class increases thanks to a clear improvement of the recall from 0.213 to 0.400. This is even better than the recall obtained by the much more complex ResNet50. In terms of ROC AUC values, ResNet50 still performs best. Notice however, that adding the pigment network channel to the input of ResNet50 actually leads to lower ROC AUC values, recall, and F1-scores.

Table 2. ROC AUC values. ME = Melanoma, MN = Melanocytic Nevus, BCC = Basal Cell Carcinoma, AK = Actinic Keratosis, BK = Benign Keratosis, DF = Dermatofibroma, VL = Vascular Lesion.

Method	ME	MN	BCC	AK	BK	DF	VL
ResNet18 (raw images)	0.893	0.927	0.940	0.929	0.877	0.840	0.986
ResNet18 (raw images + pigment networks)	0.866	0.917	0.929	0.921	0.847	0.851	0.966
ResNet50 (raw images)	**0.896**	**0.954**	**0.969**	**0.968**	**0.930**	**0.932**	**0.992**
ResNet50 (raw images + pigment networks)	0.855	0.913	0.918	0.923	0.854	0.896	0.964

Table 3. Recall, precision, and F1-score for Melanoma.

Method	Recall	Precision	F1
ResNet18 (raw images)	0.213	0.629	0.318
ResNet18 (raw images + pigment networks)	**0.400**	0.428	0.414
ResNet50 (raw images)	0.353	**0.633**	**0.454**
ResNet50 (raw images + pigment networks)	0.193	0.579	0.289

As seen in Table 4, the channel-wise attention A_c as well as the location-wise attention A_l for melanoma and melanocytic nevus are clearly higher in the case of ResNet18. This suggests that ResNet50 is not focusing its attention on the parts of the image that are medically relevant. The pre-trained ResNet50 may require more sophisticated fine-tuning if an additional channel is to be used. In our approach, only the weights of the first convolutional layer and the final fully-connected layer were learned whereas all weights in-between were pre-trained and frozen. Since the images from the 2014 ImageNet Large Scale Visual Recognition Challenge [15] are very different from dermoscopic images, it might be beneficial to use more general pre-trained feature representations from a higher layer and start learning from there. However, this is in turn computationally more expensive.

Table 4. Attention measures A_c, A_L for additional pigment network channel. ME = Melanoma, MN = Melanocytic Nevus.

Network	A_c for ME	A_c for MN	A_L for ME	A_L for MN
ResNet18	**0.263**	**0.176**	**0.161**	**0.155**
ResNet50	0.035	0.034	0.029	0.054

4   Conclusion

We showed that the recall and the F1-score for the detection of melanoma can be improved by providing a CNN with an additional input channel that contains relevant prior knowledge. Furthermore, we demonstrated that our proposed attention measures can help to identify where a CNN focuses its attention. In a next step, one might consider integrating more than just information about pigment networks in the input. Other dermoscopic structures such as streaks and dots could be used to further improve existing classifiers, e.g. for non-melanocytic lesions.

Acknowledgments. Support was provided by IBM Research Zurich, Switzerland and the Promedica Foundation, Chur, Switzerland.

References

1. Cancer in Australia 2017. Technical Report 101, Australian Institute of Health and Welfare. AIHW, Canberra, February 2017
2. U.S. cancer statistics working group. U.S. cancer statistics data visualizations tool. Technical report, Centers for Disease Control and Prevention and National Cancer Institute, June 2018. www.cdc.gov/cancer/dataviz
3. Abadi, M., et al.: TensorFlow: large-scale machine learning on heterogeneous systems (2015). tensorflow.org
4. Ancona, M., Ceolini, E., Oztireli, C., Gross, M.: Towards better understanding of gradient-based attribution methods for deep neural networks. In: 6th International Conference on Learning Representations (ICLR 2018) (2018)
5. Baumgartner, C.F., Koch, L.M., Pollefeys, M., Konukoglu, E.: An exploration of 2D and 3D deep learning techniques for cardiac MR image segmentation. In: Pop, M., et al. (eds.) STACOM 2017. LNCS, vol. 10663, pp. 111–119. Springer, Cham (2018). https://doi.org/10.1007/978-3-319-75541-0_12

6. Codella, N.C.F., et al.: Deep learning ensembles for melanoma recognition in dermoscopy images. IBM J. Res. Dev. **61**(4/5), 5:1–5:15 (2017)
7. Codella, N.C.F., et al.: Skin lesion analysis toward melanoma detection: a challenge at the 2017 International Symposium on Biomedical Imaging (ISBI), hosted by the International Skin Imaging Collaboration (ISIC). In: 2018 IEEE 15th International Symposium on Biomedical Imaging (ISBI 2018), pp. 168–172. IEEE, April 2018
8. Diaz, I.G.: DermaKNet: Incorporating the knowledge of dermatologists to convolutional neural networks for skin lesion diagnosis. IEEE J. Biomed. Health Inf., 1 (2018)
9. Esteva, A., Kuprel, B., Novoa, R.A., Ko, J., Swetter, S.M., Blau, H.M., Thrun, S.: Dermatologist-level classification of skin cancer with deep neural networks. Nature **542**(7639), 115–118 (2017)
10. Gutman, D., et al.: Skin lesion analysis toward melanoma detection: A challenge at the International Symposium on Biomedical Imaging (ISBI) 2016, hosted by the International Skin Imaging Collaboration (ISIC). ArXiv e-prints, May 2016
11. He, K., Zhang, X., Ren, S., Sun, J.: Deep residual learning for image recognition. In: Proceedings of the IEEE Conference on Computer Vision and Pattern Recognition, pp. 770–778, June 2016
12. Kawahara, J., Hamarneh, G.: Fully convolutional neural networks to detect clinical dermoscopic features. IEEE J. Biomed. Health Inf., 1 (2018)
13. López-Labraca, J., Fernández-Torres, M.Á., González-Díaz, I., Díaz-de María, F., Pizarro, Á.: Enriched dermoscopic-structure-based CAD system for melanoma diagnosis. Multimedia Tools Appl. **77**(10), 12171–12202 (2018)
14. Ronneberger, O., Fischer, P., Brox, T.: U-Net: convolutional networks for biomedical image segmentation. In: Navab, N., Hornegger, J., Wells, W.M., Frangi, A.F. (eds.) MICCAI 2015. LNCS, vol. 9351, pp. 234–241. Springer, Cham (2015). https://doi.org/10.1007/978-3-319-24574-4_28
15. Russakovsky, O., et al.: ImageNet large scale visual recognition challenge. Int. J. Comput. Vis. **115**(3), 211–252 (2015)
16. Shrikumar, A., Greenside, P., Shcherbina, A., Kundaje, A.: Not just a black box: learning important features through propagating activation differences. arXiv preprint arXiv:1605.01713 (2016)
17. Tschandl, P., Rosendahl, C., Kittler, H.: The HAM10000 dataset, a large collection of multi-source dermatoscopic images of common pigmented skin lesions. Sci. Data **5**, 180161 (2018). https://doi.org/10.1038/sdata.2018.161

Author Index

Printed in the United States
By Bookmasters